Bonaparte in Egypt

Bonaparte in Egypt

by

J. Christopher Herold

Fireship Press
www.FireshipPress.com

Bonaparte In Egypt - Copyright © 2009 by Fireship Press

ISBN-13: 978-1-934757-76-5
ISBN-10: 1-934757-76-4

BISAC Subject Headings:
    BIO008000   BIOGRAPHY & AUTOBIOGRAPHY / Military
    HIS013000   HISTORY / Europe / France
    HIS015000   HISTORY / Europe / Great Britain

This work was produced by Christina Paige of Fireship Press and is based on the 1962 edition of *Bonaparte in Egypt* by J. Christopher Herold, New York: Harper & Row

Address all correspondence to:
Fireship Press, LLC
P.O. Box 68412
Tucson, AZ 85737

Or visit our website at:
www.FireshipPress.com

1.0

To
CHRISTOPHER DAVID HEROLD

Contents

PREFACE

MY intention, when I set out to write this book, was simply to tell one of the most exciting adventures of modern times as truthfully as possible. As the work advanced, the excitement did not abate, but the difficulty of establishing the truth became increasingly evident. It would be convenient if the historian, by various 'scientific' methods of analyzing the sum of documentary evidence, could reach factual certainty about what really happened. Documentary evidence, how ever falsified, must not be ignored, of course, but whenever it is in conflict with elementary common sense it should be regarded with extreme diffidence. In the last resort the historian, like any humble member of a trial jury, is compelled to let his instinct and his experience of human affairs supplement the contradictory assertions put before him, or else he is a fool.

I have attempted, as scrupulously as I could, to present the *probable* truth. This truth does not reflect very favourably on either Napoleon Bonaparte or the French soldiers and civilians who took part in his Egyptian expedition. This should not mislead the reader into thinking that Napoleon and his men were appreciably more wicked or selfish or brutal than other men. The history of every colonial campaign, from the conquest of Mexico on, would, if properly investigated, bring no more credit upon the more civilized party in the conflict than the history of the Egyptian campaign brings on the French. Moreover, the reader must keep in mind that the French soldiers and civilians who took part in the Egyptian campaign had just emerged from the most savage revolution in history. Nothing they did in Egypt and in Syria, even in the heat of battle, equals in horror the gesture of a gentleman at Arras during the Reign of Terror, who was escorting two ladies to the theatre: the guillotine had been set up facing the theatre, and in the gutter which they had to cross there flowed a small river of blood; the gentleman bent down, dipped his fingers in the gutter, and, as he held up his hand and let the blood trickle down, remarked, 'How beautiful this is!'

The most authoritative history of Bonaparte's campaign in Egypt was written half a century ago by the Marquis de la Jonquière, in five volumes totalling more than three thousand large pages in rather small print. All writers on the subject since then have drawn most liberally on that work, but no one has adequately acknowledged his debt to it. Instead, most scholars have pretended, as scholars will, to have done all over again what La Jonquière had done before and for them. It is my theory that scholars write books so that other scholars may use them. At any rate, I have used La Jonquière's work very extensively, and I acknowledge my debt to it emphatically and unashamedly. La Jonquière was the most scrupulous historian I have ever read. He passed judgment on no one, but his five volumes constitute as complete a dossier as any court of historians could wish. I believe I may say in all sincerity that at no point in my narrative am I in contradiction with La Jonquière's work. La Jonquière was an officer in the French army and wrote under the auspices of the French Ministry of War, drawing on more unpublished documents on the subject than anyone since has seen. I stress these facts, because the Marquis de la Jonquière patriotism and respect for Bonaparte are above suspicion. Still, I do not wish to hide under his mantle, and I assume full responsibility for the conclusions I have drawn from the evidence presented by him and by my other sources.

I also wish to acknowledge my debt to the excellent book by Oliver Warner, *The Battle of the Nile* (Batsford, 1960), the most recent and, in my opinion, the best and most succinct work on that subject.

J. CHRISTOPHER HEROLD
New York,
September 1, 1962

Chapter One
Toulon

ON May 19, 1798, at six o'clock in the morning, the French flagship *L'Orient*, Captain Casabianca, signalled to the squadron and convoy assembled in the harbour of Toulon to get under sail. For the next eight hours, about a hundred and eighty vessels sailed past *L'Orient*—which towered above them like a fortress, with her three tiers of forty cannon each—and, facing a fresh breeze, struggled with some difficulty in the direction of Corsica. The spectacle must have been breath-taking. Thirteen ships of the line, carrying 1,026 cannon among them; 42 frigates, brigs, avisos, and other smaller vessels; and 150 transports of every description made up the armada. Aboard them were about 17,000 troops, as many sailors and marines, over a thousand pieces of field artillery, 100,000 rounds of ammunition, 567 vehicles, and 700 horses. Before reaching its destination—known to but a handful of men—the fleet was to be swelled by three lesser convoys, from Genoa, Ajaccio, and Civita Vecchia, bringing the total of men to about 55,000 and the number of sail to almost four hundred. On the open sea, the armada would cover two to four square miles; and when it was anchored off its final destination, the people ashore, 'when they looked at the horizon, could no longer see water, but only sky and ships: they were seized by unimaginable terror'.[1] Thus wrote

---

[1] Nicolas Turc, p. 9.

Nicholas the Turk, an Arabic poet, who chronicled the events to follow.

On the deck of *L'Orient* General Bonaparte, Member of the Institute and supreme commander of the army and navy forces constituting the 'Left Wing of the Army of England,' watched the vessels glide past the flagship, which they saluted as they passed. If anyone knew the purpose of the expedition, it was he; but what his motives were in taking its command, no one to this day could say with certainty, and perhaps he himself did not know.

He was, at that time, a lean, sallow little man whose hat and boots seemed too large for him. Women had nicknamed him Puss-in-Boots. But there was in him a compact energy that made one think of a panther ready to leap rather than of a tomcat with odd sartorial tastes; and in the cold, calm gaze of his grey eyes there was a quality that inspired devotion in some, terror in all, and love in none. In his twenty-ninth year, he had risen higher and achieved greater glory than even the most ambitious can reasonably expect in a lifetime. It was here, at Toulon, only five years earlier, that he had landed with his numerous family, expelled as a traitor from his native Corsica. It was here, only a few months after that event, that Captain Buonaparte of the artillery rose suddenly from nothingness to modest prominence; his part in the capture of Toulon from its English and royalist defenders earned him a promotion to brigadier general. It was here that the protégé of Robespierre's brother witnessed, not without disgust, the almost cannibalistic massacre of the royalist population by the revolutionary 'patriots.' Since then, after two years of obscurity, during which he had to live down his former association with the Jacobins, he had ingratiated himself with the Directory, whose existence he saved by ordering his guns to fire pointblank into a crowd of demonstrators; he had married the ex-mistress of one of the Directors; he had been appointed to the command of the French forces in Italy; he had found a tattered, starving, demoralized army and had led it from victory to victory, conquered the larger part of Italy, made peace with the Emperor, destroyed the Venetian Republic, seized the Ionian Islands, and returned triumphantly to France with the reputation of an invincible warrior, a statesman wise beyond his years, a hero in the classical mould. As Nicholas the Turk soon was to put it in his *Ode to Bonaparte*: 'The chief who marches at their head is impetuous and terrible; his name puts fear into the hearts of kings; the kings bow their heads before the invincible Bonaparte, before the lion of battle. His courage makes him the master of irrevocable destiny, and the skies of

2

glory lower themselves before him.'[1] The rhetoric is Oriental; yet it expresses a conception of Bonaparte which then was generally shared by the West.

It is dangerous to have unemployed heroes loitering about. When Bonaparte returned from his Italian triumphs in December 1797, the Directory had already appointed him to take command of the 'Army of England,' then forming along the Channel coast preparatory to an invasion of the British Isles. Evidence as to whether or not he ever seriously contemplated the possibility of a successful invasion is conflicting; if so, it was not for long.[2] After a hasty inspection of the staging areas in February 1798, he reported to the Directory that the military and financial resources available were utterly inadequate; that possibly the favourable moment for an invasion had been lost forever; that France must either make peace with England, or invade Hanover instead, or seize Egypt and thus cut Britain's lifeline to India. The latter scheme was adopted, in circumstances and for reasons that will be seen; it was by no means new, nor did it originate with Bonaparte.

The risk of total disaster must have been present in Bonaparte's mind as he impassively watched the long procession of his ships. If the English intercepted his fleet, even with inferior forces, that would be the end of the expedition. It was a risk he was willing to take, being both a gambler and a soldier, and he had calculated it soberly, despite the vistas of unlimited glory and conquests that may have filled his mind. His personal secretary and former classmate, Fauvelet de Bourrienne, who even then stood at his side, reminisced in his *Memoirs*, compiled by a ghost writer during his senility, that Bonaparte when leaving for Egypt was bursting with ambitions worthy of Alexander the Great. 'Europe is a molehill,'[3] he quoted him as saying. 'Everything here wears out: my glory is already past; this tiny Europe does not offer enough of it. We must go to the Orient; all great glory has always been acquired there.'[4] Perhaps Bonaparte really said this. Certainly, at all stages of his life, he returned to this theme, the conquest of India, which haunted his imagination. It was in Italy, he declared at St. Helena, that he first foresaw what he might be. 'Already I felt the

---

[1] Institut d'Egypte, I, 86.

[2] To be sure, there can be no question but that he seriously entertained that notion at a later time, from 1803 until the disaster at Trafalgar.

[3] Bourrienne, I, 230.

[4] Ibid., I, 221.

earth flee from beneath me, as if I were being carried to the sky.'[1] In Egypt 'I felt that I could abandon myself to the most brilliant dreams.'[2]

To Madame de Rémusat he made a more specific confession in the early 1800s: 'In Egypt, I found myself freed from the obstacles of an irksome civilization. I was full of dreams.... I saw myself founding a religion, marching into Asia, riding an elephant, a turban on my head and in my hand the new Koran that I would have composed to suit my needs. In my undertakings I would have combined the experiences of the two worlds, exploiting for my own profit the theatre of all history, attacking the power of England in India and, by means of that conquest, renewing contact with the old Europe. The time I spent in Egypt was the most beautiful in my life, because it was the most ideal.'[3] These declarations must be taken with a good deal of salt. Even if he had such dreams (and probably he did), Bonaparte never counted on their fulfillment. If he undertook the conquest of Egypt, his motives were far more limited and calculated. The one thing that was bound to be to his disadvantage was inactivity: if the conquest of Greenland had been the only way to avoid inactivity, he would have accepted command over the Army of Greenland. To be sure, Egypt offered more inspiring possibilities.

***

Whatever Bonaparte's thoughts may have been that morning at Toulon, it is indisputable that the vast majority of the 54,000 men aboard his ships did not share them. The sea was choppy, and—especially in the smaller craft—almost to a man they were seasick. They did not know where they were going or how long they would be at sea.

On May 10, immediately after his arrival at Toulon, the Commander-in-Chief had reviewed and addressed his troops. 'Officers and soldiers,' he had said, 'two years ago, I came to take command of you. At that time, you were on the Ligurian coast, in the greatest want, lacking everything, having sold even your watches to provide for your needs. I promised to put an end to your privations. I led you into Italy. There all was given you in abundance. Have I not kept my word?'

---

[1] Gourgaud, II, 56.

[2] Las Cases, II, 381.

[3] Remusat, I, 274.

According to the official *Moniteur* of May 21, the troops responded with the single shout, 'Yes!'

'Well, let me tell you,' continued Bonaparte, 'that you have not done enough yet for the fatherland, nor the fatherland for you. I shall now lead you into a country where by your future deeds you will surpass even those that now are astonishing your admirers, and you will render to the Republic such services as she has a right to expect from an invincible army. I promise every soldier that upon his return to France, he shall have enough to buy himself six acres of land.'[1]

The speech continued in this style for a minute of two. It was followed by shouts of 'Long live the immortal Republic' and by patriotic hymns.[2]

There are numerous indications in the letters written from Egypt by the officers and men of Bonaparte's army that the patriotic slogans of the time were naïvely accepted by many of them. The majority had left their families and homes years earlier as volunteers, to defend the Republic against the 'tyrants;' others were young recruits drafted in the *levée en masse*. Whatever their destination, they believed that they would earn glory by extending liberty to other countries. But, with few exceptions, they also were veterans of the Italian campaign of 1796-97, and their patriotism was mixed with both the memory and the anticipation of booty, of ample food, of wine and women in delightful profusion. On these they counted more confidently than on their pay, which had been chronically in arrears since Bonaparte's departure from Italy. Bonaparte's promise of booty and material rewards no doubt inspired his men with more enthusiasm than did anything else he said in his speech. But where was the booty to be taken? Few knew, and they did not tell. The prevailing ignorance of geography and of current politics led to some astounding guesses; the majority, however, expected to land in Naples or Sicily; only a few, by putting two and two together, surmised that their destination was the Levant. For the time being, and during most of the journey to Malta and thence to Alexandria, their main concern was their seasickness. Cramped for space, ill supplied, retching, unable to

---

[1] Belliard, Histoire, III, 43-44.

[2] The following day, the *Moniteur* put in a correction, denying that Bonaparte had made this speech, and printed another, totally different text. Yet various independent sources confirm that Bonaparte did make this speech, and the promise of the six *arpents de terre* became a standing joke among the disillusioned troops in Egypt.

change their clothes, they soon regretted that they had ever left land, and nothing of what awaited them was to make them stop regretting it. The Egyptian campaign may have been the most ideal time of Napoleon's life, but decidedly was not the most ideal time of theirs. The grumbling began almost as soon as the fleet left Toulon.

Yet those who survived and returned—and not quite half of them did, after three years—had memories to last them for a lifetime. They could tell of incredible privations, of men trampling each other to death for a few drops of water, of battles fought in distant places against Mamelukes, Arabs, Turks, Englishmen, and embattled peasants, of fabulous booty, of massacres and rape, of strange lands and sights—the Pyramids, Thebes, the Cataracts of the Nile, the holy places of Palestine—of the splendours and miseries of the East, of desert storms and mirages, of the plague, which had killed more than a thousand of them, and of the eye disease which had blinded as many, of courage and endurance, of greed and selfishness, of discouragement and despair. Few returned with enough to buy themselves six acres of land. Rarely have such epic deeds been performed for motives as frivolous or results as futile.

II

Baron de Tott's *Memoirs of the Turks and Tartars*, translated from the French, was among the books most frequently borrowed in the year 1789 by the members of the New York Society Library, a fact which tends to show that interest in the conditions of the disintegrating Ottoman Empire was endemic throughout the world in the late eighteenth century. The Baron, a French officer of Hungarian origin, had long acted as military adviser to the Turkish army; his authority on Eastern affairs was not challenged seriously by anyone except Baron Munchausen, who found occasion in the recital of his adventures to cast doubt on de Tott's veracity and asserted that he was the son of an intoxicated Savoyard prostitute and of the devil himself. Be this as it may, in 1777 the French Foreign Office sent de Tott on a secret mission to the Levant, of which he speaks with something less than candour in his book.

Officially, de Tott was to inspect the French consular and commercial establishments in the Levant. His unofficial mission was nothing less than to explore the possibility of making Egypt into a French colony. Accompanied by the naturalist Sonnini, he sailed to Alexandria on the frigate *Atalante*, went on to Rosetta, transferred to a felucca despatched to him by the Sheik el-Beled

Ibrahim, and proceeded in Oriental luxury up the Nile to Cairo, where utter chaos was awaiting him an experience familiar to almost anyone arriving in Cairo. Here ever so brief an explanation is due.

The traditional alliance between France and the Sublime Porte dated from 1536, when Francis I and Suleiman the Magnificent leagued themselves against the House of Habsburg—a time when Turkey had reached, and France was about to reach, the zenith of its power. It was Suleiman's father, Selim I, who in 1517 had conquered Egypt and Syria from the Mameluke sultans and thereby, on quite flimsy grounds, had acquired for himself and his descendants the title of Caliph, or spiritual ruler, of Islam. As Baron de Tott points out in his book, the terms by which Selim obtained Egypt from the Mamelukes were more favourable to them than to him. Each of the twenty-four provinces of Egypt was to be ruled by a Mameluke bey, or prince; the twenty-four beys were to form a governing council, or divan, over which the Turkish governor, a pasha with three horsetails, was to preside. The object of the arrangement, as far as the Turkish government was concerned, was limited, of course, to the exacting of tribute, which was levied from the peasants by the landowners, who handed part of it to the Coptic tax collectors, who handed part of it to the Mameluke kyacheffs, or subgovernors, who handed some of it to the beys, who handed a little of it to the pasha, who shipped what was left to the Grand Signior.

By the mid-eighteenth century, the central authority in the Ottoman Empire had been so weakened that, aside from the collection of the *miry* (as the tribute to the Porte was called), the government of Egypt had become a vast joke, an occasionally bloody farce acted out with colourful ceremony and ceremonious mayhem by the beys and the pashas, while the rest of the population looked on with amused indifference.

The word 'Mameluke' signifies 'bought man' in Arabic. Contrary to what has been often asserted, the Mamelukes were not slaves in the ordinary meaning of the term. They made their first appearance in Egypt about the year 1250, when the Ayyubite sultan then reigning bought about 12,000 youths from the Caucasus mountains—mostly of Georgian and Circassian—stock to form the élite corps of his army. Within twenty years, the Mamelukes took over the land; in 1252 they killed Sultan Ashraf Moussa and founded their own dynasty, which lasted until the Turkish conquest of 1517. Their power was by no means broken by the conquest. While the authority of the Turkish pashas became more and more nominal, and was at times non-existent, the beys, each with his own band of Mamelukes, were the actual lords and owners of the populated parts of Egypt. (As for the desert, no one was lord there except the Bedouin sheiks.)

The fact that the Mamelukes succeeded in dominating Egypt for five and a half centuries may be explained by the resigned subservience of the native population and by the distance of Egypt from Constantinople; but there were certain peculiarities in the customs of the Mamelukes themselves which contributed to their extraordinary staying power. Although their harems were filled with Egyptian, Nubian, and Abyssinian concubines, they married only women of their own stock—that is, Georgian, Armenian, or Circassian—and they almost never had children from them. This latter phenomenon was caused partly by the high infant mortality in Egypt but even more so by the almost universal practice of Mameluke wives of aborting themselves in order to preserve, as long as possible, their youthful looks and their hold over their husbands. Consequently, the Mamelukes replenished their numbers—which fluctuated between ten and twelve thousand—by buying boys eight to ten years old, mostly from the Caucasus, whom they trained as warriors. As soon as a young Mameluke received a military command, he automatically became a free man, was entitled to grow a beard, and was given at least two servants-at-arms, called *serradj*. It was these 'bought men' who formed the true aristocracy, and they looked down contemptuously on the few sons of Mamelukes who achieved their position by birth. Thus the arrogant Circassian warriors remained a caste apart from the supine population over which they ruled with absolute power, and at the same time they renewed them selves with ever fresh blood. Although there was among them a sprinkling of Russians, Greeks, Germans, and Negroes, by and large they kept, until their destruction in 1811, the character of Caucasian mountaineers.

Ignorant of anything except horsemanship, manslaughter, and extortion, the beys and their armies (all in all about 10,000 men) lived in luxurious splendour off the backs of the rest of the population and kept themselves in practice by sporadically exercising the noble art of war—usually among themselves and occasionally against the Turks. Their usefulness to anyone but themselves was not readily apparent. In their chronic struggle for supremacy, the beys constantly combined into hostile factions and overthrew each other in a monotonous succession of revolutions. Whenever, after a series of intrigues and secret plots and betrayals, the atmosphere was ripe for a new convulsion, the beys, with their kyacheffs and followers, converged from the provinces on Cairo and had it out with the help of muskets, pistols, scimitars, lances, and battle axes. The peasants, glancing up from their labours, would observe their gleaming cavalcades, all aglitter with steel and resplendent in multicoloured turbans and flowing silken gowns, galloping toward their equally glittering foes, skirmishing for a while, then either entering the capital victoriously or tearing south at a lightning gallop toward Upper Egypt, where they would lie low until there arose an opportunity to fight another day. The personal courage of the Mamelukes was astonishing and proverbial; but equally great was their aptitude, if they chose to exercise it, at retreating with spectacular speed.

To dignify this systematized anarchy with the name of government, the Turkish pashas were assigned a ritual role. Whenever a new pasha was appointed by the Porte and made his entry into Cairo, the beys went to meet him at the river port, greeted him with solemn ceremony, and instantly conducted him to the Citadel, where he was kept in polite imprisonment until the end of his term. When civil war broke out among the Mamelukes, the faction in possession of Cairo would occupy the Citadel and force the pasha to issue stern edicts in their favour, a procedure which often proved as academic as was the pasha's authority. Baron de Tott arrived in Cairo at the precise moment when one of these revolutions broke out. At that time, two beys shared the power—Ibrahim, who held the title Sheik el-Beled, or head of the country, and Murad, who was Emir al-Hadj, or leader of the annual pilgrimage to Mecca.[1] Both these remarkable men were again in power when the French invaded Egypt twenty-one years later. Shortly after de Tott's arrival, their careers seemed at an end. According to customary procedure, as soon as the rebels approached, Ibrahim Bey betook himself to the Citadel and forced the pasha, an old friend of de Tott's, to issue a *firman* 'by which the Insurgents were condemned to banishment; but these, little regarding vain Formalities, and firing their Pieces on their Enemies, compelled them, after a few days' skirmishing, more noisy than bloody, to fly towards the upper Egypt.'[2]

The tumult having died down, de Tott proceeded with his inspection of the French establishments. He also entrusted a

---

[1] There were two great annual pilgrimages. One started at Damascus, the other at Cairo; they joined, before reaching Mecca, under the leadership of the Pasha of Damascus.

[2] Tott, II, 44-45.

Frenchman named La Laune with an espionage mission to Suez and the Delta coast. La Laune fulfilled his task most creditably; it was on the basis of his draft that de Tott made his report to the French Minister of Marine. The military defences of Egypt, the Minister was informed, were negligible. With Crete as an operational base, the ports of Alexandria, Rosetta, and Damietta could be captured with ease, and a main landing could be effected at Abukir Bay. The seizure of Egypt, de Tott affirmed, would mean 'the peaceful occupation of a defenceless country'.[1] A proclamation would be issued reassuring the population that the French came as friends, as allies of the Sultan, as liberators from the Mameluke yoke. Every detail was foreseen; every economic and political advantage of the operation was pointed out; every difficulty was glossed over.

For twenty years, de Tott's memorandum lay gathering dust in the French Foreign Office, along with a growing number of similar proposals. The reasons why, despite this sudden interest in Egypt, the French government hesitated for two decades to adopt them, and the circumstances that eventually brought about their execution are both complex and instructive.

The acquisition of Egypt presented certain obvious advantages. Egypt controlled the land routes to Arabia and India; the construction of a canal from Suez to the Mediterranean, recommended as early as 1586 by a Turkish engineer, was a project interesting enough for Louis XIV to propose it on three occasions to the Porte—each time without result. The potential wealth of the country, and especially of the Delta, was generally known, both from ancient Greek and Roman accounts as well as from modern travellers' reports; equally well known was the shocking neglect into which Egypt's economy had fallen under Mameluke rule. By the eighteenth century, French trade with Egypt amounted to about five and a half million livres a year in combined imports and exports. The figure is unimpressive; nevertheless, France had a larger stake in Egypt than had any other European power. France also was better represented: a consul general resided at Cairo and there were consulates in the principal ports, Alexandria and Rosetta. An English consulate had been established at Cairo in 1698, but there were fewer English merchants than French, and they presented no serious competition until the late eighteenth century.

It is understandable that the fifty or sixty French merchants resident in Egypt, speaking with the voice of their consuls, would

---

[1] Charles-Roux, Origines, p. 88.

have welcomed the support of French arms, or even outright seizure of the country, to make their existence and profits more secure. They were more exposed to dangers and vexations than were
their countrymen elsewhere in the Levant. It would have been
foolhardy for them to venture, without an armed escort, anywhere
outside the cities of Cairo, Alexandria, Rosetta, or Damietta; indeed, as Bonaparte's forces, which largely relied on the merchants'
information, were to find out to their dismay, they hardly knew the
country except for these four cities and the Nile. Even in the cities,
they resided in their *funduks*—walled compounds which combined
storehouse, living quarters, and fortress. In Cairo, they had their
own walled quarter, whose gates were guarded by Janissaries.
Egypt had nothing of the cosmopolitan character that pervaded
other places in the Levant. Religious fanaticism; Bedouin raiders;
political anarchy; the unique strangeness of the country itself, a
strip of green in the middle of the African desert, extending from
the classical Mediterranean to the mysterious Sudan; the monuments of an ancient civilization which even Europeans invested
with an aura of superstition—all this combined to inspire in the
foreigner a feeling of constant danger and isolation.

The Mameluke beys, indifferent to the alliance between France
and their nominal sovereign, the Sultan, frequently inflicted vexations on the French merchants, who chronically appealed for help
to their government. There was little the French government could
do: if they tried to come to terms with the beys, the Porte protested
that its sovereignty had been ignored; if they took up their complaints with the Porte, the beys ignored whatever measures the
Porte might take to give France satisfaction.

Not only was the existence of the French in Egypt precarious,
but the very reason for their presence there was increasingly
threatened by insidious encroachments on the part of the British,
who did not scruple to by-pass the Porte and deal directly with the
beys. A trade treaty between the beys and the governor of British
India, Warren Hastings, and the appearance in Egypt of a number
of British agents and cartographers gave alarm in Paris, in Constantinople, and in the French colony at Cairo, It is true that the
beys made overtures to France, offering similar privileges, but the
French government was hampered by its Turkish alliance. Vergennes, the Foreign Minister, a Turcophile since his term as ambassador to Constantinople, particularly opposed all projects that
might further weaken the Porte.

While the grievances of the French merchants against the beys
and the British might have justified a military expedition to Egypt

in their own eyes, it took more than mere concern for their particular interests to make the French government regard such a project as a serious possibility. Yet as early as 1769—the year of Bonaparte's birth—the Due de Choiseul, Vergennes' predecessor, had made the acquisition of Egypt one of his pet projects. As Talleyrand was to explain to the National Institute in July 1797, it was Choiseul's intention 'to replace the [French] colonies in America, in case they should be lost, with colonies offering the same products and a more extensive trade.'[1] If Vergennes rejected Choiseul's plan and shelved de Tott's memorandum, he did so not only out of loyalty to the Porte but also because the American Revolution made the loss of the French West Indies less likely than it had been during Choiseul's administration. But with the British occupation of Martinique in the French revolutionary wars, the likelihood became almost a certainty.

Even more important in softening the opposition to the scheme was the consideration that if France did not seize Egypt, someone else sooner or later would. It is a moral and political axiom that any dishonourable act, if performed by oneself, is less immoral than if performed by someone else, who would be less well-intentioned in his dishonesty. Catherine II of Russia and Frederick II of Prussia—two morally reprehensible characters—were in the process of carving up Poland, and Maria Theresa of Austria, weeping with moral indignation, secured a large slice for herself in the partition, lest the wicked should obtain all and the pure nothing. A similar fate appeared to be in store for the Ottoman Empire, the 'Sick Man of Europe,' and it stood to reason that the larger the slice France could secure for herself, the less Turkey's enemies and the more Turkey's best ally would obtain. On the part of France, it was almost an act of devotion to the Sultan to take away his territory, which otherwise might fall into the hands of the barbarous Russian, the brutal Austrian, or the perfidious Briton. As it turned out, the Sick Man resisted his demise with uncommon stubbornness and lived on for another century and a half, surviving many amputations. In this respect, Vergennes' prognosis was more accurate than Choiseul's. Still, there was no question but that the Turkish Empire was cracking up, what with Russia and Austria pressing on the north and the outlying regencies—Algiers, Tunis, Tripoli, and Egypt—being virtually independent. The Porte itself was expressing fears of British designs on Egypt and deploring its powerlessness against the Mameluke beys, a circumstance which

[1] Charles-Roux, Origines, p. 40.

suggested to several Frenchmen the possibility of snatching the country ostensibly in order to do the Porte a good turn.

Throughout the 1770s and '80s, the French Foreign Office was swamped with memoranda on the Eastern Question. Some had been solicited by the government, but most of them were officious and not a few were the work of cranks. As far as Egypt was concerned, nearly all the memoranda advocated its acquisition and described it in the most glowing colours. The climate was salubrious; the potential productivity of the country was unlimited; the population was submissive; new crops, such as indigo and sugar cane, could be raised; a canal from Suez to the Mediterranean could be constructed; thousands of enterprising Frenchmen could settle there to cultivate the land and to trade in its goods; militarily the operation presented no difficulty; rumours about endemic plague and trachoma were exaggerated if not false; and so forth. Some of the memoranda had been drafted by men fairly familiar with Egyptian conditions, though scarcely paragons of candour; but most of them were the productions of eager officials who had never seen the country and who relied on second-hand reports, hoping to gain favour with their superiors by proposing bold and new policies.

The spectre of an Austria reaching all the way from the Elbe to the Nile had become an obsession by 1783, much as the fear of a Germany extending her power to Baghdad haunted the Western chancelleries in 1914. Amateur statesmen joined forces with the professionals in seeking ways to spare mankind such a disaster. Among the more imaginative amateurs was a Baron de Waldner, who proposed a joint expedition of French, Dutch, and Venetian forces to conquer Egypt, Yemen, Muscat, and the rest of Arabia, dig the Suez Canal, and partition the Ottoman Empire. The Comte de Choiseul-Gouffier, who was no amateur, displayed less originality but must be credited with a talent for phrases. 'Egypt is at our doorstep,' he wrote. 'Egypt no longer belongs to the Turks; the pasha is nothing; Egypt does not belong to anybody.'[1] These assertions were to recur almost textually in the correspondence of Bonaparte and Talleyrand with each other and with the Directory.

Despite the pressures of what would now be called the 'Egypt lobby,' Vergennes held out in his policy of loyalty to the Sultan. He even invited the European powers to join with France in guaranteeing the Ottoman Empire. But then Emperor Joseph II himself offered Egypt to France as a price for her complicity if she agreed

---

[1] Charles-Roux, Origines, p. 113

to partition Turkey. If the man from whose grasp Egypt was to be protected offered Egypt to its would-be protectors, how could the would-be protectors resist the temptation for long?

In the first years of the Revolution, France was too busy with matters of life and death to pay more than casual attention to the Eastern Question or to the interests of French trade in the Levant. By 1795, however, the Republic had made peace with Spain, Holland, and Prussia; in 1796, Britain withdrew her fleet from the Mediterranean; in 1797, Bonaparte was negotiating peace with Austria. Only England and Portugal remained in the field against France. It so happened that the continued struggle against England and the multiple considerations advanced during the preceding decades in favour of an expedition to Egypt all pointed in the same direction. Patriotism and mercantilism were welded into imperialism.

During the final phase of his campaign in Italy, General Bonaparte, invested with almost unlimited authority to negotiate peace, began to cherish projects which far exceeded the scope of his mission. As he approached the Austrian border, his perspective broadened. Italy, which he had just conquered and whose people he despised, he held to be of little value to France; the great Victorian folly, the fascination of the East, which was to obsess Disraeli and Napoleon III and William II, had begun to take hold of his mind: 'The islands of Corfu, Zante, and Cephallonia are more valuable to us than the whole of Italy,' he wrote to the Directory as early as August 16, 1797. 'I believe that if we had to choose, it would be better to keep these islands, which are a source of wealth and prosperity for our commerce. The Turkish Empire is crumbling; possession of these ... islands will enable us to support it to the degree that this is possible, or else to take our share of it.'[1]

The cynicism concealed in these few lines is admirable in its wholeness. At the cost of incredible efforts and blood, the French army, in the name of freedom and justice, had just liberated a major part of Italy from what the phrase-makers in Paris called her tyrants: these territories the victorious liberator was willing to hand back to their former oppressors for the sake of a few small islands whose possession would be beneficial to a handful of merchants. One wonders what Bonaparte's soldiers, let alone the liberated Italians, would have thought of their hero had they been aware of his musings. 'The day is not far off', Bonaparte added to his message, 'when we shall appreciate the necessity, in order

---

[1] Correspondance, III, 235.

really to destroy England, to seize Egypt. The vast Ottoman Empire, which is dying day by day, obliges us to think, while there is still time, of the measures we must take to preserve our trade with the Levant.'[1]

There is no reason to believe that Bonaparte had studied the dossiers in the French Foreign Office; yet it is certain that these ideas did not germinate in him spontaneously. Four months before he wrote this letter, on April 9, he had had a long interview with Raymond Verninac, a diplomat returning to Paris from Constantinople, where he had represented the French Republic as minister plenipotentiary. Verninac had failed to improve the rather strained relations between France and the Porte, which was naturally antipathetic to the Revolution; he had been particularly unsuccessful in his efforts to make the Turks proceed energetically against the Mameluke beys. All the same Verninac had managed to send a commissioner to investigate conditions in Egypt. The commissioner, Dubois-Thainville, an old hand at the Levant, addressed a report to Verninac from Smyrna in September 1796 in which he came to conclusions virtually identical with those expressed by Bonaparte a year later: the Ottoman Empire was in a state of dissolution and chaos (a vastly exaggerated statement), and Egypt could be had for the mere trouble of taking it. A similar memorandum had been sent to Verninac even earlier, in June 1795, by a French merchant, Charles Magallon, who was consul general in Cairo. The fact that Bonaparte echoed their ideas after his interview with Verninac cannot reasonably be ascribed to coincidence. Yet it is difficult to see why the General should have espoused so wholeheartedly the views of a handful of businessmen and consular agents who clearly had only their special interests at heart. A man's motives can never be proven, but guesses are permissible. In the case of Bonaparte, there was, most obvious of all, the romantic motivation: the campaign in Italy was at an end; peace was in the making; the proconsular authority which the Directors had granted him would soon be terminated, and after being fêted as a hero he would once again be just one general among many. Even while negotiating the peace and remaking the map of northern Italy, he was chafing at the obstacles of an 'irksome civilization,' which he was less likely to encounter in the Orient. He had just raped the ancient Republic of Venice, a neutral power, and was offering her to Austria in exchange for Belgium and the left bank of the Rhine. The liquidation of the Venetian state

---

[1] Ibid

15

brought him into direct contact with Eastern affairs. Even for a less imaginative man, it would have been difficult not to sense the excitement of new and strange possibilities as he stood in that amphibious city, the Venice which 'did hold the gorgeous East in fee,'[1] master over the mistress of the Adriatic, where the Balkans, Greece, Byzantium, the Levant, the Barbary States mingled with the prosaic Western world under the shimmering haze of an exotic sky. Here the Orient began, the only prize worthy of a conqueror and a dreamer.

But there was no more realistic dreamer than General Bonaparte. As he once put it, he 'measured his dreams with the callipers of reason.'[2] Besides, he was a politician as much as a conqueror. He knew exactly the mood of the Directory: what they wanted above all was money. The millions he had levied in the Italian states as war contributions were barely a drop in the Directory's bottomless bucket. If the war with England was to be brought to a victorious end, or at least to a draw, it seemed impracticable to attempt the most hazardous, most expensive, and financially least promising method—a direct attack on the British Isles. The other method—seizing Egypt and threatening India—though it might not bring England to her knees, was far cheaper, held few military risks, and, at worst, put France into a more favourable bargaining position should peace negotiations materialize. At any rate, it offered an opportunity for levying more contributions.

In retrospect, dictating his account of the Egyptian campaign to while away his time in St. Helena, Napoleon allowed his imagination to run wild. 'What could be made of that beautiful country [Egypt] in fifty years of prosperity and good government? One's imagination delights in the enchanting vistas. A thousand irrigation sluices would tame and distribute the overflow of the Nile over every part of the territory. The eight to ten billion cubic yards of water now lost every year to the sea would be channelled to the lower parts of the desert ... all the way to the oases and even farther west.... Numerous immigrants from deepest Africa, from Arabia, from Syria, from Greece, from France, from Italy, from Poland, from Germany, would quadruple the population. Trade with India would again flow through its ancient route.... France, being mistress of Egypt, would also regain mastery over Hindustan.'[3]

---

[1] Wordsworth, 'On the Extinction of the Venetian Republic', in Poetical Works, III (Oxford,1954), 111.

[2] Remusat, I, 267.

[3] Correspondance, XXIX, 429.

It stands to reason that so powerful a colony would sooner or later claim independence. This possibility held no terror for Napoleon. Having created his imaginary empire, he generously granted it imaginary independence and more: it would be only natural, he asserted, if the world were ruled from Alexandria rather than from Rome, Constantinople, Paris, London, or Amsterdam. As for practicability, Napoleon was no less sanguine in sweeping aside all petty objections. The distance from Cairo to the Indus was no greater than from Bayonne to Moscow. Sixty thousand men, mounted on 50,000 camels and 10,000 horses would reach the Euphrates in forty days and the Indus in four months; there they would join forces with the Sikhs, the Mahrattas, and the other Indian nations anxious to shed the British yoke. Having proved the ease with which the project could be carried out, the dreamer lets go of his reins and rides his chimera full gallop into glory: 'After fifty years, civilization would have radiated to the centre of Africa by way of Sennar, Abyssinia, Darfur, and Fezzan; several great nations would be enabled to share in the benefits of [Western] arts and sciences and in the religion of the true God—for it is from the hands of Egypt that the peoples of central Africa must receive enlightenment and happiness.'[1][2]

One cannot help marvelling at this mixture of grandiose, Faustian visions, and utter poppycock. Yet such was the stuff that the dreams of farsighted statesmen and empire builders fed on throughout the nineteenth century; one glance at Africa today will suffice to show that in the long run it is impracticable to be benefactor and profiteer at the same time.

In a more sober mood, also at St. Helena, Napoleon diagnosed somewhat more realistically the motives that pushed his government into the Egyptian venture: 'The Directory,' he wrote, 'was dominated by its own weakness; in order to exist, it needed a per-

---

[1] Correspondance, XXIX, 430

[2] These were not mere pipedreams of a bored exile. In 1808, Napoleon wrote to Caulaincourt, his ambassador to Russia: 'Tell Romanzov [the Russian foreign minister] and the Emperor [Alexander I] that I am seriously considering an expedition to India and a partition of the Ottoman Empire. To carry out this project, I would march an army of twenty to twenty-five thousand Russians, eight to ten thousand Austrians, and thirty-five to forty thousand French into Asia and thence to India. Nothing is easier than this operation' (Lecestre, ed., Lettres incites de Napoleon I, I, 144). In the same year, in a letter to Decrès, his Minister of Marine, he wrote of a planned expedition to Egypt, which, like the expedition of 1798, was to leave from Toulon.

petual state of war, just as other governments need peace.'[1] He might have added that, whatever the differences between the Directory's policies and his own, in this one respect there was none.

***

On July 16, 1797, while Bonaparte was still in Italy, musing about the East, a new foreign minister took office in Paris, thanks largely to his former mistress, Madame de Staël, and to her friend Barras, the most influential of the five Directors. He was Charles-Maurice de Talleyrand, unfrocked Bishop of Autun, recently returned from Philadelphia, where he had waited out the Reign of Terror. Only two weeks before his appointment, the ex-bishop, thirsting for political employment, had read before the Institute of France a paper on 'The Advantages to Be Obtained from New Colonies in the Present Circumstances.' It was in this paper that Talleyrand recalled Choiseul's plans for Egypt; indeed, he had long been a familiar of Choiseul and was well acquainted with Middle Eastern affairs. When Magallon, the consul general in Cairo, arrived in Paris shortly after Talleyrand's appointment, he found a sympathetic listener to his proposals. About a month later, Talleyrand received from General Bonaparte a letter almost identical with the one addressed to the Directory: Turkey was in the process of dissolution; French trade needed more colonies; the war against England must be fought in the East; France should seize Egypt.

Historians have quarrelled over the question, which of the two, Talleyrand or Bonaparte, initiated the Egyptian venture. Since it turned out to be a disaster, Talleyrand in his later years gave full credit for it to Bonaparte. Actually, it was thanks to Talleyrand's efforts rather than Bonaparte's that the Directory endorsed the plan. The true initiators of the scheme, however, were the late Due de Choiseul and the spokesmen of French commercial interests overseas. Bonaparte himself was not insensitive to the profits to be derived from colonies: his wife had, or claimed to have, property in Martinique.

Whatever Talleyrand's weaknesses, he was not a dreamer. He was, moreover, a fairly consistent Anglophile, and he had a distaste for war. In fact, he despised any form of strenuous activity; clever people could manoeuvre events their own way without the least apparent exertion, and he was cleverer than most. If Talleyrand fell in wholeheartedly with General Bonaparte's grandiose schemes, it was not because of their grandiosity. It is even doubt-

---

[1] Ibid., XXX, 231.

ful whether he really believed in the usefulness of colonies; but he had a true passion for diplomacy, which is the art of fishing tranquilly in troubled waters, and the Ottoman Empire was an ideal fishing ground. Besides, he never trusted Bonaparte. Give him employment a few thousand miles away, and there will be one troublemaker less at home; let him do the heavy work, and if he succeeds, so much the better, and if he fails, good riddance. For different reasons, Bonaparte found it to his benefit to keep away from home: like Julius Caesar when he left for Gaul, he appreciated the advantages of active absence over passive presence. Like Caesar, he could—and did—return at the opportune moment.

In the ensuing correspondence between Bonaparte and Talleyrand, one gains the impression of a perfect harmony of views. It would be a good idea, the General suggested to the minister on September 15, to seize Malta; the Knights of Malta, though French for the most part, had been hostile to the Republic; their new Grand Master was a German; to take Malta would prevent Emperor Francis II from gaining a foothold there, and the island would be invaluable for subsequent operations in the Levant. Egypt could be conquered with a force of 25,000 men and eight to ten battleships; but what effect would such an expedition produce on the Porte? Talleyrand's reply arrived a couple of weeks later: the Directory fully agreed with the General's views on Malta. As for Egypt, the General's ideas were interesting and useful; Talleyrand would write to him more fully on the subject; in any event it must be understood that the conquest of Egypt could be undertaken only in the interest of the Ottoman Sultan to protect him from Russian and English designs. (Needless to say, Sultan Selim III was not informed of these kindly intentions in his favour.)

At that time, Bonaparte was installed at Passeriano and negotiating with Austria the peace that came to be known as the Treaty of Campo Formio. He was communicative on the subject of Egypt. General Desaix, the future conqueror of Upper Egypt, kept a notebook of his conversations with Bonaparte: 'Ideas about Egypt, its resources. Project about it. Development peace with Austria, England. Embark at Venice with 10,000 [French] men and 8,000 Poles for Egypt. Seize it. Advantages. Details. With 5 divisions,

2,000 horses.'[1] As it turned out, the project was to be much delayed, and it was not at Venice that the expedition was staged.[2]

Although the Egyptian campaign failed in all its objectives, it undoubtedly had distant consequences of a most varied nature. Whether the balance sheet of these consequences shows a positive or a negative result remains a matter of opinion; at any rate, they differ vastly from the Due de Choisel's expectations, as all colonial experiments have differed in their results from the forecasts of their originators. As for the human facts of the campaign—and it is with them that this book is mainly concerned—they are facts, and nothing could contrast more grotesquely than they do with the reveries of the inventive policy-makers who called them into being.

III

If Talleyrand informed the Directors of his thoughts on Egypt in the autumn of 1797, there is no indication that he received a favourable response. The victories of French arms in Italy and Germany, mutinies in the English navy, and signs of popular discontent in Britain, let alone Ireland, encouraged the Directory to entertain exaggerated hopes of seeing English resistance collapse in the near future. Preliminary peace negotiations with England, held at Lille in the summer, had been brusquely terminated by the French, Britain having refused to return the colony of the Cape of Good Hope to their Dutch allies. A direct blow must be dealt the British homeland, supported by a rebellion in Ireland. An army of invasion was organized and General Bonaparte was appointed to its command; he seemed to have forgotten Egypt. At the same time, high French officials in Paris were conferring with a motley contingent of Swiss, Italian, and Irish agitators. Nothing would be more convenient than to stir up disorders in Switzerland and the Papal States, intervene by force of arms in the name of freedom, and confiscate the reputedly fabulous treasuries of Berne and Rome; indeed although considerable labour was required to

---

[1] Guerrini, p. 52.

[2] Bonaparte did, however, make use of several Venetian battleships which he had seized.

The Poles to whom he referred to Desaix were former fighters in Kosciusko's forces who had been driven into exile. The French army in Egypt had a large sprinkling of Polish volunteers, including General Zayonczek, of the Cavalry, and Bonaparte's aide-de-camp Sulkowski.

manufacture the necessary pretexts, this is precisely what happened in the early months of 1798. The Irish rebellion, as will be seen, was less successful, but the costs were borne almost exclusively by Irishmen.

Bonaparte returned to Paris in December 1797, ostensibly burning with zeal to proceed with the invasion project, yet posing at the same time as a man of peace who desired nothing more than to withdraw from public life and devote himself to studies. He had just been elected a member of the Mathematical Section of the National Institute; the only true conquests, he declared, were those gained by knowledge over ignorance. Yet the conquest he obviously was preparing for was that of England. Wolfe Tone, who had an interview with him at that time, described him as courteous, cold, and inscrutable.

By the end of February 1798, the invasion project was abruptly abandoned, or rather modified and postponed. The French navy was not adequate for it; Spain and Holland were unwilling to cooperate. On February 9, Magallon handed Talleyrand a detailed memorandum on Egypt; on the 14th, Talleyrand presented his plan for a conquest of Egypt to the Directors; on February 25, Bonaparte wrote his pessimistic report to the Directory which favoured abandoning the invasion and suggested, among the alternatives, an expedition to Egypt. A week later, the Directory approved that project. (Later, the Directors were to blame each other for the decision, which at least two of them claimed they had opposed.) On March 5, Bonaparte drafted a memorandum to the Directory, outlining his plans. On April 12, the Directory issued a series of resolutions; Bonaparte was instructed to seize Malta and Egypt, to dislodge the English from their establishments in the East in as far as this was possible, to pierce the Isthmus of Suez, to improve the living conditions of the native population of Egypt, and to maintain good relations with the Porte. It was generally estimated that six months would suffice to accomplish the immediate ends and to prepare the ground for the more remote ones; General Bonaparte would then return, leaving adequate forces behind, and—unless England agreed to make peace on satisfactory terms—take command over the forces destined to invade Great Britain. At that time, Ireland would rise in rebellion under the leadership of the United Irishmen. Meanwhile, concurrently with Bonaparte's expedition to Egypt, relations would be established with Tippoo Sahib, Sultan of Mysore, who was then fighting the English in India, and Talleyrand would go to Constantinople on a personal embassy. If there was anyone who could persuade the

Porte that France was occupying Egypt in the interests of Turkey, Talleyrand was the man. As it turned out, he eventually chose not to go—wisely so, considering what was soon to happen to the French *chargé d'affaires* in Constantinople.

There is no doubt that Bonaparte assured those whom he persuaded to accompany him on his venture that they would be back before the end of 1798. Whether he thought that he himself would be back by then is open to question. To Bourrienne, who asked him on how long an absence he counted, Bonaparte replied (according to Bourrienne), 'A few months, or six years. It all depends on the course of events. I shall colonize that country. I shall import artists, workmen of all kinds, women, actors, etc. We are only twenty-nine years old; we'll be thirty-five then. That's still young. Six years will be enough for me, if all goes well, to go to India.'[1] One suspects that the only thing Bonaparte firmly counted on was his ability to exploit the course of events, what ever it might be.

***

From the day the Directory approved the Egyptian project to the day the French fleet left Toulon, Bonaparte had about ten weeks to concentrate and equip his troops, assemble the transports, fit out the warships, recruit the sailors needed to bring the depleted crews to full strength, and enlist a commission of civilian experts—engineers, scientists, aeronauts, artists, archaeologists, economists, pharmacists, surgeons, writers, musicians, interpreters, printers to accompany his expedition. That some of this work had to be carried out hastily and imperfectly is hardly surprising; that it was done at all is astonishing. Haste, however, was necessary in order to prevent the enemy from, learning the purpose of these vast preparations and in order to gain control over Egypt before the Nile reached its annual flood.

It was characteristic of Napoleon to claim credit for everything that others did for him; it is characteristic of his admirers to take him at his word. From the beginning of March until his departure from Paris in the night of May 5, so historians assert, Bonaparte spent his time in feverish activity, displaying his superhuman organizational genius. To be sure, he was busy; but there is nothing superhuman in a general sitting down at his desk and ordering units to proceed from one place to another. Inability to do so would have proved him incompetent, and that he assuredly was not. The credit for the smooth functioning of the complex opera-

---

[1] Bourrienne, I, 233.

22

tions belonged to those who had shaped the French revolutionary army into an admirably disciplined, intelligent, and swiftly responsive mechanism; credit belonged, in particular, to the *commissaire ordinateur* Najac, the civilian official of the navy who supervised the preparations at Toulon. Najac's accomplishment was all the more remarkable since he had but recently succeeded in office to a senile blunderer who had left him a legacy of an astronomical deficit, dock-workers whose pay was in arrears for several months, and general chaos.

If Bonaparte tended to claim all credit for himself, he also blamed all his mistakes on others. Throughout his life, he clung to the notion that French naval officers were a fraternity of stubborn, fussy, timorous souls, forever raising technical objections, declaring whatever he demanded of them to be impossible, and inviting defeat by their excessive caution. Had he listened to them, Waterloo might have been spared him. Be this as it may, there can be no question that, compared to the British navy, the French navy of 1798 was in sorry shape. Some of its ships were excellent, but many were in disrepair; the crews were dangerously under strength; the officers' corps had been depleted (far more severely than the army's) by emigration during the Reign of Terror and, in the days of sailing ships, new officers could not be trained overnight. In five years, from 1793 to 1797, the French navy had lost thirty-five battleships and sixty-one frigates, while the British had lost only fourteen battleships and twenty frigates. To send a slow convoy of 400 ships across the Mediterranean, which Admiral Nelson had just re-entered with a large squadron, was foolhardy; it will be seen how only its slowness and Nelson's impatience saved the convoy from destruction. Still, thanks largely to Najac's energy, the men-of-war were adequately repaired, the crews brought reasonably close to field strength, and the transports mostly French and Italian merchant men assembled. The entire naval force was assigned to Vice-Admiral Brueys, whose conscientiousness and heroism were to be rewarded with defeat and death. The squadron was divided into three groups, the first commanded by Brueys himself, aboard *L'Orient*; the second by Rear-Admiral Blanquet du Chayla, aboard the battleship *Le Franklin*, the third by Rear-Admiral Villeneuve, aboard the battleship *Guillaume* Tell. Rear-Admiral Decres, aboard the frigate *La Diane*, commanded the convoy. Another Rear-Admiral, Ganteaume, served as chief of staff to Brueys. In the hands of these men, their officers and their ill-trained, undisciplined crews lay the fate of the entire expedition; their only hope was that they would be lucky.

Compared to the naval preparations, the assembling of the land forces was an easy matter. As soon as the expedition was decided upon, in early March, orders went out to the units chosen by Bonaparte to march to their several ports of embarkation—Toulon, Marseilles, Genoa, Ajaccio, and Civita Vecchia. (The Marseilles convoy joined the fleet on May 11; the other three convoys were to sail separately and to join the main convoy on the high seas.) The units were widely dispersed at the time Bonaparte selected them: some were in Switzerland, which they had just conquered; others had been left in northern Italy; others were in Rome, where they had just deposed Pope Pius VI as temporal ruler and set up a republic under French protection; yet others were in Corsica, and several divisions were in northern France as part of the 'Army of England.' The wide dispersal of the various units called upon tends to conceal the fact that nearly all of them had been part of the 'Army of Italy' during Bonaparte's campaign of 1796-97; the few that had not served under his previous command were to be left in Malta as a garrison. It was only natural for Bonaparte to prefer the men who had proven themselves under him at Arcole, Lodi, Castiglione, and Rivoli, and on whose loyalty he could count in his new hazardous expedition. They all were veterans; many had volunteered for the defence of the fatherland in 1792 and fought in the Army of the Sambre-et-Meuse and the Army of the Rhine before their transfer to Italy. Their morale, however, was not uniformly high as they marched to their various ports. It was their first overseas expedition, and though they had no inkling of where they were going, they were aware of the discomforts and dangers of a sea voyage. In some units, the incidence of desertions while marching to the ports was unusually high; it would have been much higher had they known what was in store for them and for how long they would be separated from their homes, from the comforts of civilization, from their families, wives, and mistresses. Moreover, the pay of many units, especially those that had been stationed in Italy, was long overdue; the temper of the unpaid citizen soldiers was not improved by the spectacle of the army commissioners living in luxury, partly on the illegal sale of government property, partly on loot and bribes. When Bonaparte, in his address, hinted that the Republic had not treated them right, he struck a responsive chord, and his promise of compensation as well as glory was a psychological necessity.

The civilians accompanying the expedition showed a more sanguine mood than did the soldiers. Apart from the so-called Scientific and Artistic Commission (actually, a commission of experts and technicians), the expeditionary force included at least 500 civilians, among them twenty-six army commissioners and 445 other administrative personnel. Until 1807, when Napoleon reorganized the administration of the army, all the services (finance, supplies, hospitals, etc.) were in the hands of a corps of civilian commissioners, who operated through private contractors. The appointments to the Corps du Commissariat often were purely political; thus Bonaparte's brothers Joseph and Lucien held lucrative posts in the Commissariat during his Italian campaign, as did his uncle Fesch, the future cardinal. The abuses of these officials were a constant target of Bonaparte's wrath, but only when they pushed them to extremes.

Bonaparte had offered the post of Controller General, or chief financial officer, of the expeditionary force to the Swiss Haller, who had held that post during the Italian campaign. Haller, however, was at that moment revelling in undreamt-of opportunities in Rome, despoiling the treasury of the man whom the troops called 'Citizen Pope.' (It was Haller who, when the octogenarian Pius VI begged him to be allowed to live out his life in Rome, replied, 'When it comes to dying, you can do that anywhere,' and had him carted off into exile.) The tactful Haller having courteously declined, the post of Controller General was given to Citizen Poussielgue, who had just accomplished a delicate mission to the Knights of Malta with, as will be seen, considerable success.

The civilian contingent included some less exalted members, whose duties were often ill-defined. There were cooks, servants, and, especially, a number of small businessmen and concessionaires who, scenting profit, attached themselves to any army no matter where it might go—a breed still to be found in wartime at the fringes of military training centres. Also, as Nicholas the Turk points out, there were women and children. Possibly some of the children referred to by Nicholas were apprentice seamen and midshipmen; Midshipman Casabianca, aged nine or ten, was to earn fame thanks to a useless death and a bad and factually inaccurate poem.[1] Probably there also were some drummer boys and children belonging to *cantinières*, laundresses, and the like. They and their mothers suffered, and some no doubt died, just like the others, even though historians persist in ignoring them.

Aside from officially authorized female personnel, women were Barréd by strict orders from embarking with their husbands or lovers. (It was not unusual for women to follow their men on cam-

---

[1] See "Casabianca" by Felicia Hemans; Appendix A — [Ed.]

paigns.) The orders were not absolutely effective. Thus General Verdier managed to take along his wife, 'a lively and good-natured Italian woman';[1] a few others, disguised in the uniforms of their men's units, also succeeded in slipping aboard the transports. All in all, about 500 women accompanied the expedition. Bonaparte intended to have civilians, including women, brought to Egypt once its conquest was consolidated; since the British navy spoiled this plan, he was to be grateful to those who had managed to come as stowaways and enlivened garrison life in Cairo. He was particularly grateful to that young, blonde, and pretty *chasseur*, Madame Fourès, wife of Lieutenant Fourès, who soon regretted having taken her along.

IV

General Bonaparte's house in the rue Chantereine (rechristened, since his return from Italy, rue de la Victoire), looked a little too much like a cocotte's boudoir for the taste of his wife Josephine, who was wishing him away so she could buy the chateau of La Malmaison (which she could not afford) and enjoy the company of her lover, Monsieur Charles, with whom she had been deceiving her victorious husband all over Italy. It was in these somewhat erotic surroundings that General Bonaparte, Member of the Institute, was preparing his campaign, as well as trying to make love to his wife despite the obligatory presence of her ever-snarling lap dog.[2] The full extent of his wife's disloyalty had not yet dawned on him (it was to be revealed to him in Egypt), but the incessant influx of astronomical bills for her wardrobe and jewelry was enough to appall him, and his family's systematic warfare against her proved to be equally harassing. If only for domestic reasons, another victorious campaign, with the rewards attending it, seemed imperative. As far as the domestic distractions allowed, the General devoted himself to its organization whole heartedly. The number of his official letters in the period of March—May 1798 is not impressive, but much of his activity was spent in conferences, and not all his letters have been preserved. Issuing orders for troop movements was a simple matter compared to the

---

[1] Belliard, Histoire, IV, 70.

[2] The scrupulous historian must object that Fortuné, the dog of whom Bonaparte complained in his letters, had been choked to death by the dog of Bonaparte's cook late in 1796. But it may be assumed that Fortuné had a successor.

more delicate negotiations required to appoint his staff and the members of the Scientific Commission, to which he attached equal importance. Besides, he was determined to learn, within a few weeks, all that a conqueror should know about Egypt, Syria, Turkey, and Islam. In his somewhat roughshod way, he succeeded remarkably well in all these endeavours.

In his choice of the generals to serve under his command, Bonaparte was limited by considerations of their availability and of their willingness to serve under so young and so ambitious a man. Of the thirty-one general officers he selected, twenty-seven accompanied him to Egypt.[1] Of these, two were assassinated, three were fatally wounded in action (one of these may have committed suicide), nine were wounded but survived, and two died of illness while in Egypt. This was an extraordinarily high percentage of casualties for generals, but Napoleon always regarded generals as expendable and wished them to set examples of personal courage. About two thirds of them had served under Bonaparte in Italy; they were, however, by no means the most distinguished ones. A notable fact is that, like Bonaparte, twenty-seven of the thirty-one had served in the old army of the monarchy—sixteen as officers, eleven in the ranks. Six of the generals were to become Marshals of the Empire and one of them (Murat, the son of an inn-keeper) a king. Twenty-five were older and four were younger than their commander-in-chief, the oldest was fifty-seven, the youngest twenty-five, and their average age thirty-eight—on the whole, a youthful command.[2]

The foot troops were divided into five divisions, to be commanded by Major-Generals Desaix, Kléber, Baraguey d'Hilliers (soon replaced by Menou), Reynier, and Bon. Of these men, Desaix and Kléber were the most remarkable. As generals, they were at least the equals of Bonaparte; as human beings, decidedly superior. Of these two men, and of Menou, who became a Moslem to marry a bathkeeper's daughter, more will have to be said. During the preparatory stages of the campaign, Kléber supervised the embarkation areas of Toulon, Marseilles, Genoa, and Ajaccio, and

---

[1] General Vaubois remained at Malta in command of the French garrison; Generals Chaney and d'Hennezel stayed with him. General Baraguey d'Hilliers was sent home from Malta.

[2] These data, to be sure, apply to the composition of the command at the outset of the campaign. Several officers were promoted to general rank in the course of the expedition. The title 'Major-General' is used throughout this book for convenience, to translate the French *général de division*.

Desaix was in charge of the armaments at Civita Vecchia. Desaix, at the time, was twenty-nine years old; Kléber, forty-five. They were to die on the same day, practically at the same hour, 1,500 miles from each other, one on the battlefield, the other by the hand of an assassin.

To command his artillery, Bonaparte appointed the competent General Dommartin. The command of the engineers and the supervision of the Scientific Commission were entrusted to General Caffarelli du Falga, who had lost one leg in Germany and was to lose an arm, and soon his life, in Syria. Among the military staff of the expedition, Caffarelli was no doubt the closest to Bonaparte. As for the cavalry, its command went to a Herculean mulatto, General Alexandre Dumas, the father of the novelist, a veritable one-man army but not a good general.

Among Bonaparte's aides-de-camp were Duroc, later Duke of Frioul—the only man for whom he confessed ever having experienced friendship; the Pole Sulkowski, a brilliant officer who was doubly valuable to the expedition, being a Knight of Malta, familiar with the Levant, and conversant in Arabic; Junot, later Duke of Abrantes, who was very close to the Bonaparte family; Croisier, whom Bonaparte was to humiliate with tragic results; Napoleon's brother Louis Bonaparte, later King of Holland, a syphilitic homosexual with literary pretentions; and Napoleon's stepson Eugène Beauharnais, later Viceroy of Italy but then a very innocent young man of seventeen. Of these, the first four died a violent death—Duroc, killed in Germany; Sulkowski, torn to pieces in Egypt; Junot, insane and a suicide in Dalmatia; Croisier, killed in Syria.

For his chief of staff, Bonaparte summoned the ever-reliable General Alexandre Berthier, who had served him in that capacity in the Italian campaign and continued in it until 1814. Berthier, it has been said, was born to be chief of staff—meticulous, indefatigable, and lacking any ambition except that of being Napoleon's chief of staff. Unlike Napoleon's other generals, who felt chronically slighted by their master, Berthier worked in complete harmony with his commander, who rewarded him with the principality of Neuchatel, the title Duke of Wagram, and the hand of a Bavarian princess. He, too, was to find a violent end: having failed to rejoin Napoleon during the Hundred Days, he fell dead on to the pavement from his balcony in Bavaria, after watching allied troops parade by on their way to fight against France.

***

Although the recruiting of scientists and technicians was in the hands of General Caffarelli and of the eminent chemist Berthollet, Citizen Bonaparte, Member of the Institute (Mathematical Section) took a very active personal part in it. He was not always very successful. Thus Citizen Langlès, curator of the Bibliothèque Nationale and professor of Arabic, Turkish, Persian, Chinese, and Manchu, when invited to accompany a military expedition for parts unknown, expressed his reluctance with almost hysterical vehemence; his place, he insisted, was in the rue de Richelieu, not in some bivouac. The orientalist Venture eventually took his place; he, too, did not return.

Less reluctant than Langlès but intimidated by his wife was Citizen Monge, one of the most versatile figures in the history of science. Gaspard Monge was fifty-two years old in 1798. The eldest son of an artisan, he had early developed an exceptional gift for mathematics and was admitted, at sixteen, to the school for army engineers, despite his humble birth. There he was to teach intermittently from 1766 to 1809, and there he developed a new branch of mathematics—descriptive geometry. Made a member of the Academy of Sciences in 1780, he moved to Paris and became an associate of Lavoisier, the father of chemistry, who credited Monge with the discovery that water is made up of hydrogen and oxygen. Monge's career as a pure scientist came to an end in 1787, when the Ministry of War sent him to inspect the Wendel iron works at Le Creusot; at about the same time the Ministry of Marine appointed him examiner of candidates at the naval academies, a function which forced him to undertake many journeys. From then on, despite sporadic efforts to return to pure research, Monge was caught in the machinery of administration, politics, and applied technology. An ardent republican, he put his talents at the disposition of the revolutionary government; he served as Minister of Marine in 1792—95, a rather hopeless task. He was commissioned by the Committee of Public Safety as co-author of a manual entitled *Advice to Ironworkers on the Manufacture of Steel in Puddling Furnaces,* to be distributed to all workers who wished to set up steel mills. He served on the Commission for Weights and Measures, which introduced the metric system, and on a committee for aerostatics. He took part in a balloon ascent. He devised, with Berthollet, a process for extracting saltpetre from ordinary soil, thus preventing a crisis in the munitions works, and he supervised the munitions plant at Grenelle (which blew up one evening, killing a thousand people). He served on the Committee for Public Works, wrote a work on *The Art of Manufacturing Guns,* and lectured on new methods of manufacturing munitions. He was an active member of the Jacobin Club and the chief founder of the École Polytechnique. He did about everything a patriot could do to help the fatherland in danger; but he did not lift a finger to help his collaborator Lavoisier escape the guillotine.

In May 1796, Monge's career took a new turn, in a direction even farther removed from science. Along with Berthollet and four other experts, he was appointed to a 'Governmental Commission for the Research of Artistic and Scientific Objects in Conquered Countries,' and sent to Italy. There he befriended Bonaparte, in the wake of whose army the commission examined art collections, museums, and libraries, designating the objects to be ceded to the French Republic under the terms of the peace treaties. A cursory tour of the Louvre indicates the efficiency of the commission of which Monge was the senior member. A list of the works of art thus obtained, headed by the Mona Lisa, staggers the imagination. To keep a Correggio, the Duke of Parma offered a million livres— in vain. The best that can be said for Monge in the operation is that he did not make a sou in it for himself.

Monge's relationship with Bonaparte took on a strangely intimate and confidential nature when they met at Milan in the summer of 1797. Perhaps the General was attracted by the scientist's upright character and practical outlook; there was between them an intellectual kinship that extended even to their vague feelings of deistic religiosity. However, this was also a time when Bonaparte, the victorious hero in the field, was passing through a humiliating sentimental crisis. One may imagine that Bonaparte opened his heart more than was his wont to Monge, who was old enough to be his father and whose manly earnestness offered a consoling contrast with Josephine's feminine frivolity. At any rate, no one was closer to Bonaparte throughout the Egyptian campaign than Monge.

Monge was among the first men to whom Bonaparte mentioned the possibility of an expedition to Egypt. As early as September 1797, he had begun to collect maps and memoranda on Egypt for Bonaparte's use.

On December 28, as a consequence of some riots in Rome, General Duphot, a young man on the staff of the French ambassador (Napoleon's brother Joseph), was mobbed and killed by a gang of papal soldiers. Outraged by the crime and welcoming the pretext, the Directory ordered General Berthier to march on Rome and named Citizen Monge to head a commission for the investigation of Duphot's murder. Monge's unofficial mission was to supervise the liquidation of the Pope's temporal power and the establishment of the Roman Republic; this, however, was already an accomplished fact when Monge reached Rome on February 22. (It is one of the piquant details of history that, on the day they deposed the Pope, the French ordered a Te Deum to be sung at St. Peter's to celebrate the occasion.) The looting perpetrated under Commissioner Haller's benign auspices shocked even the patriotic Monge. Under the terms of what was euphemistically called a Treaty of Mutual Assistance, Haller extorted from the Roman Republic 4,000,000 piasters in cash, not to mention church treasures, control of the shipyards and mines, etc. To convey the objects carted off to France, so Monge informed his wife, required 500 crates; it may be said that the originator of descriptive geometry was well on his way to becoming an expert appraiser of *objets d'art*.

On March 5—the very day he outlined his campaign plans for the Directory—Bonaparte also wrote to Monge, asking him to collect Arabic typographic characters, printers, and interpreters, as well as other experts and invited him to join the expedition. Monge procured the characters at the printing office of the Roman Propaganda; he also found typesetters; he acquired surveying instruments and several young people expert in their use; and he recruited four interpreters among the Levantine medical students at Rome. However, as for joining the expedition, Monge at first declined: his duties called him to Paris, and besides, he was too old.

Sensing the real reason for the refusal, Bonaparte addressed himself to the proper authority: he called on Madame Monge, in Paris. The servant who opened the door for him mistook the young and skinny general for one of Professor Monge's students. Madame Monge held out for some time, but after several more calls granted Bonaparte her reluctant consent to let her husband go. In her letters to Monge she continued to berate her 'old fool of a husband': had he lost his head, wanting to gallivant about the world at fifty-two years of age? Her old fool of a husband meanwhile had been reaping the fruits of Bonaparte's favour: he had been elected a deputy to both Chambers the Council of Ancients and the Council of Five Hundred.

No sooner had he received Citizeness Monge's authorization than Bonaparte requested the Directory to relieve her husband of his mission in Italy and to assign him to the expeditionary force. From then on, Monge assisted Desaix in supervising the preparations at Civita Vecchia. Bonaparte entrusted him with private as well as public missions: would Citizen Monge see to it that some 800 bottles of wine from the cellar of Joseph Bonaparte be embarked with the convoy; also, 4,000 bottles from Naples, and a fine city carriage with double harness, for the convenience of the commander-in-chief? Monge saw to everything—Arabic characters, wine, and carriage; he even began to take riding lessons in anticipation of the military life. All this accomplished, there was nothing for him and Desaix to do but to wait the arrival of the French courier ship which would order the Civita Vecchia convoy—some eighty sail—to join the main fleet.

***

The Commission on the Sciences and Arts consisted, according to official sources, of 167 persons, two of whom were left behind in Malta. As has been pointed out, a considerable proportion were technical personnel rather than scientists or artists. The largest contingent in the Commission consisted of civil engineers (nineteen) and surveyors and cartographers (sixteen). Bonaparte had some ambitions of taking with him eminent musicians and poets—for what purpose, it is difficult to say: his own tastes in literature and music were limited, and as for the troops, they were quite content with their regimental bands. He tried to enlist Méhul; Méhul insisted that his services were more urgently needed at the Conservatoire and the Opéra; the man who took his place was Guillaume-André Villoteau, undistinguished except for the learned research he was to do in Arabic music. Bonaparte also tried to recruit Népomucène Lemercier, a secondary but influential figure in literature, who also declined. In his stead came Antoine-Vincent Arnault, who never went farther than Malta, and François-Auguste Parseval-Grandmaison, a less than mediocre poet, but a man who possibly did not deserve all the ridicule heaped upon him by historians.

There were more competent men among the astronomers, botanists, surgeons, pharmacists, antiquarians (today we would say archaeologists), and architects. The chief interpreter, Jean-Michel de Venture, who at fifty-six was among the oldest men in the expedition, was a distinguished Orientalist. The artists Denon and Dutertre and the architect Balzac (no relation of Honoré) were excellent choices; they count among the founding fathers of modern Egyptology. But the most distinguished names were to be found among the mathematicians, chemists, mineralogists, and zoologists. Gaspard Monge already has been introduced. Besides him, in the mathematical section, there were Jean-Baptiste Say, later one of the international oracles of the liberal school of economics, and Jean-Baptiste Joseph Fourier, whose more permanent fame is founded on the 'Fourier series' of equations, with outwhich the higher forms of contemporary applied statistics would be unthinkable.

Claude-Louis Berthollet, chief recruiter of the savants, had been a physician before he devoted himself to chemistry. He had upheld the phlogiston theory of fire with uncommon stubbornness despite the findings of Lavoisier, but in 1785, he had the good grace (all too rare in scientists) to admit having been wrong. His contributions to applied chemistry—especially in the preparation of pigments and dyes—were many, and his *Essai de statique chimique* was the first systematic exposition of the problems of chemical physics. Perhaps of even greater stature was Etienne Geoffroy Saint-Hilaire, who at twenty-one had conducted the first course of zoology ever taught in Paris. He probably also was the first and only professor of zoology ever to masquerade as a prison commissioner, a feat he performed in a vain attempt to save the lives of his imprisoned teachers just before the September Massacres of 1792. Geoffrey's theories, which in some ways foreshadowed Darwin's, were to lead in 1830 to a bitter and sensational battle, still famous in the annals of the biological sciences, with his lifelong friend Cuvier, the father of palaeontology.

Nicolas-Jacques Conté, a man of forty-three when he embarked for Egypt, has two rather contrasting achievements to his credit. He was the first man to think of using balloons for military purposes, did so successfully in the battle of Fleurus, and organized the first airborne battalion; he even planned, at a later date, an airborne invasion of the British Isles. He also invented the first graphite pencil, on which he took out a patent that proved lucrative to his descendants. His mechanical ingenuity bordered on sorcery: with the most rudimentary materials, he was able to manufacture whatever tools were needed and, if necessary, the tools to make the tools—a talent which proved providential in Egypt. In the Scientific Commission, he headed the section on mechanics and aerostatics, with eleven experts under him.

If the Fourier series is named after Fourier and the *crayon Conté* after Conté, the Dolomites in the Italian Alps are called after the mineral Dolomite, which in turn is named for the mineralogist Déodat-Guy-Sylvain-Tancrède Gratet de Dolomieu, another member of Bonaparte's Scientific Commission. Quite apart from his contributions to his science, Dolomieu is remarkable for his adventurous life. He probably is the only mineralogist on record to have been tonsured and created a Knight of Malta while in his cradle, and—should this assertion be proven false—he certainly was the only mineralogist to have been condemned to life imprisonment at eighteen for having killed a man in a duel. This happened in 1768; Dolomieu was reprieved by the Grand Master of the Order, served for a while in the French army, then resigned his commission to pursue his scientific studies.

Whether Captain Etienne-Louis Malus of the Engineers was a member of the Mathematical Section of the Scientific Commission or directly attached to General Caffarelli's staff is a question which it is difficult to elucidate. Whatever his precise status, Malus was one of the most brilliant members of the body of scientists that accompanied the expedition. He was stationed at the somnolent German university town of Giessen, and about to marry Fraulein Koch, the daughter of the university's chancellor, when Caffarelli summoned him to Paris and assigned him to the expeditionary force; Malus was only twenty-three years old. In Egypt and Syria, he kept a diary of his activities, which brought him into close contact with both the combat forces and his fellow scientists. Among other things, he supervised the plague hospital at Jaffa, caught the disease, and cured himself. His chief interest was the study of the physical properties of light. Returning to France in 1801, he married Fraulein Koch, discovered the principle of the polarization of light, and was awarded, in 1811, the Rumford Medal by the Royal Society of London—a rare honour for a scientist to receive, in the middle of a total war, from an enemy nation. A year later, he died of tuberculosis.

Neither civilians nor soldiers, the medical officers of the expedition were destined to play an ungrateful but memorable role. The chief surgeon, Dr. Larrey, the originator of flying ambulances, was the man whom Napoleon in his will called the most virtuous man he had ever known. His colleague, Dr. Desgenettes, chief medical officer of the army, is less well known—possibly because his independence of judgment and his integrity brought him into conflict with 'the Hero of the expedition,' as Kléber called Bonaparte sarcastically. Perhaps it was Dr. Desgenettes who was the real hero of the expedition, at least among the noncombatants.

The presence of so many civilians of undeniable distinction and even genius in the midst of a military body was unprecedented. That these men consented to take part in the adventure was a tribute to General Bonaparte's powers of persuasion. That they were asked at all speaks for the breadth of his vision; it also suggests the scope of his ambitions. Had not Alexander the Great taken philosophers and savants with him when he went to conquer

Egypt, Persia, and India? While still a student at Brienne, Bonaparte had read and reread his Plutarch. The example of Alexander would haunt him while he stayed in the land where forty centuries of history looked down upon him. Still, as in all things, ambitious dreams and practical sense went hand in hand with him. His mission was of a colonizing as much as of a military nature. With a handful of exceptions, the men he selected—even those distinguished in the pure sciences—had a practical turn of mind, a talent for technology, administrative tasks, an Archimedean versatility and pliability that suited them ideally for the many challenges ahead of them. What lasting and beneficial accomplishments the campaign was to achieve were due to them, and to them alone.

V

General Bonaparte and his wife arrived at Toulon on May 9, about eight o'clock in the morning. Everything was ready for the departure of the fleet. There had been a brief flurry during the diplomatic crisis provoked by General Bernadotte, the French ambassador in Vienna, which almost had led to hostilities with Austria and to the abandonment of the Egyptian project. Bernadotte had refused to haul down the Republican tricolour from the embassy, in the face of a rioting mob (in this he was right) and left Vienna with dire threats (in this he was undiplomatic). The matter had been settled peacefully, however, and final sailing orders could be issued. The Bonapartes took up residence at the naval administration building. There the General shed his civilian frock coat with its square-cut tails and donned his general's uniform. Despite his wife's insistence, he had not yet sacrificed his abbreviated pigtail and his long sidelocks in favour of the fashionable haircut *à la Titus*: he had the face of an eagle and the hairdo of a spaniel. Having transformed himself from Member of the Institute into Commander-in-Chief, he proceeded to address his troops, promised them their six acres of land each, and inspected the fleet, receiving a two-gun salute from each warship. In the evening, the city Toulon was illuminated in his honour.

About the same time there arrived at Toulon 5,000,000 gold francs, liberated from the treasury of Berne—part of the equipment to be embarked for Egypt.

All the other equipment and supplies also seemed to be in readiness, at least on paper, and so did the troops. Two rather important things had been neglected, however, possibly from oversight but more probably in order to keep the army's destination secret. Although unfamiliar with disembarkation procedure, landing tactics, and desert warfare, the troops had not been given the least instruction or training; neither had their officers or even generals. What seems even more incredible, no provision had been made to supply the troops with flasks or canteens to carry water while marching through the desert. 'It would have been sufficient,' noted one of the participants in the campaign, 'to equip ... each soldier with a small flask to carry his water. The Commander-in-Chief, who knew very well to what country he was taking us, must be blamed for this negligence. The same lack of foresight made itself felt in everything.'[1]

Whatever the cause of such inexcusable carelessness, the secret of the army's destination had been remarkably well guarded, despite the fact that a considerable number of people (according to Kléber, about forty) were privy to the secret, among them the Prussian minister to Paris, to whom Talleyrand had made indiscreet revelations.[2] Many more must have guessed it: a sudden rash of official requests for memoranda on the Levant; the titles of the books selected for Napoleon's travelling library; the hiring of Egyptian and Syrian personnel by Kléber; the search for Orientalists and for Arabic typographic characters—everything clearly pointed toward Egypt or Syria. As early as April 25, Lieutenant Thurman in a letter to his parents expressed the conviction that Egypt was his destination. The Turkish government had wind of the project as early as May. It seems all the more surprising that the British government, which had no lack of informants in France and elsewhere on the Continent, were as much in the dark about the purpose of the Toulon armaments as the French hoped them to be.

The original Army of England, concentrated along the northern coast of France, had been secretly transferred to the command of General Kilmaine; however, to confuse the public, and particularly the English, the forces gathering in southern France were named the Left Wing of the Army of England, and Bonaparte officially retained the command of the Army of England until his departure. On March 31, the Directory issued a bogus order, which was leaked to the French press, enjoining Bonaparte to proceed to Brest and to take command of the invasion forces. This manoeuvre

---

[1] Vigo-Roussillon, p. 587

[2] According to Marshal Marmont, the Minister of War, Schérer, was not informed of the purpose of the preparations at Toulon; this, however, seems scarcely credible.

was almost spoiled by an article in *Le Publiciste* of 11 Germinal (March 31) which speculated that Egypt might be the target. The editors of the *Publiciste* were soon set straight and inserted a correction in a later issue: the goal, its readers were informed, was more likely to be England or Ireland.

Though unable to penetrate the secret of Bonaparte's destination, the British government took no chances. To be sure, there was a bare possibility of the Toulon fleet slipping past Gibraltar and joining the Brest fleet in a general attack on the British Isles. Unlikely as this was, *The Times* of April 27 expressed the opinion that the intelligence received about the Toulon armaments pointed to a probable invasion of Portugal or Ireland. This prognostication may have been merely in the general tradition of *The Times'* genius for prophecy, but one is surprised to find that Pitt himself wrote to Lord Mornington on May 31—twelve days after the sailing of the Toulon fleet—that 'the French will probably try a magnificent project of invading Ireland from Toulon.'[1]

Invasion hysteria had gripped England ever since Bonaparte's return from Italy. Voluntary contributions had been requested by the government in January, to defray additional military expenditures; since subscriptions proceeded at a languid pace, George III himself—though sane at that moment—pledged one third of his privy purse, and the cabinet ministers 'an ample fifth' of their income. For the guidance of his colleagues, Pitt ordered to be compiled and printed a 'Report on the Arrangements which were made, for the Internal Defence of these Kingdoms, when Spain, by its Armada, projected the Invasion and Conquest of England; and Application of the wise Proceedings of our Ancestors, to the Present Crisis of public Safety.'[2] Measures recommended to the population in the event of invasion included the erection of block houses in each square of London and of barricades in each street, the storing of hand grenades in each corner house; alarm bells to be placed in the centre of each street; 'all obnoxious foreigners to be sent out of the country'; 'no foreign servants, male or female, to be allowed' (a step which, in our days, would paralyse London in an instant); and a particularly patriotic measure—'prisoners to be put into prison ships, in the most secure situations; so that they may be destroyed instantly, in cases necessary, for the defence of the country.'[3] Semaphore telegraphs had been erected along the

---

[1] Wheeler and Broadley, I, 121

[2] Wheeler and Broadley, I, 129

[3] Ibid., I, 122.

coast, and telegraph stations had been installed at the Admiralty and atop one of the towers of Westminster Abbey. As a further precaution, prompted by the government's view that England was teeming with foreign and native subversives, radicals, and French sympathizers, the Alien Bill was revived and the Habeas Corpus Act suspended; it even was suggested that all Britons be compelled to take oaths of allegiance to the Sovereign in order to 'detect those *reformers* who seek for *revolution*.'[1] Despite the dangers of putting arms in the hands of so unreliable a citizenry, militia units of volunteers proliferated throughout the country. Thus the Bath Volunteers met on May 5 and, by vote, decided that their uniform should consist of 'a scarlet jacket with black collar and lapels, white waistcoat, and blue pantaloons edged with red.'[2] Clearly, England was ready to receive the French armada. How sincerely the government counted on an attack is a matter of surmise; certain it is that the publicity given to the danger enabled William Pitt and his colleagues to raise considerable contributions and to intimidate the liberal opposition.

The Admiralty's precautions, though less flamboyant and less publicized, proved more to the point than did the martial preparations for the defence of the homeland. On May 2, 1798, Earl Spencer, First Lord of the Admiralty, informed Admiral Jervis, recently created Earl of St. Vincent, of his decision to send a squadron into the Mediterranean. St. Vincent was, at the time, blockading Cadiz, where part of the Spanish fleet was bottled up; he would be sent a reinforcement of eight battleships, which would enable him to continue with the blockade. 'When you are apprized,' wrote Spencer, 'that the appearance of a British Squadron in the Mediterranean is a condition on which the fate of Europe may at this moment be stated to depend, you will not be surprised that we are disposed to strain every nerve, and incur consider able hazard in effecting it.' If St. Vincent should decide not to take personal command of the Mediterranean fleet, it was recommended that that task be entrusted to Admiral Sir Horatio Nelson, 'whose acquaintance with that part of the world, as well as his activity, and disposition, seem to qualify him in a peculiar manner for that service.'[3]

So wholeheartedly did Lord St. Vincent agree with Lord Spencer that, by some process of telepathy, he had anticipated his

---

[1] Ibid., I, 132.

[2] Bath Chronicle, May 3, 1798

[3] Warner, p. 45.

superior's instructions. On May 2, the very date on which Spencer had written the despatch, Admiral Nelson sailed from off Cadiz with three battle ships, two frigates, and one sloop, with orders to approach Toulon and to collect information concerning the French armaments.

Horatio Nelson, then in his fortieth year, had been in the navy ever since he was twelve. He had served in the West Indies, in the Far East, in the Polar Seas, in the Mediterranean; he had commanded ships since he was twenty; he had lost his right eye in battle; he had just recuperated from the loss of his right arm, incurred a year earlier in his stubborn and unsuccessful attack on the Canary Islands. After a long convalescence in England, he was impatient to return to active service. His ambition, his thirst for glory were perhaps even more impetuous than Bonaparte's, though in an entirely different manner, and his almost pathological hatred of the French nation in general and the French Revolution in particular made him regard himself as a God-chosen instrument for their punishment. 'He had such a horror of all Frenchmen,' declares one of his officers, 'that I believe he thought them at all times nearly as corrupt in body as in mind.'[1] He also affected, it may be added without prejudice to his glory, to entertain a peculiarly intimate relationship with the Almighty, whom he gratefully credited, along with his subordinates, for his successes. In this respect his modesty exceeded Bonaparte's, who claimed all the credit for himself.

Having left Spithead aboard H.M.S. *Vanguard* on April 10, Nelson arrived off Cadiz at the end of the month, whence St. Vincent despatched him to the Mediterranean. His small squadron was in the Gulf of Lions when, on May 17, it captured a French corvette; interrogating the crew, Nelson learned that thirteen French battleships were ready to sail from Toulon. The heavy weather of May 19-20, which caused considerable discomfort to the troops on the French convoys, inconvenienced Admiral Nelson even more. Far from being able to keep the French fleet under surveillance, Nelson barely escaped being wrecked aboard the *Vanguard*, which was dismasted in the storm. This was the beginning of a series of *contretemps* that were to plague the Admiral for the following ten weeks. Still, as Nelson wrote to his wife, thanks to the exertions of Almighty God and of Captains Saumarez and Ball, his battleships reached safety off the Sardinian island of San Pietro, and the damage was repaired in four days. By May 27, he resumed his position before Toulon, eight days after his quarry had

---

[1] Warner, p. 75.

slipped away. It was only on June 7 that he was joined by rein-forcements—eleven ships of the line sent to him by Lord St. Vin-cent. Without these, there was little Nelson could have done to stop Brueys' squadron of thirteen battleships. Unfortunately for him, he had lost his frigates and sloop during the storm. In the be-lief that Nelson would have to repair his flagship at Gibraltar, their commander, Captain Hope, had taken them there instead of re-joining Nelson before Toulon. The ensuing comedy of errors was largely due to the absence of the frigates, without which the Eng-lish fleet found it difficult to reconnoitre the course taken by the French. The brig *La Mutine*, under Captain Hardy, which joined Nelson on June 5 with instructions from Lord St. Vincent, was an inadequate substitute for the wayward frigates.

With thirteen battleships of seventy-four guns and one of fifty, the British squadron was about evenly matched in firing power with the French and superior in every other way. Admiral Nelson's instructions were unambiguous: he was to find the French squad-ron, prevent it at all costs from any movement westward, pursue it, and destroy it. The difficulty proved in finding it.

Chapter Two
To Alexandria

WHEN Lord Spencer wrote to Lord St. Vincent that the fate of Europe depended on the English squadron in the Mediterranean, he probably was right, but not quite in the sense he intended. If, during the first lap of its crossing, the French armada had not been delayed by the slowness of the transports and by the difficulty of effecting a junction with the three other convoys, if it had reached and left Malta two days earlier than it did, Admiral Nelson would have annihilated it, battleships, transports, troops, and all, off Alexandria, about June 28. If it had been even slower and taken a day or two longer to reach Malta, the same would have happened, in all probability, off Malta about June 20. If, on June 22, when the two fleets were within a few miles of one another, this conjunction had occurred during the day instead of at night, Nelson, instead of unwittingly overtaking the French fleet, would have destroyed it. If Nelson had been a more indolent man and proceeded less impetuously in his pursuit, the same would have happened. And if the Knights of Malta had followed their glorious tradition instead of yielding to the French like a half-willing maiden, they could have defended their virtually impregnable stronghold long enough to see their besiegers routed by the English fleet. That none of this happened, that Bonaparte was able to conquer Malta almost without a blow and to land his forces near Alexandria without interference, was due not to planning or calculation but to the unpredictable interplay of miscalculations on both sides and to the fortuitous effects of human behaviour. In other words, Bonaparte was lucky. He was the first to admit it. Or, as Nelson put it in his theological approach to the fortunes of war, 'the Devil's children have the Devil's luck.'[1] To be sure, when luck was on his side, he called it Divine Providence.

If Almighty Providence had prevailed over the Devil's luck and Nelson had caught the French before or during their landing in Egypt, General Bonaparte would never have become First Consul and Emperor, and undoubtedly history would have been quite different for at least a quarter century from what it turned out to be. There would be no Arc de Triomphe in Paris, no Trafalgar Square in London; neither Moscow nor Washington would have been burned. Yet to say that these things depended on the British fleet in the Mediterranean between May 19 and June 50, 1798, is not so true as to say that they depended on luck; and to assert that the fate of Europe was affected by the issue seems, *sub specie aeternitatis*, a hyperbolical statement. Perhaps a few million lives would not have been snuffed out needlessly before their time—that is all. Their fate was indeed determined by the unwitting game of blind man's buff that Admiral Nelson and General Bonaparte were playing with each other across the vast expanse of the indifferent Mediterranean Sea.

II

In his own account of the Egyptian and Syrian campaigns, dictated at St. Helena, Napoleon made this remarkable utterance à propos of the French capture of Malta: 'Napoleon made sure that he could dare, and he dared.'[2] He had made even surer than he admitted.

The Order of the Knights Hospitaler of St. John of Jerusalem, now known as the Knights of Malta, came into existence in the Holy Land almost nine centuries ago, during the First Crusade. At first a loose association for the protection of pilgrims and the care of the sick, it was constituted as a religious order by Pope Paschal II in 1113 and took on an increasingly military character, forming a kind of élite corps of the Crusaders in their losing struggle with the Saracen. In 1187 Jerusalem fell to the Mameluke Sultan Saladin, but the Knights Hospitaler continued to hold out for another century in their castles. Krak des Chevaliers, whose massive power

---

[1] Warner, p. 58.

[2] Correspondance, XXIX, 370.

still astounds the visitor to Jordan, fell in 1271; their last strong-hold, Acre, before which Bonaparte's ambitions were to be frus-trated, resisted until 1291. The Knights eventually settled on the Island of Rhodes, which they made into a forbidding fortress, and from there continued to fight the Infidel on the sea, as pirates. To Moslem seamen, the eight-pronged cross on the sails of the Knights' galleys became a sight as terrifying as that of the skull and crossbones was to the West India traders. In Gibbon's words, the Knights 'neglected to live, but were prepared to die, in the service of Christ.' Indeed, the immense wealth they amassed by means of their pious piracy, the ransoms they gathered for the release of their captives, the use they made of prisoners as galley slaves—all these things bore greater resemblance to the practices of the Bar-bary pirates than to those recommended in the Sermon on the Mount.

Late in 1522, Sultan Suleiman the Magnificent landed an army on the island and laid siege to the city of Rhodes. The defenders, under the heroic leadership of their Grand Master, Villiers de L'Isle-Adam, resisted for several months but had to capitulate in the end. In a driving snowstorm, under the eyes of the Turkish forces, they marched toward their ships, retaining their arms and followed by a long train of wagons loaded with their treasures and archives, exiles once more.

Suleiman was to repent his generosity. In 1530 Emperor Char-les V, in his capacity as King of Sicily, gave the Knights the island of Malta as their sovereign domain. Charles does not seem to have realized the strategic importance of the tiny island, from which the Knights' ships could control or at least harass all trade in the east-ern Mediterranean. Suleiman, who did realize it, attacked Malta in 1565 with everything he had. Some 30,000 Turks had lost their lives in the space of five months when Suleiman decided to lift the siege. Two hundred and thirty-three years later, General Bona-parte took Malta in one day; three of his men were killed in the operation.

Napoleon's own explanation of his success is terse and essen-tially true. The Order of the Knights of St. John of Jerusalem, he wrote, 'no longer served a purpose; it fell because it had to fall.'[1]

For more than a century after their triumph over Suleiman II, the Knights of Malta continued to terrorize Moslem shipping. They sank more Turkish and Barbaresque ships, made more slaves, and

---

[1] Correspondance, XXIX, 369.

took more booty than did any other Christian nation in the Mediterranean. Unfortunately for the Order, European affairs had taken such a turn by the beginning of the eighteenth century that a permanent crusade against the Infidel seemed an anachronism. The Ottoman Empire had become a respectable power, and crusading had become poor business. To be sure, it still was profitable to repay the Barbary pirates in kind, and the Knights continued to police the Mediterranean against them, but they also turned toward trade to compensate for the Order's deficit.

At the beginning of the French Revolution, the Order was in an advanced state of decay, though Malta itself, ruled with benign paternalism, was an oasis of prosperity in the southern Mediterranean. The complement of Knights in active service or in residence at Malta had shrunk considerably. More than half the Knights had always been French, and their conflicting attitudes toward the Revolution introduced a new element of discord. What Knights there were suffered from the effects of protracted idleness; there was little for them to do but to devote themselves to their mistresses and intrigue against each other.

As Napoleon had put it, the Order no longer served a purpose; but its island had lost none of its strategic value. France, England, Austria, and Russia had their eyes on it. In January 1797, Tsar Paul I, an eccentric who regarded himself as the champion of Christendom, took the Order under his personal protection. This step threw the chancelleries of Europe into consternation. To prevent Russia from gaining a foothold in the Mediterranean, no sacrifice seemed too heavy—not even the effort of seizing Malta for oneself. The threat of Russian influence and the election of a German, Baron von Hompesch, as the Order's new Grand Master in July 1797, convinced Bonaparte that quick action was needed to beat Russia and Austria to the post. The Directory agreed with Bonaparte's views and gave him a free hand.

To make sure that he could dare, Bonaparte sent two emissaries to Malta in late December 1797. One, a Maltese, went ashore secretly, at night: his mission was purely one of espionage. The other, on official business, was the same Citizen Poussielgue who, four months later, became controller general of Bonaparte's expeditionary force.[1] He had a good contact in Malta, one of his cousins being Guardian of the Port of Valetta. During the four months of his stay, he sounded out the French Knights, among whom he found a handful of republican sympathizers, notably Bosredon de Ransijat, the Treasurer of the Order, and Fay, its Commissioner of Fortifications. The rest of the Knights, he reported, including the Grand Master, would fight any attempt at invasion, unless they were assured of some suitable compensation. Diplomacy, rather than force, was needed. Poussielgue also approached, with some success, several officials in the service of the Order and at least two French private citizens in Malta. On March 5, Admiral Brueys, coming with his squadron from Corfu, picked up Poussielgue and the Maltese spy and proceeded to Toulon.

***

On June 6, the French convoy from Civita Vecchia hove in sight off Malta; on June 9, it was joined by the main fleet. The sight of the 400 ships was terrifying. 'Never,' wrote a witness, 'had Malta seen such a numberless fleet in her waters. The sea was covered for miles with ships of all sizes whose masts resembled a huge forest.'[2]

Bonaparte's plan was simplicity itself. He would request the Grand Master's permission for the French fleet to renew its water supply. Then, whether permission was granted or not, he would land his troops to the north and south of Valetta and on the neighbouring island of Gozo, encircle Valetta, and wait for the Knights' surrender. The population was to be assured that the French came with peaceful intentions and would respect their property and religion. Nothing in the orders issued by Bonaparte and Berthier between June 6 and June 9 indicates that hostilities were anticipated.

In the late evening of June 9, von Hompesch's reply was delivered to Bonaparte: no more than four ships at a time would be admitted. Bonaparte pretended to be indignant at such want of hospitality on the part of the Knights Hospitaler. 'General Bonaparte,' he informed von Hompesch, 'will secure by force what

---

[1] Actually, after taking over the command of the Army of England, Bonaparte had his brother Joseph, the French ambassador in Rome, instruct Poussielgue that his mission to Malta was cancelled; but Joseph's message to Poussielgue, dated December 16, did not reach Poussielgue, who already was on his way—a mishap which turned out to be lucky for Bonaparte.

[2] Cavaliero, p. 223.

should have been accorded him freely.'[1] By 10 p.m., he issued his final orders for the landing. Less than twenty-four hours later, all of Malta and Gozo save Valetta and the other fortified 'cities' on either side of Grand Harbour were in French hands.

To Bonaparte's surprise, there had been some resistance, especially on Gozo. Some cannon had been fired, and in a few spots the Maltese regulars and militia even had emptied their muskets at the French before throwing them away to expedite their retreat. This 'misunderstanding,' as Bourrienne called it, irritated the General, who blamed Poussielgue for it. After spending a few hours on the island, he returned to *L'Orient* and went to sleep.

On Gozo, according to the reminiscences of Captain Vertray, then a lieutenant in the 9th Half-Brigade, the French scaled the local defences singing the *Marseillaise* as they went. A few Knights allowed themselves to be captured; the Maltese defenders, after some resistance, were equally happy to capitulate and kiss their victors' hands. Vertray says that French and Maltese instantly began to fraternize; Quarter-master Sergeant François, also of the 9th Half-Brigade, declares that 'the island of Gozo was thoroughly looted, the inhabitants having left their homes.'[2] Probably both statements are true, and Vertray fraternized while François looted.

At Valetta, meanwhile, consternation was general among the Knights as well as among the Maltese. Women were wailing in their houses, saints were carried through the streets in procession, and Grand Master von Hompesch spent the day debating with his council of Knights what to do. None of these activities contributed materially to the defence of Valetta, a city named for the Grand Master Jean de la Valette, under whose command it had resisted Suleiman's army for five months.

Von Hompesch had had sufficient warning, long before the French appeared, that an attack was impending. A weak and irresolute man despite his sixteen quarters of nobility and the elegant suit of armour in which he had himself painted, he had done nothing to prepare for that eventuality. There were enough supplies in Valetta to withstand a siege for four months, but the defences were in poor shape. The guns, of which there were nearly a thousand, had not been used for a century except to fire salutes. The powder supplies were rotten. The Maltese militia (about 10,000 men) showed little martial spirit. They were not afraid of

---

[1] Correspondance, IV, 133.

[2] François, I, 184

the Turks, they said, but they had been told that the French were devils, and who would not be afraid of devils? a reasoning which shows that propaganda often boomerangs. There was a native garrison of about 1,500 men, hardly enough to serve 1,000 guns. As for the Knights, there were exactly 332 in Malta; of these, fifty were too old or too ill to fight. Of the remaining 272, few showed the faintest sparks of the spirit of Villiers de L'Isle-Adam or Jean de la Valette: on June 10, many of them deserted the militiamen they were supposed to command, and two allegedly were shot by their own men as deserters.

Two hundred of the Knights were French. Their reliability became dubious in the morning of June 10, when Bosredon de Ransijat informed the council that he would not fight against his countrymen and offered his resignation as Treasurer of the Order. His message unnerved the Grand Master, whose only action on that crucial day consisted in putting his Treasurer under arrest. Conflicting reports poured into the council chamber of mob violence, of Knights being killed by the Maltese, and of hidden arms supplies being distributed to the population by French agents disguised as Greeks: small as it was, the city was in chaos. In the evening, a deputation of leading Maltese nobles and burghers was admitted to the council chamber and pleaded with von Hompesch to put an end to a useless resistance.

Undoubtedly there was a fifth column of disaffected Knights and officials within the walls of Valetta. Their number, however, was small, and energetic action could have paralysed them. Yet the strength of fifth columns resides not so much in their numbers as in the vague fear and panic they inspire: nothing serves the purposes of traitors better than do shouts of 'Treason!' Conversely, nothing is more convenient to those who do not care to fight than to claim that they have been betrayed. Admittedly, the Knights could not have held out for long, but they could easily have resisted for two weeks. At worst, this would have saved their honour; at best, it would have resulted in the relief of Malta by the British fleet and the destruction of the French forces.

Von Hompesch did not know that on June 9, the day the two French convoys joined before Valetta, Admiral Nelson with fourteen battle ships had started on his pursuit of the French fleet, and that two weeks later he would be within reach of Malta. Neither, for that matter, did General Bonaparte, who knew only that Nelson was somewhere about with three battleships but had not yet learned of the British reinforce ments. Had he been aware of them, he would not have spent a week in Malta. Hompesch's ignorance

and irresolution, combined with the confusion created by a handful of disaffected men, led to the decision—made in the early
morning hours of June 11—to sue for an armistice. For twenty-four
hours, the course of modern history depended on some 500 men,
warrior monks, quaint relics of the Age of Crusades. Had their
hearts been as anachronistic as were their institutions, they would
have fought, regardless of the outcome, as had their predecessors.
But their hearts were modern: resistance seemed an empty gesture; surrender allowed hopes for material compensation. The
Mamelukes, whom the Knights had fought five centuries earlier,
and whom Bonaparte was to fight five weeks later, showed no such
signs of modernity.

The fall of Malta stirred up a tempest of recriminations. Hompesch himself was accused of having been bribed in advance and
of putting up a mere show of resistance, a rumour given substance
by Bonaparte's confidence that he could take Malta without a
blow. There is no evidence to support this view. It is almost certain
that Hompesch had not been bribed in advance; but he was only
too willing to let a bribe shorten his resistance, and this Bonaparte
had known in advance. It was thus he could make sure that he
could dare.

***

In the morning of June 11 an emissary from the Grand Master
walked up the thirty-two steps to the deck of *L'Orient* and delivered two letters—one to Bonaparte, asking for a truce, and one to
the geologist Dolomieu, begging him to use his good offices on behalf of the Order to which he once had belonged. Bonaparte appointed Dolomieu (who resented the ambiguous role thus forced
on him), along with Poussielgue and his aide-de-camp Junot, to go
ashore and confer with Hompesch. Hompesch embraced the black
sheep Dolomieu, by now his only hope; a twenty-four hours truce
was signed, pending negotiations for surrender. About midnight,
the Grand Master's emissaries—including Bosredon de Ransijat,
who was no longer under arrest—arrived on *L'Orient*. Bonaparte
was woken; half an hour later, the treaty had been drafted and
signed. Malta was ceded to the French Republic, France would use
her influence to obtain for Hompesch a principality in Germany,
and in the meantime would pay him a yearly pension of 500,000
francs; the other Knights were to receive pensions of 700 to 1,000
francs, depending on their age.

Bonaparte went ashore in Valetta on June 12 and was received
by a delegation consisting of his supporters in the Order. 'It's a

lucky thing,' observed General Caffarelli, who was with him, 'that at least there was somebody to open the gates for us.'[1]

The Knights Hospitaler, relieved at the thought that no more heroism was required of them, received the French with almost an excess of hospitality. 'They showered us with a thousand attentions and civilities,' noted Lieutenant Desvernois of the Cavalry. 'It is not surprising that they bear so easily the state of celibacy to which the rules of their Order condemn them. Most of them have mistresses who are ravishingly beautiful and charming and of whom they are not the least bit jealous.'[2] Not only was Malta famous for the beauty of its women, but also could its capital boast of a higher percentage of streetwalkers than any other European city. Grateful for their brief escape from their crowded ships, the French took advantage of their last opportunity in three years to make love to Christian women, whose language they could more or less understand. Those not engaged in that pursuit would stroll through the astonishingly tidy streets, speculate on the dark-eyed beauties hidden behind their grilled balconies or in their ample capes, or relish the juicy oranges liberated from the gardens and orchards—their first fresh food in three weeks. But only a fraction of the troops had disembarked, and most of them were ordered back to their ships on June 14.

While his troops and crews went about their various details and recreations, General Bonaparte addressed himself to the multiple tasks facing him with the impetuosity of a tornado. In the six days he spent in Malta, he dictated no less than 168 reports, despatches, and orders. In a single day—June 15—he liquidated a centuries-old state, established the basis of a new government, and confiscated close to 7,000,000 francs' worth of treasures belonging to the Order, not to mention 55,000 muskets, two battleships, one frigate, and four galleys. The administration of the island was set down in an order containing sixteen terse paragraphs. Made part of the French Republic, Malta was placed under a governmental commission of nine, eight of whom were native Maltese. A member of the Scientific Commission, Regnault de Saint-Jean d' Angély (later a cabinet minister under Napoleon) was appointed Commissioner of the French Republic. Another order, in four paragraphs, dissolved the armed forces of Malta; abolished armourial bearings, liveries, and titles of nobility; gave all subjects of enemy powers two days to leave the island; and notified the

[1] Bourrienne, Vol. I, Ch. v.

[2] Desvernois, p. 97.

Knights (with certain exceptions) that they must leave Malta within three days. In yet another order, Citizens Monge and Berthollet were deputed to inspect the Mint, the treasures of the Church of St. John, 'and all other places where objects of value might be found.'[1] Among the objects of value found were 5,000,000 francs' worth of gold, almost a million francs' worth of silver plate, and the gem-encrusted treasures of the Church of St. John, also valued at about a million. The Knights were graciously permitted to take with them a splinter of the True Cross, which lacked cash value, and one of the many hands of St. John the Baptist—they are scattered all over the Middle East, along with his several heads -but only after it had been removed from its bejewelled reliquary. All the bullion and precious objects were transferred, after inventory, to the French paymaster; a large part of them were taken to Egypt. To top off the day—all this happened on June 15—the General snubbed the Grand Master's invitation to dinner, summoned him and the Knights to his residence, and bluntly informed them that all Knights below sixty years of age had to leave within three days, none being allowed to take with him more than 240 francs, for travel expenses. Excepted from the expulsion were thirty-four Knights, all French and under thirty, whom Bonaparte had persuaded to volunteer with the French army in Egypt, and seventeen other officials of the Order (not all of them professed Knights), who had assisted the French in various ways during the preceding months. The list of the seventeen, which may be regarded as the roster of the fifth column, is headed by two Knights—Bosredon de Ransijat and Fay. Ransijat also heads the list of the governmental commissioners .

When Villiers de L'Isle-Adam and his Knights left Rhodes in 1525, they took with them their arms, treasures, and archives, and they marched out of their fortress with military honours, amidst the silent homage of their Turkish conquerors. When Ferdinand Freiherr von Hompesch left Malta on June 17, 1798, he took with him nothing beside a vain promise of a pension, and he made his way to the ship that was to take him to Trieste amidst the boos of the French soldiers and the Maltese populace. Disgraced, he resigned one year later, under the pressure of Tsar Paul I, whose heart was set on the Grand Mastership. On October 12, 1799, St. John the Baptist's withered hand arrived at St. Petersburg, where the new Grand Master, dressed in his imperial coronation robes, bowed to the ground before it. As for von Hompesch, he never re-

---

[1] Correspondance, IV, 147.

ceived the principality that had been promised him, and he had to wait six years for the first payment of his pension. He died in exile shortly afterwards, in 1805.

III

Between June 14 and 18, General Bonaparte took care of a number of odds and ends before leaving Malta to conquer Egypt. Among other things, he abolished slavery, visited the bagno of the port, freed the 600 Turkish and 1,400 Moorish slaves held there, and ordered the Turks (following their own request) to serve as crews in his convoy, pending their release in Egypt; asked the French consuls in Tunis, Tripoli, and Algiers to inform the beys of this action and to invite them to liberate their Maltese slaves in turn; ordered all Maltese men to wear the French tricolour cockade, and promised French citizenship and the right to wear the 'French national costume' to all those who showed sufficient patriotic zeal (especially in the form of voluntary contributions); decreed that all French troops left in garrison in Malta should wear cotton uniforms; formed native National Guard battalions, patterned on the French; set up a military hospital; reorganized the island's hospital and postal services; reduced the number of monasteries and of new priests to be ordained; limited the jurisdiction of the Bishop of Malta to purely ecclesiastic affairs and forbade him to appeal to the Pope; transferred the funds of charitable religious foundations to the hospitals; decreed the death penalty for all Greek Orthodox residents of Malta and the Ionian Islands who had any traffic with Russia; had the Russian and English consuls deported to Rome; ordered that sixty boys between nine and fourteen years of age, chosen from among the wealthiest Maltese families, be sent to Paris and educated there as Frenchmen at the expense of the Republic; set up a new primary and secondary school system; fixed the teachers' salaries and prescribed the curriculum (with heavy emphasis on the sciences, French, and 'the principles of morality and of the French constitution');[1] requested the Directory to send graduates of the École Polytechnique to Malta to teach mathematics, mechanics, and physics; determined the new fiscal rates and the salaries and expense accounts of administrative officers; incorporated more than 300 men of the former Malta Regiment into the expeditionary force—a useful acquisition, the Maltese language being a branch of Arabic; granted allowances for the

---

[1] Correspondance, IV, 174

maintenance of the wives and children of the Maltese soldiers embarked on his fleet, and ordered all their male children above the age of ten to join the convoy as apprentice seamen; provided for a French garrison of some 5,000 men to be left in Malta under General Vaubois; requested that all the soldiers' wives waiting at the Toulon depot to join their husbands be embarked on a second convoy and taken to Malta, to await further orders; despatched his aide-de-camp Lavallette to Albania aboard the frigate L'Arthémise, with a letter to 'his most respectable friend,' Ali Pasha of Janina, in which he hinted to that formidable governor and bandit that his envoy would make certain interesting overtures to him; and sent the frigate *La Sensible* to Toulon, with despatches to the Directory. Along with the despatches, he sent General Baraguey d'Hilliers—who was in ill health, being consumed either by lovesickness for his wife or by something worse—and a few personal gifts for the Directors, among them a sterling silver model of a galley dating from the Knights' sojourn in Rhodes ('It has,' he wrote, 'some curiosity value because of its antiquity ') and a silken altar cloth woven in China, which showed 'pretty good workmanship.'[1] He also informed Citizen Talleyrand that *La Sensible* would take him from Toulon to Constantinople.[2] Despite all these activities, the General found time to stroll in the well-kept gardens of the luckless Grand Master and to savour the delicious oranges that he and his entourage picked from the trees.

Its mission accomplished, the French armada sailed from Malta on June 18 and 19. The troops had been put on alert or re-embarked as early as June 17; nevertheless at least one officer, Lieutenant Thurman of the Engineers, managed to miss his boat. The battleship *Le Tonnant*, to which he was assigned, was just

---

[1] Correspondance, IV, 174

[2] *La Sensible* never reached Toulon and it was some time before General Baraguey d'Hilliers reached his wife. The frigate was captured by the English frigate *Sea-horse* on June 27. Except for the general and his two aides-de-camp, whom the British kept as prisoners of war, the crew and passengers were released at Cagliari, in neutral Sardinia. The despatches and trophies had been cast into the sea before *La Sensible*'s surrender, but one of the passengers released, the writer A.V. Arnault, who had quit Bonaparte's Scientific Commission in Malta, relayed the contents of the despatches to the Directors. (The most important despatches, announcing the capture of Malta, had been sent earlier, on June 14, aboard a Maltese ship, and reached the Directors on July 4.) The fate of the indomitable courier Lesimple, who brought the Directors' congratulations back to Bonaparte in Egypt, was even more adventurous.

pulling out when he reached the shore, and he had to hire a rowing boat, which caught up with the ship several hours later, on the open sea, after what must have been a grueling and expensive chase.

Admiral Nelson, though equally determined, was less lucky than Lieutenant Thurman in catching up with the French fleet. On June 17 he reached the Bay of Naples and sent the brig *Mutine* to get information from the British Minister, Sir William Hamilton. Hamilton suggested that the French might be found off Malta. The question was: had they already left Malta and, if so, for where— Sicily or Egypt? Nelson thought it was Egypt. 'I shall believe,' he wrote to the First Lord, 'that they are going on their scheme of possessing Alexandria, and getting troops to India—a plan concerted with Tippoo Sahib, by no means so difficult as might at first view be imagined.... Be they bound for the Antipodes, Your Lordship may rely that I will not lose a moment in bringing them to action, and endeavour to destroy their Transports.'[1] He lost not a moment; on June 20 he passed the Strait of Messina, about 160 miles from the position of the French fleet on that date. The same day, Bonaparte received intelligence, through one of his cruising frigates, that an English squadron of fourteen ships of the line had been observed sailing eastward. The French decided to set their course toward Crete, to elude their pursuers. The pursuers, travelling at approximately twice the speed of their prey, passed the French, at a few miles distance, during the foggy night of June 22-23. For the whole week following, Nelson was to race after a quarry which was trailing him at a leisurely pace, unaware of his presence.

Nelson had polled his senior captains on June 22, requesting their opinion as to the real destination of the French. Their replies to his questionnaire were unanimous: the English squadron must crowd sail and make for Alexandria with the utmost speed, to prevent a French landing there. Still, with only one brig to reconnoitre the whole eastern Mediterranean, Nelson was operating in the dark. 'We are proceeding upon the merest conjecture only, and not on any positive information,' wrote Captain Sir James Saumarez of H.M.S. *Orion*. 'Some days must elapse before we can be relieved from our cruel suspense; and if, at the end of our journey, we find we are upon a wrong scent, our embarrassment will be great indeed.'[2]

---

[1] Nelson, III, 31.

[2] Warner, pp. 57-58.

On June 20, the day the French sighted Crete, Nelson already was half-way between Crete and Alexandria. He sent the *Mutine* ahead with Captain Hardy; all Hardy could find at Alexandria was a few dilapidated Turkish warships. Three days later Nelson himself, with his entire squadron, anchored off Alexandria and disconsolately surveyed the empty harbour. By now, his embarrassment was great indeed: the French must have sailed west after all. Close to nervous collapse, Nelson ordered his squadron to set sail for Crete; the English had barely left when, in the afternoon of the same day, the French frigate *La Junon*, sent ahead by Bonaparte, entered the harbour of Alexandria.

Nelson did not find the French anywhere near Crete—they had passed the island about two weeks earlier. On July 19 he reached Syracuse: but the French were not in Sicily either. By this time, he was barely able to eat. He had, so he wrote, 'gone a round of near six hundred leagues with an expedition incredible' and was as much in the dark as ever.[1] Nothing is more vexatious to a man possessed by duty and ambition than to appear ridiculous in the pursuit of either. Nelson's every nerve was strained in his passionate determination not to return a failure. 'Be assured,' he wrote to Sir William and Emma Hamilton (who was not yet his mistress), 'I will return either crowned with laurel, or covered with cypress.'[2]

After spending three days at Syracuse, victualling and watering his ships, Nelson set sail for Greece; then, after receiving reliable information that the French had sailed to Egypt, he steered south. For a week, he barely slept or ate. On August 1, at Abukir Bay, a few miles east of Alexandria, his frenzied quest reached its climactic end. A spectacle of excruciating delight presented itself to his one eye—the entire French squadron at anchor. Admiral Nelson ordered dinner to be served and the French fleet to be attacked.

By that time, however, Bonaparte was in Cairo.

IV

Bonaparte's journey from Toulon to Alexandria took six weeks. Only during the last week was he aware of the closeness and strength of Nelson's squadron; at that time he was too busy with preparations for the landing to let this danger disturb his calm. One wonders whether his composure would hare been ruffled even

---

[1] Nelson, III, 43.

[2] Nelson, III, 47

if the intelligence sent him from various ports concerning the English fleet (whose strength some of the despatches vastly exaggerated) had reached him before he landed. In Admiral Brueys' opinion the French fleet, overloaded with troops and supplies, would have had as good as no chance in an encounter with even as few as ten battleships. With this danger ever present in his mind, Bonaparte throughout the voyage showed not the slightest sign of nervousness (quite unlike his pursuer); his was the serenity of the gambler who has placed his bets and can do nothing but wait for the results. It was the Englishman who was fiery and the Latin who was cool.

During most of the sea journey, Bonaparte spent his time in bed. Expecting to be seasick from beginning to end (an assumption that proved essentially correct), he had had casters attached to the legs of his bed, hoping thus to counteract the ship's motion. There he dictated most of his orders and messages and read the reports and inquiries sent him by his generals and admirals, which he frequently did not trouble to answer. Little that happened aboard his 400 ships escaped him, and when he rose to go on deck he plied Brueys, Captain Casabianca, and their officers with such quantities of questions on matters nautical that they must have felt as harassed by his curiosity as impressed with his perspicacity.

Much of his time, while lying abed, he spent having Bourrienne read to him from his travel library—mostly works concerning Egypt and the Holy Land, above all the Bible and the Koran, which he classified under the heading 'Politics.' Except during the first few days, when he kept a large table, he took his meals in his stateroom, with only Brueys, Berthier, and one or two guests. When he reached Malta, he invited Monge to join him aboard *L'Orient*; Monge, who had made the journey from Civita Vecchia to Malta on the frigate *La Courageuse*, in a stateroom lined with crimson damask, had to relinquish his luxury in order to share Brueys' stateroom on *L'Orient*.

After dinner, Bonaparte was in the habit of summoning his staff officers and whatever savants were on hand to hold what he called his 'Institutes.' These consisted for the most part of discussions on topics proposed by him; he also designated the debaters. His interests were catholic: politics, economics, government, religion, tactics, chemistry, physics—there was hardly a subject he neglected. Was the earth the only inhabitable planet? How old was the earth? Was there anything in the interpretation of dreams? (This last question he proposed after a reading of Joseph's Dream in the Bible.) A three-day debate, sparked off by a reading from

Rousseau's *Discourse on the Origin of Inequality*, revolved about the social nature of property. With Regnault de Saint—Jean d'Angély as his opponent, General Caffarelli developed some bold communistic ideas. 'I maintain,' declared Caffarelli, 'that the laws which sanctify property sanctify usurpation and theft.'[1] Would he abolish these laws? his opponent inquired. No, a compromise could be achieved, thought Caffarelli, whom Regnault promptly challenged to explain how he would go about it. At the next meeting, Caffarelli pulled a fresh manuscript from his pocket and read it aloud. Society, he proposed, could be divided into present property owners and future property owners. The latter would be the tenants of the former for a twenty-year period, during which they would work for the profit of their landlords; then they in turn would become landlords and take on tenants and so ad infinitum. The solution seems ingenious, and no doubt Arnault, through whose memoirs it is known, oversimplified it; unfortunately the manuscript, which anticipated Marx in that it regarded work as the sole origin of property, has never been published and may have been lost, along with the author's life, at Acre.

The 'Institutes'—which sometimes were held while walking on deck, sometimes in the council chamber—did not invariably rise to such levels, and although everyone was free to express whatever opinion he chose, the very institution of the 'Institutes' had a constrained character. To most of the officers, they were a crashing bore, and Junot fell asleep during the discussions with such disarming promptness that he soon received dispensation from attending. His generals' hostility to the savants amused Bonaparte, and their anti-intellectualism sometimes caused him to chaff them in a manner more reminiscent of the barracks room than of the Institute. He himself had a talent for holding forth on any subject in monologues consisting mostly of blatant banalities but punctuated by sudden flashes of intuition. Religion was among his favourite topics. It was his vague religiosity, perhaps a lingering attachment to childhood beliefs, which made him recoil from the cold materialism of Berthollet and attracted him to the more open-minded Monge. Also, religion has such obvious political usefulness! The closer he came to the African coast, the more he steeped himself in the study of Islam and speculated on the practical use to which he might put it. 'As we passed the island of Crete,' says Bourrienne, 'his imagination became exalted.... He spoke a great deal about the decline of the Ottoman Empire.... The fables of my-

---

[1] Lichtenberger, p. 270.

thology presented themselves to his mind and lent his words a poetic and almost inspired quality. The sight of the Kingdom of Minos led him to speculate which laws were most appropriate to the government of men, just as the cradle of Zeus [Mount Ida] revealed to him the people's need for religion.'[1] This sort of twaddle continued until he lost sight of Crete; behind it loomed his flirtation with Islam and, three years later, his Concordat with Pope Pius VII.

***

'The entire crew is very cheerful. We just have been singing the revolutionary hymns in chorus.'[2] Thus wrote the ever-patriotic Monge to his wife on June 5, from his crimson-damask cabin aboard *La Courageuse*. Perhaps the crew's jollity can be explained by the fact that they had left Civita Vecchia only a week before and that the sea had been calm. Also, unlike the crews and troops on the other convoys, they knew at least where they were going: General Desaix had unsealed his orders when he was forty leagues from the coast and had informed the troops without delay. Most of all, however, one suspects that Citizen Monge mistook his own patriotic enthusiasm for that of others, as civilians often will, when carried away by the martial spirit. On the whole, the troops and crews, including the lower-ranking officers and civilians, were unutterably wretched.

There is no point in dwelling on the agonies of those who suffered from seasickness; during much of the journey the weather was fairly rough, and there is superabundant testimony on that subject. 'I vomited blood every day,'[3] Captain Guillet of the 25th Half-Brigade wrote to his mother from Cairo; to multiply such quotations would be monotonous and unaesthetic. Since the men were crowded like sardines, even the hardy ones had their share of the others' sufferings. There was, apparently, little opportunity to do one's laundry or to change one's linen. As for food, even a chronic grumbler like Lieutenant Vertray had to concede that his lot was enviable compared to that of 'the poor privates who, throughout the two-month crossing, lived on salt meat, whereas the officers had fresh food.'[4] By the time the main convoy approached Malta, the foodstuffs were rotting and the water spoiling.

---

[1] Bourrienne, I, 250

[2] Aubry, Monge, p. 240.

[3] Correspondance de L'armée Française, pp. 11213

[4] Vertray, p. 35

Even for the officers and civilians, things were becoming a little rough; there was hardly any livestock left to supply their table with fresh meat. 'There was no more fuel to heat our fetid water; the useful animals were disappearing while those which were eating us multiplied a hundred-fold,' wrote the artist Denon.[1]

At least, Denon had pencil and paper and an ever-curious eye. He made sketch after sketch, with an industry and imperturbability which later served him in good stead in even less propitious circumstances. The coasts of Corsica and Sardinia, Mount Etna in eruption, the guns of Malta bombarding (with no effect) the French fleet, antique pottery found on Gozo, Mount Ida the cradle of Zeus—whatever Denon saw, he sketched. Others, lacking his resources, sought to alleviate their boredom in different ways. The more privileged visited one another, weather permitting, from ship to ship or exchanged social notes. There was a great deal of singing—not only of revolutionary hymns, one hopes. There were amateur theatricals. There were band concerts: on *L'Orient*, Bonaparte's favourite tune, something called *March of the Tartars* by Kreutzer, was performed almost as frequently as Monge's favourite, the *Marseillaise*. There also were, of course, the inevitable amateur fiddlers, vocalists, and story-tellers. The manoeuvres of the fleet often made a fascinating spectacle. The obligatory daily exercises of crews and troops, in preparation for an enemy attack, were a less cheerful occupation, but at least they killed time. But the main relief from the monotony of life aboard ship was afforded by the not infrequent cries of 'Man overboard!' and the consequent manoeuvres. General Bonaparte took a lively interest in rescue operations, even at the price of delaying the convoy for hours, and he offered cash rewards to the rescuers. (It is true that the crews were incomplete and sailors at a premium.) Cash prizes also were offered to apprentice seamen in a daily speed contest for climbing into the crow's nests another diversion. The most popular pastime, however, was gambling. Even the Commander-in-Chief indulged in card games; it is said that he delighted in cheating but always returned his winnings to his victims. The greediest among the common soldiers, says Denon, in order to supplement their rations, 'sold their property or raffled it off. Others, even more impatient, gambled and lost more in a quarter of an hour than they could pay in a lifetime. After cash, came the watches: I have seen

---

[1] Denon, I, 7

six to eight watches staked on a single throw of dice.[1] Nothing surprising—in this the world has not changed.

Whereas water could be renewed in Malta, the island proved a
disappointment as to food supplies. On June 9, before the landing,
General Baraguey d'Hilliers drew Bonaparte's attention to the fact
that in his convoy part of the biscuits was spoiled, being of faulty
manufacture; that part of the oil had leaked through the Barréls,
and part of the wine likewise; that part of the salt beef was spoiled;
and that the supplies in general had suffered much from the wind
and the sea water. After the landing the chief paymaster of the
army informed Bonaparte that 'it will be difficult to do without the
supplies now aboard, seeing the lack of resources in this country
[Malta].'[2]

Band concerts and patriotic hymns notwithstanding, the journey from Malta to Alexandria must have been an infernal ordeal
for most of the men, what with supplies giving out or rotting and
the thermometer steadily rising. Among officers and troops alike
an every-man-for-himself spirit developed which was to reach ugly
proportions after the landing in Egypt, As for relations between
army and naval personnel, they became increasingly strained,
when the troops were landed at last, in a climax of high seas, seasickness, and misery, the naval officers gave a profound sigh of
relief to be rid of the intruders.

On June 28, the proclamation to the army, drafted by Bonaparte six days earlier, was read to the troops:

Soldiers!

You are about to undertake a conquest whose effects on
the world's civilization and trade are incalculable.

You will inflict upon England a blow which is certain to
wound her in her most sensitive spot, while waiting for the
day when you can deal her the death blow.

We shall make some wearisome marches; we shall fight
a few battles; we shall succeed in all our enterprises; destiny is for us.

The Mameluke beys, who exclusively favour English
trade, who have oppressed our merchants with vexations,
and who are tyrannizing over the unhappy people of the
Nile valley, will cease to exist a few days after our landing.

[1] Denon, I, 5.
[2] Correspondance inédite, officielle et confidentielle: Egypte, I, 155

The people with whom we shall live are Mohamme-
dans. Their chief creed is this: 'There is no God but God,
and Mohammed is His prophet.'

Do not contradict them. Act toward them as in the past
you have acted toward the Jews and the Italians. Respect
their muftis and imams, as you have respected the rabbis
and the bishops.

Show the same tolerance toward the ceremonies prescribed by the Koran and toward the mosques as you have
shown toward convents and synagogues, toward the religions of Moses and of Jesus Christ.

The Roman legions used to protect all religions. You
will find here customs quite different from those of
Europe; you must become used to them.

The people of the countries where we are going treat
their women differently from the way we do: but, in all
countries, the man who rapes a woman is a monster.

Looting enriches but a few. It dishonours us, it destroys
our resources, and it turns the people whom we want to
befriend into our enemies.

The first city we shall see was built by Alexander. At
every step we shall find traces of deeds worthy of being
emulated by the French.[1]

An admirable proclamation, no doubt—especially in its plea to
the godless for tolerance of believers. However, it is difficult to see
how it could have clarified to the average soldier just why he had
been taken to Egypt. Nor are starving and seasick men overly anxious to emulate the deeds of ancient heroes. There was little enthusiasm among the troops when they landed.

V

Although the French armada stunned the people of Alexandria
by its hugeness when it hove in sight, its appearance in itself
caused little surprise. Reports of the capture of Malta had preceded it, and, as Brueys reported to the Minister of Marine, 'the
population was in a state of ferment and apprehension,'[2] There
had been a general rush to arms; repairs were made on the moth-

[1] Correspondance, IV, 182-83.
[2] Correspondance de L'armée Française, p. 53

eaten fortifications; there were scarcely any soldiers, but a militia was formed, and the Mameluke kyacheff of Beheira Province rounded up some Bedouin tribes to assist in the defence: all these measures were more frenzied than effectual. On June 27, while the preparations were in progress, Captain Hardy sailed into the port of Alexandria with the *Mutine*. He was at first mistaken for a Frenchman. Even when this error was cleared up, Mohammed el-Koraim, the commandant of the city, who came to ask what were the Englishman's intentions, refused to accept their assistance against the French. Distrusting all Europeans alike, he cagily pretended ignorance. 'It is impossible,' he told them, according to Nicholas the Turk, 'that the French should come to our country. They have no business here, and we are not at war with them.... In any event, you cannot stay in our waters, and we have no plausible reason to authorize you to do so. Water and victual your ships, if you have to, but go away. If the French really think of invading our country, as you pretend, we shall thwart their undertaking.' 'You'll see what will happen,' replied Captain Hardy, 'and you'll be sorry you refused our help.'[1] In El-Koraim's particular case, the Englishman's prophecy assuredly proved accurate. It may be said with equal assurance that it was not Koraim's impotent defiance which kept the English from anchoring outside the harbour. Yet, unless Nicholas the Turk invented this conversation out of whole cloth, a puzzling question arises. If the English thought that there was a chance of the French fleet reaching Alexandria after they themselves did (and this possibility is implied in Hardy's exchange with El-Koraim), why did not Nelson wait off Alexandria for at least a couple of days? What made him give up so suddenly his conviction, expressed in despatch after despatch, that Egypt and India were the goals of the French? For lack of a better explanation, one must assume that the motive was more psychological than strategic: in the heat of the chase, he could not bring himself to idle away two days at a standstill and risk the chance of his prey escaping in another direction.

In any event, when the English left on June 29, the tricolour was still flying atop the house of the French consul, Magallon, a nephew of the Charles Magallon who perhaps had done more than any other man to instigate the expedition and who, at the moment, was aboard *L'Orient*.

***

---

[1] Nicholas Turc, p. 8

On June 27, after nightfall, the frigate *La Junon* was ordered to the stern of *L'Orient*. 'It would be difficult,' says Denon, who was aboard the frigate, 'to convey an exact idea of what we felt as we approached that inner sanctum of power, dictating its orders amidst 500 sail, in the mystery and silence of the night, with only the moon lighting the spectacle just enough to let us take it in. We were about 500 of us on deck; one could have heard the buzzing of a fly.' Ordered aboard the flagship, the captain of the frigate received his instructions: he was to sail to Alexandria, reconnoitre the defences, pick up the French consul, and bring him back. *La Junon* set off immediately; she sighted the coast of Egypt on the 29th at dawn. The view did not cheer the troops. 'Look!' a wit among them remarked to his neighbour, pointing at the dismal, Barrén coast, 'There are the six acres of land they've promised you.'[1] At 1 p.m., the frigate reached Alexandria and anchored several miles offshore. A lieutenant was despatched in a launch to fetch the consul; while waiting for his return, Denon sketched the distant view of the fort, the mosques and minarets of the city. As he drew, he indulged himself in daydreams of Alexandria's past glories—daydreams soon to be dispelled by the realities of a wretched, filthy town whose population had shrunk to about 6,000.

The emissary and the consul having returned about midnight, *La Junon* set sail. When, at 7 a.m. the following day, she pulled alongside *L'Orient*, the calm weather had given way to a brisk north wind which soon became a gale. The French fleet, both warships and transports, was bobbing on the waves in chaotic confusion. Magallon and Denon went aboard the flagship to report to Bonaparte. The main news, of course, was that the English squadron had just left Alexandria and might be prowling in the neighbourhood. Bonaparte's countenance, so Denon assures us, remained unaltered.

On the following day—July 1—the armada sighted Pompey's Pillar, which then was the outstanding landmark of Alexandria. The proximity of the English fleet forced an immediate choice upon Bonaparte: either he must land his army that very day or he must seek safety in one or both of the city's harbours. It was clear from the younger Magallon's report that a landing in Alexandria itself was out of the question without a battle. The fleet might fight its way into one of the harbours, but only at great risk, the approaches to both ports being narrow and tricky, especially in heavy

---

[1] Denon, I, 20-21

weather; there was a danger that the battleships might run aground. The alternative—a landing east or west of Alexandria—presented equal difficulties. The ideal landing place was Abukir Bay, about fifteen miles to the east. To land there, however, would waste precious time, because of the distance, and it was exactly the spot where the enemy would expect a landing. The beach of Marabut, a fishing village about eight miles to the west, was preferable from the landlubber's point of view, but not from the seaman's. Admiral Brueys raised vehement objections to it. The operation could not begin before afternoon and would take all night; the sea was ugly; the coast and coastal waters were uncharted. It would be better not to land the same day but to wait until the following morning, since Nelson was not likely to return for some time.

As it happened, Brueys was right (Nelson returned only a month later), but he was overruled by the landlubber. Bonaparte, says Bourrienne, 'listened to these arguments with impatience and ill humour. He replied brusquely, "Admiral, we have no time to waste. Luck grants me three days, no more. If I don't take advantage of them, we're lost".'[1] Thus the question was decided on a gamble.

In the report he wrote to the Directory to explain the disaster which overtook the French fleet a month later, in Abukir Bay, Bonaparte used the words 'luck' and 'Fortune' with astounding profusion. 'When I arrived before Alexandria,' he says, 'and when I learned that the English had passed by there with superior forces a few days before, I decided to land my troops, despite the horrible storm that was raging.... I recall that just at the moment when the manoeuvres preparatory to the landing began, a warship was sighted on the horizon. As it turned out, it was [the frigate] La Justice, coming from Malta. I cried out, "Is my luck leaving me? All I need is five days!"'[2] To be sure, Bonaparte had every reason to fear that the man of war on the horizon might be the van of the English fleet. If he reckoned with luck, he did so prudently: how could he know that Nelson would give him four weeks instead of five days? Unnecessary though it turned out to be, the decision to land the troops, despite all risks, was the only rational one.

While the French fleet was still off Alexandria, casting terror into the hearts of those ashore, the Turkish commander of a caravel that was anchored in the port sent an officer to L'Orient with a

[1] Bourrienne, I, 258.
[2] Correspondance, IV, 190.

gift of two sheep and an inquiry as to what the French were doing there. The Turk was handed a copy of the Arabic proclamation, already printed, addressed to the people of Egypt. He shook his head; he could not read Arabic, he said (probably he could not read Turkish either); the proclamation was translated for him by Venture. At every disobliging mention of the Mameluke beys, the visitor leaped with joy; he requested more copies of the proclamation to distribute, consumed quantities of coffee and sweets, and left with a letter from Bonaparte to his commander. 'I shall be in Alexandria tomorrow,' wrote the General. 'You need not fear anything. You belong to our great friend, the Sultan: act accordingly. But, if you display the least hostility toward the French army, I shall treat you as an enemy, and you will be to blame for it, for it is far from my heart's intentions to do so.'[1] It is doubtful whether the Turkish commander was impressed with Bonaparte's sincerity, but he kept his own counsel and did nothing.

The landing operations off Marabut beach began about noon. Of the five divisions that made up the army, those commanded by Desaix, Menou, and Reynier were on transports, anchored about three miles off shore; the divisions commanded by Kléber and Bon were on the battleships, forming an arc at about twice that distance from the beach. The approaches to the shore were obstructed by rocks and reefs; the sea grew steadily worse, and it was eight o'clock when the first troops reached land. The operation turned out a night-long inferno. Many of the soldiers had to be lowered into the launches and longboats by ropes. The sea was covered with capsized boats, and the screams of the men could be heard above the noise of the waves; very few of the men could swim, everybody—soldiers, sailors, and marines—was desperately seasick. Some of the boats took eight hours to row three miles. It seems a miracle that only nineteen men were drowned; this, at least, is the figure given by Bonaparte, who may have minimized it.

The commander-in-chief boarded a Maltese galley about 4 p.m. A fleet of small craft collected about the galley, which had to anchor half a mile offshore, in the darkness. About 1 a.m., impatient to reach land, Bonaparte jumped into a launch, with Brueys holding him by the hand to steady him. Accompanied by Generals Berthier, Caffarelli, and Dommartin, he reached shore some distance away from Marabut. By this time, Kléber, Menou, and Bon had succeeded in landing close to 5,000 men; Desaix, to Bonaparte's annoyance, was still bobbing on the waves with his divi-

---

[1] Ibid

sion; Reynier had landed a few hundred men. After ordering a watch to be placed to guard the beachhead, Bonaparte slept for about an hour, while the drenched troops continued to make their way to shore.

At three in the morning, under a bright moon, Bonaparte passed in review what troops there were. He then gave orders for the divisions of Kléber, Menou, and Bon to begin their march on Alexandria, leaving Reynier's and Desaix's men behind as a guard.

Neither food rations nor personal belongings, nor a single piece of artillery, nor a single horse had reached shore as yet. There was no drinking water, and none was to be found all the way to Alexandria. Few of the men had had anything to eat in the first twenty-four hours from the landing. On empty stomachs, after five or six weeks of a grueling crossing, carrying nothing but their weapons and the clothes they wore, sick and exhausted by the night's exertions, the troops began their march, at dawn, through a desert, to take a fortified city by assault. 'Confidentially,' says Lieutenant Thurman in a letter to his family, 'I can assure you that it was thirst which inspired our soldiers in the capture of Alexandria. At the point the army had reached, we had no choice between finding water and perishing.'[1] Still, there were some who preferred even this to their ordeals aboard ship. 'All my wishes,' says Lieutenant Vertray, ' looked forward to the moment when I would recover the appetite I had left behind at Gozo.'[2]

There was, of course, no road; there is one now—the road from Alexandria to El Alamein, through the Libyan Desert. The troops had not marched for long when the sun rose and beat down on them. What wells or cisterns they found on their way were dry or had been filled in by the Bedouins. The heat and thirst soon became intolerable; still the men marched on—there was no choice. At their head was Bonaparte himself, on foot. At his side walked Caffarelli, stumping through the sand on his wooden leg; Dumas, commander of the cavalry, without a horse; and Dommartin, commander of the artillery, without a gun.

At dawn, on the hills, the scraggy silhouettes of a few Bedouins, mounted on their horses and armed with long spears, could be seen against the sky. Soon there were about 400 of them. Seeing that the French had no cavalry, they grew bold and, with blood-curdling screams, galloped into the intervals between the French

[1] Thurman, p. 27.
[2] Vertray, p. 30

columns. They fled at the least sign of determined resistance, but not without having made prisoner a number of stragglers, among them several women, whose weariness and misery had made them indifferent to danger. When the captives were returned several days later, they had a tale to tell which soon spread through the army and discouraged straggling on subsequent marches: the male prisoners had been much admired for their white, smooth skins and abundantly raped by their scrawny but vigorous captors; as for the women, they had merely been beaten. There is no accounting for the tastes of people who live on camel's milk all year round.

By eight in the morning, the French columns reached the outer fortifications of Alexandria. The wind had stopped. Some, like Lieutenant Vertray, fell to the ground, prostrated by the heat, when their columns were ordered to halt. Fortunately for Vertray, there was a well near the spot where he fell; not all were so lucky.[1]

General Bonaparte, after surveying the fortifications from the pedestal of Pompey's Pillar, which was to be his headquarters for several days, ordered his troops to attack without a rest. He then sat down and idly lashed away at a mound of potsherds with his riding whip. He too was thirsty, but no one could find water for him. An officer who had managed to carry some oranges all the way from Malta to Pompey's Pillar offered them to him. The General ate them greedily.

***

The preceding evening, Mohammed el-Koraim had sent the following despatch to Murad Bey, in Cairo: 'My lord, the fleet which has just appeared is immense. One can see neither its beginning nor its end. For the love of God and of His Prophet, send us fighting men.'[2] Even if he had known the wretched and perilous condition of the French army, there was little he could do. According to Nicholas the Turk, the defenders of Alexandria had but one Barrél of gunpowder for their artillery. As for cavalry, aside from the useless Bedouins, there was no more than a score of Mamelukes. As terrified of the French as the French were of the dangers and hardships facing them, El-Koraim sent no less than thirteen messengers to Cairo in the course of the night: It was, to use an

---

[1] It is strange to see that Vertray, who belonged to the 9th Half-Brigade, which belonged to General Reynier's division, should have taken part in the march to Alexandria; however, according to his Journal, whose veracity there is no reason to doubt, he did: one of the minor puzzles of history.

[2] Nicholas Turc, p. 9

expression dear to Nicholas, a night of horror 'such as will make
the hair of an infant at its mother's breast turn white in an
instant.'[1] Nicholas' fellow chronicler Abd el-Rahman el-Djabarti
asserts that, when day broke, 'the French surrounded the city like
a swarm of locusts,'[2] an exaggeration which reflects the state of
mind of the defenders.

The French were even thirstier than the Alexandrians were terrified; by 11 a.m., the city was in their hands.

---

[1] Ibid., p. 24
[2] El-Djabarti, VI, 7

Chapter Three
To the Pyramids

THE French were still in Alexandria, getting ready for their advance to the south, when Mohammed el-Koraim's thirteen couriers reached Murad Bey with their portentous tidings. 'The city of Cairo was instantly in a turmoil,' says Nicholas the Turk. 'What a dreadful day! How grave an hour!'[1] Abu Bakr, the pasha, immediately summoned a divan, attended by all the Mameluke beys present in Cairo as well as by the kyacheffs, various notables, and nine religious leaders, among them the rector of the Mosque El Azhar, Sheik Mohammed Abdullah el-Charkawi. Of the beys, only Salih, on pilgrimage to Mecca, was absent.

The bearded Murad Bey, a tall Circassian who could decapitate an ox with a single blow of his scimitar, opened the proceedings by turning on the pasha. 'The French,' he said, 'could not have come to this country without the consent of the Porte, and you, being its minister, must have had knowledge of their projects. Fate will help us against you and them.'[2] The pasha indignantly rejected the accusation. The Sublime Porte would never permit the French to invade Moslem territory, 'Cast these thoughts from you, be coura-

---

[1] Nicolas Turc, p. 13.

[2] Ibid., p, 19.

geous and forthright, rise up like the brave men you are and prepare to fight and to resist by force, leaving the outcome to God!'[1]

This settled, it was suggested by several beys and ulemas that as a preliminary to battle it would be good to exterminate all the Christians resident in Cairo—a security measure reminiscent of a proposal made three months earlier for the defence of London. Its merits were debated for some time, with the pasha and the Sheik el-Beled, Ibrahim Bey, opposing it. Incarceration, it was decided, would be sufficient. As for more positive measures, the divan resolved that Murad Bey, with a large armed force, should move south to meet the French; the pasha and Ibrahim Bey would camp with the rest of the army at Bulaq, the river port of Cairo (of which it is now a part).

While the imams and ulemas exhorted the faithful to kill the invaders, the Moslem population took up arms. Like the people of Malta, they must have done so with considerable apprehension, Ibrahim Bey having told them that the French were devils endowed with exceptionally terrifying physical characteristics. 'The Infidels who come to fight you,' he warned them, 'have fingernails one foot long, enormous mouths, and ferocious eyes. They are savages possessed by the Devil, and they go into battle linked together with chains.'[2] This, at least, is what an Italian pharmacist, whom Lieutenant Vertray later met in Cairo, quoted Ibrahim as having said; but then Italian pharmacists are prone to dramatic exaggeration.

About a couple of days after receiving news of the French landing, Murad Bey left Cairo at the head of a motley army, comprising about three or four thousand mounted Mamelukes, their servants-at-arms, Cairo militia, and Bedouins whom he had summoned to his aid against the common enemy—in all about 20,000 men. At the same time he ordered a flotilla of gunboats to descend the Nile and support his troops when needed.

With Murad's departure, Cairo fell into the grip of a silent terror. Except for thieves and robbers, the streets were deserted. To calm the spirits and to prevent looting or panic in case of a surprise attack, the police ordered the coffee houses to be kept open all night and lights to be placed before all dwellings and shops. Nevertheless, says the historian El-Djabarti (who was an ulema of the great Mosque El Azhar at the time these events took place), the

---

[1] Ibid., p, 19.

[2] Vertray, p. 64.

rich were moving their wealth to hiding places in the countryside and preparing to flee the city. As reports came in, telling of the French advance, the ulemas met daily at the Mosque El Azhar to 'read the Book of Bokhari for the success of the Egyptians. The sheiks of the [several] ... brotherhoods also assembled in that mosque and invoked God. The students did the same at the schools.' Finally, on the third day of Safar (July 17), 'the trumpets were sounded, inviting the inhabitants to leave the city and to go to the entrenchments at Bulaq.... Bands of fakirs and dervishes marched to and fro, carrying banners and playing musical instruments while reciting prayers for victory. The lord Omar effendi, head of the sherifs,[1] went forth from the Citadel holding in his hand a large banner which the people called the standard of the Prophet and thus crossed the city all the way to Bulaq. He was surrounded by thousands of men armed with clubs, all playing their instruments and reciting prayers in a loud voice.'[2] If noise could win battles, and if one's own confusion could be communicated to the enemy, the Egyptians had a decisive superiority over the French.

Only old people, women, and children remained in Cairo. All male Moslems capable of bearing arms (they must have been close to a hundred thousand) assembled at Bulaq, where food prices rose even more rapidly than did the number of warriors. Chaos and plunder spread through the surrounding countryside. Among the commanders there appears to have been as much confusion as among the populace. Information as to the route taken by the French was contradictory; according to El-Djabarti, 'none of the leaders had the idea of sending out spies to ascertain the truth.'[3]

When the French finally appeared on July 21, not one of Ibrahim's men had a chance to fire a shot or to swing his club.

II

It was about eight in the morning of July 2 when the French columns halted just beyond gun range before the outer walls of Alexandria. Some attempts were made to communicate with the defenders, who could be seen in great numbers atop the walls. 'Suddenly,' says Lieutenant Desvernois, 'they burst into terrifying screams—men, women, and children—and at the same time a vol-

---

[1] Descendants of Mohammed, entitled to wear green turban

[2] El-Djabarti, VI, 13-15

[3] Ibid., VI, 15

ley of artillery fire acquainted us with the intentions of the Arabs. Bonaparte had the bugles sounded for the charge, and the screams doubled in strength.'[1]

General Menou's division had taken position in the east, opposite the so-called Triangular Fort; Kléber's division, in the north, facing Pompey's Gate; General Bon in the west, facing the Rosetta Gate. Although the walls were defective in many places, it was difficult to breach them without artillery. While the French were trying to scale them, the defenders pelted them with rocks and bullets. General Kléber, directing his men from the foot of the wall, received a severe bullet wound above the eye; General Menou received seven wounds from rocks. It is rare to see two major-generals become casualties in the first five minutes of a campaign. This phase of the fighting was over very quickly: impetuous and thirsty, the French breached and scaled the fortifications in several places, while the defenders beat a hasty retreat to the city proper.

Since the days when the Arab conquerors of Alexandria had built its outer walls, the city had shrunk until it occupied only the narrow tongue of land separating the 'New' or western Port from the 'Old' or eastern one: at the tip of the peninsula, on the site of the celebrated ancient lighthouse, stood the inner fortress. Just what happened after the French had stormed the outer wall is not quite clear. The Lighthouse Fort, under Mohammed el-Koraim, undoubtedly held out until late at night, and there certainly was street fighting in the city. According to Bonaparte's report to the Directory, 'every house was a citadel.'[2] According to Bourrienne, there only was some desultory sniping—but Bourrienne was with Bonaparte at Pompey's Pillar, not in the streets. According to the same Bourrienne and to Thurman, there were absolutely no reprisals against the defenders, and the occupation of the city took place without any disorder. Adjutant General Boyer, a member of the General Staff, tells a different story. 'When they [the defenders] had been repulsed on every side,' he wrote to his parents, 'they took refuge with their God and their Prophet. They filled the mosques. Men and women, old and young, even children, all were massacred. After about four hours, the fury of our soldiers was spent at last.'[3] Boyer's letter is among those intercepted and published by the British for propaganda purposes; perhaps its text was tampered with. His testimony, however, is confirmed by Private

---

[1] Desvernois, p. 100

[2] Correspondence, IV, 216.

[3] Correspondence de L'armée Française, p. 158.

Millet, who was actually in the fighting with Kléber's division. 'We already thought that the city had surrendered,' Millet says in his memoirs, 'and were quite surprised when a volley of musketry was fired at us as we were passing by a mosque.... A general who happened to be there ordered us to force the gate and to spare no one we found inside. Men, women, and children ... perished under our bayonets. However, since human feelings are stronger than vengeance, the massacre ceased when they cried for mercy: about one third of them were spared.'[1]

Civilians are not supposed to shoot at soldiers, and even under the existing rules of warfare among so-called civilized nations, the action of the French might conceivably be justified. The Moslems, unacquainted with the rules of civilized warfare, were taught a salutary lesson; they also learned that one must never mistake one's liberators for enemies.

Meanwhile the commander of the Turkish caravel had offered his services to arrange for a surrender. Bonaparte told him to tell the sheiks, ulemas, and other notables that further resistance would oblige him to put them all to the sword, a severity he would rather avoid if he could. Shortly before noon, a deputation appeared at Pompey's Pillar to surrender the city and swear an oath of obedience. The scene must have been colourful. 'Generals, soldiers, Turks, Arabs, camels—all these contrasts made up an unposed picture of the upheavals that will change the character of this country,' one of the eyewitnesses wrote somewhat incoherently.[2] At that moment an incident afforded Bonaparte a chance to impress his Moslem audience with both his sternness and his justice. 'A [French] soldier was brought before him,' says the same witness, 'for taking a dagger away from a peaceful Arab. The fact was verified in an instant, and the soldier was shot on the spot.'[3] Like the unpleasantness at the mosque, this episode made it plain that General Bonaparte, Member of the Institute and commander-in-chief, brooked no nonsense. To be sure, in different circumstances the peaceful Arab might well have been shot to teach him not to carry a dagger.

Having produced his effect, Bonaparte walked into the city, escorted by his new friends and by a detachment of Guides. As he passed through a narrow street in which no more than two men

---

[1] Millet, p. 44

[2] Correspondence de L'armée Française, p. 28

[3] Ibid, p. 29

could walk abreast, a sniper opened fire from a window and grazed his left boot. Some of the soldiers returned the fire, others climbed into the house by way of the roof, found the snipers, a man and a woman, and killed them instantly.[1] No further incident occurred, and the General soon reached the house of the French consul, facing the eastern Port, where he took up residence.

Among his first actions was the order to post throughout the city, and to have read aloud, several hundred copies of his proclamation to the people of Egypt, printed in Arabic, Turkish, and French. It is a remarkable proclamation, even in the toned-down French version in which it is generally reproduced. As quoted below, it follows the Arabic text, which shows far more plainly Bonaparte's deliberate appeal to Moslem feeling, curiously combined with the libertarian catchwords of the French Revolution. Perhaps it was this strange brew he had in mind when he spoke, in later years, of the 'new Koran' he had meant to compose to suit his own needs and hold in his hand as he conquered the East:

PROCLAMATION[2]

[In the name of God, the clement and the merciful. There is no divinity save Allah; He has no son and shares His power with no one.]

[In the name of the French Republic, founded on liberty and equality], the commander-in-chief [of the French armies], Bonaparte [lets it be known to the whole population of Egypt that] the beys who govern Egypt have insulted the French nation and oppressed French merchants long enough: the hour of their punishment has come.

For too many years that gang of slaves, purchased in Georgia and the Caucasus, has tyrannized over the most beautiful region of the world. But Almighty God, who rules the universe, has decreed that their reign shall come to an end.

---

[1] This is what happened according to Bourrienne (Memoires, I, 261); according to Bonaparte, there was hut one solitary man, surrounded by six muskets (Campagnes d'Egypte et de Syrie, in Correspondance de Napoleon I , XXIX, 434).

[2] Passages between square brackets are not contained in the official French text; those in italics appear in significantly different form in the French.

Peoples of Egypt, you will be told that I have come to destroy your religion, [This is an obvious lie;] do not believe it! Answer back [to those imposters] that I have come to restore to you your rights and to punish the usurpers; *that I worship God more than the Mamelukes do; and that I respect His prophet Mohammed and the admirable Koran.*[1]

Tell them that all men are equal before God. Intelligence, virtue, and knowledge alone differentiate them from one another.

Now tell us, by what intelligence, virtues, or knowledge have the Mamelukes distinguished themselves to possess an exclusive right to everything that makes life agreeable and sweet?

Is there a beautiful estate? It belongs to the Mamelukes. Is there a beautiful slave, horse, or house? All this belongs to the Mamelukes.

If Egypt be their farm, then let them produce the deed by which God gave it to them in fee. But God is righteous and merciful to the people. Henceforth, with His help, no Egyptian shall be excluded from high office, and all shall be able to reach the highest positions; those who are the most intelligent, educated, and virtuous shall govern, and thus the people shall be happy.

Once you had great cities, large canals, a prosperous trade. What has destroyed all this, if not the greed, the iniquity, and the tyranny of the Mamelukes?

Kadis, sheiks, imams, tchorbadjis [and notables of the country], tell the people that the French also are true Moslems.[2] The proof is that they have been to Rome the great and have destroyed the throne of the Pope, who always incited the Christians to make war on the Moslems, and that they went to the island of Malta and expelled the Knights, who fancied that God wanted them to make war on the Moslems. Besides, the French have shown at all times that they are the particular friends of [His Majesty] the Ottoman Sultan (may God perpetuate his rule!) and the enemies of his enemies. The Mamelukes, on the contrary,

---

[1] Official French version: 'and that I respect God, His prophet, and the Koran more than the Mamelukes do.'

[2] Official French version: 'true friends of the Moslems.'

always have refused to obey him; they never comply with his orders and follow only their whims.

Happy, thrice happy are those Egyptians who side with us. They shall prosper in fortune and rank. Happy are those who stay in their dwellings without taking sides with either of the parties now at war. When they know us better, they will hasten to join us in all sincerity.

But woe, woe to those who side with the Mamelukes and help them to make war on us. There shall be no salvation for them, and their memory shall be wiped out.

ARTICLE 1 : All the villages situated within three hours' distance from the route of the French army will send deputations to let the commanding general know that they are obedient and to inform him that they have displayed the flag of the army, which is blue, white, and red.

ARTICLE 2: All villages that take up arms against the army will be burned to the ground.

ARTICLE 3: All the villages that have submitted themselves will fly, besides the colours of the army, those of the Ottoman Sultan, our friend (may God give him a long reign!).

ARTICLE 4: [In every inhabited locality] the sheiks will place seals on all the goods, houses, and property belonging to the Mamelukes, and they will take care that nothing is removed.

ARTICLE 5: The sheiks, kadis, and imams shall continue to exercise their functions in their posts. All inhabitants shall remain in their homes unmolested. All Egyptians shall render thanks to God for the destruction of the Mamelukes, saying in a loud voice: 'May God preserve the glory of the Ottoman Sultan! May God preserve the glory of the French army! May God curse the Mamelukes and bestow happiness on the Egyptian nation.'[1]

Perhaps,' wrote the navy commissioner Jaubert to the Minister of Marine, 'you Parisians will laugh when you see the Mohammedan proclamation of our commander-in-chief . He has ignored all our jokes about it, and it will certainly produce a very great effect.'[2]

---

[1] Correspondence, IV, 191-92; Nicolas Turc, pp. 10-12.

[2] Correspondence de L'armée Française,p. 40.

Napoleon himself, commenting on it at St. Helena, admitted that it was a piece of charlatanry 'but charlatanry of the highest sort.'[1] 'Well,' he declared to another of his St. Helena confidents, 'in this world one has got to be a charlatan. It's the only road to success.'[2] Two days after the proclamation was issued, General Desaix, writing from a village at the edge of the Libyan Desert, requested more copies: 'It produces a great effect,' he added.[3]

The night of July 2-3 was spent in negotiations with Mohammed el-Koraim. The next morning, El-Koraim capitulated, declared himself his conqueror's slave, and swore allegiance to him. Bonaparte judged it politic to be generous: he pardoned El-Koraim for resisting attack, confirmed him as commandant, and entrusted him with the main tenance of order and the procurement of supplies for the French. It was perhaps at that moment that Bonaparte, from a general, became a ruler—a transformation which requires a very superior kind of charlatanry.

***

All the troops, horses and civilians had been disembarked by July 5. The transports and several of the frigates and lesser craft had entered the Old Port. Soldiers and civilians alike were startled by the aspect of Alexandria, which hardly fulfilled their expectations. Of the ancient magnificence there remained nothing. Besides two obelisks and Pompey's Pillar, a monument imposing chiefly because of its height of seventy-five feet, there were hardly even any ruins, except modern ones. A few ancient monuments have since been unearthed; but for the most part, the Alexandria of the Ptolemies and the Caesars had neither crumbled to dust nor been covered by earth: it had simply been broken up and digested in the unceasing course of history and life. The levees of the harbour were a jumble of rocks, polished blocks of Aswan granite, fragments of hellenistic columns. The same components, covered sometimes with exquisite hieroglyphs or with Greek inscriptions, were mingled indiscriminately with unbaked clay bricks, wooden boards, and dirt to make houses and fortifications: a sad sight to the archaeologist and architect, but a moving object-lesson to the historian. Only where death had prevailed—at Palmyra, Petra, Pompeii—have ruins been preserved intact.

---

[1] Las Cases, I, 504.

[2] Gourgaud, II, 261-62.

[3] Correspondence inédite, officielle et confidentielle: Egypte, I, 212

Alexandria had come upon hard days, but death had not prevailed. The streets were unpaved and filthy; except for a few date
palms, there were no trees: but there were mosques, bazaars, and
people. At the time the French arrived, the yearly epidemic of bubonic plague had just run its course; the rich were still hiding in
their houses, in terror of the French rather than the plague, but life
quickly resumed its usual aspect. 'In the bazaars,' wrote Citizen
Jaubert to his brother, 'one could see sheep, pigeons, smoking tobacco, and, above all, quantities of barbers, who put their patients'
heads between their knees and seem prepared to decapitate rather
than shave them. However, they are very nimble.'[1] Few women
could be seen in the streets, except those belonging to the lower
classes, whose aspect struck the French as unappetizing. Their sole
garment was a shirt, usually blue and always dirty; they went barefoot and bare-calved, smeared kohl on their eye brows, painted
their fingernails red, and blithely exposed any part of their anat-
omy save their faces. As for the children, they went about naked.

The male population impressed the French more favourably.
'This nation,' wrote Bonaparte to the Directors, 'is completely different from the idea our travellers have given us of it. It is calm,
proud, and brave.'[2] His brother Louis, in a letter to Joseph Bonaparte, agreed with this judgment. The people, he wrote, 'possess
an astonishing sang froid. Nothing moves them. Death is no more
to them than a transatlantic crossing to an Englishman.... Their
appearance is imposing. Even our most strong-featured physiog-
nomies look like children's faces compared to theirs.'[3] Side by side
with the opinions given by the future Emperor and the future King
of Holland, one may place that of Private Millet: 'The costume of
the inhabitants strikes us at first as shapeless. After examining it
more closely, I realized that it is more majestic than ours. They
shave their heads and wear a small red bonnet, called tarboosh in
Arabic, around which a turban is wound five or six times. They
wear several large robes made of silk or cloth one on top of the
other, all very long, descending to their heels, like cassocks. Their
legs, and often also their feet, are bare, and they grow long beards,
which sometimes lend the old men a rather majestic aspect.'[4]

---

[1] Correspondence de L'armée Française, p. 25

[2] Correspondence, IV, 217

[3] Correspondence de L'armée Française, pp. 9, 10

[4] Millet, p. 45

These imposing and majestic men spent the larger part of their time sitting at their doorsteps or in coffee houses, smoking, sipping coffee, and scorning labour.

If the people were cool, the weather was not. After five days in Alexandria, Louis Bonaparte wrote to Joseph: 'This climate wears me down; it will change all of us. When we come back, we shall be recognized from far away.'[1] The *khamsin*, or south wind, had just begun. 'One fine morning,' says Thurman, 'we found the atmosphere darkened by a reddish haze formed of infinitely small particles of burning dust; one could barely see the disc of the sun. This intolerable air dried our tongues, burned our eyelids, and gave us an insatiable thirst. All perspiration stopped, the chest felt oppressed, the extremities grew weary and heavy, and it was barely possible to speak.'[2] All this, however, was very pleasant compared to what the troops who had begun their march through the desert were experiencing at that moment.

Bonaparte was intent on wasting as little time in Alexandria as possible and gave his troops no opportunity for sightseeing. The week he spent in that city was a time of frenzied activity for everybody. In the middle of what seemed a wild confusion of soldiers, aides-de-camp, Egyptian dignitaries, French commissioners, naval officers, and fierce Bedouin deputations, the gentlemen of the Scientific Commission disembarked and found themselves neglected. Nobody had even unloaded their personal luggage, the engineer Jollois complains in his diary; the captain of his frigate had virtually chased him from on board. Others, on other ships, had been refused food and been made to sleep on deck. Once landed, they found no beds and nothing to eat. On learning of their plight, Dolomieu protested to Bonaparte, with the result that they were given privates' rations and quarters. The artists and men of letters fared even worse than the engineers. General Caffarelli, who was in charge of the whole lot, spoke only to the military engineers and showed his disdain to all others. If they complained too much, they were put to clerical work or sent about as messengers.

While it is understandable that the savants felt slighted and betrayed—after all, they had been induced with all sorts of promises to join in the expedition, and they expected their talents and knowledge to be put to use—it is difficult to share their indignation at being treated no better than common soldiers. First things had to be seen to first: these were the provisioning of the army and the

---

[1] Correspondence de L'armée Française, p. 8

[2] Thurman, p. 89

horses, preparations for the march to Cairo, the establishment of a civil administration, the acquisition of local currency, the fixing of standard prices for goods and labour, the construction of new for-tifications and strongpoints, the disposition of the naval forces, and the organization of hospitals—for at least 200 French had been wounded in the fighting.[1] To all these things Bonaparte at-tended as best he could—which, as will be seen, was not always very well—and they left him no time to devote to the comfort of his savants. To favour them would have produced a poor effect on the morale of the troops, which was low as it was. Since even their generals shared their hardships and since, being French, they were born grumblers, the soldiers' resentment vented itself on civili-ans—the civilians of the Paris government, whom they began to accuse of having dreamed up the Egyptian expedition simply to be rid of Bonaparte and his army, and the civilians in the expedition-ary force, particularly Magallon and the other Egyptian experts, whose glowing description of the country and its resources seemed to them a bad joke at their expense. In the circumstances, it was a wise policy not to treat civilians better than soldiers. As the cam-paign continued, the civilians learned to regard themselves as part of an army and to share its hardships, and the troops came to ap-preciate their services.

There was at least one among the civilians who neither wasted his time in Alexandria nor—despite his fifty-one years—com-plained of the hardships. Vivant Denon always kept his eyes and senses open and his pencil ready. What struck him at first sight in Alexandria was the silence and the sadness of the town. 'The only thing that recalled to me the noise and activity of Europe was the noise and the activity of the sparrows.'[2] Like most others, he had had to leave his belongings aboard ship; a futile attempt to return aboard La Junon to retrieve his spare shirts left him at sundown in a deserted part of the harbour. There followed a night of horrors, when the artist tried to make his way back, clutching his sketch-book under his arm and pursued by snarling, ferocious packs of dogs, 'the sixth and most terrible of the Egyptian plagues,' which eventually forced him to wade through the water and to clamber

---

[1] The casualty figures given by Bonaparte to the Directory are 30-80 French killed and 80-100 wounded; those he gave in his *Campagnes d'Egypte et de Syrie* are 300 French and 700-800 Egyptians killed or wounded. Captain Guillot, in a letter to his mother, writes that the French lost about 300 men.

[2] Denon, I, 27

over walls and embankments. It was midnight when he reached a
French sentry. The next day, undefeated by the night's experience,
he toured the city, starting out with Pompey's Pillar. He arrived
just in time to see Mohammed el-Koraim make his submission to
Bonaparte. 'I noticed,' he says of El-Koraim, 'in the facial expression of that clever man a dissimulation which had been shaken but
not defeated by the generous trust of the commander-in-chief. He
did not know yet the extent of our resources, nor whether what
had happened was not the result of mere bluff; but when he saw
that 50,000 men and artillery had been landed, he made every effort to attach himself to Bonaparte and never left his headquarters.
Bonaparte had already gone to bed when El-Koraim was still in his
ante chamber.'[1] There was, as it turned out, duplicity even in this
fidelity.

After studying El-Koraim's physiognomy and sketching the
heterogeneous components of Pompey's Pillar, Denon crossed the
'City of the Arabs,' which at that time was an empty terrain strewn
with rubbish and punctuated by a few gardens; admired the water
reservoir; inspected the ruins of the Church of St. Catherine the
Learned 'the one that married the infant Jesus 400 years after his
death'[2] and Cleopatra's obelisk; passed by the public baths, which
then were closed to the public so that the French soldiers could do
their laundry; was distressed by the dilapidated condition of the
principal mosque; sketched everything; and ended up in the quarter by the Rosetta Gate. There he saw, sitting on a block of stone
still sticky with the blood of the preceding day's fighting, alone
amid some corpses not yet buried, a young Frenchwoman, all
blonde and pink. Denon asked her if she was lost. No, she said, she
was only waiting for her husband, who was to start that evening on
the march to Cairo, with Desaix's division. She and her husband
would sleep in the desert that night, she added casually.

III

The word 'impossible,' Bonaparte once declared, did not exist
in his vocabulary. What he meant by this was not, of course, that
he could do anything he pleased but that once he had decided that
a thing was necessary, it was also possible for others to carry it out.
Troops were still disembarking when, on July 5, Bonaparte ordered General Desaix's division to begin the march to Damanhur.

---

[1] Denon, I, 28-29
[2] Ibid., I, 33

Desaix's men, who were bivouacking just outside Alexandria, began their march at night fall, followed on July; by Reynier's division. The other three divisions were to follow in the next two days—two of them by way of Damanhur, the third by way of Rosetta; the entire army was to join at El Rahmaniya, on the left arm of the Nile Delta, The distances do not look impressive on the map; it is forty-five miles from Alexandria to Damanhur, fifteen miles from Damanhur to El Rahmaniya—altogether, a three days' march. The conditions of the march, however, were such as most men would call impossible.

Bonaparte was determined to make good his word that the French had come as friends and liberators; to do so was a military and political necessity for a small expeditionary force in an ocean of hostile, fanatic, distrustful, and excitable people. He intended to pay cash for all supplies purchased and all labour performed. Since he was low on cash and there was no mint in Alexandria, loans had to be raised and a part of the gold and silveringots taken from Malta had to be exchanged—at disadvantageous rates—for local currency. All this greatly slowed down the provisioning of the army.

Transportation was lacking. Many of the horses were in sorry shape, and at any rate there were not enough. The larger part of the cavalry had to march on foot, weighed down by their extra equipment and sabres. Supply trains and horse-drawn artillery were totally disorganized; Desaix's division left without artillery. To some extent, Bonaparte counted on a treaty he made on July 5 with several Arab tribal chiefs to remedy this situation. With the help of El-Koraim, he induced thirteen of the leading Bedouin sheiks to call on him at his headquarters. They were seated in a circle, Bonaparte in the centre, and after the usual lengthy exchange of amenities, the even lengthier bargaining began. In the end, it was agreed that, for a cash payment, the Bedouins would supply the French with 500 horses and 500 camels; that, furthermore, they would let 1,000 camels and camel drivers for hire; and that they would return the prisoners they had taken during the march of the French on Alexandria. Unfortunately, of all these things, only the prisoners turned up. Before the horses and camels could be delivered, a message reached the Bedouins from the ulemas and religious sheiks of Cairo, inviting them to fight the invaders in a holy war. Not only was the trade agreement thus nullified, but also the Bedouins instantly began to harass the French troops on their march. The freed prisoners told the grim details of their treatment at their captors' hands, which at that time still surprised

them. (They soon came to accept involuntary sodomy as one of the
hazards of war in the East.) One grenadier, rather than submit to
the treatment, let himself be killed. Bonaparte disapproved of such
excessive virtue. 'How were you treated?' he asked one of the returned captives. The man, instead of answering, burst into sobs.
'What are you crying about?' The man told him. 'Well, you big stupid, is that all you are making such a fuss about? You paid the
price of your carelessness. You should have stayed with your unit.
Come now, stop crying and answer my questions.'[1] But the man,
still suffering from shock, could say nothing more.

***

Whether it was proper for the French to call the plains of Beheira a desert is debatable. They certainly are not a part of the Libyan Desert, and—in our day at least— they form a cultivated,
though by no means lush, area. In 1798, however, they must have
resembled the landscape to be seen as one approaches Alexandria
from Cairo by the desert route. In daytime, all the traveller can
espy is a few camels and their young, grazing on some very sparse
tufts of very tough grass; at night, hundreds of lights appear out of
nowhere—the fires of the Bedouin camps. Such must have been
the terrain the French army had to cross to reach Damanhur.
Their route followed the dry bed of the Alexandria-Nile Canal.

General Desaix's men, before leaving the outskirts of Alexandria in the evening of July 5, were told that they would spend the
following night at El Beydah. That metropolis, it turned out, consisted of a few abandoned buildings and two cisterns, both of
which the Bedouins had taken care to fill with rocks and dirt. Before he began the march, Desaix had written to Bonaparte: 'I shall
do all I can to reach El Beydah in good order, but I must point out
to you that, according to the intelligence I have received, I shall
find very little water. I beg you not to wait too long before procur-
ing the things needed by my division.... Since this morning, I have
been waiting for my artillery, but in vain, although it was firmly
promised me. Since I can no longer wait, I am leaving without it....
Our horses are on short rations. We have just enough oats for two
days, and no other fodder. We have been unable to procure any.'[2]
It must be said that Bonaparte sent his generals into the desert
with as little kindliness as Abraham showed Hagar and her children. Except for promising to send the artillery after Desaix, he
ignored all the general's requests.

[1] Bourrienne, I, 261.

[2] Correspondence inédite, officielle et confidentielle: Egypte, I,

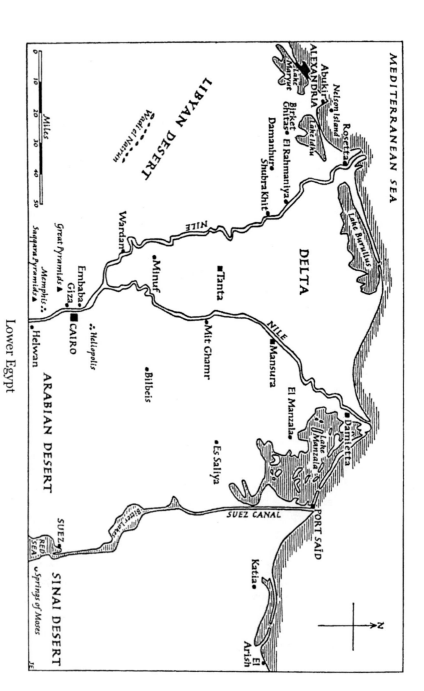

Lower Egypt

The rations distributed to the troops consisted exclusively of dry biscuits. Some had procured themselves flasks or jugs to carry water; most had not had time to do so. After marching all night, Desaix's division reached El Beydah at dawn. The sight of their resting place hardly raised the soldiers' morale. There was, Desaix learned, a village about five miles distant which had a little more water. He sent the horses there, the men being too exhausted to make another step. Eventually, the wells were cleared of the debris, and a little water of unappetizing colour appeared. Two half-empty cisterns are hardly adequate for 4,600 men. The cisterns were dry in no time, and not everybody had had his share. 'We are,' Desaix wrote to Bonaparte in a classic understatement, 'in very poor condition.' He was still waiting for his artillery, he added, and the fodder for the horses had run out. 'We manage as best we can.'[1] All that Bonaparte sent him in reply was a few copies of his proclamation. Desaix ordered his troops to continue the march in the evening. His despatches to Bonaparte became more urgent and finally desperate. He had only one day's rations left for the troops, he wrote in the evening of July 4. 'It is extremely urgent that you send me four days', or at least two days' rations of biscuits, with salt meat and, if possible, distilled liquor. The villages here are the picture of misery; nevertheless, I manage to extract from them some poor fodder for our wretched cavalry.' Still, no reply, no rations, no artillery arrived. 'I am in the greatest need as to provisions,' Desaix pleaded on July 5. 'I am distressed at being obliged to speak to you in this worried tone. Once we are out of this horrible situation, I hope I shall be able to find what I need all by myself and never to pester you again. Unless the entire army crosses the desert with lightning speed, it will perish. There is not enough to still the thirst of a thousand men. Most of the water is in cisterns which, once emptied, do not fill up again. The villages are mud huts, devoid of all resources. I beg you, General, do not leave us in this situation. The troops are beginning to lose courage and to grumble. Make us advance or retreat as fast as we can.'[2]

Meanwhile, General Reynier's division was following the same route. It was no better supplied than Desaix's. 'We lacked the most essential things,' says Vertray. 'Thus we had not even been issued any canteens.'[3] Most of their march was by day. After a few hours, barely able to support themselves, many soldiers began to throw

---

[1] Ibid., p. 211

[2] Ibid, p 213; pp. 216-17

[3] Vertray, p. 32.

away their tunics, their shirts, even their useless rations (who could eat dry biscuits when dying of thirst?), expecting to be able to replace these things in the next city. The burning dust of the *khamsin* parched their throats, and the hot sand tortured their feet. Then began a phenomenon quite novel to them: at a distance, in a haze, there appeared large, blue bodies of water. Disillusioned by the mirage, they yet were crazed enough by their sufferings to let themselves be deceived by it again and again. Gaspard Monge later was to write a learned treatise, in Cairo, explaining the phenomenon. This was small solace to those (and, by all accounts, they must have been hundreds) who lost their wits and shot themselves.

The Bedouins began to harass the troops almost immediately as they left Alexandria and continued to harass them all the way to Cairo. To prevent straggling, the units were ordered to march in squares instead of columns, a manoeuvre which slowed down the march. Still, many fell behind, dead of heat prostration or wishing to die. Those still alive were killed or captured by the Bedouins. What happened to the young pink and blonde soldier's wife? Only God knows.

When Reynier's division reached the longed-for cisterns of El Beydah, they found them virtually dry: Desaix's men had drunk them up. 'It was a pity to see men stretched on their bellies around that fetid hole, dying of thirst, panting and unable to satisfy their craving,' wrote Lieutenant Vertray. 'I have seen, with my own eyes, dying men beg and implore their comrades for pity, while those comrades were fighting among themselves over a little dirty water. I saw some of them die in torture.'[1] According to Sergeant François, the wells were emptied in five minutes. Some of the soldiers suffocated or were trampled to death. 'More than thirty soldiers died by those wells. Several, unable to get water, killed themselves.'[2]

When his division resumed its march at night, Lieutenant Vertray hit on the device of chewing on a lead bullet to stimulate his saliva. 'Behind us,' says Lieutenant Desvernois, 'we left a trail of corpses.'[3]

In his Egyptian and Syrian Campaigns, twenty years later, Napoleon summed up the situation of his troops thus: 'From Alexan-

---

[1] Ibid., p. 37

[2] François, I, 195.

[3] Desvernois, pp. 107-8

dria to Damanhur the distance is forty-five miles. Ordinarily, that plain is irrigated by the flooding of the Nile. It so happened that it had not been irrigated in 1797. We were at the time of the year when the Nile is at its lowest level. All the cisterns were dry, and no water could be found all the way from Alexandria to El Beydah. The army was not equipped to march through such terrain. It suffered much from the heat of the sun and from the lack of shade and water. It took a dislike to those immense deserted plains and, especially, to the Bedouins.'[1]

Under Napoleon's pen—as under that of too many historians—history becomes the art of stating the facts correctly while concealing the truth beneath them.

The truth is in Desvernois' recollections. 'The soldiers,' he says, 'are accusing the generals of the incredible sufferings they have endured since leaving the ships. They are crying, they are asking what wrong they have done to be led like this into the desert to die.'[2] Still, this is not the entire truth either, for the generals were no less desperate than the troops. Like Desaix, Reynier appealed to Bonaparte for help. 'We have neither ambulances nor medicines.... General Desaix has received intelligence that Murad Bey is on his march and, at this moment, perhaps at only two days' distance from us. He has asked me to inform you of this and requests that the divisions which are to support him be ordered to march promptly. It is urgent to send us medical officers, with medicines and camels, also wine, spirits, and vinegar.'[3] There was no reply to this either.

It was only at eight in the morning of July 6 that Reynier's troops came upon a cistern that Desaix's men had not managed to empty before them. 'It was filled,' says Vertray in a lyrical outburst, 'with delicious water, enough for an army of 40,000 men. What a delicious surprise! What joy!' To avoid scenes such as the one at the cisterns of El Beydah, a company of grenadiers were posted around the well of El Karioun. 'In less than half an hour,' Vertray continues, 'our whole division had quenched its thirst.' The soldiers were drunk on the water; they danced, sang, laughed, in a sudden hysterical outburst. Vertray drank twenty cups without stopping. Privates and officers gorged on their biscuits, which at last they could dissolve in liquid. 'We devoured these provisions

[1] Correspondence, XXIX, 438

[2] Desvernois, p. 105

[3] Correspondence inédite, officielle et confidentielle: Egypte, I, 219.

with a ferocious appetite. Never have I eaten a better repast....
That halt remains engraved in the memories of every soldier in my
division as one of the happiest moments in his life.'[1]

If, during the five days that he stayed in Alexandria, Bonaparte
seemed unconcerned over Desaix's and Reynier's pleas, this was
not from indifference or inactivity. To his mind, one consideration
over rode all others—speed, To meet and defeat the Mameluke
army and to enter Cairo within three or four weeks from his landing seemed to him absolutely essential. Comparing his own conduct in 1798 with that of Louis IX of France in 1250, when that
saintly king had landed in Egypt with the host of the Ninth Crusade, Napoleon wrote at St. Helena: '[Saint Louis] spent eight
months praying, when he should have spent them marching, fighting, and occupying the country.'[2] No doubt, Napoleon was right,
and he wasted no time in prayer. The flooding of the Nile would
make the terrain impassable by mid-August; besides it is axio-
matic that time always works against an expeditionary force and
favours the defenders. If the Mamelukes were not crushed at the
start, they would whittle down the French. Demoralization and
disease would do the rest.

These arguments, though unassailable, do not answer the
question why Bonaparte could not have given his troops a week to
rest at Alexandria and thus gained time to organize their supplies,
transports, and artillery. Since his expedition to Syria and his assault on Acre in the following spring were equally ill-prepared and
hasty, the answer to the question may lie simply in Bonaparte's
impatience. His impatience was of a different kind from Nelson's;
it was the ruthless drive of a man who took sacrifices for granted
and expected men to do the impossible. Except on two occasions,
his insistence on speed proved successful. The two exceptions
were notable—his failure to take Acre, which cost him his reputation of invincibility, and his decision, in 1812, to march on to Moscow instead of wintering at Smolensk, which cost him everything.

To send four divisions—about 18,000 men—with inadequate
supplies across a desert was a relatively minor calculated risk. All
four divisions reached Damanhur between July 6 and 9. On paper,
their losses looked small: a few hundred men had died, committed
suicide, or been killed by the Bedouins; the rest, to use a phrase
favoured by Bonaparte, had pushed back the limits of human ca-

---

[1] Vertray, pp. 38-40.

[2] Correspondence, XXIX, 460

pability. Despair and anguish were a small price to pay for a week gained.

At Alexandria, Bonaparte had attended to a number of things with his customary energy. His first concern was to see to the promotion of those who had distinguished themselves in the capture of the city—whether it was his aide-de-camp Sulkowski, who had twice been thrown from the wall before scaling it the third time, or 'that sergeant, whom I noticed and who was wounded. I am calling him to your [General Menou's] attention because you ... may not have noticed him.'[1] Always alert to the psychological value of generosity, he also lost no time in setting free his Turkish sailors—the ex-slaves of the Knights of Malta—each of whom was given a safe-conduct and a sheaf of proclamations to distribute on his way home. In the same benevolent mood, Bonaparte ordered the British vice-consul to be released from arrest, on condition that he did not communicate with any British subject.

Currency being in short supply, Bonaparte raised a forced loan, with the anticipated customs receipts of the port as collateral. In addition, he obtained cash from local merchants in exchange for bullion; this transaction, however, he was to repent after reaching Cairo, whence he shipped quantities of rice and grain to the Alexandrine merchants, requesting them to disgorge the bullion and to accept the goods in its stead.

The people of Alexandria were disarmed and ordered to wear, in token of their loyalty, the tricolour cockade—which must have looked peculiar on their headgear. Muftis and a few other chosen dignitaries were privileged to wear blue-white-and-red sashes just like French mayors, and to receive the military salute. It was a privilege which did not touch their hearts as profoundly as it should have, the psychology of Moslem muftis being quite different from that of French politicians.

Alexandria had to be garrisoned and provided with stronger defences. Bonaparte issued a series of orders to that effect and supervised the planning of the strongpoints to be fortified by the Engineers. A garrison of about 2,000 men, supplemented by non-combatant personnel and part of the ships' crews, was left behind.

The wounds of Generals Kléber and Menou necessitated several changes in the high command. Menou's division was placed under General Vial, and left for Damanhur on July 6 (followed by that of General Bon on July 7). Menou himself was to assume the

---

[1] Ibid., IV, 201

military governorship of Rosetta once that city was taken. Kléber, whose wound was more serious, was made military governor of the Alexandria district, an assignment he soon came to regard (not without reason) as a form of exile. His division was placed under General Dugua and ordered to march on Rosetta, following the coast by way of Abukir; from Rosetta it was to proceed along the left bank of the Rosetta arm of the Nile to join the other four divisions at El Rahmaniya. A reserve column consisting of a cavalry brigade, ordnance, bridge trains, and other equipment, commanded by General Andréossy, was to take the same route as Dugua's division. In addition, a flotilla of light ships, under Captain (later Rear-Admiral) Perrée, was despatched to Rosetta, where it was to put itself at Dugua's disposition and escort him up the Nile.

While Bonaparte busied himself with these measures and with the organization of the supply and transport services, most of the details fell within the competence of his chief of staff, Berthier. It was the disposition of the fleet which constituted Bonaparte's most burning problem in decision making. The correspondence on this subject between the commander-in-chief and Admiral Brueys, both during and after Bonaparte's stay in Alexandria, has given rise to a whole literature of controversy; it will be examined at a later place, in connection with the disaster that overtook the fleet on August 1. For the moment, it is sufficient to keep in mind that the entire squadron dropped anchor in Abukir Bay in the afternoon of July 7.

Dugua's division began its eastward march on July 6 and took possession of Fort Abukir, which was undefended, early the following morning. The topography of the road from Abukir to Rosetta was slightly different in 1798 from what it is now, although the general aspect of the country remains unchanged—a magnificent crescent-shaped beach, bordering on an arid, desert-like strip of land which separates the sea from Lake Idku, a brackish body of water. In Bonaparte's days, the road was interrupted by a narrow channel connecting the sea and the lake. With only four or five small ferries holding about fifteen men each, Dugua's divisions might have taken a long time crossing it, had not the squadron appeared just in time and detached several sloops to help him. Even so, the operation lasted all day from dawn to midnight; the horses and camels, with their loads, were made to swim across, without a single mishap.

On the whole, Dugua's troops fared better than the other four divisions. At Abukir, to their amazement, they struck clear drinking water when they dug in the sand a few yards from the sea-shore. The last few miles to Rosetta were a rough stretch, with the obligatory complement of soldiers dying of thirst or shooting themselves, but the sight of Rosetta afforded a pleasant surprise when the first foot troops reached the town about noon of July 8. The mounted cavalry had entered in the morning and met with no resistance. 'All the inhabitants were on their doorsteps; all the shops were open,' Colonel Laugier, a staff officer of Dugua, noted in his diary. 'This sight was the first pleasant impression we had since landing in Egypt.'[1] Private Millet, who was just as pleased as the colonel, recalls in his memoirs that the population welcomed the French with bread, water, and fruit for a price, of course, but the prices were reasonable and food was plentiful.

The town itself, compared to Alexandria, looked practically European. Large and well-built houses (belonging to European merchants) lined the waterfront, and the outskirts formed a belt of gardens, orchards, and fertile fields. Rosetta seemed an ideal place to stay and rest for a while; however, the troops had not tasted its delights for twenty-four hours when a message was delivered to Dugua from Bonaparte, who thought the division already had reached El Rahmaniya, twenty-five miles to the south as the crow flies. At 2 a.m. on July 10, the division resumed its march, leaving only a garrison behind.

The march of Dugua's troops would have seemed a picnic to the men of the other four divisions. 'We are following the Nile,' Colonel Laugier wrote in his diary, 'across a well-cultivated area cut by many rivers. [No doubt, he meant canals.] The inhabitants line both sides of our road to see us pass and to welcome us. Everything looks prosperous. The farmers are well dressed and show a grave and majestic countenance.... The women, to manifest their joy, produce cries that sound absolutely like the cooing of doves.'[2] But there are people who will complain even in a paradise full of cooing women; Private Millet was one of them. Before leaving Rosetta, he says, the troops were given rations for six days, consisting of about one pound of biscuits per man. Aside from the water of the Nile, watermelons, and some wormy salt biscuits that were distributed later, 'this was all we received in the two weeks it took us to reach Cairo.'[3] Of course, beyond what the troops received there was a great deal that they bought or simply took.

---

[1] La Jonquière, II, 125

[2] La Jonquière, II, 131

[3] Millet, p. 50.

The first columns of Dugua's division reached El Rahmaniya on July 11, about the same time as the last of the men of the four other divisions, who were far less blasé at the sight of the Nile and the watermelon fields.

***

General Bonaparte, with his staff and headquarters personnel, including Monge and Berthollet, left Alexandria last, at five in the afternoon of July 7. Riding all night, he overtook Bon's and Vial's divisions and entered Damanhur the following morning at eight. There he found Desaix's and Reynier's divisions, which had gone through four days of torture to travel the same distance. Vial's and Bon's divisions arrived in the course of July 8 and 9; their march, which was better organized, had taken only thirty-six hours, but their hardships had been barely less than those of the vanguard.

On the strength of assurances given by Charles Magallon and other experts, the troops had been told that once they reached Damanhur, their sufferings would be over. They expected Damanhur to be something like Milan or, at least, Verona. It was a fairly large city, the seat of a bey, and a centre of the cotton trade. From a distance, it looked quite promising, surrounded by greenery, with cupolas and minarets rising above the palm trees. On closer inspection, it turned out that apart from its mosques, Damanhur was nothing but an agglomeration of miserable hovels built of mud and straw—an aspect still retained by many Egyptian towns. Still, it was better than the desert. 'The natives,' says Vertray, 'instead of bread, offered us flat wheat cakes, about the size of a six-franc piece, baked on hot ashes. There was plenty of meat, fowl, and dry vegetables, mostly beans and lentils.... The market was crowded with soldiers.'[1] Financial transactions were of a peculiar nature, since the tradesmen put more trust in uniform buttons as legal tender than in any European coin. This preference was to startle the French in many Egyptian towns. At Damanhur, a horse-dealer to whom a French officer offered twenty-five Spanish gold piastres for a mount refused them and asked for two buttons instead. The officer accepted the deal. 'Thus,' Vertray notes gravely, 'there were deceivers and deceived on both sides in the market place.'[2] Most historians have related this phenomenon absolutely unique in Egyptian bazaars without attempting an explanation, historians being for the most part guileless people. The explana-

---

[1] Vertray, p. 42.

[2] Ibid., p. 44

tion, however, seems obvious. No Egyptian in his right senses ever confused brass buttons with gold coins. But several sources (Colonel Laugier's diary, for instance) show that the Egyptians at that time still were counting on the Mamelukes to make mincemeat of the French. If that should happen, the Mamelukes would accuse anyone possessing foreign currency of having dealt with the Infidel and, at the very least, confiscate the coins; whereas the possessor of uniform buttons could always claim that he had acquired them honourably by killing and robbing a Frenchman. If the French should win, in the majority of cases the buttons would be worth more than the current price of the merchandise sold; the man who sold the horse for two buttons probably had stolen it. The explanation may seem far-fetched, but only to those who have never been in Egypt. What is far more astonishing is the thought that, in all likelihood, the French won the Battle of the Pyramids with half of their uniform buttons missing.[1]

Bonaparte, upon arriving at Damanhur, was met by Desaix, who led him, as he recalled at St. Helena, to 'a kind of barn, without either doors or windows.'[2] (One wonders how he got in.) There the mayor, imams, principal sheiks, and other officials awaited the commander-in-chief to regale him with a feast consisting of a jug of milk and wheat-cakes. Bonaparte soon afterward despatched several units to forage for food in the countryside, while his chef requested an interpreter to help him requisition a roasting spit at the municipality.

Although Bonaparte's stay at Damanhur lasted only two days, its history is vexed by two episodes about which the truth can probably never be established. Desvernois in his memoirs tells of a council of war held by Bonaparte after his arrival. The council may well have taken place, but Desvernois could not have been present, and besides he gives an obviously wrong date. He places Damanhur on the Nile, which it is not, and gives the date as July 11, when the army was no longer at Damanhur. According to Desvermois, the meeting had barely begun when the generals gave vent to their feelings and heaped reproaches on Bonaparte: no rations had been distributed at the time of the landing (which is true) and the same negligence had cost Desaix's division more than 1,500 casualties (a

---

[1] In his Order of the Day of July 9, General Bonaparte set a price schedule for edible goods, ranging from 35 paras for a goose to 1 para for a pound of lentils. The exchange ratio between paras and brass buttons has not been reliably established.

[2] Correspondence, XXIX, 439.

vast exaggeration, but morally true). General Mireur, a cavalry commander, went as far (still according to Desvernois) as to condemn the whole expedition in a long speech as a hopeless and irresponsible adventure. Bonaparte, after listening in silence, adjourned the meeting and left without a further word. Mireur, Desvernois continues, knowing Bonaparte's susceptibility and seeing his own career at an end, fell into despondency. 'He got on his horse the next morning before dawn, rode into the desert, and blew his brains out.'[1] There is no question that Mireur was found dead in the desert, but according to the official version he was killed and robbed by Bedouins. Desvernois, who claims to have discovered the body, denies this and solemnly affirms that he found the general still clutching his pistol. According to another version, which seems more likely, Mireur was in a huff, because another cavalry general, Leclerc, had been preferred over him, and rode out into the desert seeking death at the hands of the Arabs.

Whatever the circumstances of Mireur's death, Desvernois' account, though based partly on hearsay, points up a situation which even Napoleon in his memoirs admitted to have existed: 'The generals and officers uttered their discontent even more loudly than the ranks,' Napoleon asserts. 'This kind of warfare was even harder on them, because it contrasted more with the comforts of the Italian *palazzi* and casinos.'[2] Las Cases, recording a conversation with Napoleon at St. Helena, quotes him thus: 'The Emperor said that no army in the world was less suited for an expedition to Egypt than the one he took there. It was the Army of Italy. It would be difficult to give an idea of the disgust, the discontent, the melancholy, the despair of that army during its first weeks in Egypt. The Emperor recalls seeing two dragoons leave their ranks and, running as fast as they could, drown themselves in the Nile. Bertrand [a captain of Engineers in 1798, and Napoleon's Grand Marshal at St. Helena] has seen several of the most distinguished generals—Lannes, Murat—throw their hats on the sand in a fit of rage and stamping on them under the eyes of the troops.... One day, being himself in an ill temper, Napoleon walked to a group of discontented generals and, addressing himself to the tallest among them, said to him in a vehement tone of voice, "You have been talking sedition. Be careful, or I will do my duty. Your five-foot ten inches would not save you from being shot by a firing

---

[1] Desvernois, p. 110.

[2] Correspondence, XXIX, 446

squad two hours from now".[1] The general in question probably was Alexandre Dumas, one of Bonaparte's most uninhibited critics. It is unfair, however, to see in the absence of *palazzi* and casinos the sole motive of the generals' mutinous spirit. They had been infected by the same homesickness, the same despair, the same 'spleen,' as Napoleon called it, as had their troops. There was an epidemic kind of insanity in the French army during the three weeks of its march to Cairo, and physical hardships were not its sole cause. It was a sense of isolation and of abandon, a loathing for the country and its people, which to some degree is a universal phenomenon in citizen armies taken to remote and culturally alien places. Moreover, the generals were in closer touch with their men than was Bonaparte, and their nerves were not made of steel, like his: to stand by helplessly while the men in their charge lost their minds from despair was more than they could stomach.

To raise the troops' morale, Bonaparte correctly sought but one means: a victorious battle. To make men do what he made them do requires a far from kindly character. Yet if he had been the least bit more human, the army would have perished. This even the severest critics among his generals eventually had to acknowledge.

The other curious episode that occurred during Bonaparte's stay at Damanhur has been related by Bourienne in his *Memoirs*. There is no evidence either supporting or refuting its truthfulness; however, unlike many other recollections of Bonaparte's secretary, this particular one has the ring of truth:

> A small band of Arabs on horseback came to insult our headquarters by their defiance. Bonaparte, who stood at the window ... was enraged at their insolence. As he turned about, he noticed young Croisier, one of his aides-de-camp, who happened to be on duty. 'Croisier,' said he, 'take a few Guides and get rid of that rabble over there.' Instantly, Croisier with fifteen Guides [on horseback] appeared in the field. A skirmish developed; we watched the fighting from the windows. The orders [given by Croisier] and the manner of the attack evidenced the kind of hesitation that the commander-in-chief could not endure. He shouted from the window, as if he could be heard, 'Forward, dammit! Charge!' Our horsemen yielded ground every time the Arabs returned to the attack. The outcome was that the Arabs

---

[1] Las Cases, I, 131-32

withdrew unmolested ... and without having lost a single man.... The General flew into an uncontrolled rage which he vented brutally upon Croisier when the latter came back. His language was so harsh that Croisier left the room with tears in his eyes. Bonaparte told me to follow him and to calm him. It was useless. 'l shall never survive this,' Croisier said to me. 'I shall get myself killed at the first opportunity. I cannot live in dishonour.' Bonaparte had let slip the word coward. It was not until the siege of Acre that Croisier could find the death he sought.[1]

As Napoleon often pointed out in retrospect, his rages had never been 'uncontrolled' but always calculated. His concern over the crying Croisier probably was more genuine than his fury, which was meant to impress the bystanders. To paraphrase Voltaire, it is a good thing to drive an officer to suicide once in a while, to encourage the others.

The army had barely reached Damanhur when, on July 9, Bonaparte ordered it to march on to El Rahmaniya. Desaix's division, again forming the vanguard, was to march a few miles further up the Nile to Minyet Salama, in order to head off Murad Bey.

It was at El Rahmaniya, an insignificant town, that the troops (except for Dugua's division) first saw the Nile. The river was unimpressive at that time of the year, being at its lowest level; still, the sight of it filled the men with no less joy than was felt by Xenophon's Ten Thousand when they reached the sea. 'The soldiers are throwing themselves into the river like animals to drink,' Colonel Savary noted in his diary.[2] 'At sight of the Nile,' says Desvernois, 'the soldiers broke ranks to throw themselves into it. Some kept their clothes, even their weapons. Others took the time to undress, then ran to the water, dived into it, and stayed in it for several hours. Many found their death by drinking too greedily.'[3] There were large fields covered with watermelons (about the only thing that grew at that season); the soldiers gorged themselves on them, and they continued to eat watermelons, and practically nothing but watermelons, all the way to the site of the Battle of the Pyramids, which itself was a watermelon field.[4]

---

[1] Bourrienne, I, 268-69

[2] La Jonquière, II, 144.

[3] Desvernois, p. 108.

[4] The diet did not agree with the soldiers. 'The whole army has diarrhea,' Colonel Savary wrote from Cairo soon afterward.

Once their thirst was slaked, what they craved most, being French men, was bread. (Vertray asserts that from May 19, when he left Toulon, until July 22, the day after the Battle of the Pyramids, he had not eaten any.) In this respect, they suffered the tortures of Tantalus, for although wheat was plentiful in the region, there were neither flour mills nor baking ovens. Lieutenant Desvernois solved the problem by pounding wheat with stones and baking a loaf of bread of sorts; charred as it was, his fellow officers stole it from under him while he slept, ate it, and in the morning criticized its poor quality.

On July 11, says Vertray, all five divisions were assembled at El Rahmaniya; it was announced that General Bonaparte would review them in the afternoon. 'We spent all morning putting our uniforms and equipment in shape. The soldiers cleaned, brushed, and polished until noon.' At three o'clock, a drum roll announced the approach of the commander-in-chief . The five divisions stood lined up in formation. Bonaparte with his cavalcade stopped in front of each, called its officers to step forward, and addressed them. On the morrow perhaps, he said, the army would come face to face with the Mamelukes. No doubt, the victors of the Rhine and Sambre-et-Meuse campaigns would triumph gloriously over those barbarians. His words were relayed by the officers to their units. Their effect, says Vertray, was great. 'It seemed that Bonaparte had at last convinced us of the importance and greatness of his plans. Each company commander announced to his men that a battle was near. This news was received enthusiastically by the entire army, and when the soldiers broke their ranks after being dismissed, they could be seen inspecting their arms with scrupulous care, sharpening their bayonets, testing their flints, and singing as if they were getting ready for a feast.'[1]

Bonaparte had received intelligence—probably through paid spies—that Murad Bey, with three to four thousand horsemen, several thousand foot troops, and a flotilla of gunboats, was approaching the town of Shubra Khit, about eight miles south of El Rahmaniya. Already on July 10, Desaix's division had had a brush with a Mameluke detachment of about 300 horsemen under Mohammed Bey el-Elfi; the Mamelukes' undisciplined attack had been repulsed easily and without losses by the French artillery. Reassured by Desaix's report on the Mamelukes' tactics, Bonaparte decided to meet Murad Bey at Shubra Khit. A series of nine orders, issued by General Berthier to the five division command-

---

[1] Vertray, pp. 48-49

ers, to Captain Perrée, and to Generals Dumas and Andréossy was all that was needed to prepare the army for the imminent engagement. All forces, including Perrée's flotilla, were ordered to march by way of Minyet Salama to Shubra Khit, where they were to halt before dawn of July 15. General Andréossy was instructed to go aboard the *chebek Le Cerf*, Perrée's flagship, and to direct Perrée's supporting action. Since there was a lack of cavalry mounts, all non-combatants were ordered to continue the march aboard the flotilla and its transports; among them were Bourrienne, Monge, and Berthollet, who went aboard *Le Cerf*. On one of the river boats that had been requisitioned at Rosetta as transports, was Madame Fourès, wife of Lieutenant Fourès of the 22nd Regiment of *Chasseurs*. As it turned out, it was the flotilla which had to bear the brunt of the fighting.

Except for a brief halt in Minyet Salama, the army marched most of the night of July 12-15 and came within view of Shubra Khit before daybreak. The soldiers had been warned to maintain the strictest discipline during the battle. To defeat the Mamelukes, they were told, there was but one way, and that was to face them with an orderly, immovable front. As soon as the army halted before Shubra Khit, Bonaparte ordered each division to form a square, each side six ranks deep; in the centre of the squares he placed what little cavalry there was as well as the baggage trains; the artillery was placed at the corners of the squares. These dispositions taken, there remained a little time for the men to sleep.

'At sunrise,' recalls Vertray, 'a warlike music suddenly burst out; the commander-in-chief had ordered the *Marseillaise* to be played, for he knew its effect on the troops. That admirable song excites the soldiers' courage, kindles their patriotism, and makes them understand that the time for complaining is over and that victory is their task.'[1] With the sound of the *Marseillaise*, there also burst on them the sight of the Mameluke cavalry, lined up in battle array. Desvernois in his *Memoirs* vividly recalls that breathtaking moment: 'In the back ground, the desert under the blue sky; before us, the beautiful Arabian horses, richly harnessed, snorting, neighing, prancing gracefully and lightly under their martial riders, who are covered with dazzling arms, inlaid with gold and precious stones. Their costumes are brilliantly colourful; their turbans are surmounted by aigret feathers, and some wear gilded helmets. They are armed with sabres, lances, maces, spears, rifles, battle axes, and daggers, and each has three pairs of pis-

[1] Ibid., 50-51

tols.... This spectacle produced a vivid impression on our soldiers by its novelty and richness. From that moment on, their thoughts were set on booty.[1]

This glittering line extended in the shape of a sickle from the Nile at Shubra Khit to the south and the west of the French squares. Their arms and the brass crescents and globes atop their tents and standards reflected the morning sun. Behind them there were, in no particular formation, perhaps 10,000 men on foot—their servants and a number of embattled *fellahin*, most of them armed only with clubs. Though it did not move forward, the line was by no means stationary. Horsemen dashed back and forth along it, giving the impression of much activity and preparations. There is no spectacle more graceful in its strength than an Arabian horse ridden in the Arabian style. To pace or trot is against his temperament: he must canter, especially uphill. He flies ahead and stops as if arrested by a bullet. To the weary French army, after trudging for days in utter exhaustion through the desert and through the parched, cracked land along the Nile, the sight of such dancing vigour, such weightless power, such beauty in strength, must have seemed something unbelievable. Yet, beauty, grace, and daring had not one chance against the discipline and drill of the weary pedestrians.

The Mameluke army, even with its reinforcements on foot, was numerically far inferior to the French. But every Mameluke was an arsenal on horseback. Riding Cossack-style, he first would discharge his carbine, slide it under his thigh, then fire his several pairs of pistols and throw them over his shoulder to be picked up by his foot-servants later, then throw his lethal *djerids*—javelins about four feet long, made of stripped and sharpened palm branches—and finally charge the foe with scimitar in hand. Sometimes he carried two scimitars, swinging both while gripping the reins between his teeth. Years of practice enabled him to sever a head with a single reverse blow. Torn from his parents while still a small child, a warrior from the age of twelve, usually without progeny, he knew no fear, no attachment. A mameluke was almost never captured: he either was victorious, or he was killed, or he fled with the same lightning speed with which he attacked. As a consequence, he carried with him, in jewels, clothes, and coins, a veritable fortune. Over a muslin shirt, he wore layers of bright and brilliant silken vests and caftans, the whole encased in gigantic silken trousers, in a single leg of which a large man could have

---

[1] Desvernois, 118

wrapped himself. The Mamelukes' stature was usually gigantic—they were picked as boys by experts—and their features handsome. Except for a sprinkling of Negroes among them, they were, as Desvernois put it, 'beautiful men, with a complexion of lilies and roses.'[1]

When Murad Bey, several days before his first battle with the French, was told that Bonaparte's army had virtually no cavalry, he laughed out loud; he would slice through them as if they were watermelons, he boasted. When he saw the French in their square formations he was puzzled; it was much the same puzzlement that a terrier experiences when coming upon his first hedgehog. For about three hours, the Mameluke horsemen did nothing but circle about the French in small detachments, looking for a weak spot. Then, some time between eight and nine o'clock, the two flotillas came face to face on the Nile, and a cannonade began. Shortly afterwards, the Mameluke cavalry at last began to charge.

On land, it never came to a real battle. As soon as the Mamelukes approached within range of any of the squares, a barrage of cannon balls, shells, grapeshot, and small-arms fire stopped them short. They tried one square after another, from every side they could approach: they always found the same hedgehog. After about an hour, they withdrew to their original position. Bonaparte ordered his divisions to move to the attack and to relieve the flotilla, which had fared less well than the land troops.

Not counting the transports, which kept to the rear and downstream, Perée's flotilla consisted of three gunboats, a galley, and the *chebek Le Cerf.* The Mameluke flotilla, manned by Greek sailors, consisted of seven gunboats; their fire was efficient and accurate. Within a short space of time, Perrée had to order two of his gunboats and the galley to be abandoned to the enemy. He himself was slightly wounded. Only *Le Cerf* and the third gunboat, encumbered with civilians and with the men picked up from the abandoned vessels, continued to resist the combined fire of the seven enemy ships, of a battery installed by the Mamelukes on shore at Shubra Khit, and of a pandemonium of Mamelukes, fellahin, and Bedouins, who fired from both sides of the Nile with whatever they had, including small cannon mounted on camels' backs. By about 11 a.m., says Bourrienne, Perée informed him that, unless the land forces came to his immediate assistance, the situation was hopeless. 'Already several ships had been boarded by the Turks,' Bourrienne continues. 'Their crews were being massacred

---

[1] Ibid., p. 116.

under our eyes with barbaric ferocity, and the captors displayed their heads to us holding them by their hair.'[1] It was a bad moment for Citizen Berthollet, the eminent chemist. Preferring a quick death by drowning to being massacred, he had filled his pockets with weights and was prepared to jump overboard if necessary; but seeing that the other civilians had joined the soldiers in the fight, he soon also took part in the firing. Monge, who once had supervised the cannon foundries of all France, made himself useful by helping to reload the guns. At last, *Le Cerf* scored a hit on the Mameluke flagship, which carried some ammunition. 'There was,' says Nicholas the Turk, 'a moment of intense terror: the explosion made the men fly up in the air like birds.'[2] This sight, according to another Arabic source, made the French burst out in hysterical laughter and caused a panic among the Moslems, both on land and on water. The Mameluke cavalry was just about to charge the oncoming French a second time when the explosion occurred; instead of charging, they and their followers began a head long flight. The French occupied Shubra Khit without further resistance. The land troops had suffered no losses; Perée, who was promoted to Rear-Admiral, reported to Brueys: 'Twenty of my men were wounded, and several killed. I lost my sword and a little bit of my left arm.'[3] Considering that over 1,500 rounds of artillery were fired by the two flotillas, the toll was not excessive.

Bonaparte had proved to his army that there was no cause to fear the Mamelukes, but he had let the Mamelukes escape. As he told Bourrienne when he saw him ten days later at Giza, his failure to cut off the Mamelukes' retreat was to be blamed entirely on the necessity of coming to the relief of the flotilla—'you, Monge, Berthollet, and the rest.'[4] Bourrienne could not help replying that surely this was the least thing the General could have done for his civilians, after taking their horses away and setting them up for targets on the ships.

According to Nicholas the Turk, the French divisions 'were advancing like an impetuous river, like a torrent unleashed.'[5] This impression was not shared by the French themselves, as they continued their march in the afternoon of July 13, after about three

[1] Bourrienne, I, 271

[2] Nicolas Turc, p. 22.

[3] Correspondence de Varmtefrangeise, pp. 6263

[4] Bourrienne, I, 272

[5] Nicolas Turc, p. 22

hours' rest from the battle, in pursuit of the Mamelukes. The victory had cheered them but briefly, and demoralization soon set in again. To make a short cut, the army left the banks of the Nile. The terrain, entirely dried up, was cut by deep crevasses. Limping along with twisted ankles, the soldiers began to regret the soft dust of the desert. 'The day after the combat at Shubra Khit,' says Vertray, 'our aching feet became as creviced as the ground they trod on.'[1] On July 14 at daybreak, Bonaparte caught up with the two vanguard divisions—Desaix's and Reynier's—while they were halting for a distribution of rations. Indignant at the delay, he brushed aside Desaix's explanations with ill humour and ordered the march to be resumed instantly. Most eyewitness accounts bear out Sergeant François' description of the following four days of the march: 'Men were dying, suffocated by the heat. It felt like passing in front of a very hot oven. Several soldiers committed suicide.'[2] The hardships of the artillery men and their horses were even more grueling; every few hundred yards, there were dried-up irrigation canals obstructing the progress of the gun carriages. The wheels and axles broke with despairing regularity and had to be repaired on the spot. The banks of the larger canals had to be levelled to make passage possible.

Discipline, briefly regained during the day of battle, seemed to be disintegrating completely. 'The army as a whole is discontented,' Brigadier General Belliard noted in his diary. 'The officers carelessly allow their soldiers to fan out through the various villages on their route and to take away whatever they can find.'[3] According to Sergeant François, a village which refused to supply the goods requisitioned by the French was put to the sword and burned down: 900 men, women, and children were massacred or burned to death, 'in order to teach a lesson to a half-savage and barbarous people.'[4] Perhaps François exaggerates the numbers, but such scenes were frequent. Colonel Laugier describes one in his diary: 'On 26 Messidor [July 14], we arrived at the village of Nekleh, which Bon's and Vial's divisions were in the process of looting. The cries of the men, the weeping of the women, made a horrible noise. The women climbed to the roofs of their houses and, every time they saw a Frenchman on horseback, called to him and signified their distress by waving back and forth a kind of

---

[1] Vertray, p. 55.

[2] François, I, 202

[3] La Jonquière, II, 162

[4] François, I, 203

shawl they held in both hands, ending up with a lugubrious chant. All this happened practically under the eyes of the commander-in-chief, who gave orders to General Dugua to stay at the village in order to restore discipline and to find victuals for his troops. General Dugua had incredible difficulties to overcome. The brigade commanders, instead of backing him up, increased his embarrassment by reproaching him for the want of everything and by showing their insubordination in front of the troops.... No sooner had steps been taken to stop the disorder than the inhabitants passed from fear and despair to trust and even joy. The troops received some local bread, rice, and meat.'[1]

At Wardan, where the entire army was assembled on July 18, the troops at last were given two days of rest. The march continued, with much the same hardships, on the 20th. Most of the commanders had by then resigned themselves to letting their troops go about marauding, since the supply service had virtually broken down. The officers, being unable to maraud, watched their men somewhat enviously as they roasted their stolen pigeons, chickens, and sheep. Ramrods would serve as spits. Their appetites sated, the soldiers would bed themselves down as best they could on straw or on heaps of small branches, 'forgetting the heat of the day in the dampness of the night. Horses, donkeys, camels, soldiers, officers, everything is mingled.'[2]

Such was the condition of the French Army of the East—that 'impetuous river,' that 'torrent unleashed' -when it arrived in the evening of July 20 Omm-Dinar, a village near the point where the Nile branches out to form the Delta, about eighteen miles north of Cairo. It was there that Bonaparte received intelligence of the disposition of the Mameluke forces in defence of the capital. Murad Bey was awaiting the French on the left bank of the Nile, opposite Bulaq, at the village of Embaba, which he had fortified. Ibrahim Bey with the rest of the Mamelukes and the militia was encamped at Bulaq, to head off the French in case they should arrive on the right bank. On the Nile itself, the Mameluke flotilla was awaiting the French. This news delighted Bonaparte: if Murad Bey had chosen to await him on the right bank, the difficulties the French would have experienced in crossing the Nile would have given him a decided advantage; as it was, Bonaparte had him exactly where he wanted him. At two o'clock in the morning of July 21, the army was ordered to march on Embaba and to engage the Mamelukes in

[1] La Jonquière, II, 162
[2] Ibid., II, 170.

decisive battle. It reached its destination at 2 p.m., during the worst heat of the day. About one mile from the French, the Mameluke battle line was drawn up; behind it loomed the Great Pyramids, their huge and mysterious masses clearly visible at ten miles' distance; to the left, the French could see the glittering sky-line of the domes and minarets of Cairo. They had about one hour's rest before Bonaparte ordered the attack. They used that time to quench their thirst with the watermelons which they found in profusion.

As at Shubra Khit, Bonaparte had ordered the divisions to form in squares, with the baggage and cavalry inside them and the artillery at the outer corners. According to his own account of the battle, he addressed his troops before ordering the attack and said to them, pointing at the Pyramids, 'Soldiers, forty centuries look down upon you.'[1] The fact is that he had neither the time nor the voice to address his men, who were spread over several square miles and most of whom, at that point, were still puzzled as to what the Pyramids were.

In all likelihood, he made the remark to the officers who happened to be around him. In all certainty, his whole being was quickened, at that instant, by the consciousness of making history in the presence of the most ancient monuments known to man.

**

The Battle of the Pyramids, which was fought a considerable distance away from the Pyramids, is regarded by some as one of Napoleon's great victories and by others as a mere incident, half skirmish, half butchery, the outcome of which was decided in advance by the huge tactical and numerical superiority of the French. The number of French combat troops engaged in the battle can be estimated fairly accurately at about 25,000 men; the strength of the Mamelukes is more difficult to appraise. One historian— Friedrich Kircheisen, in his biography of Napoleon—on the basis of some unfathomable mental processes, put it at about 6,000 mounted Mamelukes supported by 10,000-12,000 foot-soldiers. This estimate is either too high for the horsemen or too low for the foot-soldiers; indeed, since every mounted Mameluke had at least two servants on foot, and since by all accounts the Mamelukes were supported by Turkish regulars (mostly Albanians) under the nominal authority of the pasha, the number of infantry must have been considerably more than twice the number of cavalry. Napo-

---

[1] Correspondence, XXIX, 450.

leon, on the other hand, seems to set the strength of the enemy inordinately high. There were, he says, 12,000 mounted Mamelukes, each with three or four servants-at-arms, 8,000 mounted Bedouins, and 20,000 Janissaries—in all about 78,000 men, not counting Ibrahim's army on the right bank of the Nile. There were not 12,000 Mamelukes in all of Egypt. Whatever the correct number, the Bedouins and the foot-soldiers other than the Albanian troops were totally ineffectual and may be discounted. The French, beyond all doubt, had a decisive numerical superiority—and to have such superiority at the moment when it counts is, after all, the essence of good generalship.

The tactical superiority of the French seems evident; yet it depended entirely on the ranks' discipline in carrying out their commanders' instructions. The least weakness or panic could have resulted in disaster for a whole division or more. The ranks had to be held unbroken at all costs, or the Mameluke cavalry would have penetrated into the squares and cut them to ribbons. If one adds to this the consideration that the Mamelukes were well rested and, as it were, in their own element, while the French, exhausted, hungry, weakened by dysentery, and demoralized, fought in an alien country, one must concede that the outcome of the encounter was by no means settled in advance.

Murad Bey's knowledge of tactics was less than rudimentary, but he had the quick eye and instinct of a born military commander. As soon as he saw the aim of Bonaparte's manoeuvre—which was to penetrate through the centre of the Mameluke line and to cut off its retreat—he ordered his entire cavalry to charge the two forward French divisions, those of Desaix and Reynier. The charge was executed with incredible speed and impetuousness. Desaix's ranks, first to be attacked, had barely time to form their square. They held their fire until the Mamelukes were virtually upon them; its effect was murderous, as was that of Reynier's division. 'General Reynier gave the order, "Form your ranks",' relates Lieutenant Vertray, 'and, in an instant, we had formed our square, ten men deep, to absorb the shock. This manoeuvre was executed with truly extraordinary precision and sang-froid.... The soldiers fired with such coolness that not a single cartridge was wasted, waiting until the very instant when the horsemen were about to break our square. The number of corpses surrounding our square soon was considerable, and the clothes of the dead and wounded Mamelukes were burning like tinder.... The blazing wads of our muskets penetrated at the same time as our bullets through their rich uniforms, which were embroidered with gold and silver and floated as lightly as gauze.'[1]

Meanwhile Dugua's division had cut off the Mameluke cavalry from their fortifications at Embaba and was shelling the Mamelukes' rear with howitzers, while Vial and Bon prepared to take the fortifications by storm. For almost an hour, the Mameluke cavalry, though repulsed with heavy losses wherever they attacked, continued with suicidal bravery to test all the sides of the squares. So furious was their onslaught that the mortally wounded horses were carried by their sheer momentum inside the French ranks, where they were finished off, along with their riders, with bayonets and rifle butts. Some of the Mamelukes' individual feats of strength and bravery, though attested to by independent witnesses, bordered on the incredible. The kyacheff Hussein, a Greek renegade who later went over to the French, rode right into the enemy ranks and, with his scimitar, sliced through the Barréls of the French rifles as if they were straws; he was removed from the battle riddled with wounds but, apparently, immortal. All this was admirable but had no practical effect. Seeing that the French were immovable, Murad Bey, with part of his cavalry, retreated toward Giza and, hence, fled toward Middle Egypt. His remaining cavalry, cut off from retreat by Dugua, withdrew to the fortifications at Embaba, pursued by Bon, Vial, and Dugua.

It was at this point in the battle that a curious single combat took place between Lieutenant Desvernois and a majestic, white-bearded Mameluke, whose insolent cantering in front of Bon's division had caused the lieutenant's hackles to rise. Desvernois, on horseback, burst out of his square, and the duel began in full view of the division. With his first pistol shot, Desvernois dismounted his adversary, who, crawling on his hands and knees, his long white beard dragging on the ground, advanced toward Desvernois' horse, at the same time using his sabre like a sickle to sever the horse's feet. This astonishing manoeuvre continued for some time until Desvernois, with his sabre, broke the Mameluke's head, while soldiers stepped out of their ranks to finish off the patriarch with their rifle butts. On his dead body, Desvernois found rich booty—a 'canary-yellow turban made of cashmere ... more than five hundred gold pieces sewn into his skull cap ... a magnificent sabre, its sheath and pommel inlaid with gold; its handle was a rhinoceros horn, and the blade was black Damascus steel.'[2]

---

[1] Vertray, pp. 57, 59

[2] Desvernois, p. 124

Desaix's and Reynier's men were already busy disrobing and despoiling the corpses of the vanquished when Bon's and Vial's divisions stormed the fortifications. 'The carnage,' says Private Millet, 'was atrocious. The corpses of men and horses presented a horrifying spectacle, so bloody was the massacre.'[1] The Albanian infantry and artillery men were exterminated; the remaining Mamelukes, driven to the bank of the Nile, tried to escape by swimming. In this final stampede, Ayyah Bey the Younger was crushed under his own horse's hooves; Ibrahim Bey the Younger, while swimming, was drowned by a Greek sailor who, as he battered the Bey's head with a pole, cried out to him, 'It is you tyrants who are responsible for this disaster.'[2] Several hundred Mamelukes drowned in the Nile or were killed by their own guns, which the French had turned against them.[3]

Meanwhile, Ibrahim Bey and his host were contemplating the disaster from the opposite shore, at Bulaq. 'The eastern army [i.e., the forces on the right bank of the Nile],' says El-Djabarti, an eyewitness, 'seeing the battle in progress, began to scream at the top of their voices ... as if that were enough to be victorious. The more sagacious among them ordered them to be quiet, saying that the Prophet and his disciples fought with sabre and sword, not with screams and barks like dogs; but nobody listened to them. At that moment a great misfortune happened (who could read or understand it?): a large number of princes and of soldiers of the eastern army embarked on boats to pass to the other side; among them was Ibrahim Bey. There was an immense crowd at the embarkation point. When they arrived on the opposite shore, the rout of the western army was complete. The wind was very strong and the river very choppy. A sand-storm struck the Egyptians in the face; nobody could open his eyes; the wind came from the enemy's side, and this, in large part, is what caused our defeat.'[4]

---

[1] Millet, p. 52

[2] Nicolas Turc, p. 23

[3] According to the French official report, 2,000 Mamelukes were killed in battle or drowned; the figure sounds exaggerated: General Damas wrote to Kléber that the Mamelukes 'lost seven or eight hundred men, without any exaggeration (*Correspondance de L'armée Française*, p. 95). Admiral Perrée put the figure at 1,200 (Ibid., p. 64). As for French losses, Berthier in his official report set them at 29 dead and 120 wounded; Larrey, chief surgeon of the army, gives the number of severely wounded as 260.

[4] El-Djabarti, VI, 16

Nicholas the Turk also mentions the fatal sand-storm, but El-Djabarti is the only witness to claim that Ibrahim Bey made an attempt to cross the Nile and assist Murad. What everybody does agree upon is that Ibrahim and his Mamelukes withdrew into Cairo and, after taking with them their families and portable possessions, fled south-east toward the Sinai Desert. The Turkish pasha, whether of his own will or under duress, went with them.

'The combat,' says Nicholas the Turk, 'had lasted more than two hours—but two hours of indescribable terror! The populace was cowed and stupefied by the infernal noise of the incessant thunderous firing.... The people sobbed, struck their own faces, and screamed, "Woe to us! Now we are the slaves of the French"'[1] The panic in Cairo was indescribable indeed. Everybody who had left Cairo for Bulaq was streaming back into Cairo; everybody in Cairo tried to escape from it. Outside the city gates, the refugees were attacked, robbed, and raped by the Bedouins and the fellahin, who had been brought in from the countryside and the desert to defend the city. Some of the refugees were not even left their clothes. Meanwhile, as darkness descended, looting began, and the palaces of Murad and Ibrahim were set on fire. 'Never,' says El-Djabarti, 'had Egypt seen so many horrors. Never have we seen such things in the history of nations; to hear is not to see.'[2]

***

It is doubtful whether, in the evening of July 21, 1798, the French soldiers encamped at Embaba were aware that they had fought one of the most famous battles in history, with forty centuries looking down upon them. But they were fully aware of having won a fabulous amount of loot. 'Among the baggage left behind by the beys and kyacheffs,' Napoleon wrote in his history of the campaign, 'they found abundant stores of comfits and sweets, and quantities of rugs, china, and silverware. All through the night, the minarets of Cairo were silhouetted against the swirling flames of 300 Egyptian vessels [which the Mamelukes before their flight had set on fire]. The glow was reflected even by the distant surfaces of the Pyramids. During the days following the battle, the soldiers busied themselves fishing the corpses out of the Nile; many had 200-300 gold pieces on them.' Once despoiled, the naked bodies were thrown in again, and on their way to the Mediterranean broadcast the news of the Mamelukes' defeat.

[1] Nicolas Turc, pp. 23-24.
[2] El-Djabarti, VI, 20.

Bonaparte himself had set up his headquarters that evening at Giza, in the country house of Murad Bey. 'Not a single servant had remained behind,' he says. 'Nothing of its interior bore any resemblance to a European palace; however, the officers were delighted to find a well-furnished house, divans upholstered with Lyons silk and golden tassels, all the echoes of European luxury and craftsmanship. The garden was filled with fine trees, but there was not a single path. A large trellis covered with vines and heavy with excellent grapes proved a welcome find. Rumour of it spread through the camp, which came running *en masse*. The harvest was soon completed.'[1]

On the morrow of the battle, the sheiks and ulemas assembled at the mosque El Azhar sent a deputation to Bonaparte to sue him for terms. After some negotiations, Bonaparte appointed a commission of five, headed by General Dupuy, whom he had designated as governor of Cairo—'a valiant warrior with the courage of a thousand arms,' as Nicholas the Turk called him[2]—to take possession of the city. At nightfall, relates Malus, who was a member of the commission, the five officers, escorted by two infantry companies, with the band playing, made their entry into Cairo, a city of 300,000 inhabitants. 'We met not a single soul on our way. Only the ululations of the women that could be heard from all the houses made us realize that Cairo was inhabited.'[3] Murad Bey's palace was in flames; the commissioners retired for the night in the house of a kyacheff. The next day, they requisitioned the house of Mohammed Bey el-Elfi, on Esbekiya Square, to serve as Bonaparte's headquarters. On July 24, the commander-in-chief, accompanied by only a few troops, made his entry into Cairo and took up residence at Mohammed el-Elfi's palace. On the same day he reported to the Directory on what he had accomplished since leaving Alexandria. His general impression of Egypt he summed up in this sentence; 'It would be difficult to find a richer land and a more wretched, ignorant, and brutish people.[4]

He might have felt triumphant; Egypt was his, but for the mopping up. Instead, his mood was sober to the point of moroseness. On July 25, four days after the victory at the Pyramids, he wrote to his elder brother Joseph, 'I have many domestic disap-

---

[1] Correspondence, XXIX, 451

[2] Nicolas Turc, p. 24.

[3] Malus, p. 65.

[4] Correspondence, IV, 252

pointments, for the veil has been completely lifted.... Only you remain for me in the whole world.... It is a sad thing to concentrate all one's feelings on a single person, in a single heart.... You will understand me.'[1] If the letter had reached Joseph, he would have understood only too well: it was Madame Bonaparte's infidelities from which the veil had been completely lifted, possibly through an indiscreet revelation made by the General's aide-de-camp Junot. As it turned out, the letter never reached Joseph, having been intercepted by the British. 'See to it that you find me a place in the country before my return,' the letter continues. 'I am weary of humanity. I need solitude and isolation. Greatness bores me; my feelings are dried up. Glory is stale when one is twenty-nine; I have exhausted everything; there is nothing left for me but to become really and completely selfish.'

Only three weeks earlier, Louis Bonaparte had written from Alexandria, to the same Joseph, in a letter which also was intercepted by the English fleet: 'Until now, I believed that luck might abandon my brother; today, I believe that he will always succeed.'[2]

On August 1, at about 10 o'clock at night, at Alexandria, Louis Bonaparte could see the flash and hear the roar of an explosion that was visible and audible within a radius of at least twenty-five miles from Abukir: Admiral Nelson was in the process of proving that Napoleon Bonaparte's luck was not invulnerable.

---

[1] Du Casse, *Memoires du Joseph*, I, 188
[2] Correspondance de L'armée Française, p. 5.

Chapter Four
Abukir Bay

AFTER driving east for several miles from Alexandria along the Corniche road, past decaying palace hotels, ultra-modern beach clubs, and the indescribably fanciful nightmare of Montazah Palace, the modern traveller reaches with relief the limits of western culture as the road continues through marshlands and desolate villages to Abukir, a fishing hamlet about fifteen miles from central Alexandria. At the tip of a small promontory extending from Abukir into the Mediterranean, an old fort commands a view of the entire magnificent bay—a vast, regular curve, thirty miles long, ending at the Rosetta mouth of the Nile.

Little if anything has changed here since Nelson won the Battle of the Nile, which was fought off Abukir and nowhere near the Nile. The fort might be described today in the very terms used by Colonel Laugier in 1798: 'We rejoiced at the sight of an edifice which, from a distance, seemed to us huge and impressive.... From close by, and especially inside, one can see that it is a hovel.... We found eighteen pieces of artillery of various calibre, without mounts. The commandant was a kind of peasant who refused to let us have fodder for the horses unless paid in advance.'[1] As dilapidated as ever, the fort is still in charge of a peasant family whose chickens, children, goats, and dogs make up the garrison. A few

[1] La Jonquière, II, 124.

rusty pieces of artillery lie about in the moat, mixed with nondescript rubbish.

Nothing noteworthy happened at Abukir from the destruction of ancient Canopus, whose site is near by, until the first two days of August 1798, when Nelson won his fame and peerage here. In the following year, General Bonaparte drove a Turkish army into the sea at the very spot where Nelson had destroyed his fleet; in 1801 General Sir Ralph Abercromby landed here with 17,000 Englishmen to drive out the French; and in 1807 another British expeditionary force under General Fraser marched past the bay towards Rosetta. Then after a decade of noise and alarums, Abukir returned to the desolate torpor from which it had emerged so abruptly, and time once more ceased to have meaning.

***

As was his custom after a disaster, Bonaparte, in the report he wrote to the Directory on the destruction of the French squadron, placed the blame squarely on someone else—in this case on a man who could not answer back, since he had died at his post. In his history of the Egyptian campaign, dictated at St. Helena, he blamed not only Admiral Brueys but also Admiral Villeneuve, who could not answer back either, since he had killed himself after his defeat at Trafalgar. Besides shifting the blame on to others, Napoleon had the dossier relating to the Egyptian campaign destroyed; the documents it contained are extant only in copies, whose fidelity to the originals may be doubted. Nevertheless, when all the available evidence is sifted, it is impossible to resist the conclusion that Bonaparte's charges against Brueys are deliberate fabrications.

Bonaparte's version of the events leading to the disaster at Abukir can be summed up in four points:

1. On July 6, before leaving Alexandria, Bonaparte ordered Brueys to put the fleet in a safe place, if possible in the Old Port; if no passage could be found to permit all the ships to enter, Brueys was to unload the remaining artillery and material at Abukir and proceed without delay to Corfu, in the French-held Ionian Islands.

The fact is that no such order was given, at least not in writing. A written order, dated July 3, instructed Brueys to take his squadron to the Old Port if possible. If the battleships could not enter, Brueys was to investigate whether the squadron could defend itself against a superior force in Abukir Bay. If that was not possible either, the squadron (minus the lighter ships, which could be anchored in the port) was to proceed to Corfu. There is no indication whatever in the order that Bonaparte wished the fleet to leave the coast, unless it could not anchor safely at Abukir.

Brueys replied to this order that, judging from the soundings he had taken, an attempt to enter the port would be hazardous; whereas he believed he could take up a defensible position at Abukir. On the following day, July 7, the fleet anchored in Abukir Bay, according to Bonaparte's instructions of July 5. Nevertheless, Brueys ordered Captain Barré, of the frigate *Alceste*, to continue the soundings of the Old Port. Barré's report, of July 13, which is very technical, concludes with the statement: 'In the last analysis, I am of the opinion that the ships of the line can enter the port, provided the necessary precautions are taken.'[1] Brueys was not completely satisfied with this finding. It is not a light matter for an admiral to run a battleship aground; besides, if part of the fleet could enter and the rest had to remain outside, the position of the fleet would be worse in the event of a British attack than if the entire fleet remained at Abukir. Brueys ordered further soundings to be taken.

2. According to Bonaparte, the first news he had from Brueys since leaving Alexandria reached him in late July at Cairo. This is possible, for several French couriers were ambushed by the Arabs. Yet Bonaparte taxes one's credulity when he asserts that he was astonished to hear of Brueys' continued presence at Abukir, since he firmly believed him to be either in the Old Port of Alexandria or at Corfu; even if he received no direct news from Brueys, he was in communication with Alexandria, and news of such importance as either the departure of the fleet or its entry into the Old Port would surely have reached him.[2] Bonaparte's letter to Brueys, dated from Cairo, July 27, completely belies his later assertion. It raises no objections to the continued presence of Brueys at Abukir, does not even mention Corfu, and reassures Brueys that he will soon receive supplies from Cairo. The letter, it is true, does contain the sentence, 'I have received intelligence from Alexandria that at last you have found an adequate passage [into the Old Port] and that

---

[1] La Jonquière, II, 246.

[2] Admittedly, Bonaparte wrote to Kléber on July 27 that he had not received a single message from the latter since leaving Alexandria. While it may be true that Kléber's despatches had not yet reached him, there can be no doubt that he was well informed by other sources of events taking place in Alexandria, and it seems strange that the whereabouts of his fleet should have been the only thing on which his intelligence was faulty.

at the present moment you and your squadron are in the port.'[1] The trouble with this sentence is that Bonaparte could not possibly have received any such intelligence, at least not from an authoritative source: it is either wishful thinking or a falsification of the original text.[2] In fact, two sentences later, Bonaparte writes: 'As soon as I have received a letter from you telling me what you have done and where you are, I shall send you instructions as to what remains to be done.' How can this be reconciled with the earlier statement? Only by the assumption that Bonaparte did not know what he was saying.

3. In his report to the Directory, Bonaparte further asserts that in a letter dated July 20 and received on July 30, Brueys announced that he was strengthening his defences at Abukir and was ready for an enemy attack. Brueys' letter of July 20 says nothing of the sort: it informs Bonaparte of the admiral's poor state of health, complains of supply shortages, and deals with various routine matters. The letter in which Brueys did announce his intention to make a stand at Abukir, if attacked, is dated July 15 and must have reached Bonaparte no more than ten days later, thus giving him time to order the fleet to leave for Corfu before August 1 if he so chose.

4. Astonished by Brueys' 'strange resolution,' Bonaparte continues, he instantly despatched his aide-de-camp Jullien to Brueys, ordering Jullien to stay at Abukir until he had seen the squadron leave. It so happens conveniently for Bonaparte that Jullien was ambushed and killed on his way to Abukir by some Arabs:

---

[1] Correspondance, IV, 262.

[2] He may have gathered that impression from a letter he received on July 27 from his brother Louis, who was in Alexandria, but certainly not from Brueys himself. There can be no doubt but that the text of the letter has been tampered with by its editors, since it contains a reference to the arrest of El-Koraim, of which Bonaparte could not yet have been apprised.

needless to say, the alleged message has never been found, and even if it was written, it would have come too late.[1]

The conclusion that must be drawn is that Bonaparte was impatient for the fleet to seek safety in the Old Port of Alexandria; but as for his contention that, as an alternative, he had ordered Brueys to sail to Corfu, it rests solely on his own word and is contradicted by other testimony and by circumstantial evidence.

Among the witnesses against Bonaparte is Rear-Admiral Vence, who commanded the port of Toulon during the preparations for the expedition. Commenting on the disaster of Abukir, Vence expressed his astonishment to the Minister of Marine that Brueys should have stayed on in Egyptian waters once the army had been disembarked. 'Judging from our conversations with Admiral Brueys,' he says, 'I should have thought that he would not stay for more than twenty-four hours once the landing was completed.'[2]

Indeed it stands to reason that the natural desire of Admiral Brueys would have been to take his fleet to safer waters once its mission was accomplished, and that if he did not do so, he acted on Bonaparte's orders. This impression is confirmed by what the naval commissioner Jaubert wrote to the Minister of Marine on

---

[1] Duplicates of orders carried by Jullien and addressed to Kléber and Menou have been preserved. The official Correspondance de Napoleon I, Vol. IV, pp. 275-76, No. 2878, reproduces a letter to Brueys dated 12 Thermidor (July 30) and containing the sentence, 'In any event, you must quickly enter the port of Alexandria, or else load promptly the rice and wheat I am sending you and sail to the port of Corfu; for it is essential that, as long as no final [military] decision has been reached here [in Egypt], you should be at a location from where you can threaten the Porte.' The editors of the Correspondance erroneously indicate the French naval archives as the source of this document; it has never been found there. The original was destroyed by order of Napoleon; a copy allegedly existed at the archives of the War Office, but it was not returned by the editors and has not been seen since (see La Jonquière, L'Expédition d'Egypte, II, 315, n.2). If Bonaparte did write this paragraph, it may have been because of intelligence received concerning the hostile attitude of the Porte and not out of concern for the safety of the French fleet. Indeed the preceding paragraph reads: 'The actions of the English [squadron] seem to indicate that it is numerically inferior [to us] and that it is content to blockade Malta....' It is difficult to reconcile this with Napoleon's claim that he ordered Brueys to Corfu in anticipation of the imminent destruction of the French fleet.

[2] La Jonquière, II, 86.

July 9: 'It was generally assumed ... that once the landing was accomplished, we should sail to Corfu, where we would have been reinforced by our battleships from Malta, Toulon, and Ancona, so as to be prepared for any eventuality. The General has decided differently. The luck that makes all his operations succeed will attend this one also. Incidentally, all of us here are propelled by the wind of fatalism, which begins to affect even my convictions a little.'[1]

Several passages in Brueys' despatches to Bonaparte have been interpreted by an authoritative historian, Friedrich Kircheisen, as indicating a reluctance on Brueys' part to separate himself from Bonaparte. 'Believe me, General,' Brueys wrote on July 6, 'that my greatest wish is to assist your operations and to find opportunities to prove my sincere attachment and gratitude to you.' And again, on July 7: 'It is my firm wish to be useful to you in every possible way: as I have told you already, any post you assign to me will satisfy me so long as it is an active one.'[2] These protestations, quoted by themselves, may seem to betray Brueys' unwillingness to leave for Corfu. Actually, in their context, they merely stress his misgivings about bottling up his fleet in the port of Alexandria. There was no question of sailing to Corfu, for the simple reason that Bonaparte, contrary to his later assertions, had specifically ruled against this course, unless Brueys found it impossible either to enter Alexandria or to defend himself at Abukir. If circumstantial evidence were needed to prove this contention, it would be enough to point out that Bonaparte, by ordering Brueys to unload virtually all the victuals aboard the battleships for the use of the land army, made it impossible for the squadron to undertake a journey as distant as to Corfu—about 800 miles in a straight line. Brueys' repeated and desperate pleas for supplies, merely in order to maintain the fleet in Abukir Bay, and the unorthodox devices to which he had to resort to victual and water his ships, are a matter of record and bear directly on one of the main causes of his defeat: almost a third of his crews were on shore looking for provisions.

It is easy enough to see why Bonaparte tried to shift the responsibility for the disaster at Abukir on to Brueys. It is almost equally easy to see why Brueys remained at Abukir. The logical choice for him would have been to proceed to any French base in the Mediterranean, but to do so he required specific orders—and these, as has been shown, he never received. If he stubbornly resisted Bonaparte's pressure to make him enter the Old Port of Al-

---

[1] Correspondance de L'armée Française, pp. 46-47.
[2] La Jonquière, II, 94, 95

exandria, his reasons were completely justified. The entrance was risky, and admirals feel much more tender about the loss of a ship than generals do about the loss of a division: after all, it takes longer and costs more to build a battleship than to recruit a few thousand male humans. But even if the fleet could have entered the port safely, what was it to do there? What would it do if the English, with three or four battleships, blocked the exit? What facilities were there at Alexandria to keep the ships in repair in case of a prolonged blockade? Of what possible use would a blockaded fleet be to Bonaparte? Whereas at Abukir, as Brueys pointed out, the squadron had a good chance to defend itself against Nelson. Bonaparte, in retrospect, ridiculed this notion, but a better authority, Nelson himself, disagreed: 'If I had taken a fleet of the same force from Spithead,' he said, 'I would sooner have thought of flying than attacking the French in their position; but I knew my captains.'[1] Indeed, to any enemy other than Nelson and his team, Brueys' position at Abukir would have seemed unassailable. Nor would any man but Nelson have dreamed of attacking in the circumstances in which he came upon the French fleet.

It is more difficult to understand Bonaparte's motives in wishing to keep the squadron at Alexandria. Two reasons have been suggested, neither of them convincing:

1, Bonaparte was expecting a second convoy from Toulon, which was to bring reinforcements and supplies; Brueys' squadron might have been needed to assist it against the English forces. It is true that a second convoy was expected; but what assistance could Brueys have given it if his ships were anchored in the port of Alexandria? They would be more useful if based at Abukir.

2. Until he had captured Cairo, Bonaparte had to keep a retreat open for his army; therefore the presence of the fleet was necessary. It may be pointed out that this argument either flatly contradicts Bonaparte's contention that he had ordered Brueys to sail to Corfu or supports the view that in the unlikely event of an evacuation of Egypt, the French squadron could have been recalled in time from Corfu. Indeed, what military forces were there in Egypt, or even in Syria, that could have overwhelmed Bonaparte to the extent of making it impossible for him to hold Alexandria and Abukir for at least a month—which would have been time enough to recall the fleet from the Ionian Islands? Certainly not the Mamelukes. A numerically superior Turkish army could have marched against him from Syria, but undoubtedly the French

---

[1] Warner, pp. 166-67.

could have resisted it long enough; besides, Bonaparte at that time still firmly believed that Turkey would remain neutral. On the other hand, how could the fleet have helped him evacuate the troops if it was blockaded in Alexandria? And what could possibly have made him believe that Nelson would be so stupid as not to blockade it? Whichever way one looks at this puzzle, it is clear that Brueys was right in contending that he could be of greater use at Abukir, where he had freedom of action, than at Alexandria, where he might be locked in. The question remains: why did Bonaparte, who after all was at least as clever as this writer, set so much importance on the squadron's entering the Old Port? Why did he not wish to let the fleet go?

Captain de la Jonquière, the most thorough and conscientious historian of the Egyptian campaign, suggests a rather odd reason. Before Bonaparte's departure from Paris, it was understood that he would return from Egypt to France in the autumn and take command of the invasion forces to be landed in the British Isles; a subordinate general, presumably Kléber, would carry on operations in the Orient. In his letter of July 25 to his brother Joseph, Bonaparte himself indicated that he would be back in France in two months, that he would divorce his wife Josephine, and that Joseph should find a rural retreat for him. It is La Jonquière's argument that Bonaparte wished to keep Brueys' squadron for his return journey. This argument begs several questions: why did Bonaparte wish to return in September to invade England or to retire as a gentleman farmer? What about his Indian projects? And, most relevant of all, why did he need thirteen battleships to go back to France? After all, when he did return a year later, two frigates proved sufficient.

All that can be said of La Jonquière's reasoning is that (1) Bonaparte's real intentions probably will remain a mystery forever and perhaps were a mystery even to Bonaparte himself; and (2) that the argument has no bearing on Bonaparte's reluctance to let the fleet depart. One might, of course, form some wild conjectures—for instance, that Bonaparte considered the possibility of retaining the fleet for an expedition to India by sea. There is not a shred of evidence, however, to support this conjecture, which has

J. Christopher Herold

little to recommend itself besides its novelty.[1] Possibly Bonaparte, like many a general, simply was reluctant to let go a part of his command; or else he did not give the problem much thought, being completely absorbed by the conquest of Egypt, and left it in Brueys' s lap, screening his indecision behind a number of ambiguous instructions while hoping for the best. As Jaubert put it, everybody was 'propelled by the wind of fatalism': perhaps the true answer is contained in that phrase. According to Bourrienne, who sounds convincing on this point, Bonaparte after the defeat of Abukir had at first asked him to draft the official report on that event. When Bonaparte read Bourrienne's report, he was dissatisfied. 'This is too vague, too smooth,' he allegedly exclaimed. 'It should be more staccato, and you must mention many details—the people who distinguished themselves in action. And then, you don't say a word about Fortune. And, according to you, Brueys was blameless. You don't know men. Leave it to me, I'll dictate.'[2] The final paragraph of Bonaparte's account ends with the words, 'It was only when Fortune saw that all her favours [to Brueys] were useless that she abandoned our fleet to its destiny.[3]

Nelson attacked Brueys at Abukir Bay recklessly and became the hero of Europe overnight. Bonaparte, having left Brueys with impracticable or ambiguous instructions, shifted the blame to him and remained a hero. Admiral Brueys followed his orders, common sense, and better judgment, and died a hero.

II

Admiral Brueys cannot be blamed for remaining in Abukir Bay; he had no other choice. However, he could have made his position there much stronger than he did. To withstand equal or superior forces, he had to bring his line of battle—especially the van and the rear—as close to the beach as possible, leaving virtually no intervals between the stern of one ship and the bow of the next, and linking them together securely with cables. This disposition would have prevented any enemy ship from slipping to the land-

---

[1] All the same, one of the first things Nelson did after destroying the French fleet at Abukir was to notify the British governor in Bombay that a junction of Bonaparte's and Tippoo Sahib's forces was no longer to be feared. It would seem that, in Nelson's mind at least, a seaborne expedition to India had been planned by the French.

[2] Bourrienne, I, 296.

[3] Correspondance, IV, 361.

side of the French (which is precisely what happened) and would have created a virtually unassailable front of some 500 guns.

The French squadron was anchored more than one and a half miles from shore—at least half a mile farther than was necessary to avoid the shallows. The thirteen battleships formed a line about a mile long, with intervals of approximately fifty yards. To strengthen the rear, which he thought was most likely to be attacked, Brueys had placed two frigates and two gunboats between the battleships and the shore. As for the van, he hoped to protect it with a battery of mortars he installed on tiny Abukir Island, off Fort Abukir, and with a frigate and a gunboat; the shoals surrounding the island seemed a sufficient deterrent to anyone who thought of turning the head of his line in order to get to the landside of it. As it happened, the range of the battery was just too short for the mortars to be effective, and the shoals proved no deterrent to the British captains.

Brueys had had three weeks to rectify his position before Nelson attacked. His failure to take advantage of them is difficult to explain. Perhaps the circumstance that a large part of his crews was ashore at all times on supply details discouraged him from attempting the complex manoeuvres that would have been required. Perhaps he expected to receive at any moment the order (which Bonaparte claimed he had sent him, but actually never did send) to sail for Corfu. Almost certainly, he had not yet made up his mind whether he should fight from a fixed position at anchor or under sail. Perhaps, being a cautious man, he could not imagine that the English would take the chances they took. Whatever the reason, it cannot have been sheer negligence, for conscientiousness was Brueys' outstanding virtue.

At two o'clock in the afternoon of August 1, the working parties who were digging wells near Abukir beach were warned by signals from *L'Orient* to return instantly to their ships. Perhaps they could not see the reason for the order, since the line of battleships hid the horizon from their view. At any rate, only a fraction of them, and of the soldiers' detachments protecting them from the ever-present Bedouins, responded to the summons, even after the reason became perfectly plain—an English fleet of at least twelve sail, approaching at a very fast rate under a strong northerly breeze. Besides the working parties ashore, several hundred more sailors were absent in Alexandria and Rosetta, whence they were to bring back some desperately needed shipments of rice and wheat. As a result, at this critical moment, the French squadron was short not only of many of its sloops and launches but of about 25-30 per cent of its crews. What men there were at their stations were, for the most part, inexperienced and undisciplined. They had been recruited wherever they could be found and by whatever means, within a few weeks, from fishing craft, coastal merchant vessels, and the like, much to the despair of their officers, who realized what General Bonaparte refused to admit: that raw cannon fodder may serve its purpose in a land army, but never aboard a sailing ship. It is safe to estimate that half of the French crews were younger—and some considerably younger—than eighteen. When it came to the fighting, these children died like heroes: but how to die was about all they knew.

By four o'clock the British fleet was in full sight, bearing down under all sails, in no particular order, much like a racing regatta of gigantic sailing craft. There were fourteen ships of the line: two of them (the *Alexander* and the *Swiftsure*) trailed behind the rest, as they came from Alexandria, where they had been reconnoitring. It was only then that Brueys realized Nelson's determination to give battle that very evening. He gave the signal to clear the decks for action and to throw cables so as to secure the ships more firmly; the latter order was imperfectly carried out.[1]

***

When Captain Samuel Hood of the *Zealous* signaled, early that afternoon, that he had sighted the French squadron, Horatio Nelson's nervous depression gave way to exultation. He ordered dinner to be served for himself and his officers on the *Vanguard*. On the morrow, he said, between toasts, he would be either in the House of Lords or in Westminster Abbey.[2] The consideration that, regardless of the outcome for Admiral Nelson, none of the others aboard the ship would be in either of these places, was a thought too invidious to present itself to a Briton's mind. The general mood of the fleet was that of a football team confident of victory. From captains to apprentice seamen, everybody knew exactly what he had to do, and for over two months they had been waiting for a chance to do it.

Nelson's orders to his captains were very general and gave each complete freedom of action in carrying them out. Although

---

[1] Quantitatively, though not qualitatively, the two squadrons were fairly evenly matched. Nelson had fourteen battleships with 1,012 guns and about 8,000 men; Brueys had thirteen battleships and four frigates with 1,182 guns (not all manned) and about 8,000 men.

[2] i.e., Either he would have earned a title or he'd be dead and ready for burial. — [Ed.]

the *Zealous* had reported the French as sixteen battleships (no doubt three of the frigates were mistaken for ships of the line), and although Nelson at the moment disposed of only twelve, he made up his mind to attack immediately, concentrating on the French van and centre; once a partial victory had been won, he could bear down on the rear if there was an opportunity. He had discussed all conceivable contingencies with his captains in the preceding weeks, and each knew how to co-operate with the others as the situation developed.

After dinner, while his ships were racing each other to be first in the attack, Nelson retired to his cabin, to nurse a raging toothache. 'When I saw them [the French ships],' he reminisced three years later in Vienna, 'I could not help popping my head every now and then out of the window (although I had a damned toothache) and once, as I [1] was observing their position, I heard two seamen quartered at a gun near me, talking, and one said to the other, "Damn them, look at them. There they are, Jack, if we don't beat them, they will beat us." I knew what stuff I had under me so I went into the attack with a few ships only, perfectly sure that the others would follow me, although it was nearly dark and they might have had every cause for not doing it, yet they all in the course of two hours found a hole to poke in at.'

***

It was with some astonishment that Brueys realized Nelson's intention to attack that very evening. By all the rules, Nelson should first have reconnoitred the French position and drawn up his ships in a line of battle; this would have reduced his own risks, but it also would have given Brueys time to get ready. At five o'clock, Brueys was still undecided whether he should fight from anchor or meet the British under sail. Indeed, at first he ordered the topsail yards to be got up. His indecision may have been influenced by his debilitated physical condition: for about a week he had been suffering from colic and diarrhoea; probably he had dysentery. Which of the opposing two admirals was the more handicapped, the one with the damned toothache or the one with the diarrhoea remains an arguable matter. In any event, Brueys decided to fight from anchor only after a hasty conference with his chief of staff, Ganteaume, and with Admirals Blanquet du Chayla and Villeneuve. Ganteaume's reasoning won over Blanquet's insistent recommendation to fight under sail. His arguments seem convincing: three of the French battleships were barely seaworthy

---

[1] Warner, p. 166.

(they had been condemned three years earlier); the crews were insufficient and too inexperienced to serve the guns and the sails at the same time; fighting from anchor, the gun crews could concentrate on serving the seaward batteries; and, besides, with barely a day's supplies of water and food, the squadron could not afford the risk of being cut off from its base. The decision having been made without much enthusiasm, Blanquet and Villeneuve returned to their respective flagships, the *Franklin* and the *Guillaume Tell*. Neither was to see Brueys again.

***

The *Zealous*, Captain Hood, and the *Goliath*, Captain Foley, were in the lead of the race when the English squadron came within range of the French van, about 6.15 p.m. At the last moment the *Goliath* over took the *Zealous* , whose crew were sporting enough to greet its passage with three formidable cheers. Cheering was to punctuate the opening phase of the battle, casting terror into the hearts of the French, whose weak and unskilled attempts at retorting provoked among the English a laughter loud enough to be heard by their enemies.

The *Goliath's* victory over the *Zealous* in their race may have been decisive in the outcome of the battle. Indeed, it was Captain Foley' s idea to sail his ship past *Le Guerrier*, at the head of the French line, between the shore and the French. This he dared on the strength of a recent French chart of Abukir Bay which in fact was so inaccurate that, had he navigated by it only rather than by instinct, he would have run aground.

While the *Goliath* rounded *Le Guerrier*, the French battery on Abukir Island opened fire without effect and the battle began. The sun was about to set. From the shore, a party of Bedouins, spears in hand, were watching the show.

Captain Foley intended to anchor opposite *Le Guerrier* but missed it and halted opposite the second ship in the line, *Le Conduerant*, while Hood, amazed to see the *Goliath* pass the shoals without running aground, followed him and took his station opposite *Le Guerrier*. Three more English ships followed—the *Orion*, the *Audacious*, and the *Theseus*—and anchored opposite the French ships further down the line, the rest, beginning with Nelson's flagship, the *Vanguard*, opened fire on the French van from the weatherside.

The frigate *La Serieuse*, mistaking herself for a David, had had the temerity to fire at the *Goliath*. 'Sink that brute, what does he do here!' cried Foley, and sunk she was, by a broadside from the

Orion and a shot in her rudder from the *Goliath*, first among the French casualties.[1] Settling in the shallows, she continued to fly her colours until 3 a.m., when she surrendered.

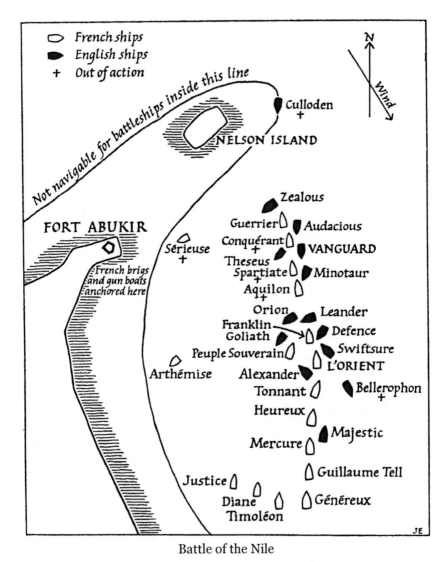

Battle of the Nile

Within an hour from the start of the battle, each of the first eight ships in the French line was raked by the fire of at least two

---

[1] Warner, p. 101.

English ships, and this despite the fact that the *Culloden*, under Captain Troubridge, had run aground in the shoals and that the *Alexander* and the *Swiftsure* had not yet joined in the battle. (The *Culloden* was to serve them as a beacon when they entered upon the scene.) This feat was made possible by the fact that the English ships were anchored at such angles in relation to their targets that they could fire at two ships at once, whereas some of the French were unable to direct both their broadside batteries against the English. In addition, since they had not expected to be attacked from the landside, the French had piled up quantities of equipment on that side of their ships, thus obstructing the operation of their landward batteries. While the French van was being destroyed and the centre pounded, the ships of the rear remained inactive bystanders. Admiral Villeneuve, who commanded them, had received no signal to get under sail and assist the other ships; the wind being strongly against him, it is doubtful if he could have done this even if so ordered.

Night had fallen and the confusion was extreme. The moon, though bright, was completely obscured by the smoke: the light signals were barely visible among the continued flashes of over a thousand guns. Both Frenchmen and Englishmen occasionally fired at their own ships. Several of the opposing vessels fought their cannon duels within pistol range from each other, and the screams of the wounded could be heard from ship to ship above the roar, mixed with the Hip! Hip! Hurrahs of the triumphant scorers.

Some time during that night, in the middle of the battle, a young woman aboard the *Goliath* gave birth to a son.

Surprising though it may seem, there were women aboard, at least on the *Goliath*, which incidentally also had some fifty Austrian troops (liberated from a French prison ship near Genoa) serving the batteries. John Nicol, a cooper aboard the *Goliath*, who left reminiscences of the battle, mentions not only the birth of the baby boy but also some other picturesque details. There was, he says, 'the gunner's wife who gave her husband and me a drink of wine every now and then, which lessened our fatigue much,' and there was the dead boy sitting on an ammunition chest, killed by blast, who would not jump up to obey the gunner's command to bring more cartridges: the gunner gave him a push and the boy fell stiffly on the deck. And there was the 'lad who had the match in his hands to fire his gun. In the act of applying it, a shot took off his arm. He looked at his arm, and seeing what had happened, seized the match in his left hand, and fired the gun before he went to the cockpit to have it dressed.[1]

***

At seven o'clock, just after sundown, Admiral Brueys, on the bridge of *L'Orient*, was wounded in the head and in one hand; he refused to have his wounds dressed and merely wiped off the blood from time to time with his handkerchief. *L'Orient* was doing well; by 7.15 p.m., she had completely dismasted the *Bellerophon*, which had had the cheek to attack the giant alone and which soon afterwards had to cut her cables and withdraw from the battle with heavy loss of life. At 7.50 p.m., a cannon ball ripped off Brueys' left thigh, nearly cutting him in two. He refused to let himself be carried to the infirmary and begged to be left where he was, so he could die on the bridge. 'He died,' reports Ensign Lachenfede, 'with the same tranquillity of soul that he had shown in combat.'[2]

About half an hour after Brueys' death, the *Swiftsure* from the outside and the *Alexander* from the inside replaced the *Bellerophon* in attacking *L'Orient*. The cannonade was becoming murderous, and at 8.50 p.m. Captain Casabianca of *L'Orient* received a head wound. He went below deck to be bandaged, then returned to his post. Although at this time the advantage lay clearly with the English, the issue of the battle was by no means decided. Two of the fourteen British ships—the *Culloden* and the *Bellerophon*—were out of action; in the French line, not counting the three remaining frigates, all thirteen ships were either still firing or as yet uncommitted. It is true that *Le Conquérant* was about to surrender to the *Audacious*: of her crew of 400, 130 were dead and eighty or ninety seriously wounded. *Le Guerrier*, though totally dismasted, was still firing back, ignoring Captain Hood of the *Zealous*, who hailed her twenty times to make her surrender. 'At last,' says Hood, 'being tired of firing and killing people in that way, I sent my boat on board her, and the lieutenant [who had replaced the wounded captain] was allowed ... to hoist a light and haul it down to show his submission.'[3] Even after the surrender of *Le Conquer* ant and *Le Guerrier*, the opponents remained evenly matched in numbers—eleven battleships and three frigates on the French side, twelve battle ships on the British side. Brueys had been killed, but then Nelson too had suffered a head wound and

---

[1] Nicol, p. 187, p. 189.
[2] La Jonquière, II, 399.
[3] Warner, p. 82.

was virtually incapacitated. If Villeneuve had been able to join the battle, the outcome still might have been a draw, if not a French victory.

At 9.30 p.m., fire broke out aboard *L'Orient*. It was, so it seemed then, easily extinguished, but a quarter of an hour later, it appeared again and, within a matter of minutes, swept across the entire deck. 'We had the crews manning the 24-pounder battery come up,' reports Ensign Lachenfede. 'But everything at that moment contributed to increase the confusion. The pump, it was found, was broken, the hatchets were hidden under mounds of debris; the buckets which we kept on the forecastle were scattered all over the place; we had to have some brought up from the holds; five ships had surrounded us and were firing at us with double intensity.[1] After incredible but futile efforts, we left the bridge deck, which was covered with flaming corpses. The mainmast and the mizzen crashed toward port.... The ship was burning fore and aft, and already the flames were reaching the 24-pounder battery. And yet in the 56-pounder battery, the men seemed to be unaware of the danger, and they continued to fire vigorously.'[2]

Midshipman Theophilus Lee, aboard the *Swiftsure*, was ten years old. The memory of that night quite understandably remained vivid all his life. 'The incessant flashes of the numerous guns,' he recalled many years later, 'discharged at nearly the same instant, [were] so vivid at times as to enable each party to distinguish clearly not only the colours of the respective contestants, but the disastrous results of battle upon them.'[3]

If Theophilus Lee retained an indelible picture of the general scene, his memory nevertheless was naturally confused as to detail. Thus he declares that Admiral Brueys was still alive. 'The brave Brueys,' he says, 'having lost both his legs, was seated with tourniquets on the stumps in an armchair facing his enemies, and giving directions for extinguishing the fire, when a cannon ball from the *Swiftsure* put a period to his gallant life by nearly cutting him in two.'[4] Lee could not possibly have seen this, even if it had happened; he probably confused Brueys' death with that of Cap-

---

[1] Presumably the *Swiftsure, Alexander, Defence, Goliath* and *Leander*. As soon as fire broke out on *L'Orient*, the English concentrated their efforts on her.

[2] La Jonquière, II, 400-401.

[3] Lee, p. 90.

[4] Ibid., p. 91

tain Thévenard of *L'Aquilon*, who had both legs shot away and died almost instantly, or with that of Captain Dupetit-Thouars, of *Le Tonnant*. *L'Aquilon*, with eighty-seven dead and 215 wounded, surrendered to the *Minotaur* at 9.45 p.m. *Le Tonnant*, whose guns were still blazing, cut her cables about that time to avoid being set on fire by flaming debris from *L'Orient*, directly ahead of her; Dupetit-Thouars, though in the process of being reduced to a rump, was still in command.

Captain Millet, commanding the *Theseus*, also could observe *L'Orient*'s fire from close quarters. He did not share Midshipman Lee's admiration for French gallantry. Although, he wrote, the blazing *L'Orient* presented 'a most grand and awful spectacle, such as formerly would have drawn tears down the victor's cheeks, pity was stifled as it rose by the remembrance of the numerous and horrid atrocities their unprincipled and bloodthirsty nation had and were committing.'[1] In Captain Millet, British principles got the better of the British sporting spirit.

Amidst this inferno, Admiral Ganteaume conferred with *L'Orient*'s officers to determine what to do. They agreed that the fire could no longer be checked; all that could be done was to try to flood the powder magazine. This proved to be impossible; the fire was gaining faster than the water. About ten o'clock the order to abandon ship was given. From that moment on, it became a matter of *sauve qui peut*—every man for himself.

About a hundred men squeezed into the sloop and pushed off. The wounded were left to burn. About 200 others sought to save them selves by swimming or, if they could not swim, by clinging to the debris floating about the ship. Some were picked up by French ships, others by the English. Lieutenant Berthellot swam off, had an after thought, returned aboard the blazing ship, and, clutching his hat in one hand, swam off again. When he appeared aboard the *Swiftsure*, stark naked but properly covered, Captain Hallowell was astounded. 'Who the devil are you?' the captain inquired. Berthellot gave his name and explained he had gone back to fetch his hat so he could prove he was an officer: there is nothing like presence of mind in unusual circumstances. The *Alexander* picked up twenty-eight men, all naked, and supplied them with 'shirts 28, trousers 28 pair.'[2]

---

[1] Warner, p. 110.

[2] Ibid., p. 94.

Where, during those fateful minutes, were the boy who stood on the burning deck—a boy nine or ten years old—and his father, Captain Casabianca? Mrs. Hemans, in her confused poem, does not say, and there is no reason to think that she knew. According to Theophilus Lee, who was about the same age as Midshipman Casabianca, the boy was in the infirmary below deck, having had a leg shot away. According to others, he and his father had sought safety by swimming and were drowned. Or perhaps they were still aboard *L'Orient* when she blew up. Together? Looking for each other? Who knows? Bonaparte, who had a flair for the dramatic, asserts in his report that young Casabianca refused to abandon ship and stayed by his father's side to the end. The only thing that is certain is that not a shred of either was ever seen again.

The explosion occurred at about 10.15 p.m.; no two accounts agree on the exact time. The concussion was felt in a twenty-five-mile radius; the flash lit up Alexandria and Rosetta. Whole sections of the ship, masts, spars, and riggings, flew sky-high, mingled with human bodies, and came down in a flaming shower. The blast was succeeded by sudden silence: all the guns, British as well as French, ceased firing for at least ten minutes. The crew of the *Theseus* tried a cheer, but it stuck in their throats. As the carcass of *L'Orient* sank to the bottom, the men who were still in the water were pulled down with it. About sixty of them re-emerged and found some floating object to cling to; they held on until daybreak, for five hours; a few were killed by cannon balls from the French ships to the rear.

With *L'Orient*, there sank or blew up the gilt and silver saints and jewelled reliquaries, confiscated from the Protocathedral of St. John of Jerusalem at Malta.

The eerie silence that succeeded the explosion was caused not only by astonishment but mainly by the apprehension, on both French and English ships, that the burning debris might set them on fire. Also, the men had been fighting for four hours; during the silent pause, they stretched out wherever they were and slept.

It was the guns of the *Franklin* that wakened them again; she was the first to resume firing. Admiral Blanquet du Chayla, whose flagship she was, had been wounded in the head at eight o'clock, and at half-past nine her captain was severely wounded too. When the *Franklin* recommenced the firing, says Blanquet in his report, she had lost two of her masts and all the guns on the main deck had been dismounted, 'two-thirds of the ship's company being killed or wounded, and those who remained much fatigued. She was surrounded by enemy ships, some of which were within pistol-shot, and who mowed down the men with every broadside.' In this condition, the *Franklin* continued the struggle for an hour; at 11.30 p.m. she struck the colours. *Le Spartiate*, though riddled through and through, with half her men dead or wounded and most of the rest working the pumps, surrendered to the *Vanguard* only at eleven o'clock. *Le Peuple Souverain*, completely dismasted by nine o'clock, slipped her cable about 10.15 p.m. and ceased firing at 11 p.m.; she was boarded by officers of the *Orion* at 4.30 a.m.

Le Tonnant slipped her cable shortly before *L'Orient* blew up, to avoid being set on fire. Captain Dupetit-Thouars was still at his post according to some accounts, with both arms and one leg shot away, though this seems scarcely credible. Lured to the seafaring life by a childhood reading of Robinson Crusoe, he had fought (like Brueys) under de Grasse in the American Revolution, had emigrated to the United States, during the Reign of Terror, and had just resumed his naval career under the Directory. His sensitive, aristocratic, intelligent features bear out the judgment of his contemporaries that he was among the ablest and most promising officers in the French navy. At some time that night, while the guns of his ship were still firing, seeing that he was losing too much blood despite the tourniquets applied to his stumps, he said to his lieutenant, 'I might lose my head along with my blood and do something foolish if I keep the command. It is time I gave it up.'[1] Which said, he blew his brains out with his pistol.[2] *Le Tonnant* continued firing until 3.30 a.m. and struck colours only late on August 2, having had 120 men killed and 150 wounded. The ship, at the time of Dupetit-Thouars' death, was a complete shambles.

***

Citizen Poussielgue, Controller General of Finances for the Army of the Orient, stayed up that entire night, with most other Frenchmen at Rosetta, about twenty-five miles away, watching the battle from a tower. Of course, he could not tell at that distance which ships were French, which British. He was shaken by the dreadful explosion of *L'Orient*, and he confirms, in a letter to his wife, the ten-minute silence that followed it (about the only thing

---

[1] La Jonquière, II, 425.

[2] This account of Dupetit-Thouars' death follows that given in the diary of General Damas; it is true that Damas had his information from second hand, but then all accounts of the captain's death are either second-hand or vague. What Damas tells seems to have been the gossip of Cairo, which probably was closer to the truth than the official versions.

in the battle on which all witnesses agreed). After that significant pause, he says, 'the firing resumed and continued uninterruptedly until three o'clock in the morning, when it ceased almost entirely until five. Then it continued with as much fury as before.'[1]

About eight in the morning, says Poussielgue, there was another explosion, similar to that of *L'Orient*. This must have been the frigate *L'Artemise* blowing up, which had drifted ashore and was ordered to be burned by her captain. However, though there undoubtedly still was some firing throughout the morning of August 2, Poussielgue's assertion that it was as furious as during the night is quite incredible. Probably, by that time, he was four-fifths asleep and could not tell the difference. Indeed, when the sun rose that day, six of the French battle ships had struck their colours; a seventh, *L'Orient*, was no more; *Le Tonnant*, *L'Heureux*, and *Le Mercure* were still flying their colours but had ceased fire and were grounded or beached; so was *Le Timoldon*, last in the French line, which was burned by her crew on July 3. The only French ships still undamaged and capable of firing were Villeneuve's flagship *Guillaume Tell*, the battleship *Le Gendreux*, and the frigates *La Diane* and *La Justice*. The English, though they had not lost a single ship, also had taken severe punishment, especially the *Bellerophon* and the *Majestic*, which had suffered the heaviest casual ties. What fighting there was between these remnants cannot have approached the night's battle in intensity.

It was only at 2 p.m. of August 2, says Napoleon somewhat unfairly, 'that Admiral Villeneuve seemed to take notice of the fact that there had been a battle going on for the past eighteen hours.'[2] After taking aboard part of the crews of the abandoned ships, Villeneuve cut his cables at about that time and sailed from the scene, followed by the *Genereux* and the two surviving frigates. The English made a half hearted effort at pursuit but soon gave up, being far more battered than were those four ships, which had taken only a small part in the battle.

Nelson, in Napoleon's opinion, 'owed his victory to the ineptness and the negligence of the captains of *Le Guerrier* and *Le Conquérant*, to the accident of *L'Orient*, and to the poor conduct of Admiral Villeneuve.... It was in Villeneuve's power to turn the battle into a French victory even as late as daybreak.'[3] Whether

---

[1] Correspondance de L'armée Française, p. 222.

[2] Correspondance, XXIX, 469.

[3] Ibid., XXIX, 469-70.

Captain Trullet the elder and Captain Dalbarade were inept and negligent or not, it is hard to tell; there can be no question that the fire of *L'Orient* was the decisive and climactic event of the battle; and it is difficult to explain Admiral Villeneuve's lack of initiative. The curious thing is that Bonaparte waited for twenty years before he blamed the admiral for the loss of the battle. His report of August 19, 1798, to the Directory contains not a single word of censure directed against Villeneuve, and in a letter of August 17, he even asked General Chabot, commanding the French forces in Corfu, to convey his congratulations to Villeneuve for preserving himself and two excellent ships. If Villeneuve was as incompetent as Napoleon made him appear in his history of the Egyptian campaign, why did Napoleon put him, in 1805, at the head of the fleet which Nelson destroyed at Trafalgar?

When Bonaparte received news of the disaster at Abukir, his comment on Brueys' death was, 'He did well to die.'[1] When he dictated his report to the Directory, in which he blackened Brueys' memory, he followed it up with a letter of condolence to Brueys' widow 'the wife of my friend.'[2] Napoleon respected neither winners nor losers, except himself. According to him, the Duke of Wellington, at Waterloo, committed every possible blunder and won only because General Grouchy blundered even more; as for the Battle of the Nile, 'Nelson's conduct ... cannot be held up as a model, but he and the English crews displayed the utmost possible skill and vigour, whereas half of the French squadron showed as much ineptness as pusillanimity.'[3]

Of these pusillanimous officers and crews, one admiral, three captains, and 1,700 men had been killed in the action, and one admiral, six captains, and 1,500 men had been wounded. No English naval officer criticized Brueys and his staff as severely as did Bonaparte. The English had the better ships, the better captains, and the better crews; they had no need to belittle their enemy's intelligence or courage in order to prove this to themselves.

III

Admiral Nelson was wounded early in the battle, before *L'Orient* caught fire. A fragment of shot from *Le Spartiate* laid his cra-

---

[1] La Jonquière, II, 425

[2] Correspondance, IV, 362.

[3] Ibid., XXIX, 471.

nium bare for more than an inch above his blind eye; the eyelid fell over his good one, and for a while he was totally blinded. Undoubtedly he also suffered from severe concussion; two weeks after the battle he wrote to Lord St. Vincent, 'My head is so upset that really I know not what to do.'[1]

At first, Nelson thought he was fatally wounded. 'I am killed!' he exclaimed. 'Remember me to my wife.'[2] Led below to the surgery in the cockpit, which was full of wounded, Nelson insisted on waiting his turn. His eyesight was barely restored when he ordered his secretary to take down a despatch. Mr. Campbell, the secretary, being too shaky to comply, and the chaplain likewise, the admiral himself drafted the opening lines of his victory bulletin: 'Almighty God has blessed His Majesty's arms in the late Battle.'[3] By what intuitive process Nelson could have known at this point that the battle was won it is difficult to see, but not quite so difficult as the connection between the Almighty and the mangling of 4,000 human bodies, men and children, by means of cannon balls, chain shot, and fire.

When, the next day, the wreckage and the corpses were sorted out, it was found that the victory, although almost complete, had been costly. Captain Barré, who went aboard the *Vanguard* on August; to arrange for a return of the French prisoners, took a good look at the British ships: three were completely and six partially dismasted; two others were temporarily out of action. British casualties, though far inferior to the French, nevertheless amounted to 218 killed and 677 wounded, almost half of them on the *Vanguard, Majestic* and *Bellerophon*. When John Nicol of the *Swiftsure*, a veteran seaman to whom such horrors were not new, went on deck after the battle to survey the scene, he found it 'an awful sight.... The whole bay was covered with dead bodies, mangled, wounded and scorched, not a bit of clothes on them except their trousers.'[4]

At 2 p.m. of August 2, thanks was given to God for all this aboard the *Vanguard* and the other English ships. In the afternoon, the English buried their dead on Abukir Island, which the French had evacuated; it is now known as Nelson Island. Among

---

[1] Warner, p. 104,

[2] Ibid., p. 92.

[3] Nelson, III, 56.

[4] Nicol, pp. 186-87,

those buried, there was one of the women aboard the *Goliath*, who had succumbed to her wounds.

The British had taken about 5,200 prisoners, a large part of whom were wounded. 'One thing I observed in these Frenchmen quite different from anything I had ever before observed,' says John Nicol. 'In the American war, when we took a French ship ... the prisoners were as merry as if they had taken us, only saying "Fortune de guerre"—"you take me today, I take you tomorrow." Those we had on board were thankful for our kindness, but were sullen, and as downcast as if each had lost a ship of his own.'[1]

To feed the prisoners and take care of the wounded was beyond the capacities of Admiral Nelson; within a few days, all save about 200 officers and specialists were returned to shore. Undisciplined and riotous, they were to create a severe problem for General Kléber in Alexandria until Bonaparte organized them into a 'nautical legion.' The legion proved to be of no particular use, since the Directory never sent Bonaparte any ships to replace the lost ones.[2]

As Kléber's and Menou's despatches to Bonaparte and to each other reveal, there was considerable anxiety during the days following the battle that the English might follow it up by forcing the entrance into the ports of Alexandria and Rosetta. If Nelson could have entered Alexandria, captured the French transports in the harbour, and possibly even destroyed the garrison with the help of the Arabs, his victory would have been complete indeed. But Kléber and Menou apparently had no idea how weak the British were, and Nelson had no idea how weak were the defences of the French.[3] The English admiral's main concern was to repair his own ships (partly with wreckage from the unsalvable Frenchmen) and to determine which of the French ships to tow away as prizes and which to destroy. On August 6, he sent H.M.S. *Leander* to take his message of victory to England; a duplicate of the despatch was sent to Naples with the brig *Mutine*. Since the *Leander* was cap-

---

[1] Ibid., p. 188.

[2] The English had released all prisoners on parole. When they caught three of them aboard a French aviso, Commodore Hood regretfully had them shot. However, the parole did not forbid the released sailors to take arms against enemies other than Englishmen.

[3] His attempt to make the population of Alexandria rise against the French was foiled by the sheik el-Messiri, who brought the scheme and Nelson's letter to the notables of Alexandria to General Kléber's attention.

tured off Crete on August 18 by *Le Genereux*, one of the two French battleships that had managed to escape from Abukir Bay, it was through Naples that Europe first heard of the victory.

On August 17, Nelson sent his senior captain. Sir James Saumarez, to Gibraltar with seven of his ships and with his six French prizes.[1] He himself, following orders from Lord St. Vincent, proceeded to Naples on August 19 with the *Vanguard*, the *Culloden*, and the *Alexander*. To blockade the Egyptian coast, he left behind the *Zealous*, the *Swiftsure*, the *Goliath*, and three frigates that had joined him, rather belatedly, several days after the battle. Cruising between Damietta and Alexandria, this small fleet, under Commodore Hood, effectively cut off all communication between Bonaparte's army and the rest of the world.

***

For several nights after the Battle of the Nile, the whole coast of Abukir Bay was illuminated by the bonfires the Bedouins were lighting to celebrate a victory which had cost them no effort. This illumination was nothing compared to the outbursts of joy that took place when the news became known in Naples and in London. Nelson was still at sea when Lady Hamilton wrote to him from Naples, 'If I was King of England, I would make you the most noble, puissant Duke Nelson, Marquis Nile, Earl Alexandria, Viscount Pyramid, Baron Crocodile and Prince Victory, that posterity might have you in all forms.'[2] Actually, he received only a barony, thus becoming Lord Nelson of the Nile and Burnham Thorpe, and was awarded a life pension of 2,000 a year. Foreign potentates showered honours on him; Sultan Selim III sent him the Plume of Triumph, a diamond-encrusted horror whose centre revolved by clockwork and which—one refuses to believe it—Nelson wore in his hat.

When Nelson arrived in Naples on September 22, the population, in his own words, was 'mad with joy.' Queen Marie Caroline's transports were spectacular: 'She fainted, cried, kissed her husband, her children walked frantic about the room, cried, kissed and embraced every person near her, exclaiming, "o brave Nelson! Oh God bless you and protect our brave deliverer"!' Lady Hamilton 'fell apparently dead and is not yet properly recovered from

---

[1] *Le Peuple Souverain, Le Conquerant, Le Spartiate, L'Aquilon, Le Franklin*, and *Le Tonnant*. It may be noted that the first two of these ships, which Nelson judged to be worthy of being repaired, had been condemned by the French Ministry of Marine two years earlier.

[2] Warner, p. 145.

her severe bruises.' King Ferdinand himself—a man with the countenance (and mentality) of a prosperous village idiot, but whom Nelson respected as he did all kings—took him by the hand, calling him 'his deliverer and preserver.'[1] No matter how steady a hero's character, such sudden and surely well-deserved glory easily goes to the hero's head; yet Admiral Nelson, near the end of the letter in which he reports these events to his wife, redeems his vanity with a phrase that expresses the noble and romantic side of glory hunting in three simple words. If King George should give him a peerage, he wrote to Fanny Nelson, she ought to go to Court, without minding the expense. 'Money is trash.'[2]

To the conquering hero, money may look like trash compared to adulation, but often it is far less corrupting. Intoxicated with his new role, Nelson soon became the evil genius of the king who had called him his 'deliverer and preserver.' No doubt he was convinced that he served England, humanity, and the Almighty in inciting the Court of Naples to send an army against the French troops in the Papal States, without a declaration of war. Actually he merely tarnished his own glory by making himself the instrument of the clique headed by the Queen and Lady Hamilton; moreover, he proved himself a poor politician and an even poorer judge of military affairs. By November 29, the Neapolitan army under Field-Marshal Mack (borrowed from Austria) had taken Rome; two weeks later, the French under General Championnet recaptured Rome and pushed on south toward Naples. On December 25, the royal family, the Hamiltons, Sir John Acton, and their whole *camerilla* took refuge on Nelson's ships, to be conveyed in all haste to Palermo. Among the refugees, only King Ferdinand kept his serenity. Sicily, it occurred to him, would present marvellous opportunities for hunting and shooting; the idea enraptured him so that he requested Nelson to send a transport back to shore for additional dogs and shotguns. The same day, the French entered Naples, and on Christmas Eve, the kingdom was proclaimed a republic. Only Sicily proper was left to the King of the Two Sicilies.

***

---

[1] Nelson, III, 125.

[2] Warner, p. 141.

IV

The news of Abukir was brought to Bonaparte on August 13 near Es Saliya, a town at the edge of the Sinai Desert, where he had gone in pursuit of Ibrahim Bey. Ibrahim with his followers had escaped into Syria, and Bonaparte, leaving the occupation of the north-eastern provinces in the hands of his generals, was on his way back to Cairo.

There are various accounts of Bonaparte's first reaction to the news; it does not matter which one is correct, since Bonaparte never betrayed his real feelings on such occasions, supposing he had any. Keeping his thoughts to himself, he was content to act a part. In his own history of the campaign, he quotes himself as having said to his officers, 'Well, gentlemen, now we are obliged to accomplish great things: we shall accomplish them. We must found a great empire, and we shall found it. The sea, of which we are no longer master, separates us from our home land, but no sea separates us from either Africa or Asia. We are numerous; we have enough men to form our cadres. We have no lack of munitions; if necessary, Champy and Conté will manufacture more of them.[1] This speech, he says, electrified his men; they ceased their complaints.

In essence, no doubt, this is what he said, and it was the right thing to say, although it is not true that the men ceased their complaints. But at bottom, one suspects, the destruction of his fleet did not strike him at first as a fatal turn of events.

His situation was not nearly as hopeless as his enemies believed and as later historians judged it to be. 'This army is in a scrape, and will not get out of it'[2] Nelson wrote to Sir William Hamilton, speaking of Bonaparte's forces. He was quite mistaken. In the first place, Bonaparte had not lost his transports, which were still at Alexandria; all he had lost was eleven battleships, three of which were about to go to the scrapping yard. Only a few months later, the French Atlantic fleet sailed into the Mediterranean; combined with the Spanish squadron there, it would have had an overwhelming numerical superiority over the British; that the two would never agree to co-operate was some thing neither Nelson nor Bonaparte could have foreseen. If Nelson's victory turned out to be decisive in nullifying the French conquest of Egypt, this effect was due not to the victory itself but to remotely

---

[1] Correspondance, XXIX, 458.

[2] Nelson, III, 95.

related developments in Madrid, Ireland, and Constantinople. No matter what history textbooks say, the British victory at Abukir did not condemn the French expedition to failure. Bonaparte himself never thought that it did, and he was right.

***

If Bonaparte, upon first hearing of the defeat, emphasized the resulting isolation of his army, he did so because this suited his purpose, which was to shock his men into accepting the probability of a long stay with fortitude. He did not expect his prediction to be fulfilled to the letter, for he had no reason to believe that the Directory would abandon him completely to his fate. His military position seemed secure for some time to come, unless Turkey and England should combine against him; but he still counted on Talleyrand's coming to Constantinople to prevent this and to regularize his position in Egypt in the eyes of the Porte.

As for Bonaparte's reputation of invincibility, even that was untouched by Nelson's victory: after all, Abukir was Brueys' defeat, not his. In his report to the Directory, Bonaparte managed to relate the naval disaster as a mere unfortunate episode, a long footnote to his own victories at Malta, Alexandria, Shubra Khit, and the Pyramids. (It may be suggested in passing that if Nelson and Bonaparte had named their victories with less flair for the dramatic, public opinion would have been less stirred. 'Abukir' and 'Embaba' lack the magic of 'the Nile' and 'the Pyramids.') As luck would have it, the news of Brueys' defeat reached Paris at the same time as the news of the capture of Cairo—another magic name. To sugarcoat the catastrophe of Abukir, the Directory had no choice but publicly to celebrate another of the invincible Bonaparte's victories.

***

It frequently happens in politics that an event, if erroneously evaluated by a sufficient number of responsible people, produces precisely those effects which the erroneous evaluation ascribes to it. Nelson's victory of the Nile is a classic example. Aside from costing France eleven battleships and from renewing every Englishman's pride in his navy, that event need not have affected the course of history. Nor did it do so in the long run; in the short run, however, it had tremendous consequences, all of them due to an international epidemic of erroneous reasoning.

The complexities of a naval battle, intricate as they are, are simplicity itself compared to the complexities of diplomacy and power politics. It will be recalled that when Bonaparte started out on his expedition, France had just made peace with Austria. Only England and Portugal remained at war with her, Russia, though increasingly hostile since Tsar Paul had succeeded his mother Catherine on the throne, had not yet declared war on France. Nevertheless, with French forces scattered from the Vendée (where they still were fighting a civil war with the royalists) all the way to Corfu and to Egypt, it was easy to foresee that the powers hostile to the French Republic would form a coalition as soon as France suffered an important setback. The French government, quite aware of this likelihood, had sought to strengthen their strategic position by occupying Switzerland and the Papal States and by bringing pressure on Spain to become a more active ally in the war. Further more, it was understood that the Directors would do their utmost to ensure Turkish neutrality by sending Talleyrand as ambassador to the Porte, and that in September an uprising in Ireland, supported by French forces, would keep England busy at home. By that time, Bonaparte would return and direct the invasion of Ireland and, if possible, of England, while his successor in Egypt would establish contact with Tippoo Sahib to agree on joint action in India.

Such far-flung operations required a precision of timing and a speed of communications which were scarcely possible until a century later.

Things began to go wrong simultaneously in Ireland and in Turkey. Instead of waiting until September, the United Irishmen rose in the southern counties in May, a few days after the French fleet left Toulon. The insurrection was ill-organized; by early July, the English forces had the situation well in hand. Meanwhile, however, the representatives of the Irish Union in Paris had besieged Talleyrand and the Directors with requests for aid. Wolfe Tone, one of the founders of the Union, had been commissioned an adjutant general in the French army as early as March; he now offered to go to Ireland to fight even if only a corporal's guard was sent there. Though the French government responded a little more generously than that, the help they gave fell far short of what was needed. On August 6, three frigates with 1,020 troops aboard left La Rochelle under the command of General Humbert; they reached Killala Bay on August 22. Pathetic though it was, Humbert's little legion caused renewed alarm in England for a fortnight; on September 8, it was obliged to surrender to General Sir John Moore at Ballinamuck. Among the prisoners was Wolfe Tone's brother Matthew, who was hanged at Dublin for treason three weeks later.

Wolfe Tone himself left Brest with a second, somewhat larger, expeditionary force, under General Hardy, a few days before his brother's hanging. Driven off by a storm, the squadron (the battleship *Hoche* and eight frigates) sighted the Irish coast only on October 10. They were met by Admiral Warren with superior forces, which obliged the *Hoche* and six of the frigates to surrender after a gallant battle. Wolfe Tone, who commanded one of the batteries of the *Hoche*, was made a prisoner and taken to Dublin to be court-martialled. He, too, was sentenced to be hanged. His petition to be allowed to die before a firing squad was turned down by General Cornwallis. On the eve of the scheduled execution, Wolfe Tone cut his throat with a pen knife; he died on November 11. Thus ended the projected Irish uprising; two weeks before Tone's death the French government had called off all further aid. Thus, also, ended the 'Army of England,' which from then on was used exclusively to fight the royalists in the Vendée. The renewal of warfare in Italy, the news that Turkey had declared war on France, and the drawing together of the Second Coalition diverted the Directory's attention to the Continent; all these developments had been sparked off by Nelson's victory at Abukir. The invasion of the British Isles having been abandoned, the French Atlantic fleet was ordered in March 1799 to leave Brest and to enter the Mediterranean; combined with the Spanish Mediterranean fleet, it could have dispersed Nelson's squadron, saved Malta and Corfu, and given Bonaparte overwhelming superiority. But the Spanish refused to co-operate with the French in any project other than an invasion of Ireland, and France would no longer hear of Ireland. Wolfe Tone's death was as futile as anything connected with the Egyptian campaign.

***

'Is Talleyrand in Constantinople?' Bonaparte inquired at the end of his report of August 19 to the Directory. It was a question he had asked several times before; to reach an understanding with the Porte concerning Egypt was an urgent necessity, and only a diplomat of the first rank could negotiate it.

But Talleyrand, whose motto was *Surtout pas de zéle*, was not at all anxious to go to Constantinople. The ciphered despatches he received from the French *chargé d'affaires* Ruffin did nothing to diminish his distaste for the mission.

It was only on May 11, just before the departure of the French fleet, that Talleyrand wrote to Ruffin to inform him of the expedition to Egypt. Ruffin was to convince the Porte that no hostility against it was intended and to announce the imminent arrival of a French negotiator with full powers. The letter reached Ruffin only on June 28, on the eve of the French landing at Alexandria. Unlike Ruffin, who until then had been kept utterly ignorant of the project, the Turkish government had been informed of the French preparations as early as May, through the Turkish ambassador in Paris. (Apparently Turkish intelligence agents, a team of astute Greeks, were more efficient than the English ones.) Ruffin spent a rather embarrassing three hours on June 19, when the Reis Effendi (the foreign secretary of the Turkish government) grilled him about the expedition to Egypt, of which Ruffin had not even heard. Ruffin did his best to reassure him that France could not harbour any hostile intentions toward the Porte. This was precisely the reply Talleyrand had made in Paris, in April, to Esseid Ali, the Turkish ambassador, who had questioned him on the purpose of the Toulon armaments. As the Reis Effendi pointed out to Ruffin at a later inter view, this reply was a little too implicit to be reassuring.

The Reis Effendi's attitude was, on the whole, friendly and under standing. The destruction of the Order of Malta was welcome news to the Turks, and they had no love for the Mamelukes. Yet he was also very worried. To abandon Moslem territory to the control of a non-Moslem power without a struggle was completely contrary to fundamental Turkish policy; such an action was likely to discredit the Ottoman government with their Moslem subjects and to cause further disruption in the Empire. It also might involve Turkey in war with England and Russia, and surely it was unreasonable to expect a country to go to war to defend its right to abandon a province to an invader; it seemed more reasonable to fight the invader, though he might be one's best and oldest friend.

There were other things that worried the Turks, and they made them increasingly plain to Ruffin in the weeks following Bonaparte's landing. If the intentions of France were friendly, why did she not send a fully empowered ambassador to Constantinople who could explain them? Why had General Bonaparte meddled for the past year in the internal affairs of the Ottoman Empire, carrying on mysterious negotiations with Ali Pasha of Janina? Why had Bonaparte sent messages to Greece, announcing the 'liberation' of Malta as a preliminary to the liberation of the Greeks? It was difficult not to regard these actions as indicative of France's intention to dismember the Ottoman Empire. Prince Constantine Ypsilanti, then Dragoman of the Porte,[1] was particularly perturbed by Bonaparte's interest in Greece. 'As Dragoman of the Divan,' he told a

---

[1] The highest position in the Ottoman foreign office under the Reis Effendi; it was traditionally held by a Fanariot Greek.

French embassy official on June 25, 'I cannot approve of Citizen Bonaparte's ambitious views on Ottoman territory; but as a Greek, I curse a vainglorious boast that will cost the lives of ten thousand Greeks whom the Turks are about to massacre.'[1] The remark is not without interest, in view of the part the Ypsilanti family were to play in the achievement of Greek independence.

To all this, Ruffin could reply little, except plead ignorance and deplore Citizen Bonaparte's independent views, which surely could not have the approval of his government.

The Turks' apprehensions mounted as the first news arrived of Bonaparte's actions in Egypt. Special council meetings were held by the Grand Vizier and the Mufti; the faces of the councillors, as they left the meeting, showed consternation. Food prices rose alarmingly. The population displayed mounting hostility toward foreigners, particularly the French, and seemed disposed to begin a soul-satisfying massacre at any moment. The panic spread throughout Turkey. Citizen Choderlos, the French consul general at Aleppo (and a brother of the author of *Les Liaisons Dangereuses*) reflected the nervous irritation of all his fellow citizens in the Levant when he complained to Talleyrand of Bonaparte's inexplicable failure to inform the French consuls of his intentions; how were they to calm down the Turks if they themselves were kept in ignorance?

It was disturbing enough for the Turkish government to see a friendly power occupy one of its most important provinces without warning or explanation, save the implausible protestation that the action was meant in a friendly way and should cause no alarm. It was positively vexatious to learn that in all his speeches and proclamations General Bonaparte represented himself as having come with the consent of the Ottoman Sultan and that, at the same time, he had placed an embargo on all Turkish ships in the port of Alexandria. The report of the Turkish ambassador in Paris on his interview of July 21 with Talleyrand cannot have contributed to the Turks' peace of mind: Talleyrand had assured Esseid Ali that no permanent conquest of Egypt was intended and had proposed a joint Franco-Turkish naval expedition to the Crimea, which Turkey had but recently lost to Russia. Whatever the Turks may have thought of this new piece of effrontery when it reached them, there was no need for them to reply to it, since the fleet that was to help Turkey reconquer the Crimea had been destroyed in the meantime.

---

[1] La Jonquière, II, 600.

In the afternoon of August 6 before the news of Abukir had reached Constantinople the Reis Effendi summoned Ruffin to his office. General Bonaparte's conduct, he said, had roused public indignation to such a pitch that the Porte had to take measures to protect French citizens in Turkey. As a consequence, Ruffin must not leave the precincts of the French Embassy in Pera; he must take down the armorial bearings of the French Republic and place them inside the building. All Frenchmen must avoid showing themselves in public places. Ruffin's first dragoman must no longer present himself at the Porte; if he had any communication to make, he should call at the Reis Effendi's house during the dark. All this, the Reis Effendi added, was meant in a friendly spirit, to avoid the kind of incident that Bernadotte had had to contend with in Vienna. 'When I took my leave from him,' concludes Ruffin in his report, 'I was given neither sherbet, nor perfume, nor handkerchief. The absence of these marks of honour confirmed my impression that I had not had a conference but a ministerial scolding.'[1]

According to a Turkish proverb quoted by Ruffin, 'An Ottoman hunter, if he wants to chase a hare, goes by oxcart'—the implication being that Turks are averse to precipitate action. While imposing severe restrictions on French citizens throughout the Ottoman Empire, the Porte was still awaiting the arrival of the much-heralded French ambassador and in the meantime tried to calm the population by issuing a series of bizarre *firmans* affirming that 'the French were still the allies of His Highness [the Sultan] and should be treated as such, although a certain Buonaparte had invaded a part of Egypt. Indeed, that rebellious general had abused the trust of the French Republic; on his own private initiative, he had invaded Ottoman territory with ships and troops that had been put in his charge for an entirely different purpose. Consequently, the hostilities occasioned by the defection of General Buonaparte should in no manner affect the friendly disposition of the Porte toward the French nation.'[2] While the Porte issued these *firmans*—intended, no doubt, for the protection of French residents but possibly also to afford the French government an opening to disavow Bonaparte, call off the Egyptian expedition, and thus save face—Bonaparte himself surpassed even the Porte in the art of white lying: to minimize the effect produced on the sheiks of Cairo by the destruction of his fleet, he blithely told them that Nel-

---

[1] Ibid., II, 602

[2] Ibid., II, 603

son's fleet had been obliged to leave Abukir Bay to escape pursuit by a fresh French squadron.

Two days after Nelson's victory, Talleyrand, in a very interesting confidential letter to Ruffin, clarified the real intentions of the French government: 'All trade in the Mediterranean must ... pass into French hands. This is the secret wish of the Directory, and, moreover, it will be the inevitable result of our position in that sea.... Egypt, a country France always has desired, belongs of necessity to the Republic. Fortunately the consistently insolent and atrocious attitude of the beys toward us and the Forte's powerlessness to give us satisfaction have allowed us to introduce ourselves into Egypt and to fix ourselves there without exposing ourselves to the charges of lawlessness and ambition.... The Directory is determined to maintain itself in Egypt by all possible means.'[1]

Since the Turks were not in possession of the French cipher, they probably never had the satisfaction of seeing this barefaced avowal of Western duplicity. Still, they knew enough not to be taken in by the naïve lies of the French. Until the news of Abukir, they avoided a break with France and resisted the arguments of the British and Russian ambassadors. When the full extent of the French defeat became known in Constantinople toward the end of August, the Russians and English intensified their pressure, leaving the Turks no choice. Yet even in declaring war, Turkish manners remained exquisite.

At 2 p.m. on September 2, Ruffin received a polite invitation from Prince Ypsilanti to call on the Reis Effendi at the Seraglio. He went there, accompanied by his dragomans Dantan and Kieffer, and was received in solemn audience by the Reis Effendi and several other ministers. Coffee was served, for nothing of importance could be transacted without coffee. No sooner had Ruffin put down his cup than the Reis Effendi made a little speech. The Sublime Porte, he said, was pained to see an allied power seize, without warning, her most precious province, 'which must be regarded as the navel of Islam' because of its proximity to Mecca and Medina. The Sublime Porte had long been unable to believe any reports to that effect. Unfortunately, 'the glorious imperial divan, having ascertained the fact to be true, has resolved that, following the custom in case of a break of diplomatic relations, and by an order written in the Emperor's own hand, you shall be taken immediately to the Fortress of the Seven Towers; that all the French consuls and merchants resident in the well-guarded territories of

---

[1] Ibid., II, 607-8.

His Highness shall be arrested and their merchandise sequestered; and that you and the officials of your legation shall be detained until ... with God's help Egypt has been restored to the authority of our invincible Emperor and master.'[1]

Everyone having finished his coffee, a detachment of Janissaries escorted Ruffin, Dantan, and Kieffer to the Seven Towers 'through a crowd of curious bystanders who lined the streets, shops, and windows without allowing themselves a single shout or threatening gesture.'[2] In his prison, Ruffin had ample leisure to relate these events to Talleyrand in the report just quoted. On September 9, the Reis Effendi handed the formal declaration of war to the Spanish ambassador, who transmitted it to the French Foreign Office.

To Citizen Ruffin belonged the distinction of being the only representative of France ever to be locked up in the Seven Towers. It was a treatment traditionally reserved by the Sublime Porte for ambassadors of nations on which war had been declared, on the theory that ambassadors were not representatives but hostages. One might think that their prison was comfortable if not luxurious: a cursory inspection of the Seven Towers will dispel this illusion. They are a grim complex of dungeons forming part of the great wall that surrounds Stamboul—windowless, chilly, and medieval. General Bonaparte might well be angry with Citizen Talleyrand for not having gone to Constantinople, but Citizen Talleyrand had every reason to congratulate himself on his lack of zeal.

On the same day, September 2, while Ruffin was drinking coffee with the Reis Effendi, Talleyrand at last appointed an ambassador to Constantinople. Before Citizen Descorches, the ambassador designate, had time to leave France, Turkey's declaration of war reached Paris. Yet as late as December, Bonaparte still refused to believe—or pretended not to believe—that the Sultan had declared war and that Talleyrand was not in Constantinople. For four months he persisted in proclaiming himself the best friend of Sultan Selim, thus giving the most brilliantly successful example on record of ostrich policy.

***

On July 25, 1799, almost a year to the day after Nelson's triumph, a large Turkish army, recently landed on Abukir beach, was

---

[1] Ibid., III, 232.

[2] Ibid., III, 233.

destroyed there by Bonaparte's forces. Several thousand Turks—
10,000, according to Bonaparte—were drowned as they tried to
swim out to their transports through the sparkling surf which
breaks on that splendid sun-drenched beach. The circumstances
leading to that grim bathing party will be related in their proper
place. It was, by a seemingly fatal chain of events, the direct result
of the nocturnal fire works of August 1-2, 1798; it also was the immediate cause of another chain of events leading to Bonaparte's
return to France, the *coup de état* of 18 Brumaire, the Consulate,
the Empire, and an infinitesimal rock in the middle of the South
Atlantic.

Every happening contains an infinity of potential consequences; the actual consequences are determined, not by a fatal
necessity inherent in the event itself but, very often, by a number
of only remotely related and usually trivial circumstances. Thus it
may be said that Nelson's victory did not at all bring about the results he expected from it, though of necessity it brought about important results. His victory was as great a military success as any
man can achieve in a single battle.

How could he foresee that by paving the way for a formidable
coalition against France he was offering Bonaparte the opportunity to defeat the coalition and gain all Europe? The only thing
that can be foreseen is that a hundred, two hundred years after an
event, whatever it may be, even the faintest ripples of its consequences will have vanished as completely as the impact of cannon
balls and the struggles of dying men have vanished from the surface of Abukir Bay. There, nothing remains but a cross on a tiny
Barrén island, to mark the spot where the victors buried their
dead.

Chapter Five
Policy of Peaceful Coexistence

CAIRO, which has more than 500,000 inhabitants, has the world's ugliest rabble,'[1] Bonaparte wrote to the Directory the day he entered that fabled city. If not the ugliest populace, it was, at any rate, the most polychromatic, ranging from black Nubians to milky-white Circassians. Whatever his colour, the average Egyptian towered about a head above the average Frenchman, wore far more picturesque clothes, and displayed a physiognomy which, though it might conceal the gentlest of souls, presaged the slitting of throats, regardless of whether it scowled or smiled.

The most conspicuous feature of Cairo, however, was the total absence of such amenities as even the least spoiled of Parisians took for granted. 'This city,' declared the paymaster Peyrusse, 'does not deserve its great reputation. It is filthy, badly built, and populated by horrible dogs.'[2] Major Detroye describes the filth with expansive lyricism: "Once you enter Cairo,' he asked, 'what do you find? Narrow, unpaved, and dirty streets, dark houses that are falling to pieces, public buildings that look like dungeons, shops that look like stables, an atmosphere redolent of dust and garbage, blind men, half-blind men, bearded men, people dressed in rags, pressed together in the streets or squatting, smoking their pipes,

---

[1] Correspondance, IV, 252.

[2] Charles-Roux, Bonaparte, p. 254

like monkeys at the entrance of their cave; a few women of the people ... hideous, disgusting, hiding their fleshless faces under stinking rags and displaying their pendulous breasts through their torn gowns; yellow, skinny children covered with suppuration, devoured by flies; an unbearable stench, due to the dirt in the houses, the dust in the air, and the smell of food being fried in bad oil in the unventilated bazaars. When you have finished sight seeing, you return to your house. No comfort, not a single convenience. Flies, mosquitoes, a thousand insects are waiting to take possession of you during the night. Bathed in sweat, exhausted, you spend the hours devoted to rest itching and breaking out in boils. You rise in the morning, unutterably sick, bleary-eyed, queasy in the stomach, with a bad taste in your mouth, your body covered with pimples, or rather ulcers. Another day begins, the exact copy of the preceding one.'[1]

A visit to the poorer quarters of Cairo even today will convince any one that Major Detroye's description of Cairo in the summer of 1798 is not exaggerated, though it betrays his determined blindness to the city's more beautiful features. The streets were not only unpaved and filthy; they were also impassable during the day and unlit at night. A personage of any consequence would never ride out without a troop of runners armed with sticks, who cleared the path with indiscriminate blows; at night, he would be escorted by torchbearers. Sanitation and hygiene were unknown. Packs of wild dogs, often rabid, roamed about without interference; when the French had several thousand of them poisoned one night, it was an event that El-Djabarti deemed worthy of including in his chronicle, as was the French edict that corpses could no longer be buried in streets and public squares, be the deceased ever so holy. Blindness from trachoma, still prevalent, was even more common then. The rate of infant mortality was staggering.

Even the houses of the rich, despite the profusion of luxury, lacked certain elementary comforts. One of the few exceptions was the palace inhabited by Bonaparte, belonging to Mohammed Bey el-Elfi, who had just finished building it when the arrival of the French forced him to flee to Upper Egypt: apart from its staircases of marble, alabaster, and polished granite from Aswan, aside from its mosaic floors and the monumental fountain in its reception room, it had a bath on every floor, and there were glass panes in the windows.

---

[1] Ibid., p. 256

As for entertainment, the French found nothing on a level higher than snake charming and belly dancing. The snake charmers, Denon found, were clever frauds; the dancing girls, he conceded, were pretty and graceful, but their dance, 'voluptuous at first, soon became lascivious, and conveyed nothing but the gross and indecent expression of sensual intoxication;' also, 'they drank hard liquor in tall glasses as if it were lemonade.'[1] One suspects that the majority of the French soldiers were less prim than Denon in their appreciation of this most gratifying art, which Egypt has brought to perfection. The more intellectual pursuits, however, except for the study of theology and law, had come upon hard times since the days of the caliphs. Only the Christian Copts and a handful of sheiks and imams could read and write. Until the arrival of the French, there were only two printing presses in the whole Ottoman Empire, neither of them in Egypt. Windmills and wheelbarrows were unknown until introduced by the French. The Mosque El Azhar, once the glorious centre of Moslem learning, though it retained its reputation among the pious, was infested with fanatic beggars and fakirs, and its school was a stronghold of conservatism which impeded rather than fostered the pursuit of knowledge. The richest land in the world, a cradle of civilization, Egypt had become the picture of ignorance, poverty, superstition, disease, and contempt for human dignity.

All this, General Bonaparte was determined to change.

He was preparing for a long stay. Shortly after his arrival in Cairo, he jotted down a list of items he proposed to have shipped from France, among them 'a troupe of actors; a troupe of ballerinas; at least three or four puppeteers, for the common people; about a hundred French women, the wives of all those serving in this country; twenty surgeons, thirty pharmacists, ten physicians; foundry workers; liqueur manufacturers and distillers; about fifty gardeners and their families, and seeds of every variety of vegetable; ... 500,000 ells of blue and scarlet cloth; soap and oil.'[2] Each convoy was to bring 200,000 pints of spirits and a million pints of wine. Nothing of all this ever arrived. The second convoy, which Bonaparte was expecting at any moment, was called off by the Directory in August, the ships and their cargo being deemed more essential to Italy than to Egypt. After receiving news of the Battle of the Nile, the Directory ceased to make any serious or sustained effort to assist Bonaparte or even to communicate with him.

---

[1] Denon, I, 82.

[2] Correspondance, IV, 273.

When he was making plans, in late July, for a permanent French occupation of Egypt, only three cities—Alexandria, Rosetta, and Cairo—were under his control. Yet even if he had foreseen then that his fleet would be destroyed, that Turkey would declare war, and that his own government would leave him in the lurch, he would have acted precisely as he did. His temperament—his greatness—made it impossible for him to admit the hopelessness of any situation. He began by pretending that he controlled Egypt. To make his pretence a reality he ordered Desaix to pursue and destroy Murad Bey's forces, set out himself in pursuit of Ibrahim Bey, and detached several of his generals to occupy the Delta, Damietta, and the north-eastern provinces.

Desaix's campaign, one of the most remarkable in modern times, will be the subject of a later chapter. It took him 550 miles south to the First Cataract of the Nile, always tracking, sometimes defeating, but never destroying the elusive Murad Bey; it did not establish effective, permanent control. As for Ibrahim Bey, Bonaparte mauled him at Es Saliya but could not prevent him from escaping, with his warriors, slaves, and wives, across the Sinai Desert into Syria, where he remained a constant threat. The Delta Egypt's richest and most populated region was nominally occupied without resistance. But to take a few large towns and leave garrisons in them is not the same as to control a country or its population. The townspeople made a show of friendliness, but the Delta peasants, whose villages formed veritable fortresses, were for the most part decidedly inhospitable, and even the cities were not always safe.

Here, for example, is the report made to Colonel Laugier by Private Mourchon of the Dragoons, sole survivor of the garrison of El Mansura:

> General Vial, when passing through El Mansura, left a detachment of 120 men The day after General Vial left with his battalion, three soldiers of the garrison were assassinated by the inhabitants, one being stoned while standing guard duty, another while bringing soup to a sentry, the third while returning from his post.... From then on, we barricaded ourselves in the house we used for a barracks.... [About two days later] at approximately 8 a.m., the barracks was surrounded by a large number of Moslems, carrying various weapons. One of them tried to set the house on fire ... but was killed by one of our dragoons: they then tried to tear the house down. In short, the fighting ... lasted until 4 p.m. We then marched out of the house, in which

we had lost eight men.... As we marched through the streets to leave the town, we were shot at continuously from the windows; we returned the fire as best we could. When we reached the open country, the same individuals pursued us and kept firing. Some of them ran to nearby villages to look for reinforcements.... During the retreat, a bullet traversed my left thigh.... At daybreak, there were twenty-five or thirty of us left, and we were still pursued by the enemy.... Having run out of cartridges, we defended ourselves with steel. The wounded, of whom there were ten, preferred drowning themselves to falling into the enemy's hands. When only fifteen of us were left, a multitude of infuriated peasants threw themselves upon us, stripped us of our clothes, and massacred us, my comrades and me, with clubs; I threw myself into the Nile all naked with the intention of drowning myself, but since I can swim, instinct proved the stronger and I reached the opposite shore.... I began to walk without any fixed purpose. I saw seven Moslem horsemen approaching and threw myself into the Nile again. Having noticed that two of them were beckoning to me, I returned on shore; one of them fired at me point-blank, but his carbine jammed; the other said something to the effect that I should be spared and handed me over to two armed peasants ... who tied my hands and led me to a village along a thorny path on which I suffered much, being barefoot and wounded. At the village, the inhabitants unbound me, took care of me, fed me, and showed me much kindness. I remained thus ... until today, when the villagers came ... to tell me that a barge loaded with French soldiers was passing by.... I cannot omit mentioning that the person who took care of me most was a child about eight years old who secretly brought me boiled eggs and bread.'[1]

In mid-September 1798, Generals Menou and Marmont, accompanied by a number of civilians of the Scientific Commission and an escort of some 200 men, crossed the Nile to reconnoitre the Delta east of Rosetta. The friendly reception the population had given Menou until then made him a little careless. Riding ahead of his escort with only fifteen men, seven of them, civilians, he was suddenly attacked by a swarm of armed peasants. The geologist Dolomieu, the musician Villoteau, the artist Denon defended themselves with their swords and pistols while retreating

---

[1] La Jonquière, II, 468-69.

with the rest; not so the painter Joly. 'Citizen Joly,' Menou reported to Bonaparte, 'having lost his head completely, threw himself from his horse and screamed in terror.... We begged him insistently to get back on his horse or to get up behind someone else, but he had lost his head to such a point that he would not listen to anything.... We were finally obliged to leave him behind; he was taken and killed.'[1]

The Alexandria region, after two months of occupation, was just as unsafe as the Delta; this the passengers of the courier ship *L'Anemone* found out immediately after landing, *L'Anemone* had left Toulon on June 17, carrying the courier Lesimple, to whom the Directory had entrusted despatches for Bonaparte. At Civita Vecchia she picked up several other passengers, including General Camin. On September 2, she came within sight of Alexandria. To avoid being captured by the English squadron, her captain decided to beach her near Marabut. No sooner had the passengers reached shore than a party of Bedouins attacked them. Those who resisted—among them Camin—were killed and stripped. One officer, under the impression that his clothes were all the Arabs wanted, stripped himself and started to run, forgetting in his excitement that he was carrying his trousers in his hands: he too was killed. Another passenger, Citizen Devouges, ran stark naked into the surf for safety, although he could not swim. Whenever he came up for air, several Bedouins, in the water to their waists, fired at him. Gamin's adjutant Bella turned up next to him in the strong surf. 'We remained thus,' says Devouges, 'holding each other embraced, for a quarter of an hour, during which we saw several of our comrades being massacred.' A high wave knocked Devouges down; when he re-emerged after some struggle, both his pursuers and Bella had vanished. 'Soon,' he says, 'I felt a corpse floating by my side.... I lifted his head: it was Bella's. A poor drowned child, twelve years old, was floating next to him.'[2]

The Bedouins spared about twenty members of the party, including Lesimple, to ransom them off. General Kléber bought them back. On September 8, the intrepid Lesimple handed what was left of his despatches to Bonaparte in Cairo: it was the Directory's congratulations on the capture of Malta, and nothing else.

---

[1] Ibid., III, 114.

[2] La Jonquière, III, 61-62.

On the day of Lesimple's arrival in Cairo, Bonaparte wrote to the Directory: 'All goes perfectly well here. The country is under our control and the people are becoming used to us.'[1]

To be a conqueror requires unusual optimism and an outsize pair of blinkers.

II

Nothing indicates that Bonaparte either enjoyed or disliked reprisals. He was neither cruel nor kind, neither inhuman nor soft. Outrages had to be punished, lest they be encouraged: and thus entire communities were sacked and burned, Bedouin tribes had their flocks and cattle, their only means of livelihood, taken away, and individual heads fell by the score. 'Everyday,' he wrote to Menou on July 31, 'I have five or six people beheaded in the streets of Cairo.'[2] He applied equally severe measures against French marauders. A student of Machiavelli, he held that severity consistently applied does not breed hatred but respect and, in the long run, causes less bloodshed than ill-advised leniency. His main objective was to win the confidence of the people—confidence in his severity as well as in his good intentions—and the co-operation of the ruling class, which desires nothing more than order and stability. No European colonizer went farther in his attempts to win the natives to his side (rather than to put them in their place) than did Bonaparte. If his efforts were crowned with total failure, the fault lay not with his policy, which deserved to succeed, but with the improvisatory, inconsistent, and seemingly capricious methods which circumstances forced him to adopt in the details of its execution. Above all, it lay in the impossibility of the task set before him.

The chief obstacle to establishing an atmosphere of mutual trust was, of course, Islam. Bonaparte might proclaim three times a day that he was not a Christian, nor were his men; that the French had imprisoned the Pope and closed the churches, that they respected Islam—all of which was more or less true. To Moslems, the difference between Christians, Deists, worshippers of the Goddess of Reason or of the Supreme Being, Theophilanthropists, Atheists, or Jews, was insignificant: none were Moslems, consequently all were Infidels. The Mamelukes, the Ottoman Turks were Moslems: they might squeeze the people dry and let their domains

[1] Correspondance, IV, 475.
[2] Ibid., IV, 286.

go to seed, but they were brothers. As soon as the French had humbled the hated Mamelukes, the hated Mamelukes became objects of compassion. When, upon the intervention of the sheiks of Cairo, Bonaparte released his Mameluke prisoners, many of them went, 'in a pitiful state of poverty, to the Mosque El Azhar and installed themselves there. They fed on the alms distributed to them by the poor students. In this those who have eyes to see will observe a beautiful example.'[1] Thus wrote the sheik El-Djabarti, an enlightened Moslem, who in that single phrase conveys much that is most admirable in Islam: the oppressed feeding their fallen oppressors, not so much out of pity as out of a sense of brotherhood.

Still, although the people of Egypt, high and low, were justified in doubting Napoleon's sincerity when he advertised himself as a virtual Moslem, their fear that he might destroy their religion was unfounded. What he did wish to destroy was their inertia, their traditionalism, their submissiveness to a fate that was not fate, their reluctance to emerge from the Middle Ages and help him improve their lot. (The fact that French colonists would have profited from such a change does not signify that the Egyptians would not have profited even more.) It took a century and a half longer for Islam to realize that Moslems could keep their religion and traditions intact and yet move with the times. Bonaparte was in a poor position to teach them that lesson: his propaganda was sincere as far as ultimate aims were concerned, but patently hypocritical in its play on religious sentiment and popular superstition. Even more important, his military situation after Nelson's victory was so precarious that all his appeals to Moslem sentiment had the sound of desperate makeshifts rather than sincere persuasion. The insane lengths to which he eventually carried his religious policy lend some plausibility to this invidious interpretation.

With only a small expeditionary force at his disposal to control as vast and dangerous a country as Egypt, Bonaparte had to rely on the local élite to govern it for him. His first choice as local administrator, the sherif Mohammed el-Koraim of Alexandria, turned out a fiasco. El-Koraim's patent treachery and lack of cooperation forced Kléber to replace him, in July 1798, with the more reliable sheik El-Messiri and to send him under guard to his protector Bonaparte, for final disposition. On September 5, Bonaparte sentenced El-Koraim to death but left him the alternative,

[1] El-Djabarti, VI, 26-27.

according to local custom, of buying his life for 50,000 talari.[1] El-Koraim, from fatalism or avarice, refused to pay. He was shot in the Citadel of Cairo, and his head was paraded through the streets. Since he was a descendant of Mohammed, remarks Nicholas the Turk, this produced an unfavourable effect on the people.

Despite this inauspicious beginning, Bonaparte persisted in setting up local government with the help of Moslem notables. The day after his entry into Cairo, he created the general pattern by appointing a municipal divan, or council, chosen from among the principal sheiks; a French commissioner was assigned to the divan as observer.[2] The role of the Divan of Cairo and of the provincial divans patterned on it was essentially to legalize French policies and to sanction them with the prestige of the ulemas and law sheiks who composed them. 'By gaining the support of the great sheiks of Cairo,' Bonaparte wrote to Kléber, 'one gains the public opinion of all Egypt. Of all the leaders that nation could have, none are less dangerous to us than the sheiks, who are timid and incapable of fighting and who, like all priests, inspire fanaticism without being fanatics themselves.'[3] Aside from this primary function, the divans transmitted popular grievances to the French authorities and served as a sounding board of public opinion. In that last capacity, they were exceedingly unreliable, as any body of compliant yet secretly hostile men must be.

On September 4, Bonaparte went one step further and summoned a 'General Divan' for all Egypt to meet at Cairo a month later. Each regional deputation was to consist of three law sheiks, three merchants and three representatives of, respectively, the fellahin (peasants), the sheiks-el-beled (mayors), and the Bedouin tribes. Although the deputies were chosen by the French provincial commanders, the General Divan, a representative assembly without precedent in the Orient, might well have become the Estates

---

[1] The talaro was the equivalent of the Imperial Thaler. At 4 gold francs to the talaro, it was approximately equivalent to 5 shillings in 1798.

[2] This office eventually fell to Citizen Tallien, the man who had led the Convention in overthrowing Robespierre on 9 Thermidor, 1794. The one thing Bonaparte and Tallien had in common was that both their wives had been mistresses of the Director Barras. Having come upon hard days, both politically and maritally, Tallien managed to have himself attached to the Economic Section of the Scientific Commission; he arrived at Alexandria aboard the aviso (courier ship) *Le Vif* August 13 and received a pointedly chilly welcome from Kléber, who detested politicians.

[3] Correspondance, V, 574.

General of Egypt; it will be seen that the deputies preferred to reduce its importance to nil.

By creating the divans, Bonaparte secured the outward support—though by no means the loyalty or trust—of the most influential and stable elements in Egyptian society. But there were certain unpopular functions of government whose execution neither the French nor the native Moslems wished to assume—tax collecting and police. Before Bonaparte's arrival, the Mamelukes had collected their taxes through Coptic agents. The Copts remnants of the Christian population of Egypt before the Moslem conquest were qualified for that task by their education, subservience, and financial experience. Although Bonaparte estimated that a large part of the moneys the Copts collected from the fellahin stuck to their fingers, he had no choice but to continue employing them in their former capacity. A hierarchy of Coptic tax gatherers was created; each provincial 'intendant' had an office staff under him and a French commissioner at his side, and the whole Coptic pyramid was headed by an Intendant General, Moallem Girges el-Gouhary.[1] These fiscal agents, now endowed with an official capacity, 'conducted themselves,' says El-Djabarti, 'like high officials—that is to say, they beat the people and had them thrown in prison.'[2]

As for the police, Bonaparte created Janissary companies composed of Turks, Greeks, Moors, and various riffraff. Among the more colourful figures under the French occupation was a Christian Greek adventurer, named Barthelmy or Bartholomew, whom Bonaparte appointed lieutenant of police for Cairo. Flamboyant in appearance and disposition, he headed a corps of about a hundred fierce Greeks, Algerians, and Moroccans. His stature was Herculean. His bronze complexion set off by a gigantic white turban, his eyes flashing, his lips twisted in a spine-chilling smile, dressed in a gold-embroidered Greek tunic, a crimson sash, immense trousers, and a dolman surmounted by a colonel's epaulets, Barthelmy presented an unforgettable sight as he sallied forth at the head of his ruffians. His wife, a formidable Amazon, occasionally cantered at his side. Barthelmy loved combat, which afforded him an opportunity to display his valour and clothes; but what he loved best was a good execution. It has been said that when he could not find any recalcitrant Bedouins whose heads he might take back to Cairo for souvenirs, he consoled himself with the

---

[1] The title Moallem, generally applied to Christians, signified something between 'Mr.' and 'Dr.'

[2] El-Djabarti, VI, 36.

heads of some luckless fellahin who chanced on his way as he returned to the city. Once he presented General Dupuy with a whole sackful of Bedouin heads while Dupuy and some guests were at dinner; he was pained to see that he had spoiled their appetite. As an early historian of the Egyptian campaign put it, 'When one saw him marching toward the Citadel, his naked scimitar in hand and followed by his garroted patients, the spectacle was well suited to suppress all evil intentions in many a heart.'[1]

Although the employment of Christians as tax collectors and security guards was justifiable on grounds of expediency, it tended, as El-Djabarti points out, to give the non-Moslem population a mistaken notion of equality. Christians and Jews were seen riding on horseback, just like their Moslem betters; they carried arms; they no longer effaced themselves; their wives set a wicked example by going unveiled and imitating European customs.[2] The Moslems' complaints eventually forced Bonaparte to order native Christians and Jews to resume wearing their distinctive dark turbans, plain belts, and black shoes. 'No matter what you do to the Christians,' he wrote to Kléber, 'they will always be our friends. You must prevent them from becoming too insolent.'[3]

**

Bonaparte's policy of controlling Egypt by conciliating the Moslem was deceptively successful at first. None of the Egyptian notables who held office under him imitated Mohammed el-Koraim's example. Yet his religious policy was not completely founded on mere expediency. His respect for Islam was sincere because it resulted from his purely practical attitude toward religion. 'In religion,' he told the *Conseil d'Etat* in 1806, 'I ... see the mystery of the social order.'[4] Without religion, there could be no government, no polity. Islam, in his eyes, was better suited to the needs of the political order than was Christianity because it did not encourage conflict between the material and the spiritual worlds. When, in 1797, Bonaparte wrote to the bishop of Como that 'the morality of the Gospels is ... the morality best suited to the republican form of government,'[5] he probably was less sincere than

---

[1] Belliard, *Histoire*, cited in Ivray, p. 33

[2] Until 1798, all non-Moslem women except consuls' wives were obliged to conform to the Moslem custom of veiling their faces.

[3] Correspondance, V, 574.

[4] Pelet, p. 223.

[5] Correspondance, III, 24.

when he informed the sheik El-Messiri a year later of his intention 'to establish a uniform government, based on the principles of the Koran, which alone are true and capable of bringing happiness to men.'[1]

To respect the religion and traditions of a conquered country is sound policy; Bonaparte, however, pushed his courtship of Islam far beyond respect. The sacrilegious histrionics to which he eventually resorted were forced on him—or so he thought—by two highly embarrassing circumstances: one was a chronic lack of cash, the other was Turkey's declaration of war. Of his financial predicament more will be said later; as for the Sultan's declaration of war, it was so inconvenient to Bonaparte that he chose to pretend for almost four months that it had not happened, although he must have known of it since early October.

At the beginning of his administration in Egypt, Bonaparte believed in good faith that Talleyrand had gone to Constantinople and that an amicable arrangement with the Porte would be worked out. He wrote repeatedly to the Pasha of Cairo, who had fled with Ibrahim Bey, begging him to return. 'I beseech you to assure the Porte that it will suffer no loss whatsoever;' he added, 'I promise that it will receive the same tribute as before.'[2] He also wrote directly to the Grand Vizier, offering the same assurances and an alliance against Russia. All these letters remained unanswered, and not a word arrived from France concerning Talleyrand's mission.

Although Bonaparte's professed aim in coming to Egypt was to humble the Mameluke beys, he sought to come to terms with them shortly after the Battle of the Pyramids. On August 1, the day of the Battle of the Nile, he gave full powers to Carlo Rosetti, the Austrian consul in Cairo, to negotiate with Murad Bey and offer him the government of Girga province in Upper Egypt. Murad received Rosetti, of whom he had always been very fond, with much cordiality and gave him the following reply to take back to Bonaparte: 'Tell the commander-in-chief to assemble all his troops and go back to Alexandria. I shall pay him 10,000 gold purses to cover his army's expenses. In doing so, he will spare his soldiers' lives and save me the trouble of fighting him.'[3] It was after receiving this

---

[1] Ibid., IV, 420.

[2] Ibid., IV, 243-44.

[3] Nicolas Turc, cited in La Jonquière, II, 474-75.

answer that Bonaparte ordered Desaix to pursue and destroy Murad's forces.

Since the Bedouins co-operated with them, the Mamelukes received news faster than did Bonaparte. In all likelihood Murad Bey already knew of the destruction of the French fleet when he made his haughty reply. Ibrahim Bey, to whom Bonaparte made similar overtures on August 12 at Es Saliya, undoubtedly was informed of the naval defeat (which was still unknown to Bonaparte) and did not deign to answer. As the beys saw it, the eventual expulsion of the French from Egypt was merely a question of time.

Ignored by the Porte and insulted by the beys, Bonaparte patiently probed in yet other directions. On August 22 he sent one of his staff officers, Major Beauvoisins, to deliver a letter to Ahmed Pasha, governor of Acre. Better known as Djezzar 'the Butcher'—a surname in which he gloried—the seventy-year-old Ahmed had lorded it over Syria for several decades. His savage cruelty was legendary, as was his violent hatred of the French. Capable of raising and arming 100,000 men, Djezzar Pasha presented the most immediate threat to Bonaparte. He did not receive Beauvoisins but read Bonaparte's letter, in which the French commander proposed a treaty of amity and commerce: it threw him into a towering rage. Beauvoisins was lucky to leave Acre alive. Both Jaffa and Acre, he reported after his return, were seething with ferment, and the Porte had given Djezzar the military command over all Syria. Beauvoisins did not know that during his stay at Acre the Porte had resolved to make war on France.[1]

Bonaparte's letters to the Bey of Tripoli and to the Pasha of Damascus also met with silence. Only the Sherif of Mecca, who depended for his revenues on the pilgrim caravans from Cairo and on coffee exports to Egypt, responded reassuringly; yet even his reassurances turned out to be somewhat deceptive. Bonaparte's protestations of friendship for the Sultan and for Islam must have struck all these potentates as a piece of impudence bordering on insanity, especially since they reached them days or even weeks after the Sultan's Tartar couriers had brought them His Highness' proclamation of war on the French.

---

[1] Captain Mailly de Chateaurenaud, whom Bonaparte sent to Syria to establish contact with the French consuls at Latakia and Aleppo, met a worse fate: Djezzar had him thrown into prison as soon as he landed and had him executed in 1799, when Bonaparte invaded Syria. See below, Chapter IX.

The Turkish declaration of war almost instantly set in motion a series of catastrophes of which Bonaparte became fully aware only in December and January. Early in September, a Russian fleet entered the Bosphorus and was cheered by the Turks, which was about the same as if the Montagues had cheered the Capulets. Also in September, Hassan Pasha of Rhodes received orders to join the British off Alexandria with a Turkish squadron. In October, Ali Pasha of Janina, on whose Francophile sentiments Bonaparte had counted, seized the French mainland installations opposite the Ionian Islands, while the Russian fleet captured Zante, Ithaca, and Cephalonia and blockaded Corfu, which held out until March 5. In the meantime the population of Malta had risen in rebellion against the French, whose commander, General Vaubois, decided to evacuate the countryside and to defend the cities and forts only. On September 19, a Portuguese squadron under Admiral de Niza arrived off Malta; it was soon reinforced by English ships. Vaubois succeeded in holding out for two years, but Malta had become a liability rather than an asset to the French.

By early October 1798, the fact that France's dear friend and ally, the Sultan, had declared war on France was known to every Egyptian above the mental level of idiocy; General Bonaparte continued to ignore and to deny it as a malicious rumour spread by Mamelukes, English men, and fanatic fakirs. His virtuosity in the art of applying blinkers when needed was truly astounding. As late as October 30, after every imam and muezzin in every mosque of Egypt had read the Sultan's *firman* against the French to the people, Bonaparte still doubted its authenticity. It was on that day that he ordered the interpreter Bracevich and a Moslem dignitary of Turkish extraction to present themselves aboard the Anglo-Turkish fleet off Alexandria on the pre text of a routine parley and to gather what news they could. The Turks and English were astonished and amused to see the emissaries arrive under the Turkish flag. They received them with polite irony and let them have all the political news they wanted. The news was so appalling that neither Bracevich nor General Marmont, who was then about to take command in Alexandria, believed a word of it. The ships flying the Turkish flag off Alexandria undoubtedly were *bonafide* Turkish ships, they admitted, but they could not have been sent there by the Porte: the English had merely picked them up at Rhodes after duping the senile Hassan Pasha into believing that the Porte had declared war.

Still plagued by a feeling of uncertainty, Bonaparte sent another emissary, Lieutenant Guibert, aboard the *Zealous* in November, with a letter to Hassan. Commodore Hood was amused. 'So you doubt whether the Porte has declared war on you?' he asked Guibert. 'Well, I give you my word of honour that it has. And Monsieur Bonaparte, what is he doing?' When Monsieur Bonaparte's letter to Hassan was translated for him, Hood 'pretended to shake with laughter.'[1] Hassan himself declared that he would answer neither verbally nor in writing; and so Lieutenant Guibert went back to shore.

Still Bonaparte pretended to be unconvinced. As late as December 11—three months after Citizen Ruffin had been taken to the Seven Towers—he wrote a letter to 'Citizen Talleyrand, ambassador in Constantinople,'[2] and to the Grand Vizier. Surely he was not as ill informed or naïve as he pretended to be. Yet, since he had nothing to gain by acknowledging the state of war, the ostrich policy seemed the best.

III

The yearly cycle of life in Egypt is marked by the cross-rhythm of the sun and the moon. The Nile, whose annual swelling fertilizes the land, obeys the sun: it rises in summer and recedes in autumn, leaving a rich deposit of loam. The Moslem calendar of religious feasts follows the lunar cycle. It so happened that in 1798 the feast celebrating the flooding of the Nile and the feast commemorating the birth of the Prophet fell less than a week apart, on August 18 and August 25, only a month after the capture of Cairo by the French. The conquerors themselves computed their year by yet another system, based on exact astronomic calculations—the French Revolutionary calendar, which replaced the Gregorian calendar from 1792 to 1804, when it was abolished by Napoleon. The revolutionists, Nicholas the Turk observed judiciously, had introduced the new system 'in order to overthrow old habits.'[3] The French year VII began on the sixth anniversary of the First Republic, the 1st Vendémiaire, which fell on September 22, the autumnal equinox.

The possibilities offered by the close conjunction of these three feasts did not escape General Bonaparte, who was the first statesman to make full use of propaganda in its modern sense. He would associate himself and his army with the celebrations greeting the

---

[1] La Jonquière, III, 398-99.

[2] Correspondance, V, 203.

[3] Nicolas Turc, p. 5.

events that gave the people of Egypt their bread and their faith; and he would associate the people of Egypt with the ritual by which the First French Republic commemorated its own birth and the new era of progress and reason. Thus the fraternal relationship of French and Egyptians would be symbolized, and, incidentally, the shock of the disaster at Abukir would be cushioned.

On August 18, shortly after sunrise, General Bonaparte took his seat on a tribune erected in a kiosk at the junction of the Nile and the Khalidj Canal in order to preside over the first of these three feasts. Beside him sat his generals, in dress uniform, mingled with the members of the Divan of Cairo and with other Moslem notables, richly beturbaned, opulently bearded, and covered with the fur-trimmed caftans denoting their dignity. That either Moslems or Frenchmen could bear up in this attire under the Egyptian August sun seems incredible. Part of the French garrison stood by in parade formation, their sonorous bands alternating with the shrill instruments of the Egyptian musicians. Then the music stopped and a dignitary read out a proclamation: the 'blessed Nile' having risen above sixteen Cubits according to the Mekyas (the Nilometer on Rodah Island), thanks were due to Allah and the miry to the tax collector. This announcement was greeted with an artillery salvo from the French batteries on shore and those aboard the Nile flotilla; so was the curious pagan ceremony by which the statue of a woman was cast into the river. (In ancient times, a real virgin, supposedly the most beautiful in all Egypt, used to be sacrificed to the river god, a custom which persisted into early Christian times. The Moslem conquerors, either because they had better use for beautiful virgins or because they found it difficult to find any, substituted the symbol.)

While the bands were playing, the dike separating the Nile from the canal was cut, and another gun salute greeted the rushing water as it filled the canal bed, taking with it a flotilla of boats and barges. Soon the inundation covered the countryside and many of the streets and squares of Cairo, which was transformed into an African Venice. At night the coloured lanterns of the boats illuminated the city. Normally, at this time of the year, Esbekiya Square, where Bonaparte had his headquarters, became a vast basin on which, in the words of a poet, 'one could see birds floating on the water's surface like stars in the celestial vault.'[1] Not so in 1798: wishing to use the square as an ordnance park, Bonaparte had

[1] Ivray, p. 19.

taken measures to prevent the waters from reaching it. Instead of birds there were guns.

Although popular enthusiasm was manifestly absent, Bonaparte chose to regard the celebration of the Nile Festival as a great personal success. According to the *Courrier de L'Egypte* (the first newspaper printed in Egypt), he was escorted on his return to Esbekiya 'by an immense crowd of people chanting the praises of the Prophet and of the French army'[1] a journalistic hyperbole flatly contradicted by the sober El-Djabarti.

The festivities commemorating the birth of Mohammed were to begin on the night of August 20. They took place on Bonaparte's command, the religious leaders having decided to omit public celebrations that year on account of the 'critical times.' For three nights and days pandemonium went crescendo. The streets of Cairo turned into a nocturnal bazaar, while thousands marched in procession, carrying torches and enormous candelabras, singing 'baroque chants accompanied by an even more baroque music' (the words are Major Detroye's), and 'shouting, screaming, and making an infernal racket.' On August 23 the rejoicings reached their climax. 'The public squares,' Detroye noted in his diary, 'are covered with small sideshows—trained bears and monkeys, male and female singers performing scenes in dialogue, women singing poetry, jugglers making snakes disappear, children performing extremely lewd dances.... Toward evening the holy men appeared: the populace shows much veneration for these fanatics, who wear their hair long and go practically naked.... The devout gathered in groups, forming circles of men sitting close together, their arms linked. Then they began to sway in a violent motion, each man individually and the entire circle collectively from side to side; this motion was accompanied by strenuous spasms and lasted until their strength was exhausted.'[2] The holy fakirs rather astonished the French. Many of them ran around stark naked, 'in permanent ecstasy,' as a report of the Scientific Commission puts it, and nothing was forbidden to them: women regarded themselves sanctified by sexual contact with them, and on feast days they often formed a protective circle around a holy man and his chosen vessel.[3]

While Major Detroye, a trifle bewildered, was watching these scenes, General Bonaparte attended gravely and impassively at the

---

[1] Courrier de L'Egypte, 12 Fructidor, Year VI

[2] La Jonquière, II, 481-2.

[3] Cited in Malus, p. 90.

prayers held in the house of the sheik El-Bekri, whom he had just invested with the ermine caftan of the nahib al-ashraf or head of the sherifs. Seated on a cushion, cross-legged, his black uniform buttoned to the chin, solemn-faced, his slight and nervous figure must have contrasted strangely with the sheiks in their robes and turbans as they swayed rhythmically to the verses of the Koran and told their prayer beads. His mind undoubtedly strayed toward other matters than those being transacted, as a selective list of his activities during these days must suggest:

On August 22 he dictated, among other things, instructions to General Desaix concerning operations against Murad Bey; instructions to General Dugua, recommending that he have at least nine or ten heads chopped off in Mansura, by way of reprisal; instructions to General Vial for the protection of pious foundations and holy places; a letter to the Grand Vizier, protesting friendship for the Sultan; instructions to Major Beauvoisins regarding his mission to Djezzar Pasha, and a letter to Djezzar Pasha; several severe orders concerning illegal financial transactions; an order requesting that the physicians and surgeons who had failed that day to visit one of the wards in Military Hospital No. 1 be sent to the guardhouse; the list of members and the by-laws of the Institute of Egypt, founded by him that day for the purposes of '(1) the progress and propagation of the sciences in Egypt; (2) research, study, and publication of natural, industrial, and historical data on Egypt; (3) advising on various questions concerning which the Government shall consult it;'[1] and an order fixing the pay rate of the Company of Janissaries in Alexandria.

On August 23, the General dictated an order establishing in the Citadel of Cairo two baking ovens, a food depot, and a hospital to be used in the event of siege; an order requisitioning 5,000 horses; and an Order of the Day prohibiting all subordinate commanders from levying contributions on the population and instructing them to prevent the peasantry from appropriating more than their share of water from the Nile and the canals. He also attended, before going to El-Bekri's house, the first meeting of the Institute of Egypt and proposed, for its consideration, the following questions: (1) Can the army's baking ovens be improved, and if so, how? (2) Is there a way of brewing beer without hops (which were not grown in Egypt)? (3) What methods were in use to purify Nile water? (4) Which was more practical in Cairo—windmills or water mills? (5) Are there any resources in Egypt for the manufacture of gunpow-

[1] Correspondance, IV, 283.

der? (6) What was the general situation in Egypt concerning civil law, criminal law, and the teaching of law, and were there any possible improvements that would be acceptable to the population? Besides asking these questions, which range from the trivial to the sublime, Bonaparte had himself elected vice-president of the Institute, thus modestly taking second place to Monge, who became president.

From the Institute of Egypt to the prayers of the sheiks of the Mosque El Azhar it was a long way; but to Napoleon Bonaparte, a human chameleon who, in an instant, could change from warrior to legislator to academician to theologian, the distance seemed non existent. On the following day, August 24, he would tranquilly issue instructions for the transformation of the mosque of Es Saliya into a fort, and on the day after that, he would order the village of Alqam, where sixteen Frenchmen had been ambushed and murdered, to be burned to the ground, its cattle and grain to be confiscated, and its notables to be taken to Cairo as hostages. Perhaps these were the matters he was meditating with a pious air while the sheiks told their prayer beads.

The prayers terminated, Bonaparte took his place as guest of honour at the sheik's banquet, heroically overcame the nausea that inevitably assailed him in the presence of mutton fat, and plunged his hand into the huge mounds of rice, meats, and delicacies served on gigantic round copper trays. To wash all this down, there was lemonade. This feast was followed by a military parade; then the entire general staff, preceded by a military band and escorted by torchbearers, went in procession to El-Bekri's house. A 'wretched display of fireworks,' according to Detroye, concluded the festivities.

Similar celebrations were held in other cities, and the French commanders had been ordered to take part in them. In Alexandria, when feasting at the sheik El-Messiri's house, General Kléber was startled to see that in deference to the French Republic the rice was served up tricoloured.

Unfortunately for Bonaparte's expectations, the Franco-Islamic *rapprochement* proved a one-way affair. When Bonaparte honoured the chairman of the Divan of Cairo, sheik Abdullah el-Charkawi, by placing a tricoloured shawl on his shoulders, the sheik turned red with rage and threw it to the ground, while Bonaparte paled in anger. Venture, the interpreter, explained to the sheiks that the shawl was meant as an honour which would raise them in the eyes of the French. 'But we shall be lowered in the eyes of God,' the sheiks replied, 'and in the hearts of our fellow believers.'¹ Bonaparte gave way over the shawls, but insisted that the sheiks must wear at least a tricoloured cockade pinned to their chests. It became customary for them to pin one on before entering Bonaparte's room and to take it off immediately after leaving. Gradually, the whole matter was quietly forgotten, but not without a struggle on Napoleon's part. One day his horrified staff officers found him all done up in 'Turkish' clothes, in which he wished to receive the Divan, to shame his sheiks into wearing at least the cockade. Tallien, it is said, talked him out of it. 'He cut such a poor figure in his turban and caftan,' recalls Bourrienne, 'he looked so gauche and self-conscious in that unfamiliar garb, that he soon left the room to take it off and never felt tempted to repeat this masquerade.'²

The French New Year celebrations of September 22 offered an opportunity, so Bonaparte thought, to associate the Egyptian people with French institutions. The proceedings were an elaborate farce. They have been described, from rather divergent points of view, by the *Courrier de L'Egypte* and by the sheik El-Djabarti. The day was greeted, at sunrise, by three gun salutes, followed by a drum roll summoning all troops to converge upon Esbekiya Square. There a large circle had been traced, marked by 105 columns (El-Djabarti calls them 'poles'), each decorated with a French flag and symbolizing one of the Republic's 105 *departements*. A festoon linked them together to signify the Republic's unity and indivisibility. (El-Djabarti calls it a rope.) At one end of the square an arch of triumph had been erected, on which the painter Rigo had represented the Battle of the Pyramids; at the opposite end, a portal with the Arabic inscription, 'There is no God but God, and Mohammed is His Prophet ' in the centre, an obelisk seventy feet high, with suitable inscriptions in Arabic and in French, and (quoting the *Courrier*) ' seven altars in antique form, intermingled with candelabras, supporting the trophies of war, which were topped by tricolour flags and civic crowns.'³ While the commander-in-chief, his staff, the principal administrative officials French, Moslem, and Coptic and the members of the Scientific Commission took their seats on a platform covered with precious rugs, the united regimental bands 'executed warlike marches and performed the patriotic airs and the songs of victory that are so dear to all republicans.' 'The band played incessantly,' reports

---

¹ El-Djabarti, VI, 56.

² Bourrienne, II, 167.

³ Courrier de L'Egypte, 6 Vendemiaire, Year VII

El-Djabarti. 'The French cavalry and infantry, drawn up in the square, executed several exercises and fired their muskets and guns. Then the soldiers gathered around the mast [i.e. the obelisk], and one of their chief priests read out to them something written in French. Only they could understand it. This speech apparently was a collection of advice or a sermon.'[1] The sermon was Bonaparte's proclamation, read by a staff officer, which ended with the words: 'Forty million fellow citizens are thinking of you. They all are saying, "It is to their labours and their blood that we shall owe general peace, security, prosperity, and the benefits of civil liberty".'[2] One doubts whether such remarks ever were spoken in unison.

The proclamation was followed by shouts of *Vive la Republique!*, an interminable cantata especially composed for the occasion,[3] and a banquet for 150 guests, given by Bonaparte. For once, French customs took precedence over local ones, and the host had his revenge in making the sheiks eat with knives and forks. Among the toasts, two were remarkable. 'To the improvement of the human mind, to the progress of reason!' said Monge. 'To the three-hundredth anniversary of the French Republic!' said Bonaparte, who was to bury the Republic six years later.

There was a horse race in the afternoon, which is not mentioned by the Arabic chronicler, possibly because a French horse won. 'In the evening, lanterns were lit, and fireworks were shot off for about two hours; the lanterns remained lit until dawn.' Unlike the *Courrier*, El-Dajabarti goes on to relate the morning after: 'Then all the lanterns, ropes, and poles were carted away, but the triumphal arch and the big mast were left. The French placed sentries about the mast, because they pretend that it is the symbol of their country's victories and greatness.'[4]

Bonaparte had also planned a balloon ascent for the occasion, but his chief aeronaut, Conté, was not ready in time. It was only on December 1 that an unmanned balloon was sent up—unmanned, no doubt, because no one cared to volunteer for a flight that might end in the middle of a Bedouin encampment. Everything went wrong. The balloon caught fire; the gondola (or 'cup,' as El-Djabarti calls it) came down, scattering a quantity of printed proc-

---

[1] El-Djabarti, VI, 40

[2] Correspondance, V, 1

[3] Words by Parseval-Grandmaison, music by Rigel.

[4] El-Djabarti, VI, 40.

lamations. The Egyptians felt that they had been had. 'The French turned red with shame,' says the eyewitness El-Djabarti, 'for this was not a ship on which, as they pretended, one could travel through the air from one country to another: it was a mere kite, such as our people fly on weddings and feast days.'[1] Vexed by this reaction—after all, people had crossed the English Channel several times by air—Conté made another attempt some time later. 'The balloon,' reports El-Djabarti, 'rose and travelled in the direction of the Barkiya Hills, where it fell. If the wind had driven it a little farther and out of sight, the trick would have worked and the French would have claimed that it had travelled to a faraway country.'[2]

As propaganda, the balloon ascents were a total fiasco. It takes bigger magic than this to impress a people that invented the Arabian Nights' Tales.

It was not only with the Egyptians that Bonaparte's showmanship fell flat. Malus, the physicist, who had been put in charge of organizing the patriotic pageantry of September 22, found his task 'a weak palliative to the melancholy that had afflicted me for some time.' (He was pining for his German fiancée in Giessen, from whom only one letter got through to him in three years.) 'At that period,' he continues, 'this moral epidemic was spreading rapidly through the army. We were beginning to lose our illusions about the Sultan's attitude toward the expedition, and the future offered us neither hope nor peace of mind. The feast of 1 Vendémiaire was celebrated without enthusiasm.'[3]

IV

When the French troops first arrived, in July 1798, Cairo seemed a ghost city, with no one but stealthy looters abroad. Those of the merchants and wealthy citizens who had not fled were barricaded in their houses. Others, among them many of the Mamelukes' wives and slaves, were roaming in the countryside, trying to elude both the French Devils within the city and the Bedouins outside. The whole of Cairo must have looked very much like that vast and strange City of the Dead, which still extends along its eastern edge—a maze of empty, narrow streets, lifeless but for some stray dogs and cats, a few veiled old women going furtively about their obscure business, and an occasional funeral proces-

---

[1] Ibid., VI, 69

[2] Ibid., VI, 86.

[3] Malus, p. 92.

sion, with the mourners carrying the shrouded corpse on a bier, almost at a quickstep.

The first elements to emerge into daylight after the French arrived were those one might expect: a few European residents, grateful for their rescue, and peddlars of all sorts of wares, including prostitutes. Sergeant François, always quick to size up the lay of the land, managed to have himself invited to breakfast, at 8 a.m. of July 26, by an Italian pharmacist. The breakfast consisted of a large bowl of *café au lait* made with goat's milk and mixed with whiskey. François' testimony should establish once and for all that the ancestor of Gaelic coffee was served by an Italian to a Frenchman in Cairo in 1798. Made expansive by his spiked goat's milk, the pharmacist gave François the lowdown on life in Egypt: 'Everybody is afraid. All they talk about is troubles, public misery, thefts, and murder. Nothing is safe—neither life nor property. They shed a man's blood as if he were an ox. The police officers, on their rounds day and night, judge, condemn, and execute their sentence in an instant and without appeal. They are accompanied by executioners; the instant the order is given, some poor devil's head falls.'[1] As for women, the situation was rotten. However, there was a Turkish proverb that could serve as a rule of thumb: Take a white woman for the eyes, and an Egyptian woman for pleasure.

The liquor situation was positively tragic; witness the heartbreaking appeal, which takes up six printed pages, addressed on July 24 by Colonel Savary, Desaix's aide-de-camp, to a commissioner in Alexandria. After enumerating the personal items to be forwarded to Desaix and his staff (among them Colonel Rapp's possessions—'one cow, one trunk, and his hammock'), the future Duke of Rovigo continues: 'If you can possibly buy a few bottles of good rum, send it.... We have no cook, if you find one, bring him.... We live worse here than we ever did in all our lives. Not a drop of wine or liquor.... Remember: wine, liquor, and rum. We have been needing it desperately for centuries. What little there is of it here is exceedingly bad, exorbitantly priced, and impossible to find.... Adieu, we are expecting you. Do your best. Above all, remember that there won't be any wine or liquor except what you bring along, and that of the sixteen pinewood crates [containing wine], fourteen belong to General Bonaparte. In God's name, bring some wine from aboard the transports, and liquor. The whole army has

---

[1] François, I, 213.

diarrhoea by dint of drinking water. For the love of God, wine, liquor, rum, and don't forget General Belliard's belongings!'[1]

Savary's thirsty litany never reached its destination: it fell into the hands of some Bedouins, who relayed it to the British, who printed it with other intercepted letters to prove to the world that the French army was doomed. While the wine and liquor shortage was relieved somewhat in the course of time with the help of French ingenuity, it remained serious throughout the period of occupation and contributed greatly to the low morale of the army.

It did not take the Egyptians long to realize that the French soldier, far from being a devil with fingernails one foot long, as Ibrahim Bey had told them, was (unless provoked) a good-natured lad, unimpressive of stature, drably dressed, careless of his dignity, willing to spend his pay, and thirsty. 'Our soldiers walked about the streets just as if they were in garrison in France,'[2] says Lieutenant Vertray, who went sight seeing in Cairo every day. El-Djabarti, for once, confirms French testimony. 'The French soldiers,' he says, 'walked about the streets of Cairo unarmed and molested no one. They joked with the people and bought whatever they needed at very high prices. They paid one dollar for a chicken, fourteen paras for an egg—in other words, what they would have paid in their own country.... Thus the shops and coffee houses reopened by and by.'[3]

During the first week of September, on Bonaparte's request, General Kléber despatched from Alexandria all the civilian personnel not specifically needed there. Among them were not only engineers, scientists, and clerks, but a number of enterprising tradesmen who had accompanied the expedition on speculation. Kléber, writing to Berthier, referred to them as 'that numberless vermin which follows our armies as sharks follow ships and for which there are no words.'[4] Some of this vermin set up shop in Cairo to cater to the French clientèle. El-Djabarti describes a new kind of institution introduced by them: 'The cooks of those establishments bought meat, vegetables, fish, honey, sugar, etc,, and prepared dishes in the manner of their country.... In the middle of the establishment was a wooden table on which plates were placed; around that table was a row of chairs on which people sat

[1] Correspondance de L'armée Française, pp. 98-102.

[2] Vertray, p. 63

[3] El-Djabarti, VI, 23.

[4] La Jonquière, III, 91.

down. The servants brought the dishes to the customers. Thus everyone ate, and everyone paid what he owed, neither more nor less.'¹ A somewhat different establishment was set up by one of the Maltese slaves liberated by the French. Until his pioneering effort, the coffee houses of Cairo had been shops rather than what is understood in the West by a café. The ex-slave, who hailed from Aleppo, opened a café where, says El-Djabarti, 'people gathered in groups and spent part of the night.... The population of the whole quarter took part in these amusing gatherings, because the crowd always is drawn to foolishness and pleasure. Such also is the character of the French. At these gatherings ... people chatted, jested, and laughed. The officer [whom the café-owner served as interpreter] also came there very often with his wife, who was very gay and who was an Egyptian.'²

The officer mentioned by El-Djabarti was by no means the only one to take an Egyptian wife. Whether married at home or not, it was a common practice for the French in Egypt to marry a Moslem girl, a ceremony which the sheiks declared to be legal provided the bride groom pronounced the profession of faith, 'There is no God but God and Mohammed is His Prophet.' If Paris was worth a Mass, a bedmate was worth six words in Arabic.

For those Frenchmen who wished neither to marry nor to burn there were other resources, most of them inadequate. About 300 women had accompanied the army to Egypt, the majority as stowaways, but the few pretty ones among them were either overworked or monopolized. Local prostitutes were in ample supply and cheap, but, except for a few young ones, unappetizing, ugly, and diseased. Some of the high-ranking officers had their problems solved without effort on their part—Admiral Perée, for instance, who could inform his friend, Captain Le Joille: 'The beys have left us some pretty Armenian and Georgian women, whom we have requisitioned for the welfare of the nation.'³ (One wonders what Madame Perée thought of this when she read it in the collection of intercepted letters published by the English.) According to El-Djabarti, black slave women were even more willing than Georgians or Armenians. 'The Negresses,' he declares, 'seeing the Frenchmen's fondness for women, escaped over the walls of the houses in which they served and joined the French en masse. They introduced the soldiers into their masters' houses and showed

¹ El-Djabarti, VI, 26.

² Ibid., VI, 86.

³ Correspondance de L'armée Française, pp. 15758.

them the treasures that were cached there.'¹ The Frenchmen's fondness for women was generally remarked upon by El-Djabarti and other Arabic chroniclers, who would have found it less noteworthy if the French had preferred boys. Strangely enough, there is no evidence of the French in Egypt having imitated local customs in this respect—which goes to show that France has changed a great deal since.

As the austere El-Djabarti remarked, the Frenchmen's odd preference for the female sex brought with it a dangerous relaxation of public morality, due mainly to the licentious freedom they allowed their women. 'The Frenchwomen,' he says, 'went about the city unveiled.... They rode horses and mules, wearing cashmere shawls over their shoulders. They rode through the streets at a gallop, laughing and joking with the native population of the lowest class. This indecent freedom appealed to those women in Cairo who had not been well brought up; and since the French prided themselves on their slavery to women and showered them with gifts and largesse, the women began to enter into relations with them.... Indeed, the French disposed of all the money in the country and always showed themselves submissive to their women, even if the women beat them with their slippers.'²

Although the 'moral epidemic' mentioned by Malus continued to afflict the French forces in Egypt, those garrisoned in Cairo and the other larger cities made the best of their situation and tried to settle down to a routine as little different as possible from what it would have been at home. A random sampling of advertisements published in the *Courrier de L'Egypte* suggests how a bit of Paris was transplanted to Cairo: 'At the end of the rue Venitienne, at the house of Citizen Wolmar, M.D., there is a manufacture of syrups, fine liqueurs of all kinds, ratafia, spirits, and many other European-type goods.' 'Citizens Faure, Nazo & Co., manufacturers of all kinds of liqueurs and syrups, Birket-el-Fil Square, near Hospital No. 2. Everything priced right.' 'French baths ... behind Birket-el-Fil Square.' 'French tobacco of all varieties manufactured at Mehemet Kyacheff's house, rue Petit-Thouars, opposite the Milanese restaurant.' 'The French Hatters inform their fellow citizens that they have established their hat factory behind the Post Office.' 'Fine playing cards, sold at the Army Printing Office.' 'Faure, Guichard & Co., manufacturers and retailers of all kinds of liqueurs,

¹ El-Djabarti, VI, 306.

² Ibid., VI, 304-5.

syrups, imported spirits, wine, coffee, sugar, perfumery, etc., etc.'[1] (Citizen Faure, earlier associated with Citizen Nazo, appears to have changed partners and expanded his line of goods.)

Even the units stationed in remote places—or at least some of them—enjoyed improvised amenities reminiscent of home. Sergeant François, encamped at Bilbeis, asserts that the canteens were supplied with everything a man could desire, including French pastry and wine and brandy made with dates, not to mention the *cantinieres*. Those athletically inclined could practise various sports. Their favourite pastime, however, was to hunt ostriches; almost the entire army, declares François, wore ostrich plumes in their hats.[2] Even organized trips to the Pyramids were arranged for soldiers. (Individual visits were forbidden, since the Bedouins made the area unsafe.) Private Millet found it 'incomprehensible how stones of such enormous size could have been hoisted to such prodigious heights.'[3] Sergeant François scratched his name, birth-place, rank, unit, and the date of his visit on the wall of the King's Chamber.[4]

Despite such diversions, the soldiers remained unhappy, and the absence of letters from home, because of the British blockade, made their homesickness acute. In some, the disease manifested itself in physical symptoms, not all of which were feigned; in others, it led to suicidal melancholia; in the majority, it took milder forms—sullen discontent, occasionally relieved by a sour sense of humour. As is usual among occupation forces, discontent combined with idleness and a false sense of security brought about a general relaxation of discipline. Guard duty was neglected; subaltern and noncommissioned officers found it more elegant and less burdensome to carry pistols instead of muskets or carbines (some went entirely unarmed); soldiers left the cleaning of their weapons

---

[1] Charles-Roux, *Bonaparte*, p. 258.

[2] 'The ostrich,' wrote Napoleon, 'has all the characteristics of a child of the desert. It is large, ill-proportioned and bony. It bears, in its own way, some resemblance to the camel' (*Campagnes de L'Egypte et de Syrie*, in Correspondance de Napoléon I, XXIX, 389).

[3] Millet, p. 53.

[4] This author has been unable to discover the origin of the popular belief that a French soldier shot off the nose of the Sphinx. It is possible, of course, that this happened, although only a piece of field artillery would have answered the purpose, but it seems more probable that the story originated in the same sort of source as the tales of George Washington and the cherry tree, the Dutch boy and the dike, etc.

to native servants; extortion from the population, sales of government property for private gain, even robbery and murder, were common occurrences, despite the drastic measures taken against them.

Even more serious was the high incidence of disease. A breakdown of the French forces in Egypt on August 18, 1798, reveals that at least 10 per cent—and in Reynier's division 15 per cent—of the men were in hospitals. By October 22, the average for the whole army had risen to 15 per cent, and this was before the outbreak of the plague. Of course, many of the ill were not even put into hospital. The hospitals were overcrowded and understaffed, and they often lacked the most elementary equipment, despite the heroic efforts of Desgenettes, Larrey, and several of their colleagues,[1] The most prevalent diseases were dysentery and trachoma, the worst of the Egyptian plagues.[2] Trachoma, which, if inadequately treated, easily leads to blindness, was generally ascribed to the night air. 'Nothing is more disagreeable than to sleep under the open sky at this season in Egypt,' Colonel Laugier notes in his diary in October. 'The strongest rainfall in France does not get you as wet as the night dew does here. And so it happens that, on every march requiring more than three nights, one may be sure that one third of the men will be incapacitated for some time because of an eye ailment.'[3] In late September 1798, more than fifty out of the 171 officers and men of a cavalry unit stationed at Es

---

[1] The civilian administrators who operated the hospital as a business enterprise were often blamed for the shortages. Citizen Rutty, in a letter dated November 14, 1798, lodges a vigorous protest against such accusations: 'According to the terms of our contract, I should receive 30,000 francs per month; last month, I received only 18,000; this month, 5,000.... [To procure the supplies needed], I have used my credit, I have gone into debt ... in a word, I daresay, I have exceeded by far my means and resources. I am not responsible for either the costs or the transportation of meat to Rosetta; yet, when the meat supply broke down, I took care of it.... And yet I am the target of the most insulting reproaches. Everybody is in the right and I alone am to blame, although I am the only one who has nothing to reproach himself with.' (Correspondence inédite, officielle et confidentielle de Napoleon Bonaparte: Egypte, II, 136-37).

[2] Egyptian ophthalmia, trachoma, or granular conjunctivitis is an infection caused by a nonfilterable virus, extremely widespread in Egypt. Though easily cured when treated from the start, it causes blindness or severely impaired vision if neglected. It remains one of the major health problems of Egypt.

[3] La Jonquière, III, 163-65.

J. Christopher Herold

Saliya had ophthalmia, and its commander requested more copper sulphate for their treatment. In Upper Egypt, the rate of blindness and half-blindness—few of the patients were completely cured—soon reached staggering proportions. 'If the number of your sick does not exceed eight or nine hundred.' wrote Napoleon to Desaix on November 2; Desaix's entire forces were less than 3,000 men.[1]

There are no statistics on those classic occupational hazards, syphilis and gonorrhoea, but all those who mention the matter at all agree that their incidence was high. To fight it, the French occasionally resorted to rather drastic means, borrowed from local practice. 'The prostitutes are a plague in the [French] quarters,' General Dugua, then governor of Cairo, wrote to Bonaparte in 1799. 'To keep them away, it would be necessary to drown those caught in the barracks.' Bonaparte's comment in the margin was: 'Put the aga [of the Janissaries] in charge of this.'[2] An early history of the Egyptian campaign makes the assertion that 400 prostitutes were beheaded, sewn into sacks, and thrown into the Nile on the aga's order. The authors gloss over Bonaparte's responsibility for this atrocity; according to them, he merely ordered the aga to have the women rounded up and treated in hospitals, and was incensed when he learned how his instructions had been interpreted. The documents flatly contradict this attempt to exonerate the General.

There were other occupational hazards, less murderous in their effect but more characteristic of the country. Thus, in Cairo, traffic accidents due to the excessive speeding of donkeys were commonplace enough to warrant mention in an Order of the Day, admonishing all donkey-borne French personnel 'to moderate their speed when riding through the crowds.'[3] Indeed, next to the Pyramids and Karnak, the most remarkable thing in Egypt is the Egyptian donkey; he has endeared himself to visitors in all times by his friendly expression (shared by neither camels nor humans) and has astonished them by his speed. To see an Egyptian six feet tall, his galabiya flying in the wind, gallop on a spirited ass is an exhilarating spectacle. Donkeys were the taxicabs of Cairo in 1798 and were popular with soldiers and civilians alike. 'They loved to ride on donkeys.' says El-Djabarti, 'and they hired them at generous rates. Some spent their entire day riding a donkey. Others gathered in groups and went on excursions, singing and laughing.

---

[1] Ibid., V, 231.

[2] Belliard, Histoire, IV, 113-15

[3] La Jonquière, III, 49.

175

The donkey drivers associated themselves with them in their joy.'[1] Since the members of the Scientific Commission were known among the soldiers as 'donkeys,' donkeys were called 'scientists,' and mules 'half-scientists.'

***

Good-natured at bottom, a Frenchman will easily overcome his more melancholy moods by means of wine, song, and jibes at those in power.

'As a rule,' concedes El-Djabarti, 'the French drank only to be gay, and if one of them drank more than was good for him, he stayed at his house, for if he went out and acted in a disorderly way, he was punished.'[2] Congregating at their canteens, restaurants, and cafés, they would dispel their spleen after a few glasses, joining in patriotic hymns and other songs of lighter nature, deciding matters of high policy and strategy, pouring their scorn on commissioners, hospital administrators, scientists, and the government, swapping rumours of fabulous caches of wine or of Mameluke hoards that had been discovered, giving a modest account of their part in past military actions, and commenting on Egyptian *morés* and on their superior's military competence and love life. General Caffarelli, who had a wooden leg, could easily afford to be cheerful, they said, since he had one foot in France; the scientists were responsible for the whole expedition, which they had instigated out of scientific curiosity; General Bonaparte was having an affair with the daughter of the sheik El-Bekri (soon to be replaced by 'Clioupâtre' Fourès —but of this more later); and the sheik El-Bekri was having a bloody feud with the aga of the Janissaries over *la Belle Helène*—a handsome Mameluke lad.[3] The *Courrier de L'Egypte* supplied them with more official but less reliable news, mixed with whimsical observations on the quaintness of Egyptian ways and with patriotic rhetoric.

To raise the troops' morale and keep their amusements within bounds, Bonaparte had his savants organize amateur theatricals (the women's parts being mostly played by men), established con-

[1] El-Djabarti, VI, 92.

[2] Ibid., VI, 95.

[3] The dispute over the slave boy (who formerly had belonged to Murad Bey) led to virtual warfare between the sheik's and the aga's retainers. It was terminated by a Solomonic judgment handed down by Poussielgue: El-Bekri kept the slave, in exchange for some real estate to be made over to the aga.

valescent hospitals, and ordered that, every day at noon, the bands of the various units post themselves opposite the military hospitals and play 'the tunes which will give cheer to the sick and recall to their memories the finest moments of their past campaigns.'[1] Late in November, he licensed his former schoolmate Dargevel to establish what must have been the first service club in history, named Le Tivoli after a popular amusement spot in Paris. It offered a dance band (though few partners), billiard tables and other games, a library, the two newspapers published by the army, coffee, European food, a pleasure garden, and similar comforts of home. At the grand opening, the *Courrier de L'Egypte* reports, what 'produced the most agreeable sensation ... was the presence of fifteen or twenty women dressed with some splendour—an absolutely novel sight in Egypt.'[2] The main trouble with Le Tivoli, says Lieutenant Vertray (among many others), was the difficulty of organizing a ball, owing to the shortage of ladies. 'Thus the gatherings never were very brilliant,' he concludes.[3]

Bonaparte cannot be accused of neglecting the morale of his troops. He spared no effort to offset their homesickness with ingenious substitutes, such as theatre without actresses and beer without hops. Helpful though they were, these makeshifts succeeded only temporarily in dispelling the universal gloom. Until the last day of their sojourn in Egypt, the French soldiers had one single thought: to return to the fleshpots of Europe.

---

[1] Correspondance, V, 224. In St. Helena, he wrote: 'The drum imitates the sound of the cannon: it is the best of all instruments.' (Correspondance de Napoleon I, XXXI, 313)

[2] 18 Frimaire, Year VII.

[3] Vertray, p. 68.

Chapter Six
The Institute and
El Azhar

TO assert that the scientists and artists attached to Bonaparte's army did not share the soldiers' urge to return home would do violence to the truth. In the summer of 1799, when rumours of Bonaparte's imminent departure for France spread among them, their agitation was great. The poet Parseval-Grandmaison, frantic at the thought of being left behind, raced after Bonaparte all the way from Cairo to the beach and surely would have swum after him if he had not been taken aboard. Nevertheless, in the majority an enthusiastic spirit of adventure more than counter-balanced their intermittent attacks of homesickness. Misfits, like Parseval, were the exception. Unlike the average soldier, the members of the Scientific and Artistic Commission were conscious of a positive purpose they could serve in Egypt. Here, opportunities were unlimited; everything was yet to be discovered, everything remained to be done. The ardour of battle, the heightened sense of existence which the soldiers knew only in combat, the scientists, technologists, artists, and physicians experienced at almost every moment of their stay.

During the first few days after their landing, they had a rough time. Except for a handful of senior members of the Commission, they had to shift for themselves in the shuffle and confusion. Only Monge and Berthollet left Alexandria with Bonaparte on July 7; their tribulations aboard *Le Cerf* during the fighting at Shubra

Khit have been mentioned in an earlier chapter. Some twenty others sailed to Rosetta a week later; the bulk remained in Alexandria until early September.

Their manner of living varied according to the 'assimilated ranks' assigned to them. Citizen Jollois, one of the junior engineers, showed no enthusiasm over the accommodations provided for him and his colleagues at Rosetta. Their house, he says, was infested with vermin and full of 'refuse and disgusting filth.'[1] No rations were distributed, and there was no cook. Banding together, the Rosetta scientists organized a communal kitchen and took turns shopping and cooking. By and by, relative comfort returned: bread, meat, and wine rations arrived, and servants were hired.

Through their stay in Egypt—and especially in the beginning—many of the Commission's members were given administrative duties that had little to do with the professions for which they had been trained; they fulfilled them more or less willingly. Monge and Berthollet, who in the course of their past experience in Italy and Malta had raised the art of confiscating property to a new branch of the exact sciences, were employed exclusively on 'administrative commissions,' ferreting out concealed Mameluke treasures and devising various methods of imposing fines on the rich. There is no indication that they resented this: their reputation as men of science remained intact even though they had become civil servants at heart. In Alexandria, General Kléber found appropriate employment for the civil and military engineers, cartographers, and other technicians who made up the bulk of the Alexandria contingent. They built barracks, devised a new type of furnace to make red-hot cannon balls, constructed a floating fire engine, made topographic surveys, studied the Nile-Alexandria Canal. Though he generally had little use for civilians, Kléber soon came to regard his scientific 'donkeys' as indispensable and was reluctant to let them depart when they were summoned to Cairo. Always humane and sympathetic, he tried unsuccessfully to help the homesick and the misfits to be repatriated. The architect Norry, he wrote to Bonaparte, was 'ill in body and in mind' and wished to return to France; so did the astronomer Quesnot, the antiquary Pourlier, and the surgeon Dubois, who 'never stops thinking of his four children, whose mother is dead and whom he left in Paris.'[2]

---

[1] Jollois, p. 50.

[2] La Jonquière, III, 80.

Before the French arrived in Alexandria, not a line had ever been printed in Egypt. Bonaparte brought two printing plants with his army. One, operated by the Orientalist Marcel and a staff of thirty-one, remained at Alexandria until the end of 1798 (although Marcel preceded it to Cairo). It had three sets of type—French, Arabic, and Greek. On its presses all Bonaparte's proclamations were printed, as was the first book ever printed in Egypt—*Exercises in Literary Arabic, Extracted from the Koran, for the Use of Those Who are Studying That Language.*[1] In addition to Marcel's press, there was another, privately owned, which was shipped to Cairo soon after the French occupied the capital. Its owner was one Citizen Marc Aurel, whose father's bookshop young Lieutenant Buonaparte had patronized during his garrison days at Valence. Marc Aurel was one among the numerous private concessionaires who accompanied the French armies at that time. In Cairo, he published the more or less weekly newspaper, *Le Courrier de L'Egypte*, and the literary and scientific periodical, La Décade Égyptienne, the organ of the Institute of Egypt. Thus, although he had no official connection with the Scientific Commission, his name became forever linked with its labours.

The Rosetta contingent of the Commission could not be employed as easily in their normal capacity as could their colleagues in Alexandria. The mathematician Fourier and the bard Parseval-Grandmaison served on a supply purchase commission; the composer Villoteau volunteered to be Menou's secretary. Most of the others kept themselves busy as best they could: Jollois, armed with a shot gun and a pair of sun glasses, roamed the countryside collecting birds, botanizing, and studying ruins; the zoologist Geoffroy Saint-Hilaire, with an escort assigned to him by Menou, penetrated into the Delta. 'I have found a number of interesting birds,' he writes. 'My chief occupations have been to observe them alive, to describe them zoologically and anatomically, and to have them and their skeletons mounted.'[2] For bird watchers, the Delta is a paradise. Denon, inseparable from his sketchbook, went on sketching and helped the naturalists by drawing their plants and birds; the botanist Nectoux made a study of local agriculture. All were on cordial terms with General Menou, with whom they spent their evenings philosophizing and grumbling about the high command in Cairo. 'I have here,' Menou writes to Caffarelli, 'as my faithful companions, and often also as witnesses of my penury,

[1] Charles-Roux, Bonaparte, p. 144.
[2] Ibid., p. 137.

Citizens Denon, Nectoux, and Villoteau.... I know that you want all the members of the Commission on the Arts [and Sciences] to join you in Cairo. But, General, take pity on a man who feels a need to be with somebody who understands French and with whom he can have an intelligent conversation in the evening.'[1] Caffarelli and Bonaparte showed no pity, however, and by mid-September most of the scientists were reunited at Cairo, where Monge, Berthollet, and Caffarelli had prepared more than adequate living and working quarters for them.

In creating the Institute of Egypt by his order of August 22, Bonaparte had a number of diverse but by no means contradictory motives. Still flattered by his election, in 1797, to the French National Institute (the body which replaced the French Academy during the revolutionary period), he also was aware that science leaves more lasting monuments than does war. He never was content to be a great general; in fact, he declared repeatedly, and no doubt sincerely, that he was an antimilitarist. To be great, he had to be more than a general, more than a dictator, more than an emperor. Unless he left behind him a monument of legislation, of industrial and scientific progress, of artistic achievement, he never would rate more than a paragraph in history. To these ends, Egypt would serve him as an experimental laboratory. His understanding of art and science was primitive; but his penetrating intelligence enabled him to use them for his purposes.

The ability to combine self-aggrandizement with usefulness was among his many special talents. He created the Institute of Egypt as an auxiliary, a kind of brains trust, whose information, research, and advice would help him administer the country and lay the basis of its future development. This purpose in itself was something unprecedented. The 'practical' work he expected from the Institute fell into two categories. To fill the needs of the moment, windmills must be constructed, the canals must be repaired and maintained, articles unobtainable from France (because of the blockade) must be locally manufactured, and the fiscal system must be reformed. To prepare the economic development of Egypt in the future, studies must be made relating to the construction of a canal linking the Red Sea with the Mediterranean, to the construction of barrages and to the better use of the Nile, to the introduction of new crops, to the improvement of agricultural methods, to the prevention of epidemics, to the creation of an educational system, etc. To all these tasks, the members of the Scientific

---

[1] La Jonquière, II, 454.

Commission and of the Institute addressed themselves with astounding energy and productivity. The results of their labours can be found in that monument of collective scholarship, the *Description de L'Egypte*, ten volumes of text and fourteen volumes of plates, published between 1809 and 1828. Never before or since has a study of such scope and thoroughness been accomplished on the basis of field-work carried out in so short a space of time (three years) and under such inadequate and harrowing circumstances.

But Bonaparte had something even greater in mind. Not all the Committee members were engineers, technologists, and economists. There were architects, musicians, archaeologists, painters, mathematicians, physicists, zoologists. Although some of them occasionally were put to work on purely utilitarian tasks, the fundamental purpose of their presence was to explore every aspect of that fabled but little-known land—its history, its monuments and arts, its geological structure, its fauna and flora—in other words, to pursue pure know ledge as well as usefulness. There is no evidence that Bonaparte ever showed the least personal interest in the classification of the fish in the Nile, which Geoffroy Saint-Hilaire collected with passion, or even in the temples of Luxor and Karnak, which he never bothered to visit. His personal suggestions of possible fields of research were invariably utilitarian, if not trivial. Yet, supreme utilitarian that he was, he appreciated the usefulness of the useless: thus, for instance, it is difficult to conceive of any practical application that could be made of Egyptology; but it was with his expedition that that science originated, and his name will forever remain linked with it, just as the style called empire, which is based on Egyptian monumentality, served to enhance the pageantry of his imperial rule. There is nothing he ever wasted, except human lives.

When, shortly after the Battle of the Pyramids, Monge and Berthollet joined Bonaparte at Giza, the General, after eyeing those monuments, from which forty centuries of history were looking down upon him, came out with the stupefying declaration that, with the stones of the Great Pyramid, a wall one metre wide and three metres tall could be built around France—a calculation which Monge later confirmed. The Pyramids and the Sphinx were the only ancient monuments Bonaparte ever inspected in Egypt. He refused, however, to enter the Pyramid of Cheops, because to do so he would have had to crawl on all fours; in this, he showed great sagacity, since there is nothing to be seen inside, as everyone who has gone through that infernal ordeal will confirm. Instead of entering, he egged on his suite—among them Berthier and Monge, no longer youths—to climb to the top, which they did, fearing his jibes more than the September sun. At the summit, Monge shared his bottle of brandy with his fellow-climbers.

Although the impetus leading to the foundation of the Institute of Egypt must be credited to Bonaparte, its organization was largely the work of Monge, whose experience, outlook, and administrative gifts ideally suited him to the task. Monge represented the epitome of what Napoleon expected from a scientist: to serve the fatherland seemed to him the ultimate aim of science. Egypt inspired him with imperialistic dreams, which he communicated to his wife. If 20,000 French families settled in Egypt, Monge wrote to her, 'in order to engage in commercial ventures, industrial establishments, etc., this country would become the finest, the most brilliant, and the most happily situated of our colonies.'[1] His was the spirit which made possible the French colonization of Algeria and its aftermath. Fortunately, many of the other members of the Scientific Commission, especially the younger ones, did not share their leader's colonial enthusiasm; they were less interested in making Egypt into a French colony than in studying it and in using their knowledge for the benefit of its people.

The organization of the Institute was drawn up on August 21 by a committee consisting of Generals Bonaparte, Caffarelli, and Andréossy, and of Citizens Monge, Berthollet, Geoffroy Saint-Hilaire, Costaz, and Desgenettes. Four 'sections' were created, and their members designated.[2] It should be noted that only the most

---

[1] Aubry, *Monge*, p. 256.

[2] Mathematics: Bonaparte, Andréossy, Monge, Fourier, Costaz, Horace Say (later replaced by Lancret), Malus; the astronomers Nouet and Quesnot; the civil engineers Le Père and Girard; the chief naval commissioner Le Roy.

Physics: Berthollet, Conté, Dolomieu, Geoffroy Saint-Hilaire, Dr. Desgenettes, the surgeon Dubois (later replaced by Larrey), the entomologist Savigny, the chemist Descotils, the botanist Delille, the engineer Champy. Two seats vacant. (Beauchamp was added later.)

Political Economy: General Caffarelli (replaced, after his death, by Corrancez), Poussielgue, Tallien, Sulkowski, Gloutier, and the chief army commissioner Sucy (replaced later by Bourrienne). Six seats vacant.

Literature and Art: The poet Parseval-Grandmaison, the linguist Venture (replaced by Ripault), the composer Rigel, the architect Norry (replaced by Le Père *fils*), the artists Denon, Dutertre, and Redouté; and a Greek priest, Don Raphael de Monachis. Four seats vacant. (The painter Rigo was added later.)

distinguished and promising members of the Scientific and Artistic Commission were selected (the poetic and musical contingent, to be sure, was chosen *faute de mieux*); that several high military officers (Bonaparte, Caffarelli, Andréossy, Sulkowski), administrative officials (Poussielgue, Sucy, Le Roy), and one outsider (the Greek priest de Monachis) were included; and that only the Mathematics Section was complete, twelve seats remaining vacant in the other three sections. Some of the choices might be criticized (and undoubtedly were by those not chosen), but on the whole the roster included the cream of the civilian personnel. Among his fellow academicians, Bonaparte was treated as an equal among equals; when he forgot to keep his place, Dr. Desgenettes reminded him. One day, talking out of turn on some question of chemistry, Bonaparte remarked petulantly that 'chemistry is the kitchen of medicine, and medicine is the science of killing,' to which Desgenettes retorted suavely, 'If this is so, how would you define the science of generalship?'[1] A quick-witted retort invariably restored Napoleon's good humour; but the memorable clash that took place between him and Desgenettes at the Institute a year later left him permanently ill-disposed toward the forthright physician.

***

The importance Bonaparte attached to the Institute and to the Scientific Commission was reflected in the accommodation he provided for them. They occupied, in the suburb of Nasriya, a complex of buildings and gardens centering on the palace of Qassim Bey—a delightful structure in the Turkish style, with a shaded garden, an open-air colonnade, and lovely fountains. (The owner, meanwhile, was fighting the French in Upper Egypt.) The main drawing-room of Qassim's harem became the meeting room of the Institute. In the other rooms of the palace and in the neighbouring houses the scholars lived and worked, unless they were away on their various field trips. 'Our houses,' Geoffroy Saint-Hilaire wrote to his friend Cuvier, 'seem to offer us more comfort and at least as much luxury as can be found in the Louvre. A huge garden ... with several raised terraces ... will serve us to grow plants and to study botany.'[2] By and by, the scientists also installed a zoological garden and an aviary; another part of the domain was set aside for agricultural experiments. There also were a chemical laboratory, a small museum of natural history, a library, an observatory, a min-

[1] Charles-Roux, *Bonaparte*, p. 219.
[2] Ibid., p. 159.

eralogical collection, an archaeological collection—a very poor one, but, all the same, the ancestor of the Cairo Museum—a printing plant, and Conté's fabulous workshop. A large part of the instruments the scientists had taken with them had been lost aboard one of the ships destroyed in Abukir Bay; Conté and his assistants, in their workshop, fashioned the tools to make the instruments that had to be replaced and many other new ones: surgical apparatus, compasses, telescopic and microscopic lenses; dies needed for the printing plant, for the Mint, and for the replacement of uniform buttons; surveying instruments; drawing tools; even sword blades, bugles, cloth, and hats. There was no problem Conté's ingenuity could not solve, nor was there ever a single man as useful to an army.

Never, until the most recent times, were so many excellent people working in such a variety of fields brought together in such close cooperation. Of course, specialists continued to pursue their specialities, mostly on the side, but no less assiduously for all that, yet each man had to do the work of several, and sometimes it was work he had never dreamt of doing. This reawakening of latent faculties, this stimulating interplay produced an exhilarating atmosphere that infected even non-scholars. 'Besides the regular sessions of the Institute,' reminisces Jomard, one of the savants, 'informal gatherings of forty to fifty people took place every evening in the garden of the Institute. They would talk about their travel projects, about discoveries they had made, and about a variety of fascinating questions concerning the physical geography of Egypt, ancient Egypt, the government of the country, and the mores of its people.'[1] Generals, high officials, and even some of the sheiks were frequent visitors. Among the sheiks was the chronicler El-Djabarti, who left a remarkable account of his visit:

> The French installed [in the house of Hassan Kyacheff] a great library, with several librarians who kept guard over the books and handed them to those readers who needed them. This library was open daily from ten o'clock. The readers assembled in a large room next to the one where the books were kept. They sat down in chairs around large tables and started to work. Even simple privates went to work in the library. When a Moslem wished to visit the establishment, he was not prevented from doing so, but on the contrary, was made very welcome. The French were particularly pleased when a Moslem visitor showed interest

[1] Ibid., p. 225.

in the sciences.... I myself repeatedly had occasion to visit that library. I saw there, among other things, a large volume on the history of our Prophet (May God bless him!); his holy features were shown in it as faithfully as the artist's knowledge permitted.... On another page, there were pictures of the first four caliphs; on another, the Prophet's ascension to Heaven; he was riding his horse Borak.... I have seen many other books, dealing with natural history, medicine, and applied mechanics. There also were many Moslem books in French translation.... Some of the French were studying Arabic and learning verses from the Koran by heart; in a word, they were great scholars and they loved the sciences, especially mathematics and philology. Day and night they applied themselves to learn Arabic....

[In the observatory] there were instruments remarkable for their great precision.... Some of them were very expensive.... There also were telescopes that could be disassembled and packed into small boxes....

The painters were installed in the house of Ibrahim Bey the Black [one of the Negro Mameluke chiefs]. Among them was Rigo, who painted portraits; he was so skillful that, seeing the portraits, one would have thought they were in relief and about to speak. He had painted all the sheiks and other notables.... Another artist drew animals and insects; another, fish.

When an animal or a fish unknown in France was discovered, it was placed in a liquid which preserved it indefinitely....

[The pharmacist Royer] installed himself in the house of Zulficar Katkhoda. There he stored all his instruments and drugs. He had furnaces constructed to distill water and to prepare unguents and salts. He had two laboratories, one on the ground floor, one on the first floor; in them, one could see many pots and bottles of all shapes.... Here are some of the curious things I saw [in the chemistry laboratory]. One of the experimenters took a flagon containing a certain liquid and poured part of it into an empty glass; then he took another flagon and poured it into the same glass: a coloured smoke arose from it, and when that smoke disappeared, the liquid solidified and kept a yellowish colour. I touched this solid and found it to be as hard as stone. The same experiment was repeated on other liquids, and a blue stone was obtained; a third experiment produced a red stone, like a ruby. The man then took a white powder and placed it on an anvil; he struck it with a hammer, and instantly a loud explosion, like a rifle shot, was heard. We were terrified, which made the onlookers laugh.... We were also shown a machine in which a glass was rotating; at the approach of a foreign body, the glass emitted sparks and produced a crackling sound. If a person held in his hand an object, even a mere wire, and touched the rotating glass with it, his body instantly received a shock that made the bones in his shoulders and arms crack....

We were shown other experiments as well, all as extraordinary as the first ones, such as intelligences like ours can neither conceive of nor explain.[1]

According to the unanimous testimony of French eyewitnesses, the Moslem visitors at the Institute seemed utterly unimpressed by what they saw. El-Djabarti's account gives them the lie. With characteristic Western arrogance, the French expected the sheiks to react to the marvels of technology with the childlike astonishment of savages. It did not occur to them that, perhaps, it was they, the technologists, who were naïve and less sophisticated than the impassive sheiks. Undoubtedly the sheiks were impressed—and, if El-Djabarti was in the least typical of them, they were more impressed by the dedication to learning than by the display of cheap tricks; but they refused to let themselves be dominated, A century and a half later, Asia and Africa had learned all the tricks, and shook off the domination. Who of the two was more naïve—the Oriental who had never heard of electricity, or the European who thought that the discovery of electricity gave him a permanent title to mastery?

It is true that Egypt, which forty centuries ago accomplished marvels of technology that still astonish us, had sunk to an incredibly primitive level. 'The native population,' Napoleon wrote twenty years after his expedition, 'were very slow in understanding what was that assembly of grave and studious people [the scientists], who neither governed, nor administered, nor served any religious function. They thought that they were making gold. Eventually, however, they formed a correct opinion of them. Not only the sheiks and notables but even the lowest class of the people held the savants in high esteem. Indeed, the savants were frequently in contact with working men, to whom they taught some

---

[1] El-Djabarti, VI, 70-71.

elements of mechanics and chemistry while directing them in their work.[1] The work mentioned by Napoleon included road building, fortification, and various civic improvements. How primitive were the working methods of the time may be gathered from this passage in El-Djabarti's chronicle: 'The workers were paid generous wages—much more than they were used to; they received their pay every day in the afternoon. They were given highly improved and simple tools. Thus, instead of baskets and jars, they used little carts with two handles, which the workingmen filled with dirt or stones, and then pushed on a wheel. Each wheelbarrow had a capacity of five baskets. The labourers filled, moved and emptied these wheelbarrows with the greatest ease.'[2] And these were the people who had built the Pyramids!

***

While the majority of the military never ceased wondering what the devil they were doing in Egypt, the scholars only wondered where to begin with all that had to be done. Freed of the social distractions of Paris and faced with unlimited opportunities to make themselves useful, they displayed an activity more diversified than has ever been seen before or since in such a body of men. The practical questions submitted to the Institute by its vice-president, Citizen Bonaparte, never ceased: was it possible to grow vinyards in Egypt? How many grains did each grain of wheat yield in Egypt and how many in France? Could wells be dug in the desert? How could the aqueduct leading to the Cairo Citadel be improved? No sooner did an idea occur to Bonaparte than he proposed it to the Institute for study. Each question was referred to a committee. The same men sat on an ever-increasing number of committees. Many served in administrative capacities at the same time: Poussielgue not only was in charge of the army's finances but also headed the entire civil administration of Egypt. Monge and Berthollet were so ubiquitous that the bewildered troops merged them into a single mythical unit named Mongéberthollet; they served on the 'Administrative Commission' (a board specializing in soaking the rich), as inspectors of the Cairo Mint, as commissioners at the General Divan, and in a dozen other capacities. Conté, the Jack-of-all-trades *par excellence*, served on at least four administrative commissions. Malus and Jollois were in charge of organizing patriotic celebrations. Fourier, the mathematician, served

---

[1] Correspondance, XXIX, 493.

[2] El-Djabarti, VI, 70-71.

as permanent secretary to the Institute and as editor of the *Courrier de L'Egypte*. Desgenettes headed the army's medical service—a Herculean task in itself—edited the *Décade Égyptienne*, and headed a commission on the establishment of a hospital for the native population. Examples could be multiplied almost indefinitely.

As if the questions and projects assigned to them by Bonaparte were not enough to keep them busy, the savants pursued various projects of their own, on which they reported at the sessions of the Institute, held approximately every five days. Berthollet read papers on the formation of ammonia and on the Egyptian method of manufacturing indigo. General Andréossy reported on his explorations of Lake Manzala and of the Wadi el Natrun—the 'soda lakes' in the Libyan Desert south of Alexandria—throwing in descriptions of the Coptic monasteries near the lakes and a dissertation on the living habits of Bedouin tribes. Sucy read a paper on the need to explore the sources of the Nile, Duertre, on the project of founding a school of fine arts for Egyptians; Nectoux, on the desirability of establishing agricultural colleges and experimental stations; Dolomieu, on the 'selection, conservation, and transportation of ancient monuments' to be shipped from Egypt to France. Conté, in addition to making pencils, also used up a few of them, making more than fifty painstakingly detailed drawings of the various processes used by Egyptian artisans and craftsmen.

Even today—and how much more so in 1798!—the traveller in Egypt cannot escape the impression that what the country needs most is doctors, drugs, and public education. Of all the members of the Institute, Dr. Desgenettes was perhaps the most active. He read papers on the causes of ophthalmia and of infant mortality. He investigated the only hospital in Cairo, where he found seventy-five beds—fifty of them made of stone—and about forty starving and neglected patients of both sexes, about fifteen of whom were demented and locked in chains. An inspection of local pharmaceutical practice revealed equally appalling conditions. Desgenettes drew up plans for a civilian hospital with 500-400 beds, for the creation of a central pharmacy in Cairo, for a school of medicine and a school of pharmacy, and for a primary school to teach the population French, so that they could attend the courses to be given in the higher schools by European instructors. These projects remained unrealized, for lack of funds and time, but they were carried out not long afterwards, under Mehemet Ali, by the Frenchman Clot Bey. Meanwhile, Desgenettes had manuals printed in French, Arabic and Italian on the treatment of bubonic plague and of small-pox. Yet, with the modesty of a true man of science, he hoped to learn as well as to teach: in a circular letter to the medical officers of Bonaparte's army, he reminded them that Egypt was the cradle of medicine; traces of ancient medical lore had, perhaps, survived. 'Therefore, study the local practices carefully. However little one may think at first of this empiricism, one must know it before judging it.'[1]

Pure research was not neglected, even though the applied sciences were favoured. Monge read papers on mirages and on capillary attraction; Fourier and Corrancez on higher mathematics. Malus, with the advance elements of Desaix's division in Upper Egypt, drafted a memorandum on the nature of light.

Marcel studied Arabic poetry; Savigny, insects and worms. Geoffrey Saint-Hilaire wrote a paper on the wing of the ostrich; later, being done with birds, he addressed himself to reptiles and to fish. One day, when he had finished reading a paper on the fish of the Nile to the Institute, a sheik in the audience asked for the floor and pointed out the vanity of such research: the Prophet had settled the matter by declaring that God had created 30,000 species, 10,000 of which inhabited the land and the air, and 20,000 the water.

***

The two fields to which the Scientific Commission made the greatest contributions were geography and Egyptology. The map of Egypt, which Bonaparte ordered to be collated in 1799, was completed only in 1806. Classified secret until the end of Napoleon's reign, that monument of cartography was included in the *Description de L'Egypte* and forms its atlas. As for Egyptology, it owes its birth to a handful of civilians who accompanied Generals Desaix and Belliard to Upper Egypt and to a chance discovery made by a captain of Engineers. The civilians in Upper Egypt had copied, with painstaking accuracy, thousands of hieroglyphic inscriptions. The meaning of the characters, however, was totally unknown. At their session of July 19, 1799, the members of the Institute were electrified when a letter from Citizen Lancret was read to them, announcing 'the discovery at Rosetta of some inscriptions that may offer much interest.'[2] The inscriptions, chiselled into the polished surface of a large block of basalt, were in Greek characters, in hieroglyphics, and in an unknown writing (since then

---

[1] Charles-Roux, *Bonaparte*, p. 163.

[2] Ibid., p. 364.

called demotic). Captain Bouchard, the discoverer of the stone, instinctively realized that here, perhaps, was the key to the Egyptian language and to hieroglyphic writing, which indeed it was. His discovery not only offered much interest but, when Champollion deciphered the hieroglyphic and demotic inscriptions thirty-two years later, they created a sensation. How the Rosetta Stone found its way into the British Museum will be seen in time.

**

In the prospectus he wrote for the *Décade Égyptienne*, Tallien defined the purpose of that periodical: 'The aim we propose to our selves is to make Egypt known not only to the Frenchmen who happen to be here now but also to France and to all Europe.' A scrutiny of the tables of contents of the *Décade* will convince anyone that this announcement was no vain boast. Its contributors were aware that the *Décade* was a preliminary clearing house for the data and information that eventually would find their place in a comprehensive work—the *Description de L'Egypte*. This aim was clear to the military, too. Desaix and Belliard, it will be seen, cooperated with the scholars and displayed an understanding rarely found in generals. General Menou insisted that 'all birds [of the Rosetta region] not yet drawn should be painted for the book projected by the government.'[1] Anonymous officers and soldiers, by capturing specimens of animals, by pointing out ruins, inscriptions, artifacts on which they had stumbled, or simply by risking their lives to protect the wayward scholars, contributed their share to the great work.

The aim of Bonaparte's expedition was to make Egypt into a profitable colony for France. To achieve that end, the Scientific Commission was as essential as the army. Most of the members of the expeditionary force realized almost from the start that they were doomed to failure, that the horrors they were perpetrating and suffering would be utterly futile. For the scientists, whose essential goals were the conquest of knowledge and the application of knowledge to the improvement of man's lot, there could be no such sense of futility. In the middle of what seemed a nightmare to others, Geoffroy Saint-Hilaire could write to Cuvier: 'Here I once again find men who think of nothing but science; I live at the centre of a flaming core of reason.... We busy ourselves enthusiasti-

---

[1] Ibid., p. 163.

cally with all the questions that are of concern to the government and with the sciences to which we have devoted ourselves freely.'[1]

II

General Bonaparte was known to the Egyptians as Sultan Kebir—'the Great Sultan.' Actually, the title was merely a hyperbolic rendering of 'commander-in-chief,' but Bonaparte accepted it in a more flattering sense. Already he saw himself as a sovereign ruler rather than a general. Since he intended to be not only a ruler but also great, he made very sincere efforts to base his rule on high-minded principles: respect for the customs and beliefs of the population, development of natural resources, equitable distribution of the tax burden, a stern but fair-minded and uniform application of the law, and gradual restoration of self-government to a people used to enslavement since pharaonic times. All these excellent intentions were vitiated by one single but all-important factor—lack of cash.

Even though there is no indication that Napoleon ever uttered the famous axiom that an army travels on its stomach, it was his practice, as it was the Directory's, to make the territories he conquered pay for the expense of conquering them.

In Egypt, which, at least until Turkey declared war, was not considered enemy territory, the system had to be modified, since no special taxes could be levied there, as was the practice elsewhere. The expeditionary force had left Toulon with 4,606,908 francs in its treasury; perquisitions in Malta added about half a million in coin. Since the monthly payroll of the army and navy forces amounted to about a million francs, this sum obviously could not stretch very far. Regular taxes could not be collected in Egypt before late autumn, since they were based, at their source, on payments in kind. Thus, from the moment he set foot in Alexandria, Sultan Kebir had to resort to every conceivable means known to cashless man to obtain money. The accounting rendered by the Chief Paymaster Esteve on September 21, 1798, on receipts and expenditures is something that must be seen to be believed. All in all, the balance shows receipts to the amount of over 4 millions, realized from the piecemeal sale or melting down of the treasures of the Knights of Malta; from the sale or melting down of the Knights' bullion; from confiscated property of the Mamelukes;

[1] Ibid., p. 164.

from punitive levies imposed on the Mamelukes' wives; from forced loans obtained from the European, Syrian, Coptic, Jewish, and Moslem business communities; from fines imposed for illegal hoarding of arms and various other transgressions of the law; from the sale of confiscated property belonging to enemy nations; from the sale of stocks of wheat, rice, soda, sugar, etc.; from levies raised on warehouses; from customs receipts; and even from such sources as a 'payment made by Citizen Frantz, Second Lieutenant in the 88th Half-Brigade, to be credited to his wife, 144 francs.'[1] (There is no record to show that Citizeness Frantz ever received that amount, saved by her husband from his pay.) The expenditures showing a total of more than 8 million, there remained a balance of 1,517,467 francs and 12 sous to welcome the Year VII of the Republic.

The methods used to raise cash up to that point, though not always dignified, were fairly orthodox compared to those used afterwards. Forced loans succeeded forced loans, the merchants thus tapped being given promissory notes on customs receipts (which never materialized, since all ports save Suez were blocked) and on anticipated taxes (which were spent even before they were collected). Any indication of treason, rebellion, or disloyalty among the richer citizens was welcomed with glee by the French fiscal authorities, since it enabled them to impose fines or to confiscate property. Fees were introduced for the registration of property, for proof of ownership, for purchases and sales, in short for almost as vast a number of transactions as those requiring a stamp in England. More than half of El-Djabarti's account of the French occupation is a chronicle of the unceasing variety of these and similar methods and of their daily application. The infinite ingenuity that Conté displayed in the field of mechanics had its match in the wizardry of Citizen Poussielgue and his colleagues; Poussielgue even achieved the miracle of remaining popular with the leading citizens whom he was fleecing.

To be sure, outright robbery was avoided. Men's and women's pockets were emptied by due process of law, even if the process was a bit speedy at times; food, horses, camels and other goods were never requisitioned without the owners being given a receipt or scrip. The owners were even paid when the term expired, with the help of new forced loans, backed up by more promissory notes. Still, the soldiers' pay remained chronically in arrears, and the army never lived more than a week or so removed from bank-

---

[1] La Jonquière, III, 692

ruptcy. When Kléber succeeded in Bonaparte's command in the late summer of 1799, he could write to the Directory that his predecessor had left a debt of 10 million francs, 4 million of which represented soldiers' pay in arrears.

***

Needless to say, the extraordinary measures taken by the Sultan Kebir to make the Egyptians pay for the expense of keeping an army they had not invited were not popular with them. Still, these exactions were in no manner different from those practised by the Mamelukes, and the average Egyptian is used to suffering.

The ordinary system of raising revenues under the Turkish-Mameluke regime was all the more iniquitous for being the accepted practice rather than the result of emergency conditions. The figures given by Napoleon for the fiscal structure of Egypt are no doubt very rough estimates; however, in the absence of reliable statistics, they are at least suggestive of the general situation.

The land, with a few exceptions, was in possession of the multazim, the feudal landlords, who held it in fief; when the landlord died, his heir continued in possession but had to pay the provincial governor a substantial death duty. More than 90 per cent of the multazim's land was worked by the peasants, or fellahin. The right to cultivate a parcel of land was obtained by the fellah through purchase; it had to be bought back, upon his death, by his heir. In addition, the fellahin paid the multazim annual dues which Napoleon estimated at 30 million francs per annum. Of these 30 million, collected by Coptic clerks, the multazim paid 6 million for local taxes and 6.4 million to the Sultan (this was the tribute called *miry*) thus keeping a revenue of about 17.6 million. In addition to the 30 million which they paid to their land lords, the fellahin paid 6 million in local taxation, 6 million to the sheiks-el-beled (the village mayors, actually acting as bailiffs of the landlords, who tolerated their various exactions from the peasants), 8 million to the Coptic tax collectors in excess of the amount actually disgorged by the Copts to the landlords; 4 million levied in kind by the provincial governors (horses, camels, etc.), and 9 million to the Bedouin tribes for the privilege of not being raided by them. Thus, according to Napoleon, the fellah footed a bill amounting to 63 million francs; how much the fellah kept, Napoleon does not say, but it is plain that it cannot have been much, if anything. Napoleon's conclusion is succinct, and incontrovertible: 'In the final analysis, the fellah has to pay for everything.'[1] It took a century and a half before any radical attempt was made to transform the fellah from a brutalized animal into something recognizable as a human being.

When he called the General Divan to meet at Cairo in October 1798, Bonaparte had two main purposes in mind. One was, in his words, 'to accustom the notables of Egypt to the ideas of assemblies and of government.'[2] The other was to revise criminal and civil procedure and the laws of property, inheritance, and taxation. However, the most radical of the reforms some of his advisers were contemplating was not even proposed to the Divan, since the French could not agree on it among themselves. A large number of villages (according to Napoleon, three-quarters of the total—no doubt an exaggeration) were without landlords, since the majority of the Mameluke multazim had been killed in battle or had fled. The question was, should this opportunity be used to introduce a general land reform and to make the fellahin outright owners of these lands, or should the old system be maintained?

The socialists among Bonaparte's advisers (no doubt General Caffarelli among them) pointed out that of the 5 million inhabitants of Egypt, 2.6 million were peasants; that their lot would be vastly improved by the reform, which furthermore would ensure their gratitude and loyalty to France; and that, in any event, the landlords were absolutely useless from the fiscal point of view. The conservatives' arguments in favour of retaining the old system were interesting and may be summarized thus: (1)To give the land to the peasants occupying it would make it impossible to distribute it to deserving officers of the French army or to native partisans of France. (2)Since the yearly yield depended on the extent of the annual floods, a delicate mechanism was required to determine it, and this operation was carried out best by the multazim. and their agents. (3)It was more politic to gain the loyalty of the solid, property-owning middle class than of the ignorant and volatile masses. The simple fact that no action was taken gave the victory to the conservatives. Just as, in France, the lands belonging to the Church and to the émigrés had been confiscated by the revolutionists and sold for almost nothing to patriotic speculators, so the confiscated lands of the Mamelukes were declared to be national property and disposed of to satisfy that moloch, the army's cash reserve. The fellah continued to be a fellah, and not a single French soldier got his six acres of land.

---

[1] Correspondance, XXIX, 427.

[2] Ibid., V, 32.

Although any kind of radical reform was thus ruled out by the French themselves, the questions Bonaparte submitted to the General Divan touched on very important matters: How should the provincial divans be organized, and what should be their members' salaries? How should the civil and criminal courts be organized? What laws should be introduced to ensure the right of inheritance and to eliminate arbitrariness from current practices? What improvements could be made in the existing method of establishing title to property and of collecting taxes?

An occasion becomes historic either by the participants' awareness that they are making history or by the consequences of their actions. If the deputies who attended the opening of the General Divan, at Cairo, on October 4, 1798, had been aware that they formed the first modern representative assembly in the Middle East, or if their meetings in the following two weeks had brought about any results whatsoever, the occasion might have been historic. As it was, the deputies were merely bewildered, and their only concern was to humour the French without changing one iota in the established order. Bonaparte was present at the opening session, while his interpreter Venture read his message. In it, he reminded his audience of Egypt's prosperity in ancient times, announced that he had delivered the people from the government of ignoramuses and fools, asserted that the French had molested no one, and invited the deputies to advise him in his efforts to restore order and prosperity. El-Djabarti, who was among the deputies, quotes the speech in full. 'What I like best in this composition,' he adds, 'are passages like "government of ignoramuses and fools" and "they molested no one."'

Venture then invited the sheiks to elect a chairman. Several among those present, says El-Djabarti, proposed the sheik El-Charkawi, head of the Mosque El Azhar and chairman of the Divan of Cairo. 'The French answered, "No, no, you must vote". A secret ballot was held, and the same sheik obtained the majority.'[1] Parliamentary procedure was decidedly novel to the assembly.

Steered by the French commissioners, Monge and Berthollet, the Divan sat for two weeks. Its deliberations, judging from the glimpses offered by El-Djabarti's account, bore a strong resemblance to the Mad Hatter's tea party. The deputies' conceptions of the proposed reforms and of European civil law were surrealistic. Thus, for some reason, they had the impression that in France 'only daughters inherit from their parents; as to the sons, they are

---

[1] El-Djabarti, VI, 50, 51.

disinherited because it is easier for them to support themselves.'[1] This practice was found to be irreconcilable with the teachings of Mohammed. In the end, the Divan made constructive suggestions as to the composition of the provincial councils (after all, since the French insisted on having local government, there was no way of avoiding it), but concerning all other matters before it, the assembly insisted quite firmly on the preservation of the existing order of things. All ancient customs and usages were to be maintained or restored. According to El-Djabarti, the Christian deputies were in complete agreement on this with their Moslem colleagues. The only new fiscal measure proposed was a graduated tax on urban real estate. 'When the inhabitants were apprised of this rule,' says El-Djabarti, 'most of them said nothing and bowed to fate, while others gathered in groups and grumbled. Several sheiks followed the example of the latter ... having forgotten that they no longer were masters.'[2]

The General Divan's reply was an indirect but unmistakable rebuff of Bonaparte's policy: there was nothing to be changed in the existing way of life, which was as it always had been and always would be, whereas the French occupation was a mere passing episode, a tribulation to be borne while waiting for its inevitable end. But Sultan Kebir chose to misinterpret the sheiks' meaning. In the account he dictated at St. Helena he even managed to twist the Divan's reply into an approval of his proposed reforms. It is the privilege of those who both make and write history to write it quite differently from the way they have made it. In 1798, Bonaparte had no illusions about the significance of the Divan's declaration. An uprising gave him an excuse for dissolving the Divan; as reconstituted two months later, that body retained little of its former importance.

Since Egypt was not ripe for accepting reform and the benefits of French rule, the people had to be won over by less direct methods. Since they respected only power, they must be ruled firmly; since their only driving force was religious fanaticism, that fanaticism had to be channelled and exploited. In a letter he had written to the chairman of the provisional government of Genoa in 1797, Bonaparte expressed this interesting thought: 'Never forget that whenever you bring religion, or even superstition, into conflict with liberty, the former will always win over the latter in the peo-

[1] Ibid., VI, 54.
[2] Ibid., VI, 55.

ple's mind.'¹ In other words, the legislator must tame religion, not oppose it. This principle made Bonaparte restore the Catholic Church in France after his return from Egypt, a measure which he qualified as 'a vaccine against religion.'² In Egypt, he tried the same homeopathic cure. 'We must lull fanaticism to sleep before we can uproot it,' he wrote to Kléber.³ His way of lulling fanticism to sleep was to pose as an instrument of God. The method proved to be unsuccessful wherever he applied it: people had the impression that he was a hypocritical tyrant.

In his Egyptian religious policy, he had an illustrious precedent. As he wrote in St. Helena, 'At all times, religious ideas have predominated among the peoples of Egypt.... When Alexander the Great appeared at their border, they came to welcome that great man as their liberator. When he crossed the desert, in a fortnight's march, from Alexandria to the temple of Amon, and when he had the priestess hail him as the son of Jupiter, he acted in full knowledge of the mentality of those people.... In doing so, he accomplished more to consolidate his conquest than if he had built twenty fortresses and called in a hundred thousand Macedonians.'⁴

Alexander's example had filled Napoleon's daydreams since his childhood. The parallel was obvious: only the Mosque El Azhar had to be substituted for the Temple of Amon-Ra. In his history of the Egyptian campaign, Napoleon relates his courtship of El Azhar with relish:

> The school, or Sorbonne, of the Mosque El Azhar, is the most cele-brated in the East. It was founded by Saladin. There, sixty doctors or ulemas debated theology and explained the sacred texts. It was the only centre that could set an example and carry with it public opinion of the Islamic world and of the four sects of Islam. These four sects ... differ among themselves only on points of discipline. In Cairo, each was headed by a mufti. Napoleon neglected nothing to gain their favour and to flatter them. They were old men, worthy of respect for their morals, their erudition, their wealth, and even their birth. Every day, at sunrise, they and the ulemas of the Mosque El Azhar would come to

---

¹ Correspondance, III, 367.

² Stael, p. 373. See also Marquiset, p. 71, and Pelet, p. 223.

³ Correspondance, V, 574.

⁴ Ibid., XXIX, 478.

his palace before prayer time. Their escort filled all of Esbekiya Square. They came on their richly harnessed mules,
surrounded by their servants and by many runners armed
with poles. The French sentries presented arms to them....
In the palace ... they were received with respect; sherbets
and coffee were served to them. After a moment, the General would enter, sit down in their midst, on the same divan, and seek to gain their trust by discussing the Koran,
by having its chief passages explained to him, and by displaying great admiration for the Prophet. When they left,
they went to the mosques, where the people were assembled. There they spoke to them of their hopes and calmed
the distrust and hostility of that immense population. They
rendered very positive services to the army.[1]

In his conversation with the ulemas and muftis, Napoleon
tried to convince them that he was under the special protection of
the Prophet. How else could he have defeated the brave Mamelukes? This great revolution had been predicted in several passages of the Koran. The religious leaders gave their affection to
Sultan Kebir: 'They thought that he was predestined.' This, at
least, is what Sultan Kebir asserted at St. Helena. However, he
concedes, the fact that the French were called 'Infidels' caused
'disorders and misunderstandings' in the provinces.

Sultan Kebir began to complain more bitterly, in his
conversations [with the sheiks], of the hostile sermons
made by the imams at the mosques during the Friday services; but the reprimands and exhortations the sheiks directed at these turbulent imams were inadequate. At last,
when he thought that the right moment had arrived, he
said to ten of the principal sheiks those who were the most
devoted to him: 'We must put an end to these disorders. I
need a *fetfa* [a proclamation] of the Mosque El Azhar, ordering the people to make an oath of obedience.' This request made them turn pale. Their faces showed the fright
in their souls. They became sullen and embarrassed. The
sheik El-Charkawi, head of the ulemas of El Azhar , asked
to be heard and said, after collecting himself, 'You want the
protection of the Prophet, who loves you. You want the
Moslem Arabs to enlist under your flag. You want to restore the glory of Arabia, and you are not an idolater. Then
become a Moslem yourself. A hundred thousand Egyp-

---

[1] Ibid., XXIX, 479.

tians, a hundred thousand Arabs will come to join you from
Arabia, from Mecca and Medina. With them under your
leadership and discipline, you will conquer the East and
you will restore the Prophet's fatherland in all its glory.'
When he said this, the old men's faces became wreathed in
smiles. All prostrated themselves to implore divine protection. It was the General's turn to be astonished. [1]

Offhand, it seems curious that neither this memorable scene,
so vividly described by Napoleon, nor its bizarre consequences
should deserve a single line or mention in the chronicles of El-
Djabarti and of Nicholas the Turk. On second thought one realizes
that Napoleon is rather vague as to the date when it is supposed to
have taken place. Since he thought that his history of the campaign
was superior to Caesar's *Commentaries* because it mentioned
dates, this vagueness seems even stranger. Although it would be
difficult to prove that the scene never happened, the assumption is
more than plausible. What most likely did happen was that the
reasoning ascribed by Napoleon in exile to the sheiks and ulemas
had actually been his own reasoning, propounded by him to them.
It was he who suggested to them that he and his army wished to be
converted to Islam. 'A thousand rumours,' he says, 'spread among
the people. Some said that the Prophet himself had appeared to
Sultan Kebir and had said to him, "... Profess the principles of my
faith, for it is God's own. The Arabs are only waiting for this sign; I
shall give you all Asia in conquest."' [2] Everything points to the conviction that the rumours did not spread, as he says, but that they
were deliberately spread by him. Sultan Kebir, he continues, this
time with the ring of truth, 'took advantage of these rumours to
insinuate that in his reply [to the Prophet] he had requested one
year's respite to prepare his army, which the Prophet granted him;
that he had promised to build a great mosque; that the entire army
would embrace Islam; and that already the great sheiks El-Sadat
and El-Bekri regarded him as a Moslem.'

There is no reason to doubt this much of Napoleon's much-
embroidered story: not long after his arrival in Cairo, the sheiks
put it to him that, since he claimed to be a disciple of Mohammed,
and since his army loved Islam, the best way for them to prove
their sincerity would be to become Moslems. Cut off from the outside world, Bonaparte found it politic to humour their hopes, even
if they were as insincere as his own protestations. At the same

---

[1] Ibid., XXIX, 481-82.

[2] Ibid., XXIX, 482-83.

time, being a realist, he had no wish to honour his promise unless there was an absolute necessity to do so. 'In this world,' he told his companion Gourgaud at an unguarded moment in St. Helena, 'one must appear friendly, make many promises, and keep none.'[1] The sheiks reasoned the same way; each party pretended to be the other's dupe.

A curious exchange followed between the sheiks of the Mosque El Azhar and Bonaparte. There were two obstacles to his and his army's conversion to Islam, Bonaparte informed the theologians. One was the matter of circumcision, the other was the prohibition of wine. His men, having drunk wine all their lives, would never consent to give it up, and they were tenderly attached to their fore-skins. The theologians considered their difficulties at great length. At last they came forth with a *fetfa* declaring that circumcision was merely a counsel of perfection and not essential to the Moslem faith; as for drinking wine, it was possible to do so and be a Moslem yet, albeit in a state of sin and thus not eligible for the delights of Paradise. Bonaparte considered this and declared himself satisfied as to the first point, but suggested that surely the muftis were joking as to the second: for why should a man embrace a religion that would damn him to hell for continuing a practice he has no intention of giving up? The muftis withdrew to reconsider the problem, invoking God's help to enlighten them. Eventually, according to Napoleon's account—there is no other—a second *fetfa* was issued: the French could drink wine and yet gain Paradise, provided they redeemed their sin by contributing one fifth of their income to good works, instead of the customary tenth. It is not irrelevant to mention in this connection that the sheik El-Bekri, who acted as moderator in this theological dispute, was in the habit of drinking himself into a stupor every night by imbibing a mixture consisting of a bottle of burgundy and a bottle of brandy.[2]

Napoleon does not say exactly when the second *fetfa* was issued, but it appears from the context that it must have been during his absence in Syria, in the spring of 1799. After his return to Cairo, the ulemas of El Azhar issued a declaration to the effect that Sultan Kebir 'loved the Moslems, cherished the Prophet, instructed himself by reading the Koran every day, and desired to build a mosque unrivalled in splendour and to embrace the Mos-

[1] Gourgaud, II, 151.

[2] This, at least, is what Roustam Raza, Napoleon's famous Mameluke, who had been a slave of El-Bekri, asserts in his memoirs.

lem faith.'[1] In quoting this, Napoleon refrains from saying that the declaration was issued only because he had requested it. Cynical though they were, his promises may have appeared plausible to the ulemas since General Menou had recently become a convert to Islam, for reasons more erotic and political than metaphysical.

III

'What I like in Alexander the Great,' Napoleon confided to a companion in St. Helena, 'is not his campaigns ... but his political methods.... He was right in ordering the murder of Parmenion, who like a fool objected to Alexander's giving up Greek customs. It was most politic of him to go to Amon: it was thus he conquered Egypt. If I had stayed in the Orient, I probably would have founded an empire like Alexander's by going on pilgrimage to Mecca.'[2] This was the same man who remarked to General Caulaincourt, during his headlong flight from Russia, 'When I need somebody, I am not squeamish: I'd kiss his _ [3]

In his Islamic policy, Sultan Kebir was in something of a predicament. To make the sheiks swallow it, he had to convince them of his sincerity; to make his army swallow it, he had to convince them of his insincerity. He never convinced the sheiks, and he was unable to lay some of the doubts in the minds of his subordinates. Just what did he want to do? Establish a colony for France? Create an Oriental empire for himself? Or simply stall for time?

Bonaparte's most severe critic among his subordinate commanders was Kléber, his senior both in age and in date of promotion. A professional soldier, the tall and forthright Alsatian had little use for politicians, with whom he was on chronically bad terms. He had agreed to serve under Bonaparte in order to remove himself as far as possible from the Directory. Yet, though he despised the government of the Republic, he believed in the Republic. In Bonaparte he soon recognized a man who was more politician than general but a politician whose aims were higher and far more dangerous than those of the gang that governed France. Bonaparte was an opportunist: 'Never a fixed plan. Everything goes by fits and starts,' Kléber noted in his pocket diary about his chief. 'Each day's business is transacted according to the needs of

---

[1] Correspondance, XXX, 64.

[2] Gourgaud, II, 435-36.

[3] Caulaincourt, I, 315.

the day. He claims to believe in fate.'[1] Bonaparte was authoritarian and wanted to know everything better than anyone else: 'He is incapable of organizing or administering anything; and yet, since he wants to do everything, he organizes and administers. Hence, chaos and waste everywhere. Hence our want of everything, and poverty in the midst of plenty.' Bonaparte corrupted: 'Is he loved? How could he be? He loves nobody. But he thinks he can make up for this by promotions and by gifts.'[2]

Kléber admired Bonaparte's military genius and daring; but he had not been in Egypt for more than a few weeks when he began to be appalled by his chief's utter recklessness. A general who is a true soldier does not send his troops across a desert without supplies and water; he does not take the chances which Bonaparte had taken in leading his army into Egypt. Bonaparte, Kléber once remarked, was the kind of general who needed an income of 10,000 men a month. When Bonaparte introduced a remark with the phrase, 'As for me, who am playing a game with history,'[3] Kléber was horrified enough to record the words in his notebook.

Bonaparte's bearing in Egypt was that of an Oriental potentate rather than a general of the French Republic. Perhaps he played the part out of political necessity, but he seemed to relish it too much and to overplay it. It was evident to Kléber almost from the start that the expedition was ill-advised, ill-prepared, and doomed. Hence he did not share the enthusiasm of the 'colonialists' Menou and Monge at the head. The most sensible thing, it seemed to him, was to evacuate Egypt, rather than spend more lives and make more sacrifices for nothing. If this could not be done, the best was to hold out until an honourable capitulation could be negotiated. In the meantime, to keep in control of the situation, Egypt must be ruled with firmness and fairness rather than with flamboyant proclamations on the one hand and arbitrary tyranny on the other. Kléber's own administration of Egypt, after Bonaparte's departure for France, proved that he respected Islam at least as much as had his predecessor, even though he never found it necessary to announce that he would become a Moslem and restore the greatness of the Arab nation, as Bonaparte had.

Kléber's hostility to Bonaparte, which culminated in the scathing letter of denunciation he addressed to the Directory after his

---

[1] Charles-Roux, *Bonaparte*, p. 73.

[2] Charles-Roux, *Bonaparte*, p. 74.

[3] Ibid., p. 73.

chief's departure, first flared up while Kléber was governor of Alexandria. He had never been an easy general to handle, but Bonaparte rubbed him up in an even more radically wrong way than had other superiors. The high-handed orders, the constant dressing-down he received from Cairo annoyed him all the more intensely since his head wound, though healed, still caused him violent pain. On the other hand, Kléber's constant complaints about shortages and his tendency to modify or ignore orders as he saw fit in the light of local conditions exasperated Bonaparte. On September 5, Kléber requested to be recalled from Alexandria: 'I beg you to let me rejoin my division. I see that my conduct is so much in contradiction with your orders and with the administrative policy you seem to have adopted that it cannot help displeasing you.'[1] He repeated this request four days later: 'I know nothing about administration,' he informed his chief.[2] His letter to Berthier, written the same day, was equally testy. Bonaparte's order to inscribe on Pompey's Pillar the names of the heroes who had died in the capture of Alexandria could not be carried out, he explained among other things, because Kléber had not been given a list of the heroes; besides, even if a list were sent, the names could not be inscribed before the celebration of 1 Vendémiaire, Pompey's Pillar being made of granite and not of butter. As for the *Courrier de L'Egypte*, of which Berthier had sent him several copies: 'Your paper in Cairo is not edited attractively enough to allow the hope that many subscribers can be recruited. At the very least, it should be written in French.'[3]

Kléber's courier had barely left for Cairo when the Cairo courier brought him a severe admonition from the chief. 'You will be so kind,' wrote Bonaparte, 'as not to upset the arrangements I am making. They are based on factors that you cannot appreciate, since you are not at the centre of things.'[4] There followed a blast about what Bonaparte considered extravagant expenditures, especially for the military hospital at Alexandria, and another blast about Kléber's refusal to levy an additional forced loan from the merchants of Alexandria. Obviously, Kléber did not see the grand scheme of things. Infuriated, he requested an investigation of his conduct. 'When you wrote that letter, Citizen General,' he concluded, 'you forgot that you were holding the graver of History in

---

[1] La Jonquière, III, 81.

[2] Ibid., III, 92.

[3] Ibid., III, 91.

[4] Correspondance, IV, 448-49.

your hand and that you were writing to Kléber. I expect, Citizen General, to receive by the next courier your order suspending me, not only as governor of Alexandria, but from all my functions in the army until you are more thoroughly informed of what is happening and has happened here.'[1]

Bonaparte's reply ignored this temperamental outburst: 'If I really held the graver of History in my hand, nobody would have less cause to complain than you,' he wrote.[2] But Kléber would have none of this: on September 19 he handed his command to General Manscourt, and three days later he requested to be sent back to France because of ill health. Bonaparte could not afford to lose Kléber; and, when he needed a man, he was capable of turning on his charm. 'I am distressed to hear of your indisposition,' he answered. 'I hope that the climate of Cairo will improve your health and that, after leaving the sands of Alexandria, you may find our Egypt less unpleasant than she appears at first.... Believe in the sincerity of my desire to see your health restored and in the price I attach to your esteem and friendship. I am afraid we have quarrelled a little. You would do me an injustice if you doubted my regret. In Egypt, the clouds (when there are any) never last longer than six hours. As for me, if there had been any, they would have passed in three. My esteem for you is at least as high as the esteem you have shown me at times. I hope to see you in Cairo within a few days.... I greet and love you.'[3]

There was nothing Kléber could do; on October 22, he arrived at Cairo, to enjoy its healthful climate and study the wisdom of Bonaparte's grand scheme at first hand. The first thing he saw and heard was the French guns at the Citadel shelling the Mosque El Azhar, while hordes of screaming Moslems were massacring Frenchmen and local Christians and putting up barricades in the streets. From the tops of the minarets, the muezzins were exhorting the Faithful to kill their French friends.

IV

The most remarkable thing about the insurrection that broke out in Cairo on October 21 is that it took the French completely by

---

[1] Correspondance incite, officielle et confidentielle: Egypte, II, 75-76.
[2] La Jonquière, III, 92-93.
[3] Correspondance, V, 30-51.

surprise, although its imminence had been proclaimed, quite literally, from the roof tops.

A variety of causes have been suggested for the outbreak of the
rebellion. Napoleon and El-Djabarti, in their respective accounts,
seem agreed in ascribing it to a number of unpopular French administrative measures, foremost among them the fiscal devices
already mentioned—forced loans and sales, requisitions, fines,
registration fees, etc. These, however, struck only the upper and
middle classes, which took no active part in the rebellion. Other
measures affected the populace more directly: to facilitate circula-
tion in Cairo, Bonaparte had ordered the removal of all the gates
separating the several quarters of the city from one another; he
had forced the shopkeepers to keep street lights burning all night
in front of their establishments; he had caused several blocks of
houses and a mosque to be razed because they obstructed the
ramparts of the Citadel; he had placed additional guns in the Citadel and pointed them at the city; and he had introduced certain
novel sanitary measures—regulating burials, intended to reduce
the risk of epidemics, but vastly resented by the populace. According to El-Djabarti, however, it was the real estate tax recommended by the General Divan which set off the explosion.

Although all these factors undoubtedly contributed to provoking the rebellion, they do not explain it satisfactorily. It is Nicholas
the Turk who goes to the core of the matter. His master, the emir
of the Syrian Druses, had sent him to Egypt to observe what was
happening there, and Nicholas observed well. In their hopeless
isolation, he says, the French had sought to befriend the people.
'They were doomed to diminish in numbers, and never to grow. All
that was left them was to appeal to feelings of equality and fraternity. They proffered their friendship to the population in order to
win its affection. In doing so, they disregarded human
nature....The presence of the French in Cairo was intolerable, especially when the Egyptians saw their wives and daughters walking about the streets unveiled and appearing to be the property of
the French, with whom they were seen in public and with whom
they cohabited. Before these facts, the Moslems died of shame. It
was bad enough for them to see the taverns that had been established in all the bazaars of Cairo and even in several mosques.
Such a spectacle created an irrespirable atmosphere for the Moslems.... Fundamentally, the French occupation improved the condition of the lower classes—the second-hand dealers, pack carri-
ers, artisans, donkey drivers, horse-grooms, pimps, and prostitutes. All told, the scum of the population was doing well, because

it benefited from the new freedom. But the élite and the middle class experienced all sorts of vexation, because imports and exports had come to a standstill.'[1]

Except for trade with Arabia proper, imports and exports had virtually stopped indeed, 'the English having blockaded the ports in the manner in which the English know how to do this.'[2] All the same, Nicholas admits, there were no serious shortages; in fact, food was more plentiful than usual, and the prices of staples had come down. One might wonder, therefore, why the lower classes, whose lot had improved, rose in rebellion, while the rich, who had cause to complain, generally abstained from it. There can be little doubt as to the answer: as happens frequently, the well-to-do and enlightened used the fanaticized poor as pawns.

What the population resented was not the abuses practised by the French authorities—they were accustomed to abuse—but the novelties the invaders had introduced, even if these were to their advantage. This resentment was fanned by the demagoguery of the more fanatic among the religious leaders (particularly those who held no positions under the French) and by the propaganda spread by the agents of Djezzar Pasha and of the Mameluke beys in exile. From Syria, Djezzar and Ibrahim Bey sent messenger upon messenger. Sultan Selim's firmans, calling on all Moslems to wage a holy war against the French, were thus brought into Egypt, and they were read publicly in the mosques by the imams. The French, the firmans declared, were atheists and enemies not only of Islam but of all religion. Soon the armies of the Ottoman Empire would come to crush them. 'Ships as tall as mountains will cover the surface of the seas. Cannons that lighten and thunder, heroes who despise death for the sake of victory in the cause of God will arrive to chase the French.' To Djezzar himself it was 'reserved, if it please God, to preside over their total destruction.... No trace shall be left of those Infidels: for God has given His promise. The hopes of the wicked shall be disappointed, and the wicked shall perish.'[3] Djezzar's thunder was accompanied by Ibrahim's threats against any one who collaborated with the French. These messages were known to all the members of the Divan of Cairo, who saw Bonaparte daily; they were read at prayer services; and incitements to revolt were shouted from the tops of the minarets by the muezzins five times a day. By early October, disorders broke out in the

[1] Nicolas Turc, p. 45.

[2] Ibid., p. 40.

[3] Martin, I, 243.

Delta: in the Menzala region, the peasantry conducted what amounted to guerilla warfare under the leadership of the wealthy Hassan Tubar, who was in correspondence with Ibrahim Bey but at the same time professed his friend ship for the French. In Tanta the population rose in an abortive rebellion on October 7, in response to Djezzar's proclamations.

Despite all these, storm warnings, the French seemed utterly unaware of what was preparing. 'Thanks to the moderation of our government,' wrote Poussielgue's secretary on September 6, 'a complete sense of security prevails among all classes of society.'[1] On September 14, upon leaving the house of the sheik El-Sadat (one of the members of the Divan of Cairo), Bonaparte found himself surrounded by an ugly crowd, shouting imprecations and quotations from the Koran. 'Bonaparte,' says El-Djabarti, 'asked what was going on, but the truth was hidden from him and he was told that the crowd were acclaiming him and wishing him happiness.'[2] Though it is difficult for a person ignorant of the language to tell an Arabic curse from an acclamation, it is even more difficult to believe that Bonaparte was entirely taken in. There is ample evidence that he was aware of the imams' and muezzins' inflammatory activities: it was to counteract them that he had the Divan of Cairo proclaim his sympathy for Islam. He must also have known of Djezzar's and Ibrahim's messengers, since he had the heads of two of them cut off. Whether he really believed, or only pretended to believe, that the firmans broadcasting the Turkish declaration of war were mere concoctions of Djezzar and of the Mamelukes is a question that probably can never be answered. It was opportune, at any rate, to treat them as lies and to pretend that all was well between him and the Porte.

All the same, Bonaparte was completely taken by surprise when the rebellion broke out. With the divans and the outstanding Moslem leaders ostensibly supporting him, he felt that the rabble could easily be contained. In this, he was not altogether mistaken. He probably had no illusions as to the sheiks' loyalty, but he counted on their timorousness. That they betrayed him is certain: they withheld from him their knowledge of the impending rebellion. Yet it is equally certain that they had no hand in inciting the rebellion. Being men of substance, they had too much to lose in case it failed, and being men of high standing, they could always join it in case it succeeded.

---

[1] Charles-Roux, Bonaparte, p. 198.

[2] El-Djabarti, VI, 39.

As for the middle class—the merchants and shopkeepers—they also for the most part took no active part in the rebellion; many of them even gave shelter and aid to the French. On this all witnesses are agreed. Yet the fact that the rebellious ferment reached its boiling point just when they were to be struck by an onerous new tax may have caused some of them to welcome the outbreak. The only really militant elements were the fanatics—the imams, the students of El Azhar, the holy men, the fakirs and the blind fakirs, the beggars, who were joined by the kind of rabble which forms the underworld in every large city and springs up spontaneously whenever looting and murder are sanctioned by higher pretexts. It was a crowd not very different from that which had marched to Versailles on October 5, 1789, or that which, on September 2, 1792, had paraded the breasts and privy parts of the Princesse de Lamballe on pikes through the streets of Paris.

***

'One fine day,' says Nicholas the Turk, referring to October 21, 1798, 'some sheik or other of El Azhar started to run through the streets, shouting, "Let all those who believe that there is but one God take themselves to the Mosque El Azhar! For today is the day to fight the Infidel!" Now, although most of the population was informed [of what was about to happen], the French were living in utter unconcern. In an instant, the city was boiling over, and news of it came to General Dupuy [the commandant of Cairo]. He was a very hard man. He leapt to his feet. "What is going on?" "An uprising of the beggars of the city, who are gathered in the quarters of Khan Khalili and Nahhasin." He left instantly, followed by only five horsemen.... He rode to Khan Khalili and saw the populace and some workingmen erecting barricades. A Janissary suddenly appeared from around a street corner and hit him over the back with a police stick. The general fell from his horse. His men carried him off ... but he died on the way.'[1]

According to Detroye's diary, Dupuy was killed by a lance rather than a stick; he was, at any rate, the first victim. At six in the morning, says Detroye, it became obvious that something was afoot. People armed with muskets and sticks were running toward the great mosque, while the muezzins shouted their rallying cries. The shops closed down. At eight o'clock the troops were put on the alert. Believing the situation to be well in hand, Bonaparte left Cairo with Generals Caffarelli and Dommartin and with Detroye to inspect some fortifications in progress at Old Cairo and on Rodah

---

[1] Nicolas Turc, p. 41.

Island. About ten o'clock, he received word that a general insurrection had broken out and that Dupuy had been killed. Bonaparte appointed General Bon to take Dupuy's post and immediately set out for Cairo. As the party reached the gate, they were received by a hail of rocks; they turned back and finally managed to enter by the Bulaq gate. By this time, shots could be heard from everywhere, and corpses were lying in the streets. Fire had become general by then, but Bonaparte's escort succeeded in taking him back to Esbekiya Square.

Meanwhile the mob had invaded the Greek section of the city, killing the men, carrying off the women, and looting the shops. They also laid siege to General Caffarelli's house, in which part of the scientific instruments were stored. Caffarelli was with Bonaparte, but in his absence the chief cartographer, Testevuide, and four other engineers, with a small military escort, had rushed to his residence to save their instruments. For four hours, they held out against their assailants; at last, they tried to make a sortie. Testevuide and three of his subordinates were massacred within seconds. The mob broke into the building. 'In that house,' says El-Djabarti, 'there were many instruments of great precision, such as telescopes and other astronomical and mathematical apparatus. All these instruments were unique and had much value for people who knew their uses. The mob scattered them all and destroyed many of them. The French greatly regretted their loss. For a long time they made searches to recover some of these instruments; they even gave rewards to those who brought any of them back.'[1]

While Caffarelli's house was being looted, another mob besieged the military hospital and killed two surgeons at its gate. Except for the Citadel, Esbekiya Square, the barracks, and the quarters of the Institute (all of them rather distant from one another), Cairo was in rebel hands. The kadi (chief judge), who had tried to reason with the crowd, had been stoned but managed to escape; his house was looted, as were several warehouses, regardless of whether they belonged to Christians or to Moslems.

In his headquarters at Elfi Bey's palace, Bonaparte was in a rage. He ordered the artillery of the Citadel, reinforced with howitzers and mortars, to be directed at the Mosque El Azhar and at the surrounding quarters, which formed the focus of the insurrection and whose tortuous streets and barricades made any less drastic action impossible.

---

[1] El-Djabarti, VI, 66.

In the confusion, the scholars and artists installed at Qassim Bey's palace and in the neighbouring houses were virtually forgotten by the French command, from which they were almost two miles distant. They were not, at first, exactly under siege, but a threatening crowd had gathered about the buildings. Two engineers were despatched to headquarters for help, which came only toward evening, in the form of a company of grenadiers and of forty muskets to be distributed among the scientists, with thirty rounds of ammunition for each. Few of the savants knew how to use the weapons.

The night passed rather quietly, each side preparing for the next day. About midnight, the company of grenadiers was recalled from the Institute. 'The following morning, hostilities were resumed,' says Denon, who shared a house at some distance from the Institute with Dolomieu and several other civilians. 'We had been given arms; all the savants got ready for combat; the leaders were nominated, everybody had his own plan, but nobody felt obliged to obey.'[1] At Qassim Bey's palace, Monge was in command. Several of the savants, seeing that an escape was feasible, suggested that solution, but were overruled by the eloquent Monge. 'Would you dare to abandon the instruments of science entrusted to our care?' he demanded.[2] No one dared, and the scholars sniped at the thickening crowd of assailants heroically for several hours, until two French patrols relieved them in the nick of time.

At dawn that morning, Bonaparte had despatched his aide-de-camp, Brigadier Sulkowski, with a message to General Dumas. Sulkowski never reached his destination. His horse slipped while he was crossing a village at the outskirts of Cairo; he was cut down, with nine of the fifteen Guides in his escort; according to Desvernois, the rebels threw his corpse to the dogs to be devoured. Sulkowski was a soldier of the greatest promise, a patriot who had taken up the profession of arms only in the illusion that it might eventually help him to fight for the independence of Poland, and an idealist of rather radical persuasion. As his notes reveal, his experience at the side of Bonaparte had gradually taught him to distrust his chief's ambitions. Bonaparte pretended to appreciate his gifts but was slow in promoting him. Sulkowski's death, General Belliard noted in his diary, 'distressed the commander-in-chief, who finally said "He is dead; he is happy."'[3] Also dead and happy

[1] Denon, I, 105-6.
[2] Aubry, *Monge*, p. 257.
[3] La Jonquière, III, 281.

were thirty-three military hospital patients, massacred as they entered Cairo from Bilbeis.

The bombardment of the Mosque El Azhar began about noon and lasted until evening. 'Exterminate everybody in the mosque,' Bonaparte instructed General Bon.[1] 'This bombardment was so terrible,' relates El-Djabarti, that the inhabitants of the city, who had never seen such a thing, began to cry and to pray Heaven to preserve them from such a misfortune. The rebels ceased fire, but the French continued the shelling. Houses, shops, palaces, inns, everything crumbled. One's ears were deafened by the noise of the guns. People left their houses and the streets to hide in holes. The sheiks then decided to go to the commander-in-chief and to beg him to stop this rain of bombs.[2]

The novelty of an artillery barrage no doubt caused El-Djabarti to exaggerate its effects. According to Napoleon, who sounds convincing on this point, El Azhar suffered only minor damage, and only a few houses in the surrounding quarter were destroyed.[3] Rifle fire directed at the French batteries from the minarets and dome of the Hassan Mosque continued through the afternoon. Toward evening, the shells having produced their effect, three infantry battalions and 300 horse converged on El Azhar. Everything gave way before their bayonets and sabres, and the mosque was carried by storm. Among the first horsemen to penetrate into the courtyard of the mosque was a fantastic figure: his powerful dark chest bared, General Dumas sat astride his rearing horse whose nostrils were spurting blood, and swung his sabre above his head, a picture of terror and beauty. 'The angel! The angel!' cried the Arabs or so, at least, asserts his son, whose exuberant imagination also invented the *Three Musketeers* and the *Count of Monte Cristo*.

The mosque was cleared in em instant. Several hundred rebels were taken prisoner, but none, apparently, was put to the sword. Even El-Djabarti, always eager to report French outrages, mentions no massacre—only desecration. 'They entered the Mosque El Azhar with their horses,' he relates, 'and they tied them to the

---

[1] Correspondance, V, 88.

[2] El-Djabarti, VI, 56-57.

[3] El Azhar, now in the process of being restored, must have been in rather a dilapidated condition already in 1798. The shells which fell into its precincts exploded not in the building proper but in the colonnaded courtyard, where they undoubtedly produced a murderous effect.

kiblah.[1] They broke the lamps, the candles, and the desks of the students; they looted everything they could find in the closets; they threw on the ground the books and the Koran and trampled upon them with their boots. They urinated and spat in the mosque; they drank wine in it, and they broke the bottles and scattered the pieces in all the corners. They stripped everybody inside the mosque and took their clothes away.'[2]

While all this was going on, a strange figure could be seen sneaking away from El Azhar—a middle-aged potbellied Frenchman, wearing slippers and a dressing gown, under the folds of which a bulky object seemed to be concealed. The French artillery officers could observe him through their glasses making his way toward Esbekiya and dodging horsemen, grenadiers, and corpses. When he arrived at headquarters, his appearance caused something of a sensation. It was Citizen Marcel, the printer and Arabist, who produced from under his dressing gown a magnificent thirteenth-century manuscript of the Koran, rescued from the vandalism of *la furia francese*.

Shortly after nightfall on October 22, the fighting was over in Cairo. The French had lost about 300 men; the rebels' losses have been estimated at 2,000-5,000. Generally speaking, the outbreak was limited to the capital, but there were flare-ups in several other places, notably at Bilbeis, which had a strong French garrison. Lieutenant Vertray, who was confined there at the hospital for ophthalmia (he eventually recovered his eyesight) was among the invalid and the blind who had been issued arms to defend themselves against their assailants. The insurrection, he says, 'was terminated by terrible reprisals, to our honour and glory.'[3]

There were reprisals in Cairo too, but they were concealed under a show of clemency. On the morrow of the rebellion, the sheiks and imams of El Azhar (with the sole exception of the sheik El-Sadat, who pleaded ill health), presented themselves at Bonaparte's palace. 'Their countenances,' Napoleon recalled at St. Helena, 'were those of guilty men consumed by anxiety.' Still, no specific accusations could be levelled against them; besides, Bonaparte had made up his mind not to investigate their conduct. 'I know that many of you have been weak,' he told them, 'but I like to

---

[1] The niche, usually flanked by columns, marking the direction of Mecca. It is equivalent to the altar in Christian churches.

[2] Ibid., VI, 57.

[3] Vertray, p. 86.

believe that none of you is guilty.'[1] The blood that had been shed was sufficient; the sacred books of El Azhar would be returned to them; let them purify the desecrated mosque, bury their dead, and proclaim his magnanimous amnesty to the people.

The old men, says Napoleon, fell on their knees and kissed the Holy books which he had returned to them. Bonaparte's clemency surprised not only them but especially the French, soldiers and civilians alike, who grumbled that it would be interpreted as mere weakness. Despite their criticism and their dire prognostications, Bonaparte stubbornly persisted in his forgiveness.

'Bonaparte Forgiving the Rebels of Cairo' became a favourite subject of painters and engravers during the Napoleonic era. Their representations do not give the faintest idea of what actually happened.

One day, not long after his return from Egypt, Bonaparte made some interesting comments on the clemency scene in the last act of Corneille's *Cinna*. Cinna has plotted against the life of Augustus: Augustus, instead of punishing him, holds out his hand in friendship: 'Soyons amis, Cinna.' Corneille, remarked Bonaparte, was a poet who understood politics. 'For instance, not long ago I found the explanation of the denouement in *Cinna*. At first, all I saw in it was a device for a touching fifth act. Moreover, clemency in itself is such a miserable petty virtue, unless it rests on political motives.... But one day Monvel, playing that part in my presence, revealed to me the secret of that grand conception. He said the line, "Let us be friends, Cinna," with such a cunning and wily expression that I understood that his action was merely a tyrant's feint, and what had seemed to me a puerile sentiment I now approved as a calculated ruse.'[2]

Since the sheiks were the only reliable tools he had in Egypt; since, at any rate, it would have been difficult to prove anything against them; and since he counted on their help to pacify the people, Bonaparte's clemency toward them was untainted by any humanitarian sentimentality. In fact, while he allowed them to kiss his hands in gratitude, certain orders he had given to General Berthier were being carried out at the Citadel: 'You will have the goodness, Citizen General, to order the commandant of Cairo to have the heads of all prisoners taken arms-in-hand cut off. They will be taken to the bank of the Nile ... after dark; their headless

---

[1] Correspondance, XXIX, 502-3.

[2] Remusat, I, 279.

corpses will be thrown into the river.'[1] Aside from these prisoners, eighty members of the 'Divan of Defence' (the rebellious junta) were executed at the Citadel. 'They were people with a violent and irreconcilable turn of mind,' Napoleon commented twenty years later.[2] A public show of clemency to the blameless; executions of the recalcitrant in secret and at night the formula would have won Machiavelli's approval.

One man who was blissfully in his element during the days following the rebellion was Barthelmy, the flamboyant lieutenant of police, 'Barthelmy,' says El-Djabarti, 'was in charge of disarming the population. He covered the entire city with his men, who arrested whomever they wished or whoever was denounced to them by the Christians. Barthelmy did as he pleased with those people. He fined them and pocketed their fines, he had them bound and thrown into prison. There, he tortured them to obtain confessions and to discover the hiding places of looted objects and arms. Many of those unfortunates denounced other persons, who were promptly arrested and given the same treatment.... Many people were killed, and their corpses thrown into the Nile. Only God knows how many died during those few days.'[3]

There were other exceptions to Sultan Kebir's clemency, notably the six sheiks who had been designated to Bonaparte as the ringleaders in the uprising. Under arrest at the sheik El-Bekri's house, they were removed to the Citadel, on a flimsy pretext, during the night of November 2, found guilty by a court martial, and decapitated the next morning. They were the sheik Ahmed el-Charkawi, 'learned in the law ... a tall, long-bearded man';[4] 'the learned imam, sheik Abd el-Whabel Chabrawi,' a teacher in the Mosque of Hussein, endowed with 'an agreeable diction and a great memory'; 'the young erudite, sheik Yussuf el-Musseihi ... professor at the Mosque of El Kurdi'; the sheik Ismail, who 'was not very learned but had a great deal of eloquence'; the sheik Abd el-Kasim, of whom El-Djabarti relates no particular characteristic; and 'the celebrated sheik Soliman, chief of the blind fakirs,' a man grown prosperous in a peculiar form of the grain trade, who could despatch a whole army of blind men to bring a recalcitrant buyer

---

[1] Correspondance, V, 89-90.

[2] Ibid., XXIX, 502.

[3] El-Djabarti, VI, 58-59.

[4] Not to Le confused with Abdullah el-Charkawi, the chairman of the Divan of Cairo.

or seller to reason.[1] Nine others were sentenced to death *in absentia*. There can be no question but that those fifteen men, sacrificed by their colleagues to Sultan Kebir's righteous wrath, represented the most fanatic and demagogical elements in the Moslem clergy.

Meanwhile, in all the mosques of Egypt, a circular letter from the ulemas of El Azhar was read proclaiming Bonaparte's leniency, deploring the rebellion, denouncing as fabrications all the firmans issued by the Porte against the French, and maintaining the fiction of a Franco-Turkish alliance.

Although Bonaparte's quality of mercy was not exactly unstrained, it cannot be said that he broke the spirit of his amnesty. Except for the rebels caught arms-in-hand, there were no mass executions, and no collective punitive fine was imposed. What executions did take place were carried out almost furtively rather than as glaring examples. The sheiks were not guilty of exaggeration when they proclaimed to the people that, but for the commander-in-chief's restraint, there would have been a blood bath. 'Perhaps all those whose eyes saw French soldiers give way should have been put to death without exception.'[2] wrote the normally gentle Denon, voicing a state of mind prevalent among the army and the civilians. And yet Denon acknowledges that 'all those [Moslems] in whose houses Frenchmen were billeted had been anxious to save them, to hide them, to take care of their needs.'[3] Among them he mentions an old lady who had offered asylum to Denon and his fellow savants in her harem: should she, too, have been put to death because her eyes had seen French soldiers give way? The strong show less concern for their prestige, and on this particular occasion Bonaparte proved his strength.

Things returned quickly to normal. El Azhar was purified, and services were resumed. Conté and his mechanical wizards made new instruments to replace the pillaged ones. The Divan of Cairo and the General Divan, suspended for two months, were restored in December. The Egyptians had learned that the French could not be driven out by rebellion; the French had learned to be more on their guard, despite all appearances of friendliness. Still, criticism of Bonaparte's 'softness' persisted. He ignored it utterly. Precisely because he was tougher than his critics, he realized that he had neither the power nor the right to hold a nation under his sway by

---

[1] Ibid., VI, 122-23.

[2] Denon, I, 107.

[3] Ibid., I, 108.

sheer force. Besides, his mercy was tempered often enough by the quality of deterrent justice: 'Every night,' he wrote to General Reynier, 'we have about thirty heads chopped off, many of them belonging to the ringleaders. This I believe will serve them as a good lesson.'[1]

The lesson found its way into those heads at least that had not been chopped off. The lightness of his Islamic policy could not be disproved in Bonaparte's eyes by a mere insurrection. On December 21, after announcing to the inhabitants of Cairo their full pardon and the re-establishment of the Divan, he continued in a rather, extraordinary manner:

> Sherifs, ulemas, preachers in the mosques, be sure to tell the people that those who, with a light heart, take sides against us shall find no refuge in either this world or the next. Is there a man so blind as not to see that destiny itself guides all my operations? ...

> Let the people know that, from the creation of the world, it is written that after destroying the enemies of Islam and beating down the cross, I was to come from the confines of the Occident to accomplish my appointed task. Show the people that in more than twenty passages of the holy Koran what has happened has been foretold and what shall happen has been explained....

> If I chose, I could call each of you to account for the most hidden feelings of his heart, for I know everything, even what you have told to no one. But the day will come when all men shall see beyond all doubt that I am guided by orders from above and that all human efforts avail nought against me. Blessed are they who, in good faith, are the first to choose my side![2]

In the Arabic version of this preamble, as quoted by El-Djabarti, there are several variants from the official French text, notably this one: 'The day will come when you shall see beyond all doubt that everything I have done was inspired by God. You will see then that even if all men on earth united to oppose themselves to the designs of God, they could not prevent the fulfillment of His decrees, and it is I whom He has entrusted with that fulfillment.' 'This preamble,' says El-Djabarti, could not have had any aim other than to produce a strong impression on people's minds. It is

---

[1] Correspondance, V, 96.

[2] Ibid., V, 221-22.

long, full of pretention, and inspired by a deceitful imagination.'[1]
It would be difficult to disagree with the chronicler. And yet,
thirty-six years later, when Clot Bey, a French physician in the
service of Mehemet Ali, visited Suez, an old man in whose house
Bonaparte once had slept had this to say: 'Aboonaparte was not an
enemy of Islam. If he had wanted to do so, he could have thrown
all the mosques to the ground with the point of a needle. He has
not done it. Let his name be great forever among men! ... We are
told that at the hour of his death, far away on a rock where twelve
kings of the Christians had managed to chain him after putting
him to sleep with a philtre, the warriors who were with him saw
his soul coming to rest on the cutting edge of a sword. Let him rest
in peace!'[2] Unless Clot Bey invented this story, it would seem that
Bonaparte's propaganda had produced a strong impression indeed
on some people's minds.

---

[1] El-Djabarti, VI, 79-80, 78
[2] Ivray, pp. 79-80.

Chapter Seven
Relaxations and Vexations
of a Conqueror

N December 18, 1798, three days before his announcement that whatever he did was inspired by God, General Bonaparte issued an order to Citizen Fourès, lieutenant in the 22nd Regiment of Chasseurs & Cheval, to take the next diligence to Rosetta (the institution of a coach service was one among the many French innovations in Egypt) and thence to proceed to Malta and to Paris, taking certain despatches with him. He was to remain in Paris for ten days, then to return 'with all possible speed.' The despatches entrusted to him were, all four of them, utterly insignificant; yet there was more to his mission than meets the eye.

When King David took a liking to Bathsheba, he sent her husband Uriah to the front lines, where he was slain; General Bonaparte sent Lieutenant Fourès to Paris, partly because he was too humane to want him dead, partly, perhaps, because his designs on Madame Fourès were not of so lasting a nature as to make her husband's permanent disappearance desirable.

If there is more than meets the eye in No. 5,775 in Napoleon's correspondence (his order to Fourès), there also was a great deal more in his sudden infatuation with Madame Fourès.

When Bonaparte was a very young man and still a lieutenant, he had literary ambitions. Among his manuscripts are two interesting dialogues—one a colloquy with a streetwalker whom he met in the gardens of the Palais-Royal and whom he took home for the mere purpose of lecturing her; the other, a dialogue on love in which he puts this statement in his own mouth: 'I believe love to be harmful to society and to individual happiness.'[1] Up to the time when he met Josephine Beauharnais, in October 1795, his restraint in matters erotic, though not complete, was rather extraordinary for a young man of his era and profession. 'It takes time to make oneself loved,' he once re marked, 'and even when I had nothing to do I always vaguely felt that I had no time to waste.'[2]

When he met Josephine, she was thirty-two, a widow, and the mistress, about to be discarded, of Barras. Judging from Barras' indiscreet memoirs, a close inspection of her face revealed even more than her years; yet her expression had a sweet, seductive quality, her movements had a feminine grace, her clothes, her house, her furnishings, had an aristocratic elegance, an exquisite sensuality which almost instantly subdued the rather raw young man, her junior by six years. After a few weeks, she yielded to him, and his passion was awakened. She was the only woman he ever really loved, and he loved her with an imperious sensuality which still vibrates in his letters to her. To him, she was the woman: her body, more youthful than her face, slim, long-limbed, lean, supple, drove him frenzied with desire. He knew her past; he was not jealous of it; yet he must marry her, to make her his complete possession. Josephine, concealing her pennilessness as well as her real age, soliciting the advice and help of her ex-lover Barras, and, terrified of a future of poverty, made up her mind that General Bonaparte, uncouth and a little frightening though he might be, had a good career ahead of him. She pretended to reciprocate his passion. Shortly before his departure to take command of the Army of Italy, they were married in a civil ceremony. On the certificate of marriage, he added two years to his age and she subtracted three from hers.

He expected her to follow him to Italy shortly; she found an inexhaustible variety of reasons for delaying her departure. While he won battle after battle, sending her proud bulletins of his victories, becoming the hero of Europe, Josephine went on her rounds of pleasure in the company of pretty young men. He cursed and worshipped her. 'Take note of this: you have ruined me,' he wrote to her from Milan. 'I knew it the moment my heart became yours, the moment you began to win, day by day, an unlimited power

---

[1] Masson and Biagi, II, 277.

[2] Remusat, I, 267.

over me by enslaving all my senses.'[1] Yet, four days later, from Tortone: 'I love you beyond any thing imaginable; ... every moment of my life is devoted to you; ... I do not spend a single hour without thinking of you; it never entered my mind to think of another woman; ... my strength, my arms, my mind are yours; ... my soul is in your body; ... the earth looks beautiful to me only because you inhabit it.... A thousand kisses on your eyes, on your lips, on your tongue, on your _.'[2] (The editor of this correspondence claims that the missing word is illegible.)

Still, she stayed on in Paris. There were rumours of a young lover. Bonaparte, who at that time was as moral as he was passionate, threatened to kill her if it was true. 'He is a funny man, that Bonaparte.' said Josephine, perhaps a little thrilled. At last, after he had threatened to resign his command in order to join her, Josephine arrived at Milan in July 1796. Among her escort, apart from the objectionable dog Fortuné, who once bit Napoleon in the leg while he was making love to her, was Citizen Hippolyte Charles, adjutant to General Leclerc. The reunion was volcanic in its amorous intensity. Unfortunately, there was a war to be fought. The hero shuttled back and forth from battlefield and victory to bed and ecstasy. In mid-November, he was at Verona, making war and thinking of making love: 'You know very well,' he wrote to his wife, who was in Milan (or so he thought), 'that I cannot forget our little visits; you know the little black forest. I give it a thousand kisses and I am waiting impatiently until I can get there.'[3] One week later, having pushed the Austrians rather impetuously in his impatience, he was in Milan. He rushed into his palazzo: Josephine was off, in Genoa, with maid, dog, and Citizen Charles. 'I arrive in Milan,' Bonaparte wrote to her, 'I rush into your apartment, having left everything to see you, to press you in my arms. [More 'illegible' matter follows.] You were gone. You are running after amusements. You go away when I come to you. You no longer care for your dear Napoleon. A caprice has made you love him; inconstancy makes you indifferent to him.' There follows the classic threat of suicide: 'Accustomed as I am to danger, I know the remedy to all the ills of life. The unhappiness I am experiencing is incalculable; I had a right not to count on it.'[4] In the frustrated lover, the chronic calculator was reborn.

---

[1] Napoleon I, *Lettres a Josephine*, pp. 24-25.

[2] Ibid., pp. 31-33.

[3] Masson, *Napoleon et les femmes*, p. 44.

[4] Napoleon I, Lettres a Josephine, pp. 44-45; 46-47

He neither killed her nor sought death in battle. He even refused to admit the abundant evidence to the effect that Citizen Charles was his wife's lover—though he did have Charles discharged from the army. His family—mother, brothers, sisters—neglected nothing to acquaint him with the truth after his return to France, but who wants to see the truth when he is straying blissfully in enchanted forests? Besides, the interested motives of his informants were only too patent.

The thought of a possible divorce terrified Josephine, who was deep in debt. She accompanied her husband to Toulon, where he was to embark for Egypt. General Dumas, when he reported to his commander-in-chief one morning, found him in bed with his wife, who obviously was naked under the sheets. She was crying. 'She wants to come with us to Egypt,' said Bonaparte to the embarrassed black Hercules. 'Are you taking your wife along, Dumas?' 'No, by God,' said that honest man, 'she'd be a great embarrassment to me.'[1] Bonaparte made some consoling remarks about having soldiers' wives follow later, and gave his own a soldierly slap on her lean but shapely posterior. It is reasonable to suppose that Josephine's tears were sincere; perhaps she would rather have accompanied her conquering husband than returned to her pretty Monsieur Charles. But, however great Napoleon's passion may have been for Josephine, he budgeted his time for it. 'Love.' he remarked once, 'is the idler's occupation, the warrior's relaxation, and the sovereign's ruination.'[2] If he had taken a different attitude toward love, there might have been no Monsieur Charles; of course there would have been no Emperor Napoleon either. As it was, he wanted no women to accompany his soldiers; he had integrity or sense enough to set an example.

The day after his entry into Cairo, it may be recalled, he wrote to his brother Joseph that 'the veil had been completely lifted.' How, and by whom it came to be lifted remains a mystery; but the event must have taken place some time between his departure from Toulon and his victory at the Pyramids. Somebody had convinced him at last that Monsieur Charles had been his wife's lover and was, at that moment, virtually living with her. What good is it to be General Bonaparte, or even Alexander the Great, if the person at whose feet one longs to place one's glory prefers the caresses of a young man who is on the board of directors of a business corporation?

---

[1] Maurois, p. 22.
[2] Damas Hinard, p. 21.

According to the infuriatingly unreliable but indispensable memoirs of Bourrienne, it was Bonaparte's aide-de-camp Junot who furnished the proof of Josephine's infidelity. Junot's widow, the Duchess of Abrantes, indignantly denies this in her memoirs. Indeed, Bourrienne's account cannot be accurate, for he places the episode in February 1799, at El Arish, when Bonaparte was about to enter Syria. According to him, the General's rage was extreme, and the word 'divorce' came to his lips about twenty times a minute. Now, this was half a year after Bonaparte's letter to Joseph, and at least two months after Bonaparte himself had decided that continued fidelity on his part would make him look silly. It is a fact that he firmly intended to divorce his wife after his return to France. No matter when, where, and by whom, he was informed of the full extent of Josephine's treachery—and in all likelihood this took place before July 25, 1798—one thing is certain: the revelation produced some effect on him and his career. 'There is nothing left for me but to become really and completely selfish,' he wrote to his brother. Assuredly he had not lacked ruthless ambition before the revelation; quite likely he would have become a complete cynic even if Josephine had been as faithful as Penelope. Yet there was, in his life, a transformation: the lean-featured, romantic, idealistic hero rather suddenly turned into the bloated, cynical, materialistic tyrant. The change, though unnoticed for two or three years, took place in Egypt. Citizen Bonaparte turned into Sultan Kebir; the ambitious boy and ardent lover turned into the man whose procurers brought pretty women to his bed, to be crushed like an army when he had finished dictating his correspondence.

Shortly after his arrival in Cairo, Bonaparte was presented by his friends, the sheiks, with half a dozen Oriental beauties. He examined them, found them overweight, and dismissed them, untouched. Josephine was lean. He did not like their scent either. He was very particular. Of a chance conquest he made in Vienna in 1805, he remarked, twelve years later, 'She was one of the most agreeable women I've ever met: no smell.'[1] Tradition has it—though recorded evidence is lacking—that the sheik El-Bekri's daughter Zenab, who was only sixteen, appealed to him more. He was fond of beautiful bodies and delicate limbs, and when it comes to that, none can surpass a young Egyptian beauty. Why and to what extent her father condoned the liaison cannot be established; perhaps he was too preoccupied with the pursuit of his coveted slave boy, or with the consumption of his nightly bottles of brandy

---

[1] Damas Hinard, p. 21.

and burgundy, or with the fancy that he might become Sultan Kebir's father-in-law, to maintain very strict vigilance. When, in 1801, the French were obliged to evacuate Egypt, the more zealous among the faithful wished to punish the women who had consorted with the Infidels. Among their victims was Zenab, who in her better days had been known as 'the General's Egyptian.' Her liaison with Bonaparte must have been brief; so was her life. 'on Tuesday, the 24th Rabi el-Awwal 1216 [A.H.],' says El-Djabarti, 'the daughter of the sheik El-Bekri was arrested. She had been debauched by the French. The pasha's emissaries presented themselves after sundown at her mother's house ... and made her appear [before court] with her father. She was interrogated regarding her conduct, and made reply that she repented it. Her father's opinion was solicited. He answered that he disavowed his daughter's conduct. Then the unfortunate girl's head was cut off.'[1]

On December 1, 1798, perhaps already tired of the gentle Zenab, who lacked Josephine Beauharnais' experienced refinements, Bonaparte met Pauline Fourès. He was attending, with his staff, the unfortunate balloon ascent which so disappointed El-Djabarti. Two of his young aides-de-camp, one of them his stepson Eugène, noticed the beautiful Madame Fourès among the spectators and gave vent to their enthusiastic appreciation in tones loud enough to attract Bonaparte's attention. The General scrutinized the young woman; his interest was aroused. She was twenty, extremely pretty. Her blue eyes were set off by dark, long eyelashes, and her blond hair was magnificent. (According to General Paulin, who knew her well enough to be an authority, her hair, when let down, could serve her as a cloak, as if she were Lady Godiva.) The same evening, Bonaparte condescended to visit the newly opened 'Tivoli'; sure enough, Madame Fourès was there. He stared at her throughout his visit; his courting manners were never distinguished for their polish.

Pauline Fourès was the illegitimate daughter of an unknown father and of a cook named Bellisle; hence she was known to many under the rather charming nickname Bellilotte. Until her very recent marriage to Lieutenant Fourès, she had worked as a milliner, an occupation which, in eighteenth-century France, almost inevitably brought pretty girls into the arms of appreciative gentlemen. She had loved her husband well enough to put on the boots, trousers, vest, and tunic of his regiment, conceal her Lady Godiva hair under a cocked hat, and embark with him for parts unknown. On

[1] El-Djabarti, VII, 44.

her transport, at Shubra Khit, she had had her baptism of fire. But it was easier to face the Mamelukes than to resist their conqueror. On December 17 Bonaparte issued orders to despatch her husband to Malta and Paris—a journey almost every body else in the army would have undertaken more gladly than did Lieutenant Fourès. No sooner had the husband taken the diligence to Rosetta than Bellilotte was invited, with several other European ladies, to a dinner party at Esbekiya Square. The host stared at her during the whole dinner. When coffee was served, the officer sitting at her side was very clumsy; he spilled a cup on her beautiful dress. No matter: he would take her upstairs to a room where she could repair the damage. She was still rubbing away at her dress when the commander-in-chief appeared. The guests waited for several hours before either of them returned. A few days later, Bellilotte, now known as Cleopatra, or Clioupatre, occupied a mansion next to Bonaparte's on Esbekiya Square and rode about Cairo in his best carriage.

The trouble with idylls in wartime is that the enemy constantly keeps on the lookout. Lieutenant Fourès never reached Malta, let alone Paris. Having left Alexandria on December 18, the courier ship *Le Chasseur* was captured by H.M.S. *Lion* the next day. The English captain displayed extraordinary humanity toward Lieutenant Fourès. He would not condemn him, as he condemned the rest of the crew and passengers of *Le Chasseur*, to the horrors of a Turkish prison; he would not even keep him to be exchanged; he would send him right back to Alexandria, on parole. Lieutenant Fourès, rather bewildered, arrived in Alexandria; he was even more bewildered by General Marmont's attempts to keep him there, on grounds that seemed flimsy. If he could not accomplish his mission, at least he wanted to sleep with his Bellilotte. Nothing could keep him from returning to Cairo. When he returned, he did not find Bellilotte at home, but he heard a great deal of talk about her.

His illusions dispelled, Lieutenant Fourès made a show of gross temper, not to say mental cruelty. Bonaparte had made a fool of him; his wife had made a fool of him; and, not unlikely, the British captain had made fools of all three. 'To protect herself against his brutality.'[1] Bellilotte asked for a divorce, and obtained it with miraculous ease. Her lover, for his part, had promised to divorce his wife and marry her. Perhaps, unlike Josephine, she could even bear him a child. They both tried very hard, without

---

[1] Masson, *Napoleon et les femmes*, p. 60.

success. 'What is there to do?' Bonaparte expostulated with Bourrienne. 'The stupid little _ won't make a child for me.' It was put to Bellilotte how rewarding it would be for her to become pregnant. 'Good Lord!' she replied, 'it isn't my fault![1]

Once divorced, Mademoiselle Bellisle, as she now called herself, became Sultan Kebir's official mistress, presiding at his dinners and attended by his aides. Only Eugène Beauharnais was dispensed from the obligation of escorting the carriage of his stepfather's concubine—and this only after indignantly pointing out the anomaly of the situation to his stepfather.

The idyll did not last long. After about two months, Bonaparte set out on his Syrian campaign. Many of his generals and soldiers took their wives and mistresses along—a decision they were to regret bitterly. General Bonaparte was determined to be no Mark Antony to his Cleopatra; he left Bellilotte in Cairo, where he wrote to her—presumably passionate letters—which the editors of his correspondence did not see fit to print and which have vanished since. Throughout his career, he remained faithful to the principle never to take a woman with him on a campaign.

II

Bonaparte's liaison with Pauline Fourès, intense though it may have been, was not a grand passion: rather, it was a way of getting even with his wife and a 'soldier's relaxation.' If ever there was a soldier in need of relaxing his nerves, it was General Bonaparte in the winter of 1798-99. During the eight weeks of his honeymoon with the blonde Bellilotte (two of which he spent away from her, on a trip to Suez), he had to face an accumulation of adversities such as only Job had known; yet, unlike Job, he showed no signs of strain.

According to Nicholas the Turk, the British blockade of Egypt was so tight that 'even a bird could not have passed it.'[2] Being a poet, Nicholas was given to picturesque terms of speech and to hyperbole. Not only did birds pass through the blockade, but ships did too. Still, the blockade was at least 90 per cent effective. Once in a while (usually under cover of dark), a French or neutral vessel might slip in or out. Yet on the whole, the sense of isolation among the French in Egypt was complete: a man was lucky if he received

[1] Rourrienne, Vol. II, Ch. xi.
[2] Nicolas Turc, p. 39.

a letter from home once a year. Thus, says Nicholas, the people 'knew for certain that the French had lost all hope of receiving aid from their own country.' It was a commonplace among them to say, 'All we have to do is to resist them, to hold out against them, and we'll be rid of them in the end, for whatever does not grow must diminish.'[1]

The French army was dwindling, slowly but surely. Aside from battle casualties, individual assassinations, and suicides, there was disease, and in December the plague broke out. The first recorded victim of the epidemic, one Citizen Lintrigue, died at Damietta as early as October. His case was diagnosed as 'a pestilential or contagious fever';[2] the words 'bubonic plague' remained taboo throughout the epidemic. It was Bonaparte's theory that the greatest danger of the plague was fear. 'Fear caused its spread more than anything else,' he told Las Cases in St. Helena; the 'principal seat' of the disease was 'in the imagination. During the Egyptian campaign all those whose imagination was struck by fear died of it. The surest protection, the most efficacious remedy, was moral courage.... The best way to preserve the army from the disease was to keep it on the march and occupied. Diversion and fatigue were found to be the best prevention.'[3] No great man in history ever raised ostrich policy to such heroic levels of fortitude. Still reminiscing about the plague, he told Dr. O'Meara, his physician, 'For a short time, I succeeded in persuading the troops that it was only a fever with buboes, and not the plague; and in order to convince them of it, I went publicly to the bed-side of a soldier who was infected, and handled him. This had a great effect in encouraging them, and even some of the surgeons who had abandoned them became ashamed and returned to their duties.'[4] Those surgeons who did not return to their duties had cause to regret it, witness this Order of the Day, dated January 8, 1799: 'Citizen Boyer, surgeon of the hospital of Alexandria, has been cowardly enough to refuse to treat those wounded soldiers who had been in contact with patients allegedly suffering from a contagious disease. He is unworthy of being a French citizen. He will be dressed in women's clothes and led, on a donkey, through the streets of Alexandria, with a sign on his back, reading, "Unworthy of being a French citizen; he is afraid of dying." Whereupon he will be imprisoned and

[1] Ibid., p. 40.
[2] Correspondance inédite, ojfficielle et confidentielle: Egypte, II, 105.
[3] Las Cases, I, 409
[4] O'Meara, II, 82.

sent back to France with the first outgoing ship.'[1] It turned out
that Boyer had been unjustly accused. The punishment was not
carried out, but the paragraph printed in the Order of the Day
could not be undone. Madame Tempé, the wife of a navy captain
and one of the ornaments of Le Tivoli of Cairo, 'was highly incensed over the fact that the wearing of women's clothes had been
ordered to symbolize cowardice,' Dr. Desgenettes reminisced some
time later. An athletic beauty of twenty-seven, Madame Tempé
would not tolerate such an outrage to her sex. She declared, the
Doctor continues, 'that she was ready to fight Bonaparte in a duel
and that she would show him, pistol in hand, that not all women
were afraid, not even of him.'[2] The actual epidemic agent of bubonic plague—fleas from infected rats—was unknown at the time.
Yet the methods of prevention and cure worked out by Desgenettes and Larrey and imposed on the army by Bonaparte's orders seem to have been fairly effective. There are no reliable statistics on the number of cases, deaths, and recoveries. The outbreak
was most virulent during the Syrian campaign; in Egypt, it was
generally limited to the coastal towns. All in all, the number of fatal cases cannot have exceeded 2,000. Some of Bonaparte's pre-
ventive measures sound eminently sensible. 'As for that unfortunate half-brigade of Light Infantry,' he instructed the commandant
of Alexandria, 'have them strip as naked as they were born and
take a good sea bath. Make them rub themselves from head to
foot, and make them wash their clothes.... No more parades; no
more guard duty outside their camps.... Give orders to the soldiers
to wash their feet, hands, and face daily, and to keep clean.'[3] As for
the cure: 'In consequence of the advice of the medical officers,' he
told Dr. O'Meara, 'I ordered that all the buboes which did not appear likely to suppurate should be opened. Previous to giving this
order I had the experiment made upon a certain number, and allowed an equal number of others to be treated in the usual manner, by which it was found that a much greater proportion of the
former recovered.'[4]

Private Millet, stationed at Damietta, was among those who
survived the plague. 'This illness,' he reports, 'begins with a hot
fever, followed by a severe headache and the formation of a bubo
or gland, in the groin or in any other joint, about the size of an egg.

---

[1] Correspondance, V, 239.

[2] Desgenettes, *Souvenirs*, III, 202, cited in La Jonquière, IV, 28.

[3] Correspondance, V, 282.

[4] O'Meara, II, 82.

Once the bubo appears, the patient may be reckoned as dead. If he survives four days, there is considerable hope for him, but this rarely happens.'[1] In Millet's case, the attending medical officers judged it useless to lance his bubo; Millet himself, overhearing their consultation, waited for them to leave and opened it with his pocket knife. He lived to write about it. Captain Thurman spent the plague period at the dismal fortress of Abukir, terrified of infection and stupefied by boredom. 'Of the twelve men on guard duty,' he wrote in his diary, 'four or five succumb every day.'[2] When the courier ship *Osiris*, from France, anchored in the bay, her captain was surprised at the ragged condition of the French garrison officers who came to drink his rum. Except for himself and three others, his entire crew was presently stricken with the plague.

The variety of plague that struck Damietta was less virulent than the Alexandria variety—or else hygienic conditions at Damietta were superior. Even at Alexandria the epidemic made slow progress at first and was taken surprisingly lightly. After one month, the number of dead was about 150; then, suddenly, death struck with fury. One single battalion lost six to seven men daily, Marmont wrote to Menou on January 17. 'In a month, it will be non-existent.'[3] Five days later, the death rate was seventeen a day. The quarantine slowed down the influx of supplies; the men were starving as well as dying. 'For the love of God, my dear General,' Marmont pleaded with Menou, 'do not abandon us, and send us money.... Send us some wheat; we have just about enough left to last us forty-eight hours. The discontent among the troops is extreme, and it would not be surprising if they mutinied.... They are dying of hunger.'[4] With misery there came rumours, most of them exaggerated: patients suffering from ordinary ailments had been put into hospital beds from which the corpses of plague victims had barely been removed; instead of burning the clothes of the dead, hospital attendants had sold them; corpses had remained unburied for twenty-four hours, or buried in graves so shallow that dogs were digging them up to devour them. True or not true, such rumours give an idea of the morale prevailing among the Alexandria garrison. At Abukir, things were no better. A private's daily ration consisted of one and a half pounds of bread and half an

---

[1] Millet, pp. 61-62.

[2] Thurman, p. 74.

[3] La Jonquière, IV, 38.

[4] Ibid., IV, 39.

ounce of olive oil. 'Several of my men have deserted,' reported the commandant. 'They told their comrades that they would look for a place or master that can feed them.'[1]

On January 22, a number of medical officers despatched from Cairo arrived at Rosetta, on their way to Alexandria. Among them was a Venetian physician, resident in Cairo, Giorgio Voldoni, who had advertised himself as an expert on the plague. 'Voldoni,' Menou informed Bonaparte, 'seems to be more attached to liquor than to his profession.... He is drunk from morning to night.'[2] Arrived in Alexandria, 'he kept himself prudently sequestered and was of no use whatever,' declares Desgenettes.[3] According to other testimony, Voldoni, though self-sequestered and permanently drunk, dispensed some advice that proved useful.

Apart from sending Voldoni and ordering sea baths (a chilly affair in Alexandria in December and January), Bonaparte took severe measures: 'Every day,' he ordered Marmont, 'you will have a superior officer make the rounds of the hospitals ... visit all the patients, and have all attendants and employees who refuse to give the required care and food to the patients shot on the spot in the courtyard of the hospital.'[4] Perhaps the patients' morale was raised at the sound of hospital attendants being shot, but the hospital attendants' morale was lowered. A number of them died every day, without the help of a firing squad, reported an army commissioner. 'To find replacements,' he suggested, 'it might be advisable at least to pay their salaries in cash, instead of obliging them against their will to risk their lives without paying them a penny.'[5]

Despite Bonaparte's drastic measures against the plague, it continued to rage at Alexandria when he began his Syrian expedition. As for the Damietta outbreak, he found it convenient to ignore its existence. Damietta was not even quarantined. By the end of January an infantry battalion from the plague-stricken city left with the advance units for Syria.

---

[1] Ibid., IV, 40.

[2] Ibid., IV, 41.

[3] Desgenettes, *Histoire medicale*, 1,33.

[4] La Jonquière, IV, 33.

[5] Ibid., IV, 34.

III

While Bonaparte faced the plague just as he faced the Forte's declaration of war—with fortitude and blinkers—he still had to seek some means to counteract the continuing diminution of his army. The incorporation of the naval crews into the land forces was a partial solution. There were other measures. As early as September 7, Bonaparte ordered all Mameluke slaves between the ages of eight and fourteen to be drafted, with a view toward the eventual formation of a Mameluke corps in French service. On October 5 all male European civilians in Egypt of military age were constituted as a National Guard. An order dated December 28 contains this paragraph: 'Wherever a village rises in rebellion, the general in command of the province, by way of punishment, will seize all boys between twelve and sixteen years old. A report will be sent to the commander-in-chief, who will issue orders concerning their subsequent disposition.'[1] The object, quite obviously, was to create a reservoir of recruits. After Bonaparte's return from Syria, where casualties had been heavy, his thoughts turned toward a colonial army of black Mamelukes. 'I should like, Citizen General, to purchase two or three thousand Negroes above sixteen years of age,' he wrote to Desaix in June 1799.[2] And, a few days later, to the Sultan of Darfur, in the Sudan: 'I beg you to send me, with the next caravan, 2,000 black slaves over sixteen years old, strong and vigorous. I shall buy them all on my own account.'[3] It is interesting to note that Bonaparte did not contemplate the formation of coloured units; rather, as he wrote to Desaix, he wished to incorporate about a hundred Negroes in each French battalion.

Desaix himself strongly advocated a similar project: to amalgamate the approximately two thousand young Mameluke slaves in Egypt with the French apprentice seamen, with imported Negroes, and with Arab lads, all of whom would be given military training and French schooling. The project was eminently practical and, if realized, would have obviated any need for reinforcements from the homeland. Also, it might well have changed the course of history: the racially mixed army contemplated by Desaix and Bonaparte would have borne no resemblance whatever to the colonial armies of the nineteenth and twentieth centuries.

---

[1] Correspondance, V, 192.

[2] Ibid., V, 470.

[3] Ibid., V, 490.

Frenchmen, Negroes, Arabs, and Mamelukes would have served and been promoted on a basis of equality. In a detailed memorandum he left behind when he returned to France, Bonaparte developed this idea on a large scale: envoys should be sent to Sennar, Abyssinia, and Darfur to purchase 10,000 young slaves per year; 20,000 of these could be incorporated into the army at the ratio of twenty slaves per company; the rest would form an auxiliary corps with French cadres.

But these were long-term projects, requiring about five years to come to fruition. Meanwhile, the growing shortage of manpower was remedied to some degree by recruitment into such auxiliary forces as Barthelmy's Greek and Moroccan cut-throats. The essential thing was to remain in Egypt long enough to develop its latent resources. To the overwhelming majority of his troops and officers this seemed a hopeless enterprise.

***

Not only did Bonaparte receive daily bulletins on the piecemeal erosion of his army, but he also had to face an epidemic of resignations. At about the same time as Kléber requested his recall, Menou listed his grievances in a long and caustic letter. 'If this is what you call administration, all the notions I have acquired in the course of my life must be wrong, and I must beg you to relieve me of my post,'[1] wrote the incensed commandant of Rosetta. Bonaparte paid no attention. Impervious to insult, he invariably managed to calm down those whom he needed. When he did not need a man, he was more compliant and less forgiving.

During the initial stages of the campaign, the discontented generals had selected General Dumas as their mouthpiece. Imbued with strong republican principles but no intellectual giant, Dumas was simple enough to express his and his fellow generals' feelings with ill-advised bluntness. He came close to rebellion yet Bonaparte, after threatening to have him shot, chose to forgive him. In the following months, and especially during the Cairo rebellion, Dumas performed prodigies of bravery that might seem exaggerated in one of his son's novels. It has been said that he was worth an entire army. He could perform some amazing feats of strength; there is a tradition that, sitting astride his horse, and grasping with both hands a beam in the ceiling of the stable, he could lift his horse between his thighs. He could also stick four fingers of one hand into four rifle barrels and carry the four weapons at the end

---

[1] Correspondance inédite, ojfficielle et confidentielle: Egypte, II, 88.

of his outstretched arm. His amorous prowess was commensurate; his courage was legendary. His ferocity and beauty earned him the names 'the Black Devil' in the Tyrol and 'the Angel' in Egypt. As a tactician, he sometimes displayed ingenuity. Once, in Austria, when some infantrymen were unable to scale a palisade, the general simply picked them up and threw them across it one by one, thus putting the terrified Austrians to rout. With these qualifications, he may have been regarded as a valuable man—but not as an indispensable one.

Dumas, though born and raised in Santo Domingo, felt an overwhelming nostalgia for France. The climate of Egypt was bad for his health, he told Dr. Desgenettes; could not Desgenettes issue him a certificate of ill health and help him return to France? Desgenettes reported on this interview to Bonaparte. 'I can easily replace him with a brigadier,' said Bonaparte, and let him go. But it was the end of Dumas' career.

General Manscourt, who had replaced Kléber as commandant of Alexandria, was also permitted to return to France; so was Dolomieu, who had resented his participation in the campaign ever since he was obliged to play a rather ambiguous part in the capture of Malta. Napoleon's brother Louis, neurasthenic and afflicted with a syphilitic disease, was sent to France in November, with an important mission. But when demands for repatriation on account of ill health multiplied, Bonaparte stopped most of them by publishing the following remarks in a General Order to the Army: 'It is not my intention ... to keep men in the army who are insensitive to the honour of being my companions-in-arms. Let them go. I shall ease their departure. But I do not want them to conceal their real motives for refusing to share our labours and our danger under the pretext of feigned maladies: we would risk that they might also share in our glory.'[1]

Of course, many of those who left were *bona fide* invalids—for instance, the forty wounded and blind who sailed from Alexandria on December 15 aboard a Genoese ship. With them was the chief army commissioner Sucy, who had been slightly wounded and who, according to Dr. Desgenettes' memoirs, was more anxious to cover up some shady financial deals than to recover from his wound. The ship evaded the British and Turkish blockade and entered the port of Augusta, in Sicily, on January 7. Unfortunately, the captain was not aware that the King of the Two Sicilies was at war with France. The passengers were taken to a prison hospital;

---

[1] Correspondance, V, 491.

on January 20, a mob broke into the prison and stoned them to death. Compared to Sicilians, Egyptians and Turks were lambs.

Almost, equally unlucky were Dumas and Dolomieu, who sailed with another shipment of blind and wounded. Like their predecessors, they stopped on Neapolitan territory. The prisons of Lord Nelson's friend, King Ferdinand, were pestilential. Dolomieu, who spent twenty-one months in one of them, died shortly after his return to France in 1800. During his imprisonment, he managed to write, with bits of burnt coals, in the margin of a Bible and on various shreds of paper, a manuscript which he entitled *The Philosophy of Mineralogy*, one of the pioneering works of geological theory. Dumas, though he lacked Dolomieu's intellectual resources, had more physical stamina. He survived his ordeal and, upon his return to France, sired the author of *The Three Musketeers*.

The case of General Berthier was rather special. He also requested to be sent home on sick leave: he was love-sick for Madame Visconti, a lady he had left in Italy. 'I suffer very much,' he wrote to Menou on November 1. 'I am afflicted with almost complete deafness.'[1] Since he managed to remain Napoleon's chief of staff for sixteen more years, his deafness seems to have been psychosomatic. Bonaparte granted him the leave he requested, but in the end Berthier stayed. 'I never saw a passion like that of Berthier for Madame Visconti,' Napoleon reminisced in 1816. 'In Egypt, he would watch the moon at the same time that she was supposed to look at it herself. In the middle of the desert, he put up a tent for her cult: he put Madame Visconti's portrait inside it and burned incense there. Three mules were used to transport this tent and his baggage. Often I would enter and lie down on the sofa with my boots on. It made Berthier furious, he thought it was a profanation of the sanctuary. He loved her so much that he provoked me into talking about her, although I always spoke ill of her. He didn't care; he was delighted if one talked about her at all. He even wanted to leave the army to go back to her. I had my despatches all ready, received his parting wishes, assigned him an aviso [a courier ship] when he came back to me with tears in his eyes.'[2] Bourrienne confirms Napoleon's account of the episode. Berthier was scheduled to leave Cairo on January 29 to go aboard the frigate *La Courageuse* just at the moment when Bonaparte was about to start the Syrian campaign. For some time, Bourrienne claims,

[1] La Jonquière, III, 387.
[2] Gourgaud, I, 305-6.

Berthier had been unable to concentrate on his duties, 'His amo-rous memories, which he exalted to the point of madness, reduced the feeble faculties with which nature had endowed him.... One day I brought him an order from the commander-in-chief. I found him kneeling on his small sofa before the portrait of Madame Vis-conti.... When everybody thought that Berthier was about to leave for Alexandria, he went to see Bonaparte. "So you are determined to campaign in Asia?" [he asked.] " You know very well that every-thing is ready;" [answered Bonaparte] "I am leaving in a few days." "Well, in that case I shall not leave you.... Here are my passport and instructions." Bonaparte, highly pleased with Berthier's deci-sion, embraced him.'[1]

Whatever one may think of Berthier, his decision to postpone his return to Madame Visconti in order to remain with his chief was a brave one, for the Syrian campaign was a desperate gamble. With an army of 15,000 men, Bonaparte had to face the whole might of the Ottoman Empire. The 10,000 men he left behind in Egypt, whose conquest was not yet completed, were all he had to control a country stretching for 600 miles, from the Sudan to the Mediterranean. He received neither news nor supplies from the homeland; his ports were blockaded; his treasury was empty; the plague was raging. His prospects were none too bright. And yet, after a century and a half of criticism, it is difficult to say what other course of action he could have taken whose prospects would have been appreciably brighter—save that of at least trying to pull out.

Bonaparte's confident bearing in the midst of a situation that others regarded as desperate may appear almost quixotic. Actu-ally, his estimate of the situation was soberly realistic, insofar as this was possible in the absence of recent or reliable intelligence. Although he doubted that the Porte had officially declared war, he knew that Djezzar Pasha had raised a large army and was prepar-ing to invade Egypt by land. As soon as the winter was over, the French might expect an Anglo-Turkish landing as well. The best defence was to attack Djezzar rather than to wait for him, defeat him before spring, and return to Egypt in time to prevent an at-tempt at a landing. However, though this was undoubtedly the best defence, it involved formidable risks. If possible, it would be even better to avoid war with the Porte and to use Egypt as a trump in bargaining for peace with England. As early as October 7, after reporting to the Directory on the Forte's preparations for

---

[1] Bourrienne, Vol. II, Ch. xiv.

war, he hinted at that possibility: 'It might,' he wrote, 'be advantageous to the French Republic if the conquest of Egypt were turned into an instrument by which an honourable peace with England could be secured.'[1] This important message, which he entrusted to his brother Louis, reached Paris only on February 5, 1799, when the Syrian campaign had already started.

Since it was not at all certain that England was in a mood to negotiate peace, it seemed essential to Bonaparte that the Directory make every effort to break English control of the Mediterranean and to end the blockade of the Egyptian coast. In message after message (including that of October 7) he urged the government to assemble a new Mediterranean fleet. His suggestions seemed unrealistic to the Directory; the ships he requested were either inadequate or needed for the defence of Malta and Corfu. In the letter of October 7, he made an additional suggestion: if the government should have abandoned the project of invading Ireland, perhaps it would be advisable to send the entire Atlantic fleet into the Mediterranean, thus obliging the British to fight at—a greater distance from their bases than the French. The reasoning was unassailable, and in March the Directory sent Admiral Bruix with the Atlantic fleet into the Mediterranean. Since the Irish project had been given up half a year earlier, one wonders why the Directory did not do so immediately after the news of Nelson's victory at the Nile. As it turned out, even after entering the Mediterranean, Bruix's fleet gave neither support to Bonaparte nor trouble to Nelson: lacking a target against which they could agree to unite their forces, the Spanish and French squadrons let the opportunity of victory go by unused.

Even if he had been fully aware of the bleakness of his prospects and of the Directory's nearly complete indifference to his plight, Bonaparte still would have made the decisions that he did. In a desperate situation there are only two alternatives—either to commit suicide or to wait and see whether, perchance, some unforeseen turn of events might not make the situation seem a little less desperate. The Anglo-Russo-Turkish alliance might split up, or Turkey might make a separate peace. (Bonaparte did not know that, in December 1798, the Porte signed treaties of alliance with Russia and with England by which each party pledged itself not to make a separate peace.) Perhaps even a few major victories over the Turks in Syria might win Arabic support for his side, and any-

---

[1] Correspondance, V, 41.

thing might happen then—even a march on Constantinople. In any event, what else was there to do but try?

It would have been pointless to ask the Directory to evacuate his army from Egypt: if France could have sent the ships needed to make the evacuation possible, the evacuation would not have been necessary. To sue the British for an armistice without being authorized to do so, or without an absolute military necessity, was out of the question. Not only would this have ended Bonaparte's career, but it also would have been totally contrary to his conception of honour. He could, however, have informed his government of the seriousness of his situation and requested powers to negotiate. This he did not do. In fact, he painted his situation in the rosiest of colours. All he asked of his government was, if possible, to send a fleet in order to break the blockade if not permanently, then at least temporarily. He requested drugs, spirits, surgeons, entertainers, and above all, news. The absence of political news was a serious handicap to him, and the absence of letters from home was one of the chief causes of the troops' low morale. As to the rest, he asked for nothing. 'We lack nothing here,' he wrote in the letter of October 7. 'We are bursting with strength, good health, and high spirits.'[1] Why this colossal lie? Possibly because he realized that the weaker his government believed him to be, the less reason it would see to help him. Possibly, also, because the nature of his ambitions demanded that he return to France a conquering hero rather than a beggar.

***

The Directory made a number of attempts to communicate with Bonaparte, either by official couriers or through neutral merchants, the Barbary states, and various other haphazard channels. A handful of messages got through—usually too late to be of use. The majority of emissaries never reached their destination, and their odysseys would fill volumes. On the strength of these attempts it has been asserted even by historians partial to Napoleon that the Directory did all they could to establish contact, and that their failure merely demonstrated the complete control the English were exerting over the eastern Mediterranean. This contention is utterly indefensible.

Bonaparte indicated various means by which French ships could penetrate the British blockade. He himself managed to send a number of ships out of the Egyptian ports under cover of dark.

---

[1] Ibid., V, 42.

Some, to be sure, were captured: it was a risk which the French government apparently did not feel worth taking for the sake of remaining in touch with about 50,000 isolated Frenchmen. Perhaps they were justified in this; but then it would have been possible to send a force of six to seven battle ships to break the blockade at least temporarily now and then, with only very slight risks. The French government never even contemplated this possibility. It is easy to accumulate an impressive number of reasons why such operations were not undertaken, but such an explanation, while plausible in every detail, merely obscures the glaring fact that nothing was attempted at all.

Still, though regretting their powerlessness to give any help or cooperation, the Directors wished at least to give good advice. On November 4, 1798, Talleyrand presented for their approval a long letter of instructions to Bonaparte. The letter begins with two barely disguised rebukes—one for having careless couriers who let their despatches fall into enemy hands, the other for letting Nelson destroy his fleet. The document then proceeds to an assessment of the political situation: Russia and Turkey have declared war; Austria is about ready to join them; Naples is arming; the Dutch are poor allies; Prussia stands on neutrality; Spain has promised help but is doing nothing. The horizon is dark, but France will withstand whatever storms are brewing. Now, as concerns Bonaparte and his army: in the foreseeable future it will be impossible to communicate with him or to send reinforcements. 'Consequently you must, at least for some time to come, manage to shift by yourself. In this respect, everything you have done to attach the native population to your cause, to conciliate the Arabs, to win numerous partisans among both, deserves our approval. Since we cannot send you any help, the Executive Directory knows better than to give you any orders or even instructions. You will determine your line of conduct according to your own position and to the means you dispose of in Egypt.... Since it would be difficult, at the present moment, to make possible your [i.e. your army's] return to France, there are three choices open to you: either to remain in Egypt and to establish yourself in such a manner as to be safe from a Turkish attack (but you are aware that for part of the year the country is extremely unhealthy for Europeans, especially if they receive no assistance from the homeland); or to march to India, where, if you get there, you will no doubt find men ready to join you to fight English domination; or, finally, to march on Constantinople and to meet the enemy who is threatening you. The choice is up to you and to the brave and distinguished men who surround you.'[1] The document is signed by Treilhard, then the chairman of the Directory, but its author was Talleyrand, the man primarily responsible for the presence of the French army in Egypt. His good advice was scarcely necessary. Of the three choices offered to Bonaparte, the first was obvious. The second to march on India was preposterous, and the third to march on Constantinople only barely less so.[2] All in all, Talleyrand's advice amounted to saying: Your situation is desperate, so do the best you can.

Although the message was not exactly helpful, it was important inasmuch as at least it gave vital news. One would think that an effort might have been made to convey it to Bonaparte with all possible speed. One copy was entrusted to Brigadier Lucotte, who managed to dally with it in Spain for three months and then went to Ancona, which was under siege; this copy never reached its destination. Another copy was entrusted to a businessman on his way to Tunis; two days after his arrival there, the Bey of Tunis declared war on France. This second copy never reached Bonaparte either. A third emissary, named Wynand Mourveau, left Genoa on February 9 (three months after the despatch had been signed) and reached Damietta on February 26; at this time Bonaparte, having taken his own counsel, was in Syria. He received the letter on March 25, while besieging Acre. The conclusion that the Directory had not taken great pains is not far-fetched. If they had sent the message with a courier ship, it probably would have reached Egypt early in December, Commodore Hood notwithstanding.

The suggestion that the Directory deliberately abandoned Bonaparte and his men, in order to be rid of an ambitious general and of an obstreperous army of radical republicans, was first made by English propagandists in 1798; it has been repeated by many historians. There is no evidence to back up this assertion. The palpable truth is that the Directors were faced with formidable difficulties at home where they risked going bankrupt or being overthrown at almost any moment, and abroad, where a mighty coalition was gathering against France. They were too preoccupied with their own situation to worry unduly over Bonaparte's, especially since there was little they could do for him in any case. The French army in Egypt was merely one piece on the chessboard, and an ex-

---

[1] La Jonquière, III, 266-68.

[2] It is true that, in his history of the campaign, Napoleon himself mentions these last two possibilities as having been in his mind at the time, hut then he was merely indulging in retrospective daydreams.

pendable one at that. If Bonaparte, the miracle worker, could save it, so much the better. If not, the loss was less costly than would have been an attempt at rescue.

***

Throughout November and December, intelligence poured into Egypt of Djezzar's preparations for war. By November 19, Djezzar's hostile intentions could no longer be blinked, and Bonaparte sent him an ultimatum: 'I do not want war if you are not my enemy; but it is time for you to explain yourself. If you continue to give asylum, at the borders of Egypt, to Ibrahim Bey, I shall regard this as an act of war and shall march on Acre.'[1] Nothing could be plainer. As before, Djezzar did not deign to answer except, a little later, by deeds.

Among the despatches Bonaparte gave to the hapless Lieutenant Fourès, the report to the Directory contains one significant passage: 'A merchantman just arrived at Suez had an Indian passenger aboard, who had a letter for the commander of the French forces in Egypt; this letter has been lost. It seems that our arrival in Egypt has produced a great impression of our power in India.... There is fighting there.'[2] Whether the Indian passenger who was so careless about letters that might change the course of world history was an emissary of Tippoo Sahib or of the French Governor of the Isle of France (now Mauritius) is not at all clear.

Tippoo, who had succeeded his father Hayder Ali as Sultan of Mysore, was a ferocious enemy of the English and, hence, an admirer of France. His favourite pastime was to watch the performance of a curious automaton constructed for him by a French mechanic a life-sized tiger in the process of clawing an English officer to death and containing in his entrails a musical mechanism simulating the tiger's snarl and the Englishman's moans. It is now one of the most popular exhibits of the Victoria and Albert Museum, where, for some whimsical reason, it has been placed opposite the entrance to the concert hall.

Tippoo's fanatic hatred of England was so extreme that, in 1797, he gave his auspices to a Jacobin club founded by the French colony at his capital, Seringapatam. The first session took place on May 5, in the Sultan's presence; the members set up a Tree of Liberty and swore death to all tyrants, excepting Tippoo Sahib. In January 1798, two of his envoys arrived at the Isle of France to ex-

---

[1] Correspondance, V, 148.

[2] Ibid., V, 213.

plore the possibility of a French alliance leading to the expulsion of the British from India. About the same time the representatives of the United Irishmen were conducting similar negotiations in Paris; the French government may be forgiven for reaching the conclusion that the sun never set over the unpopularity of British rule.

The Indian traveller's report from Suez sounded interesting to General Bonaparte, who until then does not seem to have given much serious thought to establishing contact with Tippoo.

Suez had been occupied without resistance on December 7 by General Bon. The commander-in-chief 's interest in the port had several reasons. In the first place, apart from the small Red Sea port of Kosseir, Suez was the only port of Egypt not blockaded by the British; the customs revenues for goods from India and Arabia were of some value to the cash-starved French. In the second place, Suez was said to be the terminus of an ancient and ruined canal that had once linked the Red Sea with the Mediterranean; to investigate the possibility of cutting a new canal was among the missions assigned to Bonaparte. Moreover, Bonaparte had received, on November 7, a deputation of Bedouins from Tur, in the Sinai Peninsula, accompanied by a monk of the famed monastery of St. Catherine on Mount Sinai, The Arabs of Tur wished to obtain guarantees for the security of their caravans to Cairo, which supplied the city with coal. Bonaparte gave them the desired assurances and produced a strong impression on them. 'His arm is strong and his words are honeyed,' they said.[1] At the same time, Bonaparte granted virtually sovereign privileges to the monks of Mount Sinai. The idea of winning over the Arab world, both Moslem and Christian, cannot have been very far from his thoughts. The Arabs of Tur were the first important tribe to offer their friendship, and their location at the junction of Egypt, Syria, and Arabia made the alliance very valuable.

On December 24, accompanied by an armed escort, several staff officers and scientists, and a number of Cairo merchants, Bonaparte set out for Suez. Behind him he left not only Pauline Fourès but even his cook. 'He took with him neither servants, nor cook, nor tent, nor mattress,' says El-Djabarti. 'For food, all he took was three roast chickens wrapped in paper. The soldiers carried their bread on the points of their bayonets and water in a flask suspended from their necks.'[2] El-Djabarti exaggerates; according

---

[1] La Jonquière, III, 444.

[2] El-Djabarti, VI, 81.

to the *Courrier de L'Egypte*, Bonaparte took 'only' three servants with him for his personal service. Improbably enough, this frugal safari was accompanied by one of the General's carriages—surely the first, and possibly the last, vehicle of its kind to cross the Arabian Desert. Bonaparte made no use of it, but possibly Monge and Berthollet did.

During the few days he spent in Suez, Bonaparte's main activity (though not the most advertised one) was to receive in audience the merchants of Hedjaz, Yemen, and Muscat, with a view toward establishing friendly contact with their rulers, and to gather intelligence concerning the military preparations in Syria. More publicized was his excursion to the 'Fountains of Moses,' several natural springs near the coast of the Sinai Peninsula, a few miles south of Suez. Bonaparte and his party forded the Red Sea on horseback at low tide to reach the springs. When they returned, after sundown, their Arab guides, whom the soldiers had plied with liquor, lost their way, and the party very nearly met with the same fate as Pharaoh in pursuit of Moses. Caught by the tide, the horses had to swim for a stretch; General Caffarelli came close to perishing, and lost his wooden leg.

On the day he began his journey back to Cairo, Bonaparte—with his generals and scholars—left the main column of the march to investigate the remnants of the old Suez Canal bed. Surely it was not difficult to find; everybody knew that it was there. Still, Bonaparte claimed for himself the merit of being the first to find it. His small party followed the canal bed toward the Bitter Lakes for about fifteen miles, at considerable risk, and rejoined their column only long after nightfall. In the following two days, they also found traces of the canal which once linked the Nile with the Bitter Lakes. The direct result of these excursions was the appointment of a party of engineers and surveyors, led by the chief engineer Le Pére, to survey the Isthmus of Suez. The work was carried out conscientiously under harrowing conditions. Unfortunately, a slight error crept into the engineers' calculations, which made them conclude that the level of the Red Sea was thirty feet above that of the Mediterranean. The work had to be done over again when, sixty years later, Ferdinand de Lesseps began the construction of the canal.

***

On the way back to Cairo, Bonaparte ordered his column to attack a hostile Bedouin tribe which threatened his communications with Suez. The French burned the Arabs' camp, took hostages, and confiscated all the cattle, goats, and camels. Preceded by these beasts, Sultan Kebir made his entry into Cairo on January 6. Behind the French column, according to El-Djabarti, the Bedouin villagers men, women, and children mournfully followed their cattle all the way to Cairo. Together with the carriage drawn by six horses, this must have made a bizarre procession.

Stealing cattle and camels from the Bedouins on any pretext whatsoever (except from certain tribes allied with the French) had become a matter of high policy. A number of Bonaparte's orders during that period were devoted to this subject. Major Detroye noted the phenomenon in his diary entry for January 18-21: 'The Arabs are being pursued in the desert everywhere. Every day is marked by some capture of a prize from them. One time, our soldiers take their women by surprise and carry them away as hostages; another time, they take their herds, their horses, and their camels. The camels are invaluable, now that we shall undertake an expedition across the desert.'[1] Indeed, Bonaparte's camel-stealing campaign was in preparation for his expedition to Syria. To supplement the cavalry, he had created a Dromedary Regiment. Its men were to carry spears in addition to the usual infantry equipment, and their uniform had already been designed 'gray, with a turban and an Arabian cloak.'[2] On first acquaintance, a camel looks, sounds, and occasionally acts like a ferocious beast: the newly created and beturbaned camel riders approached their mounts with diffidence but soon became used to them. Camels also were needed desperately for the transport of supplies, artillery, and even wounded—for camel-borne ambulances were another recent innovation. The cattle and sheep were stolen partly in order to replenish the army's supplies, partly in order to encourage the Arabs to be more friendly toward the French. 'When returning from their expeditions,' noted Detroye, 'these raiding parties offer a strange sight. Each horseman carries, underneath his cloak, a bleating lamb or kid, which he takes furtively into some alley. One man will sell a stolen horse for a few piastres; another absconds with a camel. Others bring back with them some extremely ugly women, on whom they already have asserted the right of conquest.'[3]

While Bonaparte countenanced robbery when expedient, he made a spectacular show of frowning upon murder. On the night of January 5-4, three Moslem women were assassinated in Cairo

---

[1] La Jonquière, IV, 63.

[2] Correspondance, V, 240.

[3] La Jonquière, IV, 63.

by one or several robbers; a fourth woman saved her life by hiding under her bed. Public opinion accused some French soldiers of the crime. On January 8, having just returned from Suez, Bonaparte ordered, on rather flimsy evidence, the arrest of ten men belonging to the 3rd Company of Grenadiers of the 52nd Half-Brigade. After inquiring into the matter, and without bothering to call a court-martial, the commander-in-chief sentenced two of the ten suspects to be executed by a firing squad. They were shot the same day. Detroye recorded the following circumstance in relating their execution: 'Before they died, they drank to the health of the commander-in-chief, saying that he had been led into error; after which, they added, "You will see how the grenadiers of the 32nd can face death." There was neither a trial nor a verdict.'[1]

A few days later the aga of the Cairo police arrested the actual murderer, a servant in the household, who confessed his crime. A great sultan who must make many quick decisions and take high policy into consideration is bound to blunder once in a while. Bonaparte was to blunder again, five years later—only that time the victim was not a grenadier but the Duc d'Enghien, of whose hasty execution Fouché remarked: 'It is worse than a crime—it is a mistake.'

Having impressed the population with his speedy justice, Sultan Kebir presided over the ceremonies marking the beginning of the month of Ramadan, enjoyed another fortnight with the ex-Madame Fourès, and on February 10 left Cairo to make war on Ahmed Pasha, the Butcher, in Syria. At about the same time, after half a year of tireless campaigning, General Desaix in Upper Egypt was making his single division do the work of three to hold his conquest against almost desperate odds.

---

[1] La Jonquière, IV, 18.

Chapter Eight
To the Cataracts

ON the night of August 25-26, 1798, General Desaix set out from Giza in pursuit of Murad Bey with 2,861 men on foot and two guns. Thus began a campaign that lasted nine months and took Desaix and his division on marches and countermarches whose total length may be estimated at a minimum of 5,000 miles. They tracked Murad up the Nile, inland to Oxyrynchus, into the Faiyum, up the Nile again, past Asyut and Girga, through the colossal ruins of Tentyra, Karnak, and Luxor, up through the narrowing gorge of the Nile to Aswan, where Eratosthenes some twenty centuries ago had measured the earth, and beyond Aswan to Philae, within a day's march from the Tropic of Cancer, then back again, with a side trip across the Arabian Desert to the Red Sea, while Murad raced before them, sometimes fleeing, sometimes turning to attack, disappearing across the desert into an oasis, reappearing behind the French, sometimes reduced to a following of a few hundred faithful, but invariably raising new allies and armies, and ending, still uncaught, at the place where he had started—the Pyramids.

It was a futile campaign, but it was one of the great adventures of modern times—an adventure of which almost every man under Desaix was conscious. On the granite cliffs along the Nile, men named Poudrat, Tricot, Guibourg, their clothes and shoes in shreds, their eyes filled with pus, found the energy to chisel their prosaic names beside those of their predecessors—Julius Tenax,

Valerius Priscus, Quintus Viator—and thus to mark the fact that they too had been there.

Of the two main protagonists in this epic—Desaix and Murad—Desaix is by far the better known. The lives of French military heroes are more fully documented than those of Mamelukes. Nevertheless, his figure remains as elusive as that of Murad Bey.

Louis Desaix de Veygoux was born on August 17, 1768—one year before Bonaparte—in the mountains of Auvergne. His family belonged to the petty nobility; they were country squires. When he was eight, he entered the military school of Effiat, on a scholarship. Only that year, the school run by the Brothers of the Oratory had been reformed by the new Minister of War, a remarkable man, the Comte de Saint-Germain. Among the Minister's instructions was the following: 'The pupils must never be subjected to abusive language and even less to blows.... Men whose entire life should be guided by honour must be brought up with the principles of honour. The most commendable form of punishment, then, is to awaken their sense of shame and to deprive them of whatever they like best.... But even those means of humbling them must be used sparingly, lest the children become accustomed to humiliation. Rewards must be based on the same principles ... on honour and distinction, so as to make these a necessity to their souls.'[1] Perhaps these idealistic notions were not entirely lost on the pupil who came to be known as Sultan el-Adel—the Just Sultan. All the same, Desaix's school reports were appalling. He probably was the worst student in his class.

At fifteen, he tried to enter the naval academy; his application being rejected, he obtained a sub-lieutenant's commission in the Regiment Bretagne-Infanterie. Still a lieutenant at the outbreak of the Revolution, he chose—like the majority of the nobles serving in the army—to continue in the service, regardless of political opinions, rather than emigrate and fight his country. War broke out in 1792, and with it there came an unlimited opportunity for glory and meteoric promotion. Desaix, who served with the Army of the Rhine, was made a Brigadier-General on August 20, 1795, thus rising from a sub-lieutenancy to a generalcy in seven months. In the campaigns of 1796-97, although subordinate to Moreau, he won a reputation second only to that of the commander-in-chief of the Army of Italy: the names Desaix and Bonaparte were idolized alike by the victorious French and the defeated Austrians.

---

[1] Sauzet, p. 18.

No matter how great a general's reputation might be in the French Revolutionary army, his position was never secure: the Committee of Public Safety, and later the Directory, were just as ready to cashier or even shoot a general as to make one. During the Reign of Terror, while Desaix was rising to fame in the ranks of the Revolution, his brothers and cousins fought on the opposite side, in Condi's army of *émigrés*, and his mother and sister were jailed. In January 1797, the Committee of Public Safety ordered General Desaix's arrest as a political suspect; Desaix's men received the commissioners who came to arrest him with their bayonets; the Committee changed their minds. There were other difficulties later, but somehow Desaix always managed to elude them. Was he a republican, a monarchist, or simply a careerist? Whatever he was, he never felt the least urge to disclose it. Compared to him, the ever-communicative yet enigmatic Bonaparte was an open book.

When Bonaparte, in April 1797, took it upon himself to sign an armistice with Austria at Leoben, General Desaix decided to visit Italy and see how the other half had lived and won their laurels. In part, his journey to the battlegrounds of Lombardy and Venetia was motivated by his intense desire to learn, to draw lessons from the greatness of others, whether contemporary or past, which was one of his outstanding characteristics. 'Desaix knew every detail about every great military action,' the mathematician Fourier said of him; 'and, when there was no opportunity for him to share in a victory, he wished to see at least the battlefield. He seemed compelled to associate himself with everything great or useful that had been accomplished.... He would have liked to be the contemporary of every hero in history.'[1] On the other hand, he also had less disinterested motives. 'I am convinced,' he told a confidant about that time, 'that Moreau will never accomplish anything great and that we must always play an inferior role under his command: whereas the other one [Bonaparte] is destined to rise to such fame, to acquire so much glory, that some of it will have to reflect on his lieutenants.'[2] In other words, Desaix deliberately sought out Bonaparte to attach himself to a rising star.

Travelling incognito and in civilian clothes, Desaix studied the battlefields. There was nothing Bonaparte had done, he concluded, that he would not have done himself and with a lesser expenditure of lives. It was a common saying in the Army of the Rhine that

---

[1] Ibid., p. 131.

[2] Ibid., p. 132.

when a man went into battle under any other commander, he must say 'Adieu' to his comrades, if he went under Desaix, he could say, 'Au revoir.' Desaix did not need an income of 10,000 men per month: he was a soldier's soldier. To Bonaparte, glory was a means to power; to Desaix, an end in itself.

Although Desaix tied his career to Bonaparte's and even died to save him, his first impression of the hero, when he met him at Passeriano, was not altogether favourable. 'He is proud, dissembling, vindictive, and never forgives,' Desaix noted in his diary. 'Extremely addicted to intrigue. He is very rich, as well he might be, since he draws on a whole country's revenues.... He believes neither in probity nor in decency; he says all this is foolishness; he claims that it is useless and doesn't exist in this world.'[1]

Whatever his reservations concerning Bonaparte, Desaix was in the General's confidence from the start. 'Egypt. Isthmus of Suez,' he jotted in his diary after one of their first interviews: it was the time when the Egyptian project was maturing in Bonaparte's mind. Shortly after his departure from Italy, Desaix was appointed to the temporary command of the Army of England, pending Bonaparte's return to France. Their fates were linked.

The fact that Desaix rarely, if ever, felt any urge to communicate his opinions of anyone or anything, unless they bore on some specific decision to be made, probably contributed as much to his cult as did his heroic death at thirty-one. His scholarly tastes, his neutrality in politics, his sense of fairness, his dedication to duty and honour, his soldierly simplicity, his stoicism, his avoidance of all ostentation—all these qualities make him the embodiment of a certain military mystique, of Vigny's *Grandeur et servitude militaires*. 'Desaix,' Napoleon reminisced at St. Helena, 'was wholly wrapped up in war and glory.... He was ... always badly dressed, sometimes even ragged, and despising comfort and convenience. When in Egypt,, I made him a present of a complete field-equipage several times, but he always lost it. Wrapped up in a cloak, Desaix threw himself under a gun, and slept as contentedly as if he were in a palace.... He was intended by nature for a great general.'[2]

Like many self-contained and uncommunicative men, Desaix was something of a mystifier and a practical joker. While incognito at Trieste, he once dined with some Austrian officers in a hotel; he was almost challenged to a duel by one of them for making dispar-

---

[1] Ibid., p. 144.

[2] O'Meara, I, 153-54

aging remarks on General Desaix, whom they were praising. He would have delighted in the knowledge that posterity has not the faintest idea of what he really looked like. His several portraits do not bear the least resemblance to one another. Napoleon remembered him as 'a little black-looking man,' about an inch shorter than himself—which would have made Desaix about five foot tall; others described him as very tall; and one witness declares his height to have been five feet five inches. All agree that he was ugly, and that the sabre wound he received in his face in 1795 did not improve his looks. All agree that he was careless of his appearance, ill-dressed and unkempt; they also agree that he was vivacious, loved to joke with his officers, could talk with brilliant charm, and had a phenomenally retentive memory. All this does not add up to a recognizable portrait.

A certain trend in nineteenth-century thinking, confusing the ideal with the sexless, produced an image of Desaix so 'wholly wrapped up in war and glory,' so dedicated to duty, honour, and justice, so impervious to the needs of the flesh, that Desaix, had he known it, would have found it a quite colossal joke to be enjoyed in silence. His intellectual curiosity was lively, but there is no evidence of any deep scholarly inclinations in him; and although his life was dedicated to the travail of soldiering, he did not disdain the soldier's coarser pleasures. His most recent biographer makes something out of the fact that he suffered from a venereal infection and that a woman claimed that her illegitimate daughter was his; and Desaix himself, while in Egypt, wrote to his beloved in France that he was surrounded by a harem. While these facts may prove that war was not the only subject on his mind, their importance should not be exaggerated. It does not take a Casanova to contract gonorrhoea or to make a child, and people have been known to brag. His more serious love affairs appear to have remained platonic—whether because of timidity (perhaps due to his consciousness of being ugly) or because of his dedication to war, it would be presumptuous to say.

There were less casual attachments in Desaix's life. To the last, Marguerite Le Normant, he wrote some rather frank letters, one of which, written after he left Egypt in 1800, deserves a page in any anthology of wit: 'You want me, my lovable lady, to give you the details of my adventures martial and amorous.... So be it, I shall tell you, then, that all went well at my departure from Europe. You know that I was aboard *La Courageuse*, accompanied by *La Capricieuse* and by *L'Amoureuse*, by *La Coquette*, *La Victoire*, *L'Esperance*, and *La Constance*. I must warn you that *La Con-*

stance broke down on the way, Madame.... She stayed behind at Malta. *L'Amoureuse* was raped by the Turks, who sacked her. *La Coquette* escaped them. *La Capricieuse* got into English hands. *La Courageuse* foundered. *L'Esperance* remained with us. *La Victoire* stayed true to us, and we are bringing her back.'[1]

In another letter, he is less witty and more informative. Here is what the soldier who 'despised comfort and convenience,' who slept as contentedly under a gun as if he were in a palace, has to report on his love life in Egypt: 'I have loved the young Astiza, a nice Georgian girl, beautiful as Venus, blonde, and gentle. She was fourteen years old.... She belonged to me by right of succession: her master was dead.... I received as a present Sarah, a madcap Abyssinian, fifteen years old; she was my companion during my journeys. I also possessed Mara, a naïve child from the Tigris, and Fatima, tall, beautiful, well-shaped, but very unhappy.... Such was my seraglio.' 'To these,' he continues, 'one must add three Negresses, a young black boy, Baqil, and a little Mameluke, Ismail, as beautiful as an angel.'[2] One suspects that Desaix exaggerated his account to tease Marguerite; still, the madcap Abyssinian Sarah did accompany him on his epic expedition. The thought may seem disillusioning to those who see in Desaix a military saint. He was a soldier, take him all in all.

***

Murad Bey was more than twenty years older than Desaix. Physically, no two opponents could offer a greater contrast. Desaix—slight, ill-favoured by nature, debilitated by disease—was the pursuer. Murad, his quarry, combined the strength of an ox with the cunning of a fox. Stoutly built, his pale Circassian face framed by a thick blond beard, his cruel, fiery eyes surmounted by fierce eyebrows, dressed as magnificently as Desaix was shabby, he was the picture of manly power, to which a long scar on one cheek only added a warlike touch.

Of Murad's youth, nothing is reliably known. Presumably, he was bought or kidnapped by slave merchants in his native Caucasus, and stopped being a child at about the age at which Desaix was admitted to boarding school on a scholarship. A Mameluke slave became a man very young—at about eight or ten. Though a slave, he was taught to be a lord. He was trained in the use of arms, in horsemanship, and in arrogance. When a Mameluke rode

[1] Sauzet, p. 188

[2] Ibid., pp. 245-46.

through the streets of Cairo, all others had to get off their mules or donkeys at his passage. As soon as a Mameluke slave obtained a military command, he became free, had slaves of his own, and grew a beard—a privilege allowed to free men only.[1] His relationship to his master became one of feudal allegiance rather than slavery in the usual sense; while a boy, however, he was his master's slave indeed, and as often as not he was his mistress too, which did not necessarily prevent him from being a father before he was fourteen. Power, pride, and lust were the principles of his conduct: the human body was a thing to be exploited, killed, or possessed.

Murad had been the slave of a slave of Ali Bey, who ruled Egypt like an independent sovereign from 1765-73. In the beys' struggle for power after Ali's death, he and Ibrahim rose to share supremacy. Murad married Ali's widow, Lady Nafissa, a woman of enormous wealth (inherited from Ali) and endowed with a strong personality. It was with his money, rather than by force of arms, that he achieved his position. His generosity was proverbial, says El-Djabarti in his obituary of Murad; he distributed fortunes to his followers, but what he gave them he took from the people. 'He preferred men who were hard, brave, and cruel,' the chronicler continues. 'As for him, he was unjust, cruel, and proud to excess. Sometimes he pushed bravery to the point of madness; at other times, he acted like a coward. Despite all his boasting, he never won a battle.'[2] On the other hand, Murad seems to have been a good organizer and free of prejudice. He founded an arsenal at Cairo and imported craftsmen to cast cannons; he also created the Mamelukes' Nile flotilla, which he placed under the command of a Christian Greek. This Greek, Moallem Nicholas, enjoyed the same privileges and honours as the beys; so did Murad's favourite and lieutenant, Ibrahim el-Sennari, a black Nubian, who built himself a fine palace in Cairo, was fond of Circassian slave girls, and improved his mind by studying Turkish and necromancy.

While his lieutenant Ibrahim and Ibrahim's own lieutenant governed in his name, Murad lived in splendid isolation at Giza, 'becoming more and more prideful and prodigal.' He was, says El-Djabarti, addicted to pleasure, but he respected religion, was fond of music and of chess, and 'made men of letters and of taste his confidants and boon companions; he was never bored in their

---

[1] Also a sign that one is not on the receiving end of amorous attentions from other men.— [Ed.]

[2] El-Djabarti, VI, 314.

company.'[1] He once spent six years without setting foot in Cairo—perhaps because his pride could not bear his obligation to share power and honours with Ibrahim Bey, who governed the capital as Sheik el-Beled.

Distinguished, even among Mameluke beys, for his arrogance and cruelty, Murad offered, in these respects, a dramatic contrast to Desaix, the 'Just Sultan.' As a tactician, his military knowledge was limited to two principles: charge, and, if necessary, run. Desaix, a student of history, had every aspect of military science at his fingertips. Yet as strategists, the two opponents were evenly matched. Desaix's genius was scientific; Murad's instinctive.

There were, despite all the contrasts, some other similarities. Both were uncommonly obstinate, never discouraged, bold, cold-blooded, and tough. Both lived for war—Desaix for the sake of some abstract, romantic glory, Murad for concrete power and wealth. In the contest, neither won, neither lost, and both added to their stature in history.

II

Murad Bey felt that Napoleon had mauled him rather badly at Embaba, but it never entered his mind that he had been defeated. He simply withdrew to the south, with the three or four thousand Mamelukes he had left and with whatever treasures he could carry with him. In the provinces of Beni Suef, El Faiyum, and Minya, he had no difficulty in raising new foot troops, new supplies, and even money. Through the Bedouins, he remained in close touch with Cairo, French-occupied Egypt, the English squadron off Alexandria, his colleague Ibrahim Bey at Gaza, and Djezzar Pasha at Acre. With their luxurious and dazzling tents, the Mamelukes moved about from place to place, while the peasantry did their bidding. After all, there was no question for a fellah as to who were his true masters: the true masters were not the French newcomers but the people who had beaten him all his life, beaten his father, his grandfather, and all his ancestors for the past 500 years.

It has been seen in an earlier chapter how haughtily Murad rejected Bonaparte's proposals, transmitted by the consul Rosetti. While Murad offered to pay Bonaparte for the expense of evacuating Egypt, Murad's wife Nafissa, in Cairo, paid into the French treasury the equivalent of well over a million gold francs in fines,

---

[1] El-Djabarti, VI, 318.

exacted on various pretexts. This amount made hardly a dent in the couple's finances. She also sheltered and nursed wounded French soldiers and maintained with the French authorities a dignified relationship of wary mutual courtesy.

The continued presence of Murad Bey in Middle and Upper Egypt was intolerable to the French, even if it presented no direct threat to their possession of Cairo and the Delta. As long as Murad remained at large, the population of the occupied provinces would expect his eventual return, whether they desired it or not, pay only lip service to French authority, and let themselves be either intimidated or fanaticized by his propaganda. Moreover, it was essential to drive Murad out of Middle and Upper Egypt before he had time to collect taxes there, lest that desperately needed resource escape the French treasury. Desaix's epic campaign was not only a chase after Murad, it also was a race between competing tax collectors. Even in the Delta and the other French-controlled territories, military detachments were needed to lend authority to the Coptic revenue agents. About twenty centuries ago, Diodorus Siculus observed that the Egyptians regarded themselves as dupes if they paid what they owed without being beaten first. 'I had occasion to notice,' adds Denon after quoting this observation, 'that, while they never refused to pay, there was not a single ingenious device they did not resort to in order to postpone by a few hours their parting with the money.'[1] In Middle and Upper Egypt, that year, the fellahin required an extra strong dose of beatings, since in most places they were made to pay what they owed twice.

Desaix's campaign against Murad began on the night of August 25-26, when his forces left Giza aboard a flotilla composed of several gunboats, galleys, chebeks, and djerms (the characteristic sailing craft of the Nile). With fewer than 5,000 men, only two guns, and no cavalry, his division seemed pathetically inferior to the Mamelukes' strength. It should be kept in mind, however, that the Mameluke forces were rarely united in a single body, each bey operating pretty much on his own, unless Murad called them together to give battle. Even then, French tactical superiority was such that a division of 5,000 men could easily defeat a disorganized horde several times its strength. This lesson Murad himself had learned at Shubra Khit and the Pyramids. Therefore, like Kutuzov fourteen years later, he made it his strategy to avoid pitched battles and to draw the enemy further and further away from his supply bases, counting on his slow destruction by attrition.

---

[1] Denon, I, 118.

Against almost any adversary other than Desaix, this strategy might well have succeeded.

After sailing 125 miles up the Nile, Desaix with part of his troops marched inland, hoping to catch Murad's Mamelukes at Bahnasa, the ancient Oxyrynchus, at the edge of the Libyan Desert. Crossing the flooded terrain, the French spent three hours up to their waists in water and up to their knees in mud, and arrived at Bahnasa just in time to see the last of the Mamelukes' camels ford Joseph's Canal and disappear in the desert. Back to the Nile went Desaix, and another 155 miles up the river to catch Murad's flotilla, which he had heard was at Asyut. He found no flotilla, but he heard that a Mameluke detachment was camping fifteen miles inland, at Beni Adi. When he reached Beni Adi, the Mamelukes with all their wives and chattels had been gone for twenty-four hours. Back to the Nile once more, and down the river, went Desaix: Murad, it seemed, was in the fertile basin of El Faiyum and Desaix was determined to catch him there.

After only three weeks' campaigning, the condition of Desaix's expeditionary force was deplorable. To Desaix's desperate pleas for replacements, additional rations, medicines, and ammunition, Bonaparte responded with 50,000 rations of biscuit (a fraction of what was needed) and eighty men. 'We have had more sickness than usual these last days,' Brigadier Donzelot, Desaix's chief of staff, wrote to Berthier. 'More than three hundred men have the eye disease. Dysentery has reappeared.... Tomorrow we shall send back to Cairo all the men with acute venereal infections, and some who have a fever. All our ambulance surgeons, except the chief surgeon, have eye infections.... Of the 155 hundredweights of biscuits promised from Cairo, all we got was 83 The division lacks shoes. I beg you, General, have some sent to us. The troops are suffering excessive hardship, having to march bare foot on the burning sands.'[1]

On September 24, the flotilla entered Joseph's Canal at Dairut.[2] Navigation was very difficult, for this waterway is very tortuous, and its level was beginning to sink. On October 1, the division was back at Bahnasa, about seventy miles from Dairut as the crow flies. Two days later, the French met the first Mameluke detachments. Desaix disembarked his men and had them proceed on foot, skirmishing as they went. On October 7, at last, he caught

[1] La Jonquière, III, 206.

[2] Several of the gunboats were left to cruise on the Nile; the largest of the barges were also left behind.

up with Murad, who was awaiting him at the Coptic monastery of Sediman, near El Lahun.

Desaix estimated Murad's strength at about 4,000-5,000 cavalry, including both Mamelukes and Bedouins. The French having formed their usual square, flanked by two platoons of riflemen, Murad's cavalry threw themselves upon them with their accustomed speed and impact. 'Our intrepid troops watched them approach with the greatest *sang froid*,' Desaix later reported to Bonaparte. "Go ahead, fire!" I called to the grenadiers of the 61st. "Not until they are at twenty paces from us, General", they answered.'[1] Despite the point-blank fire of the French musketry and grapeshot, the horsemen charged with such savagery that they made several severe dents in the French squares. The ferocity of the resulting hand-to-hand fighting staggers the imagination. Wounded and dying men continued to stab at each other. 'One of our men, stretched out on the ground, crawled toward a dying Mameluke and slit his throat,' reports Denon (who had the story from an eyewitness). 'An officer asked him, "How can you do such a thing in the state you're in?" "It's easy for you to talk," the soldier answered, "but me, I've only a few more minutes to live, and I want to have fun while I may".'[2]

The battle had lasted for well over an hour when four or five guns, which the Mamelukes had concealed behind a hillock, opened fire on the French. Unless Desaix stormed the Mameluke battery immediately, the result was certain disaster; yet Desaix hesitated an instant, for to charge meant leaving behind the wounded, who were sure to be mutilated and massacred by the Mamelukes; then he ordered the charge. The men had to step over the wounded, who were pleading with their comrades to take them along or to shoot them. 'One of them,' says General Belliard in his diary, 'covered his eyes with his handkerchief and turned over, face to the ground, awaiting death.... A mortally wounded soldier grabbed a comrade by the coat-tails and would not let him go; the other, seeing he himself would be killed without being of help to his comrade, took his knife, cut off his coat-tail, and left the wounded wretch, who was finished off by the Mamelukes.'[3] But the charge was successful: the French carried three or four of the guns by storm, while the astonished Mamelukes and Arabs fled in utter confusion. The victors were not in a condition to pursue

---

[1] Ibid., III, 213.

[2] Denon, I, 127.

[3] La Jonquière, III, 218.

them. They had lost forty-four dead and a hundred wounded, the
Mameluke casualties were estimated at 400. Murad withdrew into
the Faiyum.

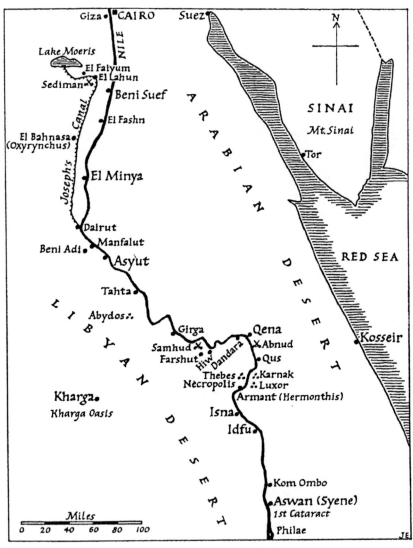

Middle and Upper Egypt

In a letter he wrote almost immediately after it, General Friant, who took part in the action, remarked, 'I believe that General Desaix is ten degrees cooler than ice.'[1]

Desaix allowed his men to rest at El Lahun, evacuated the wounded, and then marched on into the Faiyum—the fabled, lush oasis whose sacred crocodiles, huge artificial lake, temples, labyrinth, and other mysteries had fascinated men ever since Herodotus wrote of them. Desaix found none of these marvels; he did not find Murad either. Murad was back at El Lahun when Desaix sought him in the Faiyum, and he was on his way back to Bahnasa when Desaix returned to El Lahun only four days after leaving it. 'I would be glad to continue the pursuit of them,' Desaix wrote to Bonaparte, 'but really this would be very difficult at the present moment. The inundation, which cuts me off from the villages, would make it impossible for me to feed the troops.... The canal is no longer navigable, and my sick cause me a great deal of embarrassment. The eye disease is truly a horrible plague; it has deprived me of 1,400 men. In my last marches, I have dragged with me about a hundred of these wretches who were totally blind.... We are practically naked, without shoes, without anything. The troops really need a rest. Give us the supplies and the means, and we shall go on.... What do you want me to do?'[2]

For once, General Bonaparte agreed that the troops needed rest. Desaix should leave Murad alone for a while, he replied, and 'organize' the Faiyum. (To 'organize' meant to levy taxes and to requisition food and horses.) Toward the end of October Desaix re-entered the Faiyum, which had been organized but recently by Murad. The population felt that they were being organized too much. On November 8, while the bulk of Desaix's division was out organizing the province, some 500 French troops, one third of whom were ophthalmic patients, had to hold the capital against several thousand embattled fellahin. They lost four men and killed about 200. By November 20, all the Faiyum having been thoroughly organized, Desaix evacuated it, leaving neither a garrison nor a provincial divan, and established his division at Beni Suef, on the Nile, to await reinforcements. He himself went to Cairo, to see that he got what he needed. Meanwhile Murad was writing letters to various chieftains in Arabia, across the Red Sea, and beginning to organize Upper Egypt.

---

[1] Ibid.

[2] Ibid., III, 224-25.

While Desaix's men were chasing Murad back and forth between the Faiyum and Asyut, Lieutenant Desvernois of the Cavalry was entrusted with an equally difficult task, whose performance, however, turned out to be less strenuous.

Since Murad relied mostly on the Bedouin tribes in and near the province of Beni Suef to facilitate his communications, escort his supply and baggage trains, and supplement his forces, it was of some importance to persuade the various tribes to become the allies of the French. For this delicate diplomatic mission somebody at headquarters selected Lieutenant Desvernois. Leaving Cairo with an escort consisting of two hussars, a Bedouin sheik, and the sheik's son, he rode into the desert, visited twenty-three tribes in nineteen days, and had a very interesting time. Whether he signed many treaties of friendship he neglects to say, but that he made many personal friends cannot be doubted.

Although his two Bedouin escorts guaranteed that, as long as he was under their protection, his safety was assured, Desvernois had good reason to be apprehensive when he set out on his tour. An episode, which he relates in his memoirs (confirmed by independent sources), was then still very fresh in his memory. When the French were marching to Cairo, a young staff officer, Denanots, was captured by Bedouins. An emissary, sent by Bonaparte, gave the tribal sheik a hundred piastres for Denanots' ransom. The sum was probably more than the tribesmen ever had seen; before the emissary's eyes, they came to blows over the division of the shares, a not uncommon occurrence among Arabs. More out of the ordinary was the reaction of the sheik. He pulled his pistol from his belt, shot his prisoner dead, and returned the hundred piastres to the emissary: a Solomonic adjudication if ever there was one. No doubt this story was on Desvernois' mind, but he soon found out that being the Bedouins' guest was quite a different thing from being their hostage. 'Wherever I went,' he says, 'I had occasion to appreciate the kindness and solicitude lavished on me by the Bedouin sheiks, their wives, and their daughters.'

Desvernois' account contributes little to the store of knowledge of ethnologists, but it presents a refreshing contrast to the harrowing experiences of his comrades in Desaix's division. It also reveals him as one of the most adaptable men in Bonaparte's army. 'Whichever tribe I visited,' he says, 'I took part in the amusements of those Bedouins. I would be seated beside the sheik and his sons, and was quite satisfied with their cookery and with their coffee. A corner in the chieftain's tent was reserved for me and my two hussars day and night, for our repose. The women and young girls would busy themselves milking the sheep, making cheese, or preparing unleavened bread; they take care of the cooking and of serving the meals. A simple blanket of sheep's or camel's hair separates the women's quarters from the men's during daytime. At night, that blanket disappears, and the sexes are mingled, but only within the same family. We slept in many tents, but everywhere we found the same customs. The women and girls would sing most of the time. They were jolly and sometimes rather free in the way they inspected our clothes and persons. They absolutely wanted to remove the hair on our stomachs, and from elsewhere too, in places where Westerners usually don't remove it.... I must add that many of them were very pretty, usually well-shaped, and that they have very beautiful eyes.'[1] If this is not very informative about the Bedouin way of life, it gives a fairly good idea of Lieutenant Desvernois. He was rewarded for his services, upon his return from his mission, by being promoted to a captaincy on November 21. Two weeks later he was assigned, with a thousand other cavalry men, to General Desaix's division. On his way to Beni Suef, Desvernois stopped at the Pyramids, and there he revealed a different side of his personality. Not all Frenchmen appreciate Oriental feminine beauty, but almost every Frenchman appreciates a fine piece of painting or sculpture. Desvernois was shown some of the exquisite reliefs in the tombs near the Great Pyramid. They represented various rustic activities in the incredibly pure, precise, and stylized lines characteristic of ancient Egyptian art. 'What is most worthy of admiration,' comments Desvernois, 'is the exquisite perfection of the smallest details.... These glorious sights moved me so strongly that, after fifty years, the memory remains completely fresh in my mind.'[2] Not bad, for a hussar.

***

On November 8, the day when 150 half-blind Frenchmen helped to defend El Faiyum, General Belliard left Giza with a battalion sent by Bonaparte to reinforce Desaix. After joining Desaix, he was to resume command of the 21st Half-Brigade of Light Infantry, one of Desaix's units, which he had been obliged to abandon temporarily because of a severe case of ophthalmia. He arrived at El Zawiya, in Beni Suef Province, on November 15, and left

---

[1] Desvernois, p. 153, 154.
[2] Ibid., p. 158.

a week later for Beni Suef.[1] While stopping at El Zawiya, he was joined by a graying civilian fifty-one years old, an inveterate travel-ler whose stamina surpassed that of any hussar or grenadier— Vi-vant Denon, the illustrator, once a popular young man at the Ver-sailles of Louis XV and Madame du Barry. Denon was to remain with the 21st Half-Brigade for nine months; in the course of their common adventures, he and it discovered, for Europe, the glories of ancient Egyptian architecture and sculpture.

Since his arrival in Cairo from Rosetta, Denon had been watch-ing the local scene, taking notes, sketching, visiting the Pyramids and the Sphinx, sketching, attending the sessions of the Institute, sketching, almost fighting during the Cairo rebellion, and sketch-ing. Few men ever had their eyes so wide open.

He was the only man, to this writer's knowledge, who suc-ceeded in describing in words the beauty of the Pyramids and of the Sphinx, which strike most people only by their size. 'I should have liked,' he says of the Pyramids as seen from a distance, 'to show them in that refined and transparent colouring they owe to the immense volume of air surrounding them.... The great distance from which they can be perceived makes them appear diaphanous, tinted with the bluish tone of the sky, and restores to them the perfection and purity of the angles which the centuries have marred.'[2] As for the Sphinx, whose beauty is elusive at best, Denon captured it better in words than with his pencil: 'Although its pro-portions are colossal, those contours which have been preserved are as supple as they are pure: the expression of the face is gentle, graceful, and serene.... The mouth, with its thick lips, has a sensu-ality in its sweep and a refinement of execution that are truly ad-mirable; it is living flesh. If one feels that this head lacks what by convention is called style—that is to say, the proud, straight forms the Greeks lent to the images of their gods—one does not do jus-tice either to the simplicity or to the grand and gentle passage of nature that one must admire in that figure.'[3]

He was less appreciative of Arabic music and dances, but his powers of description retain their high standard when he recalls the Feast of the Prophet as he saw it celebrated at Rosetta. After

---

[1] This author has been unable to determine just where El Zawiya is or was. Perhaps it is Esh Shanawiya, a village shown on maps but barely visible to anyone who passes by it.

[2] Denon, I, 92.

[3] Denon, I, 98.

supper, he says, the French guests of honour were invited to a popular entertainment whose stage was in the street, illuminated by lamps and large candles. 'On the one side, there was a military band, consisting of short and strident oboes, small tympani, and large Albanian drums; on the other side were the fiddles and the singers; in the centre were the Greek dancers, and servants laden with coffee, syrup, rose water, and water pipes.' After describing the alternating strident chants, choruses, and orchestral accompaniments, Denon continues: 'The nasal voice of an inspired singer enhanced the monotonous sensuality of the fiddle's half-notes, which, forever avoiding the tonic, played about the second and always ended on the dominant, like a Spanish seguidilla: which tends to prove that the Moorish occupation of Spain has acclimated this kind of music there.... The dance which followed was of the same kind as the song. It suggested neither joy nor gaiety, but a voluptuousness which quickly changed into a lasciviousness all the more repulsive because the dancers, who are always men, express in the most indecent manner such scenes as even love between the two sexes allows only in the mystery of darkness.'[1] A trifle priggish, a trifle romantic, but always observant and articulate, such was Denon, and it would be difficult to say what other man would have been worthier of the thrill of being the first European in 2,000 years to take a close look at the revelations of Karnak and Luxor.

Having reached El Zawiya, Denon received General Belliard's offer to share his dwelling. This, Denon points out, amounted to splitting the atom: Belliard's quarters were so small that, in order to put in a table, the beds first had to be removed; and when they wanted to wash and dress, the table had to be removed. The second night, the kitchen and the stable collapsed: everything was built of unbaked clay, but it was the best house in the village. Fortunately, they both had a sense of humour, otherwise their nine-month association might have suffered from a poor start. 'I hope,' says Denon, 'that Belliard has kept as pleasant a recollection of me as the gentleness, even temper, and unshakable amiability of his character have left with me.'[2]

Belliard and Denon were at Beni Suef with the rest of Desaix's division when Desaix returned from Cairo on December 9. About 800 replacements had arrived earlier, and on December 10 a cavalry-corps of a thousand men, for which Desaix had been

---

[1] Ibid., 1, 71-72.
[2] Ibid., I, 117.

pleading for months and which he had virtually extorted from Bonaparte, joined his 5,000 foot soldiers. It was commanded by General Davout, later Marshal of the Empire, who routed the Prussian army at Auerstädt in 1806. Desaix had also been given some additional light artillery pieces, food rations, and other supplies. On December 16, his division set out on the march that was to take it beyond Aswan; his flotilla, which was soon to fall behind, left at the same time, under the command of Captain Guichard. At Desaix's side rode a remarkable man, without whose tact, ability, and courage Desaix, despite all his genius, probably would never have won his laurels in Upper Egypt. He was the Copt Moallem Jacob, officially in charge of tax collection in Upper Egypt but in fact the joint commander of Desaix's expeditionary force. In his early fifties, the son of John and Mary Gazalle, Jacob was eminently suited for an adviser in a campaign against Murad Bey, whom he knew quite thoroughly, having once been the steward of Murad's colleague Soliman Bey. He knew the country, he knew the people, he had connections everywhere, he was exceptionally shrewd and diplomatic even for a Coptic tax collector, and he possessed a quality rare among his people military courage and ability. In Upper Egypt, the population regarded Desaix's division as 'the army of Moallem Jacob .' Any other commander might have resented this, but Desaix, a lover of incognito, saw the advantages of the error and did nothing to discourage it. In fact, there was hardly a decision Desaix made throughout the campaign without first consulting 'the Copt,' as Jacob was known in the army; and when, after Bonaparte's departure from Egypt, a Coptic Legion was created, Moallem Jacob became its commanding general.

III

The first lap of the march took the division to El Fashn, on the Nile. During the first halt, near a village, there occurred the pathetic kind of incident that does more to reveal what war is than would any description of battle and gore. Both Denon and Belliard recorded it—Denon, in his book, with some literary frills; Belliard, in his diary, with complete sobriety. Here is Belliard's account: 'During our halt, a young boy, seeing a dragoon asleep, crept up to him and stole his rifle; another dragoon, having noticed the theft, ran after the child, who ran as fast as he could, concealing the weapon under his gown: the boy could not be stopped until after he had received a sabre wound in the arm. He was brought before General Desaix, who interrogated him. He answered, looking up to the sky, that God had commanded him to commit the theft, and that Desaix was free to dispose of his life. He then took off his cap, handed it to the general, and asked him to decide his fate. All this time, he remained unbelievably calm and displayed a rare strength of character. The general, considering his youth and his submissiveness, sentenced him to receive thirty lashes of the whip. The child bent down of his own will and took the lashes on his behind without a sound or a tear. He is about eight to ten years old, and has a lovely face. If he could be given some education, he would go far.'[1]

***

Marching twenty-five to thirty miles a day on the average, the French reached Asyut on Christmas Day. They did not find Murad, as they had hoped, but they found and captured his flotilla. At this stage, after only nine days of marching, their shoes were wearing out, and there were already 200 sick. They were also cold; the sun was hot during the day, but at night there was frost.

Meanwhile Murad, preceding the French by only a day, went from village to village collecting the *miry*. He was not always well received, especially in those towns and villages where the Christian Copts—more numerous in Middle and Upper than in Lower Egypt—were in the majority. 'We learned,' says Belliard in his diary, 'that the Mamelukes had a battle with the villagers of Sanabu. The Mamelukes asked for stiff taxes, cattle, and camels; the inhabitants refused. The fighting started. Eighty villagers were killed; the Mamelukes lost eight men, among them Murad Bey's treasurer.... The village was sacked.... It has sent a deputation to General Desaix, to ask for his protection.'[2]

What protection could Desaix give them? He, too, had to levy the *miry*, to seize cattle, camels, and horses, and then move on, as likely as not to be replaced by the Mamelukes. The villagers' pleas to be exempt from taxes, as they already had paid them to Murad, were invariably rejected at headquarters in Cairo. Although many a village paid its *miry* twice that year, Sultan Selim III, in whose name it was levied by both sides, never saw a penny of it. After observing these fiscal operations for several weeks, Denon began to pity 'the inhabitants, for the sake of whose welfare we had come to Egypt.... If fear made them leave their village at our approach, they found nothing upon their return but the mud their walls are made

[1] La Jonquière, III, 506-7.
[2] La Jonquière, III 509.

of. Tools, ploughs, doors, roofs—everything had been used for firewood to cook our soup. Their pots had been broken, their wheat eaten, their chickens and pigeons roasted.... Whenever we made a halt in their village, we ordered those wretches to return, lest they be treated as rebels or as allies of our enemy and, consequently, be made to pay the double of the tax rate. If they gave in to our threats and came to pay the *miry*, it sometimes happened that because of their large numbers and because of the sticks they carried they were mistaken for an armed mob; in that case, they invariably were shot at by our patrols before they had time to explain their purpose. Then the dead were buried, and we remained friends until they saw an opportunity to take revenge without a risk. It is true that, if they remained at home, and paid the *miry* ... they saved them selves the trouble of taking a trip to the desert, had the satisfaction of watching their provisions being eaten up in an orderly manner, received their share to eat, kept parts of their doors, sold their eggs to the soldiers, and had relatively few wives and daughters raped: on the other hand, this made them guilty of co-operation with us, so that when the Mamelukes arrived after we departed, they left the peasants not one penny, not one horse, not one camel, and often the mayor paid with his head for his alleged partiality to us.'[1]

Let self-pitying taxpayers compare their troubles to those of the fellahin of 1798! But the fellahin had been used to this sort of thing for several thousand years. If forty centuries of history were looking down upon anyone, it was upon the fellahin— with compassion rather than on the proud Mamelukes or the glory-hunting French. And yet, as if they had not troubles enough, the villagers were in a state of recurrent warfare with neighbouring villages over a stolen goat, a tampered-with irrigation canal, and similar *casus belli*. Their warlike expeditions invariably resulted in several deaths. On the local as on the national level, the government of Egypt at that time may be defined as anarchy aggravated by rents and taxes. Shortly after leaving Asyut, General Desaix, the Just Sultan, found the opportunity, for once, not to make war and to pillage, but to restore peace between two warring villages. He confronted the two sheiks. 'Each stated his case,' says Belliard, 'the *pros* and *contras* were weighed in the balance of justice, and the men who, half an hour before, wanted to destroy each other ended by appreciating the wise reflections, opinions, or orders of the

---

[1] Denon, I, 252-53.

conqueror and went away as good friends. It was a happy day....'[1]
Unfortunately, there was no Just Sultan to do the same for the
heads of state of Europe.

***

At Asyut, the Nile valley begins to narrow. Wedged between
two forbidding mountain chains, the cultivated area extends for
only about ten miles, sometimes broadening a little, sometimes
narrowing to a gorge. There was, the French found, more prosperity than in Lower Egypt. The fields, orchards, and palm groves
were fertile and well-tended; the roads and canals were kept in
relatively good condition. Yet everywhere war had left its traces.
Denon visited a Coptic monastery, built by Saint Helena, mother
of Constantine the Great, and burned down by Murad's men the
day before the French marched past it. The monks had fled, leaving behind only a few lay brothers, 'covered with rags and still under the shock of the agonies they had suffered on the eve,' Denon
recalls. Part of the ancient wood panelling of the choir had been
charred: 'yet the insatiable needs of insatiable war made our men
remove even those leftovers of misery, those vestiges of a devasta-
tion which we had caused.'[2]

According to intelligence received by Moallem Jacob, Murad
had boasted everywhere that he would await the French at Girga,
then the chief city of Upper Egypt, to give them battle. When Desaix arrived at Girga, he discovered that Murad had left the preceding night. Though eager to continue the chase, Desaix was
obliged to make a halt. The north wind had stopped and his flotilla
had fallen behind. Since the ships carried the division's supplies, it
was essential to wait for their arrival before venturing farther
south.

The delay had serious and, for many members of the expedition, fatal consequences. During the three weeks that the French
remained at Girga, Murad Bey, encamped about thirty-five miles
to the south, displayed even more than his customary energy and
built up an army of 11,000 horse and 3,000 infantry. He wrote to
his sworn enemy, the Mameluke Hassan Bey, who governed Isna,
and persuaded him to bury their feud: Hassan joined Murad's
1,500 Mamelukes with 400 of his own. Murad had already written
to the sherifs of Yamho and of Jidda, on the Red Sea coast of Hejaz, asking them to bring warriors to help his fight against the In-

---

[1] La Jonquière, III, 512.
[2] Denon, I, 159, 158.

fidel; in Nubia, his agents were buying up slaves to serve in his corps; and everywhere, from Aswan to Asyut, his emissaries carried messages, inciting the peasantry to kill the handful of French invaders in a bath of blood. He enlisted even children in his cause; at Girga, small boys were stealing the Frenchmen's weapons by the scores.

Most redoubtable among Murad's reinforcements were the Arabian warriors from Hejaz, who came sailing across the Red Sea by the thousands. They all claimed to be descendants of the Prophet, wore green turbans, were armed with muskets, sabres, lances, and daggers, and were as ferocious as they looked. Many of them turned out to be Moroccan pilgrims snapped up *en passant,* but by far the larger—and certainly the more fanatic—part of them were genuine Arabs from Arabia. While the Sherif of Mecca did not exactly encourage them to join Murad, he did nothing to stop them either. At the same time, he sent friendly messages to Bonaparte, since his revenue depended largely on his coffee exports to Egypt.

By all accounts, the bronzed and skinny 'Meccans,' or 'sherifs of Yambo,' as the French called them, bore out Bonaparte's dictum on the Arabs: 'Their ferocity is equalled only by the misery of their standard of life, exposed as they are, day after day, to the hot sand, the burning sun, without water. They have neither pity nor faith. They are the picture of savage man in the most hideous form imaginable.'[1] They were also of the same stock as that which, eleven centuries earlier, had conquered half the world. In 1798, they came to fight the godless French with the same faith and the same lust for loot.

Murad's skill at acquiring unlimited cannon fodder was awe-inspiring. He persuaded the peasants, whom he had just fleeced, that the French were decimated, isolated, and doomed; to attack them involved no risk. He then placed the peasants between himself and the French, watched them being butchered, regarded it as a gain if they killed one Frenchman for every hundred of their own dead, and, instead of coming to their aid, dashed off somewhere else to start the same manoeuvre all over again. What he promised Hassan Bey is anybody's guess, but it must have been a great deal. As for the Arabs of Yambo, 'they came running to Egypt on the rumour that there was a band of Europeans who were covered

---

[1] Correspondance, V, 71.

with gold and silver, and that all the Arabs had to do was come and beat them and grow wealthy on the spoils.'[1]

All the Arab reinforcements landed at the small port of Kosseir. It so happened that when the first contingent arrived, Bonaparte had just sent a small squadron from Suez to occupy the port. His squadron and the Meccan fleet arrived at the same time, a coincidence Bonaparte could not have foreseen. The French squadron was badly mauled and returned to Suez, where its captain ended his report with a request not to be sent on such impossible missions in the future.

**

While Murad built up his forces at Hiw, a couple of days' march to the south, the French were waiting at Girga, with increasing irritation, for Captain Guichard to show up with his flotilla. At least, they could console themselves with the abundance and cheapness of food. A goose fetched the equivalent of about two shillings; a chicken, one shilling; half a dozen eggs, or a pigeon, sixpence. 'Never,' noted Belliard, 'have we found a country where food was cheaper.... At first, one thinks that such low food prices mean poverty. But when four to five thousand soldiers stay in a town for ten days and the prices do not rise, then the conclusion is that abundance is the cause.'[2] Well reasoned, General! And yet, with all this abundance, all this cheapness, why was there so much poverty? In Egypt, the same question might still be asked today.

Besides eating pigeon at sixpence instead of army biscuit, the French relieved their tedium with a number of diversions, not all of them involving rape. They would listen to the marvellous tales of Arabian story-tellers, translated sentence by sentence by an interpreter. On New Year's Eve there arrived the yearly caravan from Nubia. The brother of its leader dined with General Desaix. 'He was,' says Denon, 'lively, passionate, and intelligent.... He was darker than bronze and had beautiful eyes.' He had just come back, he said, from a two-year journey to Mecca and to India. He had eighty brothers, all princes, all sons of the Sultan of Darfur. His caravan of 2,000 camels carried elephant tusks, gold dust, senna, tamarind, and male and female Negro slaves to Cairo. The French were bemused; they also got ideas, which they carried out a few weeks later. Meanwhile, they plied the dark prince with questions. What was the cost of a Negro slave to the traders? One rifle

---

[1] La Jonquière, III, 515.

[2] La Jonquière, III, 513.

for a woman, two for a man. Was there really a place named Timbuktu, 'that famous city whose existence remains a problem in Europe?'[1] Yes, certainly there was—at a six-month journey from Darfur, to the south-west. The merchants of Darfur went there regularly, sold the goods they had purchased in Cairo to the natives (who were 'very small and good-natured'), and received gold dust from them in payment. The prince added, acording to Denon (who swears that his account is a word-for-word transcription of the interview) that Europe had an unlimited market for its goods in Africa; 'that we [the Europeans] would be welcome if we made Africa our dependency; that by doing so we would not do any harm to their own trade; and that we would link them to our interests by supplying their needs.'[2] This, too, one suspects, did not fall on deaf ears, as the history of the nineteenth century tends to show.

Thus passed the three weeks at Girga. 'Every evening,' records Belliard, 'we [i.e. the staff officers] have a party at the general's house, and thus we spend two agreeable hours of the day among friends, discussing and arguing about various questions of more or less importance.'[3]

On January 19, Citizen Guichard arrived at last with his flotilla, the military band aboard it playing gay tunes of France; two days after that, Desaix and his division—3,000 infantry and 1,000 horse—left Girga; the following day, January 22, Murad Bey welcomed them at Samhud with 3,000 foot soldiers, 7,000 mounted Arabs from Upper Egypt, 2,000 'Meccans,' on foot, under Sherif Hassan of Yambo, and 2,000 Mamelukes. It was an occasion Desaix had been dreaming of for the past fifteen weeks.

***

The battle went as usual. This time, Desaix formed two infantry squares instead of one and placed a cavalry square at the centre; the artillery was on the flanks. The Mameluke cavalry tried various points of attack and, being repulsed everywhere, left the business to the Meccans, a large number of whom were slaughtered, and fled toward the desert. French casualties: one hussar. To be sure, there were a number of wounded, among them Captain Desvernois, who was with an advance platoon ahead of the squares. 'I received eighteen unimportant wounds,' he reminisced with a casual air, 'but the enemy picked me out as their main tar-

---

[1] Denon, I, 163

[2] Ibid., I, 165.

[3] La Jonquière, III, 517.

get. A sabre blow cut the tendons of my right forearm, obliging me to take my sword in my left hand, which put me in a perilous position....I shouted to Savary to come to my assistance.... "Help yourself as best you can", he shouted back.[1] This reply infuriated Desvernois. Charging blindly through the melée, he made straight for the ambulance, so he says, where the surgeon made an inventory of his wounds: left index and middle fingers cut, right arm cut to the bone, a severe bruise on the forehead, and nineteen minor cuts, not counting a dozen or so on the croup of his horse. No one, with the possible exception of Baron Munchausen, ever combined understatement and exaggeration with an artistry as consummate as Captain Desvernois'. Desaix, reporting on the combat to Bonaparte, has no more to say of Desvernois than this: 'Citizen Desvernois had his wrist cut by a dagger, but without any permanent damage to him.'[2]

The Mamelukes were fleeing to the south, with the French in such hot pursuit that they neglected to despoil the corpses on the battle-ground; once again, Murad had escaped. This time, however so Desaix wrote to Bonaparte the French would chase Murad out of Egypt, occupy the southernmost provinces, and wait until Murad and his men were destroyed by hunger and want. Already Murad's allies, and even some of his own men, were abandoning him, and the beys were quarrelling among themselves: this, at least, was what a Mameluke deserter—a native of Saxony, of all places—reported to the French. More deserters joined the French in the days following. Nevertheless, as Desaix himself was soon to recognize, 'the Mamelukes are like the Hydra of Lerna; as you cut off their heads, new ones keep growing.'[3] When, after marching 250 miles in ten days, the French reached Aswan, Murad was already deep in the Sudan, growing new heads.

IV

When Denon volunteered to join Desaix's division, his expectations were as boundless as his enthusiasm. He knew that he 'would be the first to see, and to see without preconceived ideas,' he reminisced later. 'I was about to tread the soil of a land covered since immemorial times with a veil of mystery and closed for the past two thousand years to all Europeans. From Herodotus to our own

[1] Desvernois, p. 162.
[2] La Jonquière, III, 531.
[3] Ibid., III, 607.

times, all the travellers were content to sail up the Nile rapidly, not daring to lose sight of their boats, and leaving them for a few hours only in order to inspect, hastily and uneasily, the objects closest to shore.... Encouraged by the cordiality with which General Desaix received me, and aided by all the officers who shared my love for the arts, I had no fear except that I might lack time, pencils, paper, and talent.'[1]

His talent was limited, perhaps, but it was of the precise, painstaking kind best suited to his task, and his enthusiasm and artistic under standing more than made up for his shortcomings. As for pencils, he and the scientific commissioners who joined the division later ran out of them all the time. New shipments were constantly requested from Cairo, where Citizen Conté manufactured them; while waiting for them to arrive Denon and his companions would melt down lead bullets and improvise pencils out of them.

The real shortage, at least during the first six weeks, was time. Denon had to move with the division, or he would have lost his life. The division had to move fast, in forced marches, in the pursuit of the elusive Murad. The only place where it halted for any length of time was Girga—and there was nothing very remarkable to be seen in it or its neighbourhood. Hermopolis had tantalized him; its temple, he recalled, 'was the first monument to reveal to me the ancient architecture of Egypt; its stones ... had been waiting for me for four thousand years.'[2] Belliard gave him a few minutes to make a sketch. On they marched, at twenty-five to thirty miles per day. At Asyut, the tombs of ancient Lycopolis beckoned to him; he snatched a few hours for them. The funerary grottoes, carved out of the granite of the Libyan Chain, were covered with hieroglyphs: 'It would take months to read them, supposing the language was known, and years to copy them.'[3] Reluctantly, Denon moved on. By the time he reached Girga, his eyes were burning from ophthalmia—the eyes that still had so much more to see. He relieved the symptoms by taking Egyptian baths, to which he was addicted. At only twelve miles from Girga, at the edge of the desert, are the nuns of Abydos, 'where Ozymandias had built a temple, where Memnon had his palace.' Denon, during the three weeks of enforced idleness, begged Desaix every day to send a detachment on reconnaissance there. 'And every time Desaix said to

[1] Denon, I, 138.

[2] Ibid., I, 147.

[3] Ibid., I, 153.

me, "I want to take you there myself. Murad Bey is at a two-day march from here. He'll be here the day after tomorrow, there will be a battle, we'll beat his army, and two days later we'll think of nothing but antiquities, and I'll help you measure them".'[1]

Desaix did not quite keep his word. After the battle of Samhud, the headlong chase after Murad took his division past Abydos, Tentyra, Thebes, Hermonthis, and Apollonopolis Magna to Syene, sometimes without stopping, usually stopping just long enough to exacerbate Denon's frustration. At Tentyra, however, the soldiers temporarily forgot the chase and lingered at the magnificent temple. 'Without any orders having either been given or received, every officer, every soldier left the road and rushed to Tentyra; spontaneously, the whole army remained there for the rest of the day,' recalls Denon. 'What a day! What bliss to have braved all to find such a feast!'[2]

His first reaction was astonishment. Whatever he had been taught of the classical rules of the Dorian, Ionic, and Corinthian orders, he had to discard. 'Nothing could be simpler or better calculated than the few lines that compose this architecture. Having borrowed nothing from other nations, the Egyptians added not one extraneous ornament, not a single superfluity to the lines dictated by necessity. Order and simplicity were their principles, which they raised to the sublime.' Even the profuse reliefs, inscriptions, and paintings that cover their edifices leave these lines unbroken: 'The lines are respected; they appear to be sacred; whatever seems ornamental, rich, or sumptuous from close by disappears when seen at a distance, and only the principle remains.' Painting was used to ornament architecture. 'Sculpture was emblematic or, as it were, architectural. Thus architecture was the art par excellence, determined by usefulness.... One must avoid the common error of thinking that Egyptian architecture represents that art in its cradle; on the contrary, one must say that it is its standard.'[3]

In his excitement, Denon sketched furiously among that embarrassment of riches. 'Pencil in hand, I passed from object to object, drawn away from one thing by the interest of another.... I had not eyes or hands enough, my head was too small to see, draw, and classify every thing that struck me. I felt ashamed at the inade-

---

[1] Ibid., I, 172-73.

[2] Ibid., I, 182.

[3] Ibid., 1, 178

quacy of the drawings I made of such sublime things.'[1] Unaware of
the setting sun, terrified lest Tentyra 'escape' him, he discovered
suddenly that he was all alone but for the patient General Belliard,
who, loath to interrupt such ecstasy, kept a protective eye on him.
They rejoined the division at a gallop. In the evening, an officer
went up to Denon. 'Ever since I came to Egypt,' he confessed, 'I
have felt cheated in every way and been constantly depressed and
ill. Tentyra has cured me. What I saw today has paid me back for
all my misery. I don't care what happens to me during the rest of
this expedition; I shall always be happy to have been in it.'[2]

***

Above Tentyra—the modern Dandara—the French came upon
the first crocodiles. Denon claims to have seen one twenty-eight
feet long, which is very long, and that 'several trustworthy officers'
had seen a forty-footer—which is preposterous. However big the
beasts may have looked to them, the soldiers soon discovered that
crocodiles did not deserve their reputation for ferocity. They
bathed calmly in the Nile within a few feet from those sluggish
creatures, and neither life nor limb was lost. The men were still
discussing crocodiles when, at nine o'clock in the morning of
January 27, they rounded a bend and saw before them, on both
sides of the Nile, the full panorama of ancient Thebes—the temples
of Luxor and Karnak. The entire division spontaneously came to a
halt and clapped their hands in applause. 'Without an order being
given,' says Desvernois, 'the men formed their ranks and presented arms, to the accompaniment of the drums and the bands.'[3]
It was a moment comparable to Balboa's men sighting the Pacific
Ocean—with this difference, that the Pacific was the Spaniards'
goal, whereas Thebes was a pure gift unsought.

Amidst this martial tribute to the genius of man, Denon was
already sketching this first sight of Thebes. Soldiers volunteered,
in their enthusiasm, to let him use their knees for a drawing
board; others surrounded him to protect him from the blinding
sun while he drew. 'I wish to give an idea of this scene to my readers,' he says, 'so as to make them share in the feelings I experienced in the presence of such majestic objects, and in the electrify-
ing emotion of an army of soldiers whose refined sensibility made

---

[1] Ibid., I, 183.

[2] Ibid., I, 184.

[3] 46 Desvernois, p. 169.

me rejoice in being their companion and proud of being a Frenchman.'[1]

A hundred and sixty-five years later, the mere description of that moment remains indescribably moving. Denon's ensuing predicament, however, has something indescribably comical about it. For months, he says, he had been vegetating in holes like Zawiya, Beni Suef, and Girga, where there was nothing of what he had come to see; now he was at Thebes and had to move on at a gallop. At the Necropolis, the City of the Dead, where he rode with Desaix, his party was assailed by a band of very live Arabs armed with javelins. Back he galloped to the main body of the army; sketched a temple; tore after the troops, who had already left; stopped to draw a fallen and shattered colossus (Ozymandias? he wondered); was left alone once again; raced on to a plain where the troops had stopped to admire two seated colossi (one of them commonly identified as the statue of Memnon; but in Denon's opinion they represented Ozymandias' wife and son); jumped back on his horse to catch up with the troops, still observing and reflecting as he rode; and left Thebes behind him in a rage of frustration. Fortunately, in the following months, he was able to visit it more at leisure several times.

At Hermonthis, Denon slept in a temple, surrounded by figures of the jackal-god Anubis. He sketched it at dawn, and continued for Isna, the ancient Latopolis. Then on, past the ill-preserved sandstone ruins of Hieraconpolis, at the tail of Mohammed el-Elfi's Mamelukes, to Idfu (Apollonopolis Magna). He reached it just before sunset: time enough to make a sketch of its fortress-like temple, filled with wretched mud huts—'like swallows' nests in our houses,' he says. On again through a narrowing granite gorge and then, by barge, across the Nile to Aswan, the ancient Syene, where the division arrived on February 2, two days after the Mamelukes had left it. Two hundred and fifty miles, in ten days, through wild and hostile territory, for an exhausted, ill-shod army, with almost every man suffering from eye disease, is a remarkable record of endurance. General Belliard surveyed the scenery of Aswan, while his troops were crossing the Nile, from a rocky lookout point. 'Toward the west,' he wrote in his diary, 'the eye discovers a huge desert; to the south, the awesome sight of the steep rocks forming the cataract. They seem to signify that here are the limits of the civilized world. Here nature seems to bar our route and to say to us, *Stop, go no farther.* To the east is Elephantine Island, its

---

[1] Denon, I, 186.

verdure and palm groves contrasting with the arid mountains that surround it.'[1]

V

General Desaix did not tarry long. On February 4, leaving only Belliard's 21st Half-Brigade of Light Infantry at Aswan, he marched back north, following the right bank of the Nile. Once again he passed Thebes, this time on the Luxor and Karnak side. 'Ecstasy at the sight of the temple and the obelisk,'[2] the ordinarily prosaic Savary, Desaix's aide, noted in his diary on February 18, (The obelisk now stands in the Place de la Concorde, where hardly anybody looks at it.) Desaix continued downstream to Asyut, where he arrived on March 8 and stayed for ten days; then he marched up the Nile again for 180 miles to Qena (not far from Thebes), the terminus of the caravan route from the Red Sea port of Kosseir. The total of Desaix's marches and countermarches in the fifty days between February 4 and March 27 amounts to about 550 miles. Sight-seeing was not his primary purpose.

When Desaix started out from Beni Suef on December 16, he had 4,000 men. With these, Bonaparte expected him to hold a strip 600 miles long of hostile territory, wedged between two deserts. To accomplish this, he could not leave garrisons, which would have been massacred by the Mamelukes, Arabs, and peasants. All he could do was to make himself virtually omnipresent—hence the perpetual marches. Was Desaix aware of the impossibility of the task? Probably. Yet, the more impossible it was, the more glory was to be won in it. He pretended that it was possible but he did not push the pretence so far as not to ask for help. In a letter to Bonaparte, dated February 18, he described his situation: constant combats with the fellahin and with the Meccan volunteers; Murad Bey about to pass to the counterattack, cutting across the desert and behind Desaix's line; disastrous shortages of ammunition, boots, drugs, and light artillery. 'We are here at the end of the earth, as it were. It is a sad situation. Remember that we are lacking everything and that the kind of war we are fighting is rather difficult. I shall not go into the details of our situation. I don't like to complain.'[3]

---

[1] La Jonquière, III, 539.

[2] Ibid., III, 566.

[3] Ibid., III, 578.

When Desaix wrote this, Bonaparte was besieging El Arish and about to enter Syria. He could spare nothing, and he fully relied on Desaix's ability to hold Upper Egypt with next to nothing. None of the essentials Desaix asked for were sent to him. By early March, Desaix began to see the unpleasant truth. To Dugua, who commanded at Cairo during Bonaparte's absence, he wrote on March 9: 'The commander-in-chief, when he ordered us to conquer Upper Egypt, was completely preoccupied with his own expedition and gave us absolutely nothing. My division, by way of reward for its travails, has been left without pay one month longer than the rest of the army.... We have no shoes, no clothes, no cash. We are exhausted with fatigue. But we shall go on, beating the Meccans, the Mamelukes, and the peasants. I have had no news from General Belliard for twelve days. I have asked the commander-in-chief for many things I need, but I give up, since I'll never get anything from him.'[1]

In writing this, Desaix understated his and Belliard's plight.

***

For the first couple of weeks, Belliard's occupation of Aswan seemed a picnic spiced with a bit of fighting and raping. At last, one could rest. 'To take off one's clothes, to sit down, to lie down to sleep seemed positively sybaritic and voluptuous pleasures to me,' Denon reminisces. 'The soldiers felt the same way. We hadn't been at Aswan for two days, and already there sprouted in the streets French tailor shops, cobblers, jewellers, and barbers, with their signs, as well as restaurants with menus at fixed prices. An army's stay anywhere means the most rapid development of industrial ingenuity: every man puts to use whatever talents he has for the good of the community. But what particularly characterizes a French army is to see to the superfluous at the same time and with the same care as to the necessary. There were gardens, cafés, and public card games at Aswan. At the exit of the village, toward the north, there was a tree-lined avenue; here the soldiers put up a military signpost reading, "Road to Paris No. 1,167,340".'[2]

With Belliard, Denon visited Elephantine Island, whose temples he sketched and which he made his 'country home, pleasure grove, and centre of observations and research all in one.'[3] Belliard wanted to push even farther south and occupy the island of

[1] Ibid., III, 592-93.

[2] Denon, I, 205.

[3] Ibid., I, 206.

Philae. There was some resistance: 'The inhabitants made strident outcries,' Belliard recorded in his diary. 'The women sang battle songs, made the dust fly, and gave the signal for combat.'[1] But Belliard had rafts built and took both island and women by storm. 'Men, women, and children, everybody threw themselves into the river,' relates Denon. 'Faithful to their ferocious character, mothers could be seen drowning the children they could not take with them and mutilating their daughters in order to protect them from being raped by the victors.... I found a girl seven to eight years old who had been sewn up ... in a manner that prevented her from satisfying her most pressing needs and caused her horrible convulsions. Only after a counter-operation and a bath was I able to save the life of that unfortunate little creature, who was as pretty as could be.'[2] What an edifying confrontation of Eastern and Western civilizations! The results scarcely justified the trouble, for two days later Belliard evacuated the island, never to return. Two days, two years, two centuries—is either victory or defence worth the price of a mutilated child? How civilized were Citizens Belliard and Denon, so sensitive to the aesthetic grandeur of ruins thirty-five centuries old, so casual about the rape of living flesh?

General Belliard made lavish use of spies. The spies told him that the Mamelukes, south of the Tropic of Cancer, were starving, having consumed everything they could extort from the Sudanese population, and that, in desperation, they were about to come back and resume the offensive. Like any conscientious general, Belliard felt that it was his duty to prevent the enemy from gaining fresh food supplies: and so he sent a detachment south to the village of Qeleb Toud, where, he informed Desaix, he ordered 'all the wheat in the village to be destroyed, and there was a considerable amount of it. The poor inhabitants could watch, within an hour, the destruction of the fruit of three months' labour.... I gave the peasants who had stayed behind a few coins and told them that, if they should starve, they ought to send for some durrah at Aswan.'[3] History does not record whether the peasants sent to Aswan; if they did, they found that Belliard was no longer there. Still, the gesture was humane.

Belliard's spies also informed him that Murad Bey was about to cut across the desert from Kalabsha to Asyut—a distance of about 300 miles—to cut him off from Desaix. Rather hastily, Bel-

---

[1] La Jonquière, III, 547.

[2] Denon, I, 219.

[3] La Jonquiere, III, 545-46.

liard left Aswan in the night of February 24-25, leaving no garrison behind, to catch up with Murad or, at any rate, to avoid being cut off by him. Except for the ecstasies at Thebes, the trip to Aswan had been rather unnecessary.

***

While General Belliard let his men rape, to improve their morale, and ordered harvests to be destroyed, to depress the morale of the Mamelukes, General Desaix and Moallem Jacob received intelligence of Meccan troop concentrations at Qena, of the landing of about 2,000 more Meccan volunteers at Kosseir, and of the approach, from the south, of a body of Mamelukes under Osman Bey.

When Desaix, with the bulk of his troops, descended the Nile to Asyut in late February, he was obliged to leave his flotilla in the vicinity of Qena. At the beginning of April, Sherif Hassan, who commanded about 2,000 Meccan infantry, was informed of the flotilla's presence several miles below Karnak. On April 3, the Meccans caught up with it. They began to fire at the ships with their muskets. L'Italie, with about 200 marines, 300 wounded and blind, and a regimental band aboard, replied with a devastating cannonade. The Meccans, however, were absolutely fearless. They managed to seize some of the smaller barges and began to board L'Italie. Her captain, Morandi, seeing that the struggle was hopeless, tried to manoeuvre her away from the Arabs but only succeeded in beaching her. The Arabs were now boarding L'Italie by the hundreds. During the hand-to-hand fighting Morandi ordered the craft to be set on fire and to abandon ship. He was killed by a rain of bullets almost immediately after the order was carried out. The survivors were led ashore by the Meccans. There, the band of the 61st Half-Brigade was ordered by their captors to give a concert. To the strains of the French Revolutionary marches, the prisoners—most of them blind or wounded—were being raped, mutilated, and hacked to pieces. Then came the turn of the band.

While the descendants of the Prophet were thus amusing themselves, General Belliard with his 21st Half-Brigade was descending the Nile in forced marches, following Desaix's instructions to take position at Hermonthis (Armant) . He arrived there precisely on the day the crew and passengers of L'Italie were being massacred some thirty miles to the north. On March 4, his spies informed him that 6,000-7,000 more Meccans had landed at Kosseir; two days later he heard of the capture of L'Italie. He crossed the Nile and raced down the river along its right bank. This time Denon passed through Luxor and Karnak without stopping for so much as a single sketch. At Qus, the sheik-el-beled, whom Desaix had befriended, warned Belliard against going farther: the country was swarming with Meccans, and the French were marching to their certain death. On March 8, in the plain above Abnud, Belliard's thousand men, almost every one suffering from ophthalmia, ran into about 3,000 Meccan infantry and about 350 Mamelukes. Belliard's artillery consisted of one single light piece. The Mamelukes and Arabs had several guns, which they managed to fire quite accurately although they were not mounted on carriages.

In square formation, as usual, the French marched against the sprawling enemy line, which slowly gave way and fell back to the village of Abnud. There they barricaded themselves in the houses. 'We had been fighting for six hours without interruption,' says Denon, who saw three officers killed before his eyes while talking to them. 'Exhausted, panting from the heat, we stopped a moment to catch our breath. We had absolutely no water, and never had we needed it more. I recall that at the height of the action I found a jar of water standing against a wall and that, not having the time to drink, I poured it into my shirt as I went.'[1]

Having caught their breath, the French went on to the assault of the village, took several houses, and bayoneted some 200 Meccans. They then concentrated their attack on a building belonging to a Mameluke, where a large number of Meccans were holding out. After two hours, the French had sixty men killed and as many wounded before that single house. The sun having set, the fighting came to a lull, but it resumed at daybreak. 'I gave orders to take the house by storm,' Belliard reported to Desaix the following day. 'We succeeded in forcing our way into the courtyard and in setting the building on fire. The Meccans came running down into the courtyard naked, holding a sabre in one hand, a musket in the other, firing at our soldiers, and leaping, like madmen, on to the flames, which they tried to put out with their feet.'[2] Black and naked,' says Denon, describing the same episode, 'they ran through the flames; they looked like devils out of hell. Seeing them, I felt both horror and admiration. There were intervals of silence, when a single voice could be heard [in prayer]; a chorus would answer it with sacred hymns and battle cries; then they would throw themselves upon us despite the certainty of being killed.'[3]

---

[1] Denon, I, 238.

[2] La Jonquière, III, 598.

[3] Denon, I, 240.

J. Christopher Herold

Night fell, and still the Meccans continued their resistance both in the house and in the courtyard, which by then was littered with corpses. During the dark, they pierced a wall and escaped, but many of them were cut down by the French soldiers outside the building. On the following morning, the French entered the house, where about thirty Meccans had remained behind, too wounded or too ill to flee. 'They still wanted to defend themselves,' says Belliard. 'All were killed save three Tunisians, whom I had spared in order to interrogate them.'[1] No sooner was the fighting over than the Frenchmen began to console themselves with the women of the village, who, according to Denon, gave in to the victors without the least difficulty.

***

Desaix and his troops arrived at Asyut on March 8 the day when Belliard began his three-day battle with the Meccans. The whole countryside around Asyut was in open rebellion: Murad Bey had made his 300-mile dash across the Libyan Desert, had beaten Desaix to the race, and, with his usual boasts, had incited the peasantry to revolt. Desaix, however, was not exactly sluggish either: he traversed the 120 miles from Farshut to Asyut in four days, much sooner than Murad had expected. The familiar sequence of events was repeated once again. Having intoxicated the fellahin with their propaganda, the Mamelukes placed them between the French and themselves; then, while the French were butchering a thousand or so fellahin, they galloped off into the desert.

As Desaix was well aware, this kind of warfare could go on forever. 'If you leave this country without troops for just an instant,' Desaix wrote to Bonaparte, 'it will revert immediately to its former masters.... I shall not bore you with a recital of our hardships. They would not interest you.... I have addressed to you, General, several urgent requests for munitions. I knew how desperately they were needed,—as a matter of fact, my situation is critical. People who ask for something always sound as if they felt sorry for themselves. Nevertheless, consider what we are up against. My soldiers have no cartridges except those they are carrying in their kits. The least you can do, General, is take notice of what is being asked of you. There are 1,800 Mamelukes in Upper Egypt. I shall go and fight them.' Belliard's Half-Brigade, at that time, had 8,000 rounds of ammunition left. 'For God's sake, send us some, and

---

[1] La Jonquière, III, 598.

281

fast,' Desaix pleaded with General Dugua, in Cairo.[1] Desaix's chief of staff, Donzelot, simultaneously sent an itemized list of his minimum requirements to General Berthier, who was in Syria with Bonaparte: 300,000 rounds of ammunition, 1,100 cannon balls, 150 howitzer shells, etc. He added: 'Unless you are kind enough to send us some drugs, our patients, whose number grows daily, will perish of want. Are we exiles in the Thebaid, to be so completely forgotten? ... We are asking only for the essentials, I note with regret that our demands produce no results. My only consoling thought is that perhaps they have not reached you.'[2]

Whether they reached Bonaparte's headquarters or not made little difference. While Desaix and Donzelot were writing to him and his chief of staff, Bonaparte was at Mount Carmel in the Holy Land, having just perpetrated the worst butchery in the entire campaign and racing on to besiege Acre with a plague-stricken army and virtually no artillery.

Although the condition of his forces afforded little cheer to General Desaix, he found some comfort in the fact that—according to all the reports received by Moallem Jacob—the Mamelukes' plight was equally harrowing. Murad's men were deserting in droves and came over to Desaix—lured, no doubt, by the Copt's clever propaganda. The beys were quarrelling among themselves. The chief reason why, in every battle, the usually brave Mamelukes had been so ready to take off for the desert was that each bey hoped to husband his own forces, while his rivals' men were being decimated by the French: this kind of politics among allies in the midst of battle, though usually well concealed under various excuses, is a universal standard of behaviour in warfare. By mid-March 1799, the Mameluke forces had split up, each detachment seeking to feed itself as best it could. Murad, with Osman Bey Bardisi, Osman Bey Tamborji, and that warrior with the unforgettable name, Mohammed Bey Manfuk, had withdrawn to the Kharga Oasis. Hassan Bey, with several other beys and their forces, had gone up the Nile to Qena, as had Mohammed Bey el-Elfi with his detachment. Various other beys and kyacheffs were roaming the countryside here and there. Soliman Bey had gone south beyond Aswan. The remnants of the Meccans were somewhere between the Nile and Kosseir, waiting for reinforcements. Superficially speaking, Desaix was in control of Upper Egypt. Yet, as he wrote to Bonaparte, the minute he turned his back, the scat-

---

[1] Ibid., III, 608.

[2] Ibid., III, 610.

tered forces of the enemy would join once more and occupy the land. There was only one thing Desaix could do—continue the chase up and down the Nile and keep on cutting off the Hydra's heads.

On several occasions Desaix divided his forces to accomplish specific punitive missions. Thus, on April 5, he sent Davout with part of the cavalry down the Nile to give the chase to some Meccan troops. At Girga, Davout learned that a revolt had broken out farther north, toward Beni Suef, and that Murad was leaving his oasis to join the rebels. On went Davout, and on May 1 he put 2,000 embattled fellahin to the sword at Beni Adi. French losses: eight men, This, no doubt, was a glorious action; but Captain Desvernois, who was with Davout, did even better. Virtually single-handed, he attacked the caravan from Darfur, which happened to be passing by—the same caravan which, at Girga, had been received so hospitably by General Desaix—and captured 897 camels. When he turned up with his booty, Davout was beside himself with joy. 'Captain,' he said, 'your fortune is made. This action of yours has ruined the projects of our enemies... [1] You will have twelve shares of the booty, your lieutenant six, and each non-commissioned officer and hussar one.'[2] In his report to General Dugua, Davout was more specific as to the value of the shares: 'Several soldiers,' he wrote, 'got fifteen or even twenty thousand gold francs' worth.'[3]

VI

Meanwhile, General Belliard's less fortunate men were marching up and down the Nile between Qena and Aswan, still battling

---

[1] There is no evidence whatever that Murad was planning to attack the caravan. It is unlikely that he would have attacked it even if he could, since he had no desire to discourage trade between the Sudan and Egypt. But some excuse was needed for Davout's and Desvernois's highway robbery. Bonaparte later apologized to the Sultan of Darfur.

[2] Desvernois, p. 186.

[3] La Jonquière, III, 644

with peasants, Meccans, and Mamelukes.[1] The only people who welcomed this tiresome and homicidal shuttling were Denon and a number of civilian engineers, who had been despatched from Cairo by Dugua to join Desaix's forces. The instructions sent by General Caffarelli to the leader of this band, Chief Engineer Girard, told him to 'investigate by what means the Nile can be used to increase the fertility of Egypt, and to collect the data necessary to establish a general chart of the hydro-graphic system of this country.'[2] The project was eminently praiseworthy; it continues to be carried out in our own days, though by different hands. But Girard's crew—Citizens Dubois-Aymé, Duchanoy, Descotils, de Rozière, Dupuis, Jollois, Villiers du Terrage (all engineers), and Casteix (sculptor and engraver)—soon got out of hand. Hydrography was forgotten; archaeology became their passion. No sooner had they viewed the first temples and tombs on their way than they joined with Denon in drawing everything—architectural details, columns, statues, fragments, paintings, and enough hieroglyphic inscriptions—of which they could not understand a word—to fill several volumes, Since Belliard's marches took them repeatedly through Luxor and Karnak, they had plenty to do. Their pleas for pencils surpassed Belliard's for bullets in passionate urgency. To copy some more hieroglyphics, they would cross the Nile, unescorted, and risk their lives. They melted down Belliard's precious bullets and moulded them to make more pencils. All this 'hieroglyph-making' infuriated Citizen Girard, the only one among them who remembered the purpose of their journey. The young enthusiasts developed for Girard a deep and healthy loathing. 'I denounce him to you as a non-lover of antiquities,' Villiers wrote to a friend. 'He has been four hours at Tentyra and spent three of them asleep.'[3] They appealed to General Belliard. Had they not done whatever Girard had told them to do in connection with their hydrographic mission? They had. Then why was that peasant persecuting them? Belliard, whom Denon had converted to hieroglyph-making long before, gave them full licence to keep on

---

[1] In the course of these operations, Captain Renaud, whom Belliard had sent with 200 men to reoccupy Aswan, ran into Mameluke forces more than three times superior to his, and beat them by sheer pluck. Hassan Bey and Osman Bey were fatally wounded in this fight, which Napoleon called 'the most beautiful combat of the entire Egyptian campaign' (Campagnes d'Egypte et de Syrie, in Correspondence de Napoleon I, XXIX, 536).

[2] Charles-Roux, Bonaparte, p. 341

[3] Charles-Roux, Bonaparte, p. 340

copying hieroglyphs. They were even joined, soon afterwards, by additional hieroglyph-makers despatched from Cairo. The result of their efforts, published years later in the *Description de L'Egypte*, was a thorough survey of agriculture and trade in Upper Egypt, a number of more specialized memoranda, and a wealth of data on Egyptology, a science created with a pencil in one hand and a musket in the other.

***

With so much to look at, everybody had ophthalmia, including General Belliard, who had had it once before. The *khamsin*, the torrid dust storm which lasts several months, was not improving their condition. Nevertheless Desaix, then at Girga, kept pressing Belliard to march on Kosseir, across 150 miles of mountains and desert. To capture Kosseir was an absolute necessity if the flow of Meccan volunteers was to be stopped and normal trade with Arabia resumed. This necessity became even more evident when a British man-of-war entered the Red Sea, bombarded Suez, and began to cruise between Jidda and Kosseir. If the British gained control over the Red Sea as well as the Mediterranean, the situation of the French would grow desperate.

General Belliard appreciated the importance of Kosseir and was eager to march on that port; all the same, it seemed to him that to do so he needed more than 8,000 cartridges, and that it would be a trifle rough on him to lead a regiment across the desert while he could barely see through his pus-filled eyes. He began to feel about General Desaix much as Desaix felt about Bonaparte. 'General Desaix,' he wrote in his diary on May 11, 'believes his orders can be carried out just as fast as he thinks them up.'[1] He also wrote to Desaix. If there was anybody, he told his superior, who had insisted on the necessity of taking Kosseir, it was he, Belliard; but he had to be given the means to do so. 'I repeat to you, General, that even if nature has not endowed me with your talents and knowledge, at least she has given me a sense of honour; and even if I am not carried away by as much craving for glory as some people are—' etc.[2]

Clearly, tempers were beginning to flare among the French as well as among their adversaries. Desaix replied with some soothing remarks which did not soothe Belliard; he also replied by sending Belliard all the supplies he needed. They arrived on May 25.

---

[1] La Jonquière, III, 664.
[2] Ibid., III, 665.

On May 26, ophthalmia notwithstanding, Belliard left Qena to march on Kosseir. He took with him 350 infantry mounted on camels, 400 camels carrying the supplies, one gun, and an escort of sixty Arabs, of a friendly tribe, also mounted on camels. They crossed 150 miles of mountainous deserts in three days. On May 28, they rode for fourteen hours. The next day they occupied Kosseir, a wretched village despite its strategic importance, without a fight. From Kosseir, Belliard wrote to the Sherif of Mecca a letter which makes one rub one's eyes in bemusement. For months the Sherif's subjects had been harassing Belliard; for months General Bonaparte had been fighting the Ottoman Sultan's army in Syria. Belliard's letter to the Sherif begins thus: 'You know, Sherif, that the French Republic is the close ally of the Ottoman Empire, and that her invincible armies are protecting all Moslems wherever they are.'[1]

Leaving about two thirds of his men behind to garrison Kosseir and to fortify its harbour, Belliard left on June 1 and, three days later, was back at Qena. Denon, who was with Belliard's party, was looking forward to a refreshing swim in the Nile. The heat in the desert had been unbearable, and the sand storm infernal. He discovered, to his dismay, that during the few days of his absence, the Nile had changed personality. 'Toward the end of the *khamsin* period,' he observed, 'the flow of the Nile slows down. The river loses its usual salubrity and transparency; its waters turn green.'[2]

Khamsin, heat, and sluggish Nile notwithstanding, Denon bravely continued to draw ruins while Belliard continued to patrol the Nile up and down. Back to Tentyra, to Karnak, to Isna, to Idfu; back down again to Qena. His eyelids were glued together and his eyeballs burning; his nose bled chronically, his skin broke out in a painful rash, every pore turning into a pimple; soldiers half his age fainted from the heat by the dozens; yet no matter how often he passed through the same territory, there was always something new to sketch, to copy. He discovered the Valley of the Kings; he discovered hieroglyphic characters he had not seen before. 'I increased my hieroglyphic alphabet by more than thirty symbols,'[3] he recalls à propos of his third visit to Idfu. The only thing that could exceed his enthusiasm was the wealth, the beauty, the mystery, the overpowering harmony and elegance of that massive

---

[1] Ibid., III, 675.

[2] Denon, I, 301.

[3] Ibid., I, 310.

world of stone forty centuries old which Europe was discovering through his poor ruined eyes.

***

With the occupation of Kosseir, the flow of Murad's Meccan auxiliaries had been stopped. Upper Egypt was relatively and temporarily pacified. Without their allies, the Mamelukes kept at the periphery in the Sudan, in the desert, in the oases—impotent though undefeated. At Asyut, General Desaix at long last had a chance to consolidate his conquest and to govern instead of chasing and destroying. 'From that moment on,' says Nicholas the Turk, 'General Desaix devoted himself to the pacification and organization of Upper Egypt, with an intelligence, an administrative knowledge, a tactfulness, a courage, a zeal, and a magnanimity that were admirable; so that Upper Egypt was better governed than was the Delta.' [1]

On July 5, Denon reluctantly left Qena to return to Cairo. The Nile had risen. From his barge, he saw huge crocodiles as far north as Girga. He observed the birds on the water, more numerous and varied than he had ever seen them. He sailed once more past the Pyramids of Saqqara and those of Giza. Then, after nine months' absence, he was back at the Institute of Egypt. His appearance, his report, read to his colleagues at a memorable session, electrified his audience. If any conquest had been made, the conquest was his, and it was never lost.

The other conquests, the military ones, were more precarious. Bonaparte, back from a disastrous campaign in Syria, which his propaganda sought to turn into a victory, was about to face a Turkish task force landed at Abukir. Murad Bey, forewarned of the Turkish expedition, had re-emerged from the desert and was hiding near the Great Pyramids, waiting to join in the kill. On the night of July 13, from the summit of Cheops' Pyramid, Murad had a lively conversation, by signals, with his wife Nafissa, on the roof of her house.

---

[1] Nicolas Turc, p. 48.

Chapter Nine
The Butchers in the Holy Land

THE region of Syria, as understood in 1799, consisted of the present sovereign states of Syria, Lebanon, Israel, and Jordan. . It was divided into five provinces or pashaliks—those of Aleppo, Damascus, Tripoli, Acre, and Jerusalem. The last of these was governed under a special regime. The so-called Syrian campaign of Bonaparte was fought, not in Syria proper, but in Palestine—that is, in modern Israel and the Lake Tiberias district of Jordan.

This region is equally holy to Moslems and to Christians; it is the Promised Land of the Jews. Napoleon estimates that, in 1799, all Syria had a population of about 2 millions. Of these, about 120,000 belonged to the sect of the Druses, whose emir governed their territory autonomously, and about 320,000 were Christians. The majority of the Christians lived in the area in which the campaign took place.

In Napoleon's estimate, one fourth of Syria's revenues went to the Ottoman Treasury and to the funds of the yearly caravan to Mecca. 'The rest,' he says, 'goes to the pashas. The cities are crumbling into ruins, the ports are silting up, the roads are disappearing, the swamps are rendering the plains unwholesome.... Nevertheless, the country retains its character: "Egypt is a farm", says an Arabic author, "but Syria is a garden."'[1]

---

[1] Correspondance, XXX, 6.

If Napoleon's soldiers could return to Palestine today, they would notice considerable changes; but in the rest of Syria, very little. And everywhere they would recognize the same serene, pastoral scene, the same shepherds and flocks, the same olive groves and orchards, the most beautiful, peaceful, eternal landscape in the world. In this landscape, the Philistines offered human sacrifices to Moloch, the Jews massacred the Philistines, Herod massacred the Innocents, the Romans massacred the Jews, the Crusaders massacred the Saracens and vice versa, the Turks massacred everybody indiscriminately, and Napoleon massacred the Turks. The massacres have not stopped since then, and worse ones may come yet; nevertheless, General Bonaparte and Ahmed Pasha Djezzar may compete for a record in needless killing, at least since the days of Herod.

***

Bonaparte undertook the Syrian campaign with about 13,000 men. [1] This figure does not include a variety of Egyptian and Arab personnel attached to the army—servants, camel drivers, interpreters, labourers, etc. as well as the French civilian commissioners, medical officers, finance officers, and the like. A number of officers took their permanent or temporary wives along as well; among them was the plucky Italian wife of General Verdier, who commanded a brigade under Kléber. 'The soldiers,' says El-Djabarti, 'took quantities of luggage with them, including even beds, mattresses, carpets, and large tents for their wives and for the White, Black, and Abyssinian slaves they had taken from the Mamelukes' houses. All these women had adopted the French costume.' [2]

In addition to this picturesque group, there was another, travelling under a special military escort and headed by Mustafa, a Turkish official who had been the lieutenant of the Pasha of Cairo at the time of Bonaparte's arrival. Bonaparte had appointed him Emir el-Hadj, 'prince of the pilgrimage'—that is, leader of the annual caravan of pilgrims to Mecca. (The appointment was little more than a gesture, since no caravan left Cairo that year.) Besides

---

[1] The breakdown was as follows: four infantry divisions, totalling 9,932 men; Cavalry, 800 men; Engineers, 370 men; Artillery, 1,385 men; Guides, both mounted and on foot, 400 men; Dromedary troops, 88 men. Total: 12,975. The infantry divisions (commanded by Kléber, Bon, Lannes, and Reynier) were not at full strength, since units had been detached from each to remain in garrison in Egypt.

[2] El-Djabarti, VI, 94

Mustafa, the group included the kadi, or chief magistrate, of Cairo (also a Turk) and a number of sheiks. Bonaparte's aim in taking these men with him was threefold: their presence was good propaganda; they might be useful in negotiations with Djezzar and the Porte; and they were hostages. As will be seen, they fulfilled none of these expectations.

Lastly, a large contingent of the Scientific Commission accompanied Bonaparte to Syria; among them the inevitable Monge and Berthollet, the naturalist Savigny, the mathematician Costaz, the physicist Malus, and the Orientalist and chief interpreter Venture. The last of these, and several other members of the Institute of Cairo, did not return alive. Exactly what was Bonaparte's purpose in taking them along on a campaign which, in his opinion, would take no more than two months remains a mystery.

***

Two weeks before he left Cairo, Bonaparte wrote to the Imam of Muscat, begging him to forward a letter to Tippoo Sahib. His message to the Sultan of Mysore was more rhetorical than candid: 'You have already been informed of my arrival on the coast of the Red Sea, with an innumerable and invincible army and filled with the desire to free you from the iron yoke of England. I should like you to despatch, to Suez or to Cairo, some clever man who has your trust, so that I may confer with him.'[1] Whether or not the letter reached the Tiger, as Tippoo liked to call himself, matters little: on May 4, British forces under General Stuart took Seringapatamby storm; they found Tippoo's body under a heap of corpses. The Englishman had eaten the tiger.[2]

The circumstance that Bonaparte wrote to Tippoo at this point, combined with Talleyrand's generous suggestion that he was free to march on India, appears to give some substance to Napoleon's daydreams at St. Helena about the aims and prospects of his Syrian venture. Once he had taken Acre, he wrote, 'Napoleon hoped that the Mamelukes and the Arabs of Egypt ... would join his forces; that by June he would be master of Aleppo and Damascus, with his outposts in the Taurus Mountains and having under his immediate command 26,000 French troops, 6,000 Mamelukes and Arabic horsemen from Egypt, 18,000 Druses, Maronites, and

---

[1] Correspondance, V, 278.

[2] Mysore was restored to its Hindu dynasty, and the rest of Tippoo's lands was partitioned among Hyderabad, the Mahrattas, and the East India Company.

other Syrian troops; and that Desaix would be in Egypt, ready to
assist him with 20,000 men, 10,000 of them French men and
10,000 Negroes with French cadres. In these circumstances, he
would have been in a position to force the Porte to make peace and
to secure its consent to his march on India. If Fortune favoured his
projects, he could reach the Indus by March 1800 with 40,000
men, despite the loss of his fleet.'[1]

Most serious historians have dismissed this staggering version
as the phantasy of an idle conqueror or as a deliberate addition to
the Napoleonic legend. But, according to various witnesses, Napoleon indulged in similar retrospective reveries as early as 1805,
and on December 1, 1805—the night before Austerlitz—he said to
his staff officers, according to the Comte de Ségur: 'If I had been
able to take Acre, I would have put on a turban, I would have made
my soldiers wear big Turkish trousers, and I would have exposed
them to battle only in case of extreme necessity. I would have
made them into a sacred battalion—my immortals. I would have
finished the war against the Turks with Arabic, Greek, and Armenian troops. Instead of a battle in Moravia, I would have won a
battle at Issus, I would have made myself emperor of the East, and
I would have returned to Paris by way of Constantinople.'[2]

Did he say this, only six years after his failure at Acre and on
the eve of his greatest triumph, merely to impress his audience
with the vastness of his designs, or had he seriously thought of
carrying out this insane project? According to Bourrienne, Bonaparte confided similar ideas to him before his departure for Syria.
'But I must add,' continues Bourrienne, 'that he fully appreciated
the disproportion between these projects and the means at our
disposal.'[3] Assuredly, Napoleon never ruled out any possibility: he
could no more resist an opportunity than Oscar Wilde a temptation. His primary object in invading Syria, he declares in his history of the campaign, was to beat Djezzar, to seize Gaza, Jaffa, and
Acre, to stir up a rebellion among the Christians and the Druses,
'and then to let circumstances determine the rest.'[4] Assuredly this
was true. On the day before his departure from Cairo, he wrote to
the Directory on the aims of his expedition. They were three fold:
to consolidate the conquest of Egypt by defeating the enemies at

---

[1] Ibid., XXX, 14.

[2] Segur, I, 251.

[3] Bourrienne, Vol. II, Ch. XII.

[4] Correspondance, XXX, 14.

its borders and by thus preventing a combined Anglo-Turkish landing; to oblige the Porte to 'explain itself and, perhaps, induce it to open negotiations; and to deprive the English cruising squadron of its supply bases in Syria. These were limited and rational aims. 'We have many enemies to overcome,' he added soberly: 'the desert, the local population, the Arabs, the Mamelukes, the Russians, the Turks, the English.'[1] He chose not to add the plague to that impressive list.

Whatever private phantasies he may have engaged in, Bonaparte never lost sight of reality, except if there was no other choice, reality being unacceptable. In February 1799, he had not reached that point yet. Aside from his letter to Tippoo, which was a mere trial balloon, there is not one shred of evidence either in Bonaparte's correspondence or in his actions that he hoped to accomplish more in Syria than precisely the purposes stated in his letter to the Directory. Of course, if the opportunity had presented itself to do more, he would have seized it; as it was, he failed even in his limited objectives.

***

On December 23, 1798, Bonaparte had ordered General Lagrange, of Reynier's division, to reconnoitre the Mediterranean coast of the Sinai Peninsula and to establish a strong point at Katia, near the Syrian border. Despite adverse conditions—constant Arab raids and incessant rain—Lagrange reported on January 17 that the fortifications of Katia were completed. Bonaparte designated Katia as the rendezvous and staging point for the units taking part in the expedition. By this time, reports were coming in of growing concentrations of Mamelukes and Turkish troops at the coastal town of El Arish, inside Egyptian territory: Djezzar was taking the offensive.

The bulk of General Reynier's division reached Katia during the first days of February and left on February 6, having been ordered by Bonaparte to take El Arish. On the same day Kléber arrived with his division, of which he had resumed active command. He left Katia on February 11 and arrived before El Arish the same evening. Bonaparte, with his headquarters and with Bon's division, reached El Arish on February 17; he was annoyed to find that the place had not yet been captured. General Lannes, who had taken over Vial's division, arrived last, on February 18, after a march across the Sinai Desert reminiscent of some earlier

---

[1] Ibid., V, 311.

marches. 'Several soldiers blew their brains out,' Paymaster Pey-russe noted in his diary.[1]

The expedition was staged somewhat more carefully than the march from Alexandria to Cairo, but this is not saying much. There were numerous camels to transport supplies; provisions also had been made for ambulance and water services, and for the transportation of the field artillery. The siege artillery, however, was found too cumbersome to be moved by land across swamps and deserts. It was placed aboard a flotilla, which was to take it from Damietta to Acre, despite Conté's offer to build special, broad-wheeled carriages that might make overland transportation less difficult. Perhaps, had he listened to Conté, Bonaparte might have taken Acre.

Despite some foresight, the army was ill-equipped. To pay the soldiers their arrears, Bonaparte had to mortgage the harvests of Upper Egypt even before they were in. 'It seemed to me,' General Damas wrote in his diary, 'that this precipitately organized expedition was bound to run into a great deal of trouble. First of all the food supplies were not complete.... The cold and rainy weather ... promised much hardship during our march through the desert and should have made us fear that our soldiers would contract various diseases, since they were poorly dressed, considering the season and the country: they only had linen tunics, trousers, and cloaks.... [Apparently Bonaparte, having spent several months in Cairo, could not imagine how chill and wet the Mediterranean coast of Egypt and of Syria can be in winter.] All these reflections either did not occur to anybody or else carried no weight whatever with the commander-in-chief, although an army commander's foremost care should be the conservation of his manpower, especially in a country where there is so much disease. He should have taken care not to use up men like cartridges, because they could not be replaced as easily as in Europe.'[2]

To all this Bonaparte might well have replied that, since it was a necessity to undertake the expedition, there was no choice but to use whatever he had available. The rest depended on the 'favour of Fortune' and on stamina. 'The French are nervous machines,' Madame de Staël quotes him as having said. 'By this,' she adds, 'he

---

[1] La Jonquière, IV, 180.

[2] Ibid., IV, 118.

meant to characterize the mixture of obedience and mobility that is in their nature.'[1]

II

When General Reynier arrived before El Arish, after a rough march, on February 8, he was utterly surprised to find not only a large enemy encampment but also a well-defended fortress. The encampment included about 600 Mameluke, Arab, and Turkish horsemen and about 1,200 Albanian infantry, sent by Djezzar. The fortress was a square stone structure, flanked by hexagonal towers, with walls about thirty feet high; its garrison consisted of 1,200-1,500 men, mostly tough Albanian and Moroccan foot soldiers, with a sprinkling of Mamelukes.

Reynier's first action was to take the village of El Arish, defended by its inhabitants, who were summarily put to the sword, or rather to the bayonet. Three days later, Kléber joined forces with Reynier. By this time, Reynier's men were already beginning to starve—for El Arish, a fishing hamlet between the sea and the desert, had no resources to offer. It was a paradoxical situation: the besieged, well supplied with food but fasting from sunrise to sunset (because it was the month of Ramadan), were starving out the besiegers. An additional paradox was that the Turks' supplies came largely from the French army depot at Damietta, where enterprising employees of the commissary had sold them for their own profit to Greek merchants, who promptly transported the goods to sell them to the Mamelukes at even higher profits—a common occurrence in all wars, if the truth were said.

Reynier and Kléber invested the fortress, but there was little hope of its surrendering before additional troops and artillery arrived. Meanwhile, during the night of February 14-15, Reynier led four battalions in a surprise attack on the 1,800 men of the Turkish camp. Since Moslems, as a rule, did not fight between sunset and dawn, the Turks had taken no precautions. Shortly after midnight, the French entered the camp unnoticed and silently bayoneted the sleeping men until they reached the centre of the camp, when a dog barked. Alerted, the sleepers panicked and tried to escape, but the exits were barred. 'I went through the whole camp, and we killed everybody we found,' Reynier reported.[2] Among the 400-500 men killed were one bey and several kyacheffs; 900 were

---

[1] Stael, p. 436.

[2] La Jonquière, IV, 166,

taken prisoner; the French lost three men. Napoleon qualified this attack as 'one of the most beautiful military operations conceivable.'[1] It all depends on one's definition of beauty.

Although Reynier had captured the stores in the camp, this did little to relieve the Frenchmen's famine. 'We were eating camels, horses, and donkeys,'[2] says Malus, who was attached to Kléber's

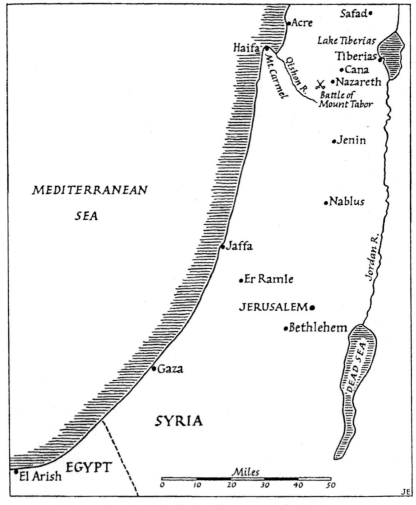

Bonaparte's Syrian Campaign of 1799

division, and other witnesses bear him out. One morning, a major

---

[1] Correspondance, XXX, 17.

[2] Malus, p. 119.

was pained to find that his stallion had disappeared from his hitching post. He rebuked his men for eating him; they answered that they had only done him a favour, the horse being vicious, but that they would defend his mare to the death.

On February 18, the commandant of the fortress began to parley. He sent word that, although he had an ample supply of ammunition and food, he was ready to surrender the fortress on certain conditions, since the aid promised him had not arrived. The conditions were that he and the garrison be permitted to leave the fortress with arms and baggage and to go wherever they chose. This Bonaparte refused, but he made a counter-proposal: if the garrison surrendered, he would return their weapons with honours of war and transport them to Egypt, whence they could take ship to any country they pleased. This the Turkish commandant refused, knowing full well that Egypt was blockaded. Having spent the day in negotiations, Bonaparte ordered a massive artillery barrage for the next morning. He had expected El Arish to fall without any difficulty, the siege had lasted ten days, and his army would starve unless it marched on to more fertile grounds.

The French artillery formed a circle around the fortress at about 300 yards' distance; its barrage lasted the entire day with almost no let-up. Many of the French shells and cannon balls, missing their target, fell into their own ranks at the opposite side, killing and wounding several men; some of the French shells, says Malus, fell into the field hospital. Toward evening a small breach was made (in the absence of any siege artillery, the field guns were almost ineffectual), and through the night the sappers worked their way to one of the towers. The French losses that day were twenty-one artillery men, seventeen sappers, and 350 infantry. 'The enemy,' noted Detroye, 'displayed extraordinary bravery; they repaired the damage and kept firing from the tower, paying no attention to our cannon balls and shells.'[1] Bonaparte had run into an enemy quite different from the sort he had dealt with in Egypt.

The cannonade was resumed the next morning, with no more effect than the day before.

Much as he loved battles, Bonaparte hated sieges. They tried his patience too much. About noon, he sent an emissary to the fort under the flag of truce and summoned the commandant to surrender, since a breach had been made. (Under the rules of warfare then prevailing, a garrison which refused to surrender once a

---

[1] La Jonquière, IV, 195.

breach had been made was liable to be put to the sword by the be-
sieger.) Bonaparte's conditions sound generous: the fortress to be
handed to the French by 4 p.m., the garrison to retain their arms
and baggage but not their horses; the garrison to march through
the desert to Baghdad and to take an oath not to serve in Djezzar's
forces for a year. Actually, it is difficult to see how the garrison
could have reached Baghdad on foot without dying on the way;
besides, Bonaparte had no intention of honouring the terms he
proposed.

The chief officers of El Arish accepted the conditions and
swore, 'by our saints Moses and Abraham, by the Prophet ... and
by the Koran,' to honour them punctiliously. There were 800-900
men of the garrison left alive; among them Captain Doguereau
noted 'two young Circassian Mamelukes, extremely handsome,
carrying arms and appearing not in the least intimidated, although
barely ten or twelve years old.'[1]

Contrary to the terms of the capitulation, Bonaparte had the
Mamelukes disarmed and sent back to Egypt, where they were set
free. As for the rest of the Turkish troops, mostly Moroccans, Albanians, and Greeks, they were surrounded, as soon as they
marched off, by General Bon's division, and a large number of
them were persuaded by more or less gentle means to join the
French forces rather than perish in the desert. 'We gave the Turks
the first example of perfidiousness,' says Malus. 'They all deserted
later on as soon as they saw a chance.'[2]

Inside the fortress, the French found ample supplies to relieve
their famine. They also found, says Malus, who had his reasons for
remembering this detail, 'an entire room filled with dying victims
of the plague.'[3]

The captured Turkish flags were sent to Cairo by Bonaparte's
orders, to be displayed as trophies at the Mosque El Azhar. This
actually was done, and the flags flew from the crescents of the
minarets of El Azhar throughout the three days of Bairam—the
feast marking the end of Ramadan. They were greeted by the
French guns at the Citadel. On the first day of Bairam, says El-
Djabarti, the French general officers in Cairo made state visits to

---

[1] Ibid., IV, 203.

[2] Malus, p. 122.

[3] Ibid., p. 124.

the notables of the city. 'They were received with a show of affability,' remarks the chronicler.[1]

No doubt the notables had learned by that time that the two chief Moslem dignitaries whom Bonaparte had taken with him to Syria— the Emir el-Hadj and the kadi—had managed to slip away from their escort even before reaching the Syrian border.

***

Leaving a small garrison behind in El Arish, the French army resumed their march the day after its capture. Kléber's division formed the vanguard; he got lost in the desert but eventually reappeared before the army reached Gaza, where Samson had been eyeless. Gaza was taken on February 24, without resistance, and was looted thoroughly. Having replenished their food and ammunition supplies with the captured stores, the French left Gaza four days later, an army of locusts travelling on their stomachs. The weather had been, and continued to be, indescribably bad, 'We are in mud and water up to our knees,' Bonaparte wrote to General Dugua. 'The weather and the cold are about the same as in Paris at this time of the year. You are lucky to be enjoying the sunshine of Cairo.'[2] On the way from Gaza to Er Ramie even the camels, hardy beasts though they are, were dying of exposure.

At Er Ramie, a town between Jaffa and Bethlehem, where they arrived on March 1, the French found that the Moslem population had fled the day before and that the Christians had stayed to welcome them. Such was the effect of Bonaparte's propaganda to the Moslem world. They also found more supplies, left behind by the Mamelukes of Ibrahim Bey. They visited two monasteries, one Armenian, the other Roman Catholic. All the Christian women of the town had taken refuge in them. (Apparently even Christian women trusted the French only so far and no farther.) 'These women,' observes the diarist Detroye, 'are very white-skinned but rather pallid; some of them are pretty; they take little care to veil their faces. All of them, and the children too, rejoiced at seeing us.'[3] In the Catholic monastery, Bonaparte established a military hospital. 'Though the largest and most commodious building in town,' says Dr. Desgenettes, 'it was still too small and lacked fresh air.... [It] was soon crowded with patients.'[4]

---

[1] El-Djabarti, VI, 100.

[2] Correspondance, V, 334.

[3] La Jonquière, IV, 237.

[4] Desgenettes, Histoire medicale, 1,45.

After two days among Christians, the French resumed their march. They arrived before Jaffa on the same day, about noon. Both the walled city and the citadel were defended by a strong Turkish force and by part of the population. 'Jaffa,' says Detroye, 'is situated by the Mediterranean shore, on top of a hill shaped like a sugar loaf. Midway up this cone, it is enclosed by a wall, flanked by towers, so that the city inside it rises like an amphitheatre above the walls.... The left and the centre [of this height] are ... covered with a large grove of orange, lemon, lime, and almond trees.'[1]

The next day, March 4, General Bonaparte began the preparations for the assault on this city, which is about fifty miles distant from. Bethlehem, where peace on earth to all men of good will had been announced by angels eighteen centuries earlier. At 2 p.m. on March 7, the onslaught began, the garrison having refused Bonaparte's terms of capitulation and detained his emissary. A breach was made by the sappers. Within a few hours, despite the defenders' determined resistance, the city was in French hands. On what happened then, eye witness accounts are only too abundant. Some are matter-of-fact, others indignant; but they all agree.

**

Major Detroye had never seen a city being taken by storm before. 'If there is any compensation for the horror of such a spectacle,' he declares, 'it is the bravery of our troops who made the assault and the sang-froid, prudence, and intrepidity of our commander-in-chief and of our staff officers, who at all times stayed within a few feet from the breach.'[2] Once in the city, these brave troops bayoneted some 2,000 soldiers of the garrison who were trying to surrender. Throughout that evening, the entire night, and the following morning, the French went berserk. Men, women, and children, Christians and Moslems, 'anybody with a human face fell victim to their fury,'[3] declares Malus, whose pages describing the sickening scene still vibrate with his shock and shame.

The behaviour of victorious troops in towns taken by storm is a phenomenon to be investigated by psychiatric medicine rather than by historians. A description of the scene is unnecessary—everybody has read several such accounts, and they are all alike. One

[1] La Jonquière, IV, 218.
[2] Ibid., IV, 263-64.
[3] Mains, p. 135.

cannot help asking, what transforms a group of fundamentally good-natured people—kind husbands, dutiful sons, sentimental lovers, and fathers of families—into ferocious, screaming beasts, sinking their bayonets into old men, young girls, and babies, raping daughters still locked in the arms of their dead mothers, redoubling their fury at the sound of cries for mercy, and keeping up their madness for twenty hours? To explain this frenzy merely by their earlier sufferings and privations, or by the tension of the assault itself, is perhaps not sufficient. The question, let it be repeated, has not been investigated scientifically. In modern warfare, it retains perhaps only academic interest, since it is possible now to kill a million humans without any excitement whatever by merely pushing a button; still, one must admit that at least in civil strife the phenomenon not only persists but in some parts of the world is likely to erupt on an unprecedented scale.

All this and worse happened in Jaffa on March 7 and 8. In his history of the campaign, Napoleon has this, and no more, to say on the subject: 'The soldiers' fury was at its height: everybody was put to the sword; being sacked, the town experienced all the horrors of a city taken by storm.'[1] Not all the eyewitnesses retained so dispassionate and detached a memory of this event.

Between 2,500 and 3,000 Turkish troops had taken refuge in the citadel. In the morning of September 8, Bonaparte sent two of his aides-de-camp—Beauharnais and Croisier, both very young men—into the city to see what could be done to restore order. Made conspicuous by their official sashes, they were hailed by the Turkish soldiers from the windows of the citadel. They were ready to surrender, the Turks shouted, if they were promised not to be treated like the rest of the people of Jaffa. The two young men, on their own authority, gave verbal assurances that the garrison's lives would be spared. On the strength of this promise the soldiers came out and surrendered their weapons. When Bonaparte saw his aides return with several thousand prisoners, he turned pale. 'What do they want me to do with them?' he muttered. 'What the devil have they done?'[2]

Trying to justify the decision he made regarding these prisoners, Napoleon and all memoirists and historians —even those hostile to him—make the following points: to send the prisoners to Egypt would have required a large escort, which Bonaparte could not afford to detach from his array; to keep them with him either

---

[1] Correspondence, XXX, 27.
[2] Bourrienne, Vol. II, Ch. XV.

as prisoners or as auxiliary troops would have been risky and cumbersome; in any event, he claimed, there was not food enough to feed them without serious prejudice to his army; and to disarm them and let them go free would merely have resulted in their going to reinforce Djezzar at Acre. Consequently, it was necessary to kill them.

Apart from moral considerations, which tend to make one condemn *a priori* the cold-blooded massacre of several thousand prisoners who have surrendered in good faith upon promises made to them, when they might have sold their lives dearly, it is difficult to accept all the parts of this argument. It is even more difficult to understand why reputable historians have accepted a reasoning which confuses mere convenience with necessity. Granted that there were not enough men to escort the prisoners back to Egypt by land, nor enough ships to take them by sea; granted that an army of 13,000 cannot lug 3,000 prisoners along with them, and even less 3,000 dubious allies. But as for the food: the only food the French army had was what they had seized from their prisoners. Perhaps they could have spared enough of it to keep the prisoners whose food they were eating more or less alive. And how many men would Bonaparte have had to leave behind to guard 3,000 unarmed, half-starved prisoners? A hundred perhaps. He could spare that many; in fact, he left more than a hundred men at Jaffa. But supposing that even this was unfeasible, that he could not spare a few guards for a prison camp nor feed his prisoners a bowl of rice per day without provoking discontent among his own men in that case, why not simply disarm and dismiss them? If they had gone to join the garrison of Acre, they would have proved more embarrassing than helpful to Djezzar, who would have had to feed and arm them without having much use for them.

Bonaparte's final argument was that about 900 men of the garrison of El Arish, whom he had allowed to depart with their arms on condition that they must not serve Djezzar for a year, had been found among the garrison at Jaffa: since they had broken their word, he need not spare them. This contention is untenable. Of the 900 men who marched out of El Arish, Bonaparte had sent a number to Egypt and incorporated an even larger number in his own forces, thus breaking his word before they had a chance to break theirs. There could not have been more than 300 or 400 of these men at Jaffa, if there were any. In the second place, what effort was made to identify them, whatever their number? The answer is, none. And lastly, even supposing that one-third of the prisoners had actually belonged to the garrison of El Arish and broken their parole, why should the other two-thirds be punished also?

One does not like to admit that a man as great as Napoleon could order a wholesale massacre without necessity. It is more comforting to accept Bourrienne's story, that Bonaparte held a council of war which reached this heart-rending decision only after every possible alter native had been weighed. Unfortunately, no one besides Bourrienne mentions a council of war, or even an informal consultation. There is no evidence that one was held. All the evidence points to the conclusion that Bonaparte alone gave the order to execute the prisoners, that no one objected or dared to object, and that the execution was carried out with complete efficiency. If there was a reason for the execution, it was of a different order than the reasons enumerated: it was Bonaparte's deliberate policy to produce a strong impression on Djezzar. If Djezzar resisted him at Acre, his men would suffer the same fate as the garrison of Jaffa. His men only—not Djezzar himself. Indeed, Bonaparte excepted a number of prisoners from the slaughter, notably all natives of Egypt, who were sent back to their country, and 300 Turkish artillery men, trained by French officers, for whom he expected to find some use. But the most notable exception was the commandant of Jaffa, Abdullah Aga, who fell before Bonaparte's feet, pleading for mercy and obtaining it readily enough. The psychological effect of Abdullah's pardon and the garrison's massacre would not be lost on Djezzar and his garrison. It is submitted that 2,500 humans were killed, not out of necessity, but out of expediency and for a calculated effect.

If the eyewitnesses of this horror mentioned extenuating circumstances, they did so only in order to live down the shame of having participated in it, or at least stood by while it was committed.

Major Detroye kept an accounting of the executions:[1]

On March 7, during the attack, there died more than 2,000 Turks

On March 8, there were shot 800 Turks

On March 9, ditto 600 Turks

On March 10, ditto 1,041 Turks

Total: 4,441

[1] La Jonquière, IV, 270.

Here is what Citizen Peyrusse, assistant to Paymaster Estève, wrote on March 10—Passion Sunday—to his mother, no doubt a kindly lady of the upper middle class, in Carcassonne:

That, in a city taken by storm, the infuriated troops should loot, burn, and kill whatever comes their way, is something demanded by the laws of war, and humanity covers these horrors with a veil. But that, two or three days after the attack, when passions have calmed down, one should order, in cold-blooded savagery, the murder of 3,000 men who have surrendered to us in good faith! Posterity no doubt will pass judgment on this atrocity, and those who ordered it will find their place among the butchers of humanity.

About 3,000 men put down their arms and were instantly led to our camp. By order of the commander-in-chief, the Egyptians, Moroccans, and Turks were separated.

The next morning, all the Moroccans were taken to the sea-shore, and two battalions began to shoot them down. Their only hope of saving their lives was to throw themselves into the sea; they did not hesitate, and all tried to escape by swimming. They were shot at leisure, and in an instant, the sea was red with blood and covered with corpses. A few were lucky enough to reach some rocks. Soldiers were ordered to follow them in boats and to finish them off.... Once this execution was over, we fondly hoped that it would not be repeated and that the other prisoners would be spared.... Our hopes were soon disappointed, when, the next day, 1,200 Turkish artillerymen, who for two days had been kept without food in front of General Bonaparte's tent, were taken to be executed. The soldiers had been carefully instructed not to waste ammunition, and they were ferocious enough to stab them with their bayonets. Among the victims, we found many children who, in the act of death, had clung to their fathers. This example will teach our enemies that they cannot count on French good faith, and sooner or later, the blood of these 3,000 victims will be upon us.[1]

Citizen Peyrusse, who wrote this, was as good a Frenchman as Citizen Bonaparte, or as any member of the O.A.S. in 1962.

---

[1] La Jonquière, IV, 271-72.

Other eyewitness accounts, some by participants, are even more sickening. One detail will suffice: the Turks, on the beach, heaped up the corpses of their dead comrades in a futile attempt to make barricades against the bayoneters. 'The bayonet.' Bonaparte has said, 'has always been the weapon of the brave.'[1]

***

The grisly beach party was still in progress when, on March 9, Bonaparte issued a proclamation to the people of Palestine: 'Remain quietly at your homes.... I guarantee everybody's safety and protection.... Religion especially shall be protected and respected ... for it is from God that all good things come: it is He who gives victory.'[2]

The same day he wrote to Djezzar: 'Since God gives me victory, I wish to follow His example and be merciful and compassionate, not only towards the people, but also towards its rulers.'[3] It was an invitation to surrender.

Among the stores seized by the French at Jaffa were 400,000 rations of biscuit and 2,000 quintals of rice. A great deal more had been looted by the troops before the commissary could seize it. But the prisoners had to be shot because they could not be fed.

On March 8, the second day of the massacre, God, from Whom all good things come, sent down the plague upon the French army with a vengeance.

***

The plague at Damietta had been relatively mild. It was worse at Rosetta, Abukir, and Alexandria, but there also it struck only at isolated garrisons, not at a whole army in the field. The plague at Jaffa was a different matter. By March 9, Desgenettes recorded, thirty-one cases had entered the hospital established at the Greek Orthodox monastery; fourteen were already dead. The following day Detroye wrote in his diary: 'In General Bon's division a disease accompanied by buboes has broken out which leads to sudden death. The doctors assure us that it is not the plague.' On March 12: 'It is a violent fever, with buboes.... Many soldiers have succumbed to it and died very suddenly. This illness has been taken

---

[1] Correspondence, II, 195.

[2] Ibid., V, 352.

[3] Ibid., V, 355.

for the plague, and this opinion is so widespread that four men, who had its symptoms, have committed suicide.'[1]

The only disease that bubonic plague can easily be confused with in its early stage is acute alcoholism. The patient is dull, staggers, loses his co-ordination and becomes delirious in a convulsive manner reminiscent of delirium tremens. The delirium is caused by a fever which has been known to rise as high as 107 F. This is accompanied by generalized pain and, particularly, by a raging headache. The subsequent symptom, which may take one or several days to develop, is the appearance of the bubo, or of several buboes, already described in the words of Private Millet. When this symptom appears, the nature of the disease is unmistakable, and its issue is likely to be fatal. The convulsive agony of the victim, the French observed, often resembles the symptoms of rabies.

Desgenettes and his staff made every effort to prevent the spread of the disease—by changing the position of the various camps, by isolating all the ill, by separating from the start the plague victims from the other patients. Yet, while he knew very well what disease he was dealing with, Desgenettes wisely insisted on hiding its real name from the army; after a few days, of course, this effort became useless.

To counteract the terror spreading through the ranks, General Bonaparte on March 11 did a thing no less extraordinary than the massacre he had ordered only three days earlier. Gros' painting, 'Bonaparte Visiting the Plague Victims at Jaffa,' is justly famous. Unlike most celebrated historical paintings, it is based on well-established facts. Dr. Desgenettes, assuredly no friend of Bonaparte, may be trusted as a witness:

On March 11, 1799, General Bonaparte, followed by his general staff, felt it incumbent upon himself to visit the hospital.... The General walked through the hospital and its annex, spoke to almost all the soldiers who were conscious enough to hear him, and, for one hour and a half, with the greatest calm, busied himself with the details of the administration. While in a very small and crowded ward, he helped to lift, or rather to carry, the hideous corpse of a soldier whose torn uniform was soiled by the spontaneous bursting of an enormous abscessed bubo.[2]

A letter by the army commissioner Daure relates the same episode; so does an entry in Detroye's diary, with this comment

---

[1] La Jonquière, IV, 284.

[2] Desgenettes, Souvenirs, III, 221,

added: 'This action, which shows a deep political instinct, has produced an excellent effect. Already there is less fear.'[1]

What kind of man is it who, one day, calmly has 1,041 humans
put to the bayonet in order to produce one kind of effect, and who
the following day, with equal calm, performs an action from which
even the greatest saints might have recoiled, merely to produce
another kind of effect? The question leaves room for much argument. What cannot be argued is that Bonaparte was very lucky: he
did not catch the plague. Six months later, on November 10, 1799,
he was to tell the upper house of the French legislature, 'Remember that the god of war and the god of luck are marching by my
side.'[2] He had every reason to believe it; but, of course, he did not.
This remark, too, was calculated—or rather miscalculated—for effect.

Two days after his visit to the hospital, Bonaparte gave orders
that Christians of the Greek rite be forcibly recruited to serve as
hospital attendants for the wounded, and Christians of the Latin
and Armenian rites to serve in the hospital for 'fever cases'—that
is, the plague-stricken. In the same order, he set up a loca divan of
mixed Moslem and Christian membership and left Adjutant-
General Grézieu in charge of the 'provinces' of Jaffa and Er Ramie.
The following day, he and his army left to march on Acre.

Adjutant-General Grézieu was not grateful for the post entrusted to him. He was terrified of the plague. He was not seen at
any time during his administration (which was brief), except when
he left his tent to lock himself up in a house. He communicated
with the outside world only through a hole in the wall, through
which he also received his food. This he did for but one day: the
next day he broke out with the plague and died.

Grézieu had been left with a garrison of 150 men and 300
plague-stricken soldiers. Attached to his staff was Malus. A few
days after the army left, another member of the Scientific Commission joined him—it was Saint-Simon, a brother of the founder
of the Saint-Simonian sect. 'He was in perfect health,' recalls Malus. 'The next day he was dead.'[3]

Malus himself was put in charge of the administration of the
plague hospital. 'For ten days,' he says, 'I went there assiduously
and spent every morning in the loathsome stench of that cloaca,

[1] La Jonquière, IV, 285.

[2] Correspondence, VI, 4.

[3] Malus, p. 142.

every corner of which was crowded with patients. It was only on the eleventh day that I noticed the symptoms of the plague. This was about the time when Adjutant General Grézieu died. Half of the garrison already had been stricken by then. About thirty men died every day.... About one man among twelve stricken survived.... The plague was in every house of the town.... The monks of the Capuchin monastery quarantined themselves, to avoid contagion. Almost all of them died.' [1]

Malus was among the 8 per cent who survived. He was evacuated to Damietta late in April and recovered during the sea voyage. When Bonaparte returned to Jaffa in circumstances rather different from his first visit, there were still about 200 plague-cases in the hospital. It will be seen how he dealt with them.

Meanwhile, Bonaparte was laying siege to Acre. The plague was in his camp as well as in Djezzar's fortress.

III

In 1785 Louis-Edmond Le Picard de Phélipeaux, aged fifteen, entered the École Militaire in Paris, where he became the classmate of a Corsican student named Napoleone Buonaparte. It seems that they disliked each other by instinct. They shared a desk in class, and their shins were permanently blue and black from the kicks they administered to each other. Phélipeaux was always ahead in class of Bonaparte, always won first prizes when Bonaparte won third prizes, and in 1785 graduated with higher honours than his rival. They were both commissioned as lieutenants in the Artillery. With the outbreak of the Revolution, their careers diverged radically, but ten years later chance brought them face to face again.

The aristocratic Phélipeaux emigrated in 1791 and served in Condi's army against the French Republic until 1795, when he returned with the scheme of stirring up a royalist rebellion in the central provinces. Arrested, he escaped with the help of a female relative, briefly left France in 1797, but returned the same year— clandestinely, of course—to resume counter-revolutionary activities. In the early spring of 1798 he decided to liberate an English naval officer held in the Temple at Paris, where Louis XVI and Marie Antoinette had been imprisoned before their execution. The Englishman's name was William Sidney Smith; he is better known

---

[1] Ibid., pp. 140-43, passim.

as Sir Sidney Smith but should not be confused with his namesake, the writer.

Phélipeaux began by making love to the jailer's daughter—always a pleasant and efficient way of getting in touch with a prisoner. He also procured himself false papers, identifying him as a police commissioner. Then, one day, he presented himself at the Temple with four friends disguised as policemen, produced a forged order, had Smith released to him, and on May 8 arrived with Smith in London. Smith obtained for him a colonel's commission in the British army.

Sidney Smith had a no less interesting career behind him. Born in 1764, the second son of a captain in the Guards, he entered the navy at thirteen, was commissioned a lieutenant in 1780, saw action in Chesapeake Bay and at St. Kitts, and in 1785 went on a prolonged leave of absence. After two years in France—a country, which, though he was to fight against it as effectively as any man, he always seems to have favoured—he decided to have a look at Morocco, where he spent most of 1788. After reporting to the Admiralty on what he had seen, he proceeded to Stockholm, impressed King Gustavus III (who was easily impressed by dashing young men), was commissioned in the Swedish navy, fought against the Russian navy and its Admiral John Paul Jones, was knighted by Gustavus (a title which George III recognized—hence the 'Sir'), and after a brief stay in England went on to Constantinople, where his brother, Charles Spencer Smith, was First Secretary at the British embassy. He stayed there happily for three years, making connections that proved highly useful later. Recalled to England by the Admiralty in 1795, he found no transportation, bought a ship, took on a number of stranded British sailors for a crew, crossed the Mediterranean, and joined the British squadron at Toulon. When, thanks to Captain Bonaparte, the English had to evacuate Toulon, Smith volunteered to burn the English ships that had to be left behind. This he did, though not too effectively. At this point, the French authorities were beginning to take notice of him; since he held no active commission in the British navy, they regarded his feat as an act of piracy.

Duly commissioned after his return to England, Smith made himself even more noticeable by raiding French shipping all along the coast of France. In fact, there was nothing he could do without becoming noticeable: his temperament tended toward that peculiarly English type of flamboyance which is a mixture of cool cheek, courage, dash, and a love for the theatre. The French captured him off Le Havre in 1796 and, since he was still under the accusation of piracy for his Toulon exploit, imprisoned him securely in the Temple. There he languished for two years until liberated by Phélipeaux, whose flamboyance belonged to the aristocratic version of the Gallic type strongly underplayed intrepidity.

Lord Spencer gave Captain Smith the command of H.M.S. *Tigre*, with eighty guns, and instructions to sail to the Mediterranean. Smith took Phélipeaux with him. Since he had received special powers of a diplomatic nature to negotiate with the Porte, he regarded himself as independent of Nelson's command, promoted himself to Commodore, and flew a commodore's flag. This Nelson resented, though he himself was not always a model of subordination; eventually, Smith had to give in and recognize Nelson's authority. In early March 1799, he relieved Hood in the command of the squadron cruising off Alexandria, thus coming by the title commodore in the accepted way. He had barely arrived when he received word that Bonaparte had taken Jaffa. He immediately sent the *Theseus*, with Phélipeaux aboard, to Acre, in order to assist Djezzar Pasha's defence, and followed shortly afterwards, appearing at Acre with the *Tigre* in mid-March.

But for Phélipeaux's timely arrival, Djezzar Pasha might well have withdrawn from Acre, which seemed an indefensible place. Phélipeaux dissuaded him from this and within a few days transformed Acre into a formidable strong point. With Phélipeaux organizing the defence on land and Sidney Smith supporting it from the sea, Djezzar's fighting spirit returned almost instantly.

The career of Djezzar, who was twice the age of his French and English saviours, makes those of the other two look pallid. Somewhere between sixty and seventy years old, he was born in Bosnia, still a largely Moslem part of northern Yugoslavia and then a Turkish border province. Because of some troubles, possibly a murder, he left Bosnia while still a youth, enlisted in the Turkish navy, quarrelled with his fellow sailors, left the navy, starved for a while, then sold himself to a slave trader in the bazaars of Constantinople. He was taken to Cairo, where Ali Bey bought him. Transformed into a Mameluke, Ahmed—for this was his real name—served Ali in a very special capacity. Ali was on his way up to becoming the virtual ruler of Egypt. To reach that position, he had to dispose of a number of other beys, and Ahmed disposed of them for him in various ways; it was thus he earned the name Djezzar, the Butcher, which he wore proudly ever after.

After a few years in this employment, Djezzar quarrelled with Ali—his was a quarrelsome temperament, flamboyant in a peculiarly Bosnian way—and left Egypt precipitately for Constantinople. Going on from there to Syria, he won the protection of Yusuf, Emir of the Druses. He served as an officer under the Pasha of Damascus, was shortly appointed governor of Beirut, quarrelled with Emir Yusuf, whom he had robbed, and, after various complicated political and murderous manoevres, managed to get himself appointed Pasha of Acre. Baron de Tott, who visited Acre in 1777, describes Djezzar as a man so true to the classic type of the Oriental despot that one suspects him of exaggeration. 'He had immured alive a great number of Greet Christians,' declares the baron, 'when he rebuilt the walls of Beirut, to defend it from the invasion of the Russians. The heads of these miser able victims, which the Butcher had left out, in order to enjoy their tortures, are still to be seen.'[1] This is not to say that the story is true, but merely to indicate what sort of stories circulated about Djezzar Pasha. It seems that he had his good sides, that he fed the poor, gave employment to the people he had maimed, and found husbands for the widows of the men he had killed. Be this as it may, Djezzar Pasha had a great deal of character, and he was beyond all doubt of all Turkish pashas then alive the most belligerent and irascible. He had also acquired, in the course of about six decades, a fairly astute political sense, which told him that General Bonaparte could not be trusted as an ally and was unlikely to keep the power long in Egypt if he, Djezzar, opposed him. Whatever messages Bonaparte sent him, whether cajoling or threatening, their only effect was either to amuse him or to throw him into a rage. It is difficult indeed to see how a man like Djezzar could have accepted to keep his post by the grace of General Bonaparte, a dangerous and ambitious man, rather than by the grace of Sultan Selim III, who was far away and left him alone.

Still, Bonaparte had good reasons to believe that at least a large part of the Syrian population—most particularly the Druses and the Christians, whom Djezzar had massacred now and then—would support him against the pasha. Citizen Peyrusse, who was not a blind worshipper of Bonaparte, wrote to his mother on April 2nd 'All the Syrians hate Djezzar.... There is no torture he has not inflicted on the Christians as well as on the Moslems of Syria, and even on his most faithful followers. He has had the noses and ears cut off some of them, and has caused others to be blinded, maimed, or shod like horses.'[2]

[1] Tott, II, 97.
[2] La Jonquière, IV, 315.

Ahmed the Butcher, Commodore Sidney Smith, and Colonel Phélipeaux made a remarkable team in opposing an at least equally remarkable adversary.

IV

At the approach of the French, Djezzar evacuated the port of Haifa, on the southern end of the Bay of Acre. On March 17, Bonaparte had his troops occupy Haifa and set up headquarters on Mount Carmel, from where he could overlook the entire lovely bay. It did not look lovely to him, for off Acre he could perceive two English battleships—the *Tigre* and the *Zealous*—several English gunboats, and some Turkish craft. He hastily sent orders to Captain Standelet, who was to bring the flotilla with the siege artillery from Damietta to Acre, asking him either to stay at Damietta, or, if he had already left, to stop at Jaffa.

The day Bonaparte dictated this order, March 18, Captain Standelet and his flotilla were approaching Cape Carmel. To arrive precisely at the same moment as the land army seemed like excellent timing, but there are occasions when it is better to be late than in time. It was a foggy day. When Standelet rounded Cape Carmel, he did not see Sir Sidney Smith's ships until they were practically on top of him. Six of his transports were captured; three escaped, among them Standelet's flagship.

On the following day, the French army took its position before Acre. The siege artillery had been lost, but to Bonaparte this did not seem critical. He had taken El Arish and Jaffa without it, and Acre, from the looks of it, was a far less defensible place. A walled city fortified by the Knights Hospitallers during the Crusades—it had been their last strong hold in Syria—Acre's defences were somewhat out of date, and besides they seemed to be crumbling. However, anyone who cares to inspect any of the Crusaders' castles in the Levant will easily convince himself that the Crusaders spared no stones to make their walls thick. More over, Acre being built on a peninsula, two thirds of it face the sea, which Sidney Smith controlled. Toward the landside, its crenellated walls jutted out at an angle. They were flanked by several towers, the largest of which soon came to be known among the French as *la Tour Maudite*—'the Damned Tower.' Djezzar 's castle, a stout, square structure adjacent to the wall, faced east. In the west, at the end of a jetty projecting into the bay, a lighthouse had been fortified to defend the small port. The entire city measured only about a thousand yards in circumference, and its population was estimated at

10,000-12,000. In addition to the 250 guns installed in the towers, the English had brought some artillery of their own, 1,200 bombs, 4,000 cannon balls, two mortars, and a vast quantity of gunpowder.

Although Bonaparte had no doubt whatever that Acre would fall to him within a few days, his lack of large-calibre guns and the nature of the terrain and of the fortifications demanded more elaborate preparations before the assault was made than had been necessary at El Arish and at Jaffa. While the troops and the Engineers, directed by one—legged Caffarelli, were working at the preparations, Bonaparte took certain political steps with a view to gaining allies against Djezzar. Seeing Djezzar 's decided unpopularity with virtually everybody under his rule, no matter whether Moslem, Christian, Jew, or Druse, this seemed an easy operation. Bonaparte summoned deputies from near-by Nazareth, Cana, and other Christian villages whose names still rang familiar to many French ears, to confer with him at his headquarters. He wrote to Emir Beshir of the Druses, promising to make his people independent and to restore the port of Beirut to them. He received Abbas el-Daher, whose father Djezzar had murdered and replaced as Pasha of Acre, and appointed him sheik of Tiberias, which the French occupied a few days later.

Bonaparte even exchanged amenities—perhaps inspired by the spirit of Holy Week—with Sir Sidney Smith. Smith had a number of French prisoners aboard his ships. Among them was Lieutenant Delesalle, sole survivor of an ambush in which his squad had been massacred by peasants. When Delesalle was taken to Acre, Sir Sidney, fearing that Djezzar would cut off the heads of all Frenchmen in his power (excepting Phélipeaux's, to be sure), had spirited him away to one of his ships, and treated him more than well, outfitting him with new clothes and inviting him to his table.

It so happened that on March 21 the French had captured a number of Englishmen whom Sidney Smith had sent ashore to Haifa in a rather dashing attempt to seize some French sloops anchored there. On March 22—Good Friday—Smith proposed an exchange of prisoners and also forwarded Delesalle's report to his unit commander; to this report Smith added a note, warning the French not to recriminate with Djezzar for the ill treatment Delesalle had received at his hands. 'I have managed the matter in such a manner that Djezzar will not claim him back from us.... Recriminations merely would remind Djezzar of the matter and cause him to request the prisoner's return, seeing his and the Turks' present animosity against the French. Monsieur Delesalle is now my guest and will remain my guest until a favourable opportunity arises to send him back to France.[1] Bonaparte agreed, returned the English prisoners, and, through his chief of staff, conveyed his thanks, 'Do not doubt my wish to be agreeable to you, Sir, or my eagerness to seize every opportunity to make myself useful to persons of your nation who are suffering misfortunes due to the hazards of war.'[2] It was the last polite or even decent word Bonaparte sent to, or spoke about, the chivalrous, eccentric, but always polite and decent Sidney Smith.

***

Meanwhile, throughout Holy Week, the French soldiers were digging trenches and worrying about the plague. A circular letter by Desgenettes advised all medical officers to see that everybody washed, rinsed his mouth, and kept warm. Experience had shown, he said, ' that the disease is not contagious.'[3] This seems an odd thing to say about the plague, but, aside from psychological considerations, Desgenettes was right in a manner of speaking, since the plague is transmitted by flea bites and not directly from person to person. It is difficult, however, to keep clean and warm and to avoid flea bites while digging trenches in Syria during March. A hospital for the plague-stricken was established at Mount Carmel. Between April 10 and April 25 (the only period for which statistics are available), 269 new cases were admitted in addition to the 152 already there. Out of these 421 cases, 57 had died by April 15; 157 had been discharged as cured or convalescent; and 250 remained. Since, during that period, several detachments and most of Kléber's division were absent on various missions, there were approximately 9,000 men in the siege camp. Thus, in a fortnight, 5 per cent of the besieging force was stricken with the plague—not a staggering proportion, but alarming all the same. The increase in the rate of cures, however, was encouraging. As Desgenettes points out in his medical history of the campaign, the death rate had fallen from 20 per cent of the new cases to 10 per cent.[4] These statistics do not include non-military victims, however—for instance, the hospital attendants, almost all of whom died of the plague.

If the rate of cures rose encouragingly during the siege, conditions in the plague hospital were anything but encouraging. Con-

---

[1] 41 La Jonquière, IV, 649.

[2] Correspondence, V, 373.

[3] La Jonquière, IV, 320.

[4] Desgenettes, Histoire me'dicetle 1,81.

firming that, toward the end of the siege, all the male nurses were either dead or dying, Desgenettes adds these edifying details: 'They [the hospital attendants] were, by the way, the scum and the disgrace of society: almost all were criminals, escaped from the bagnos of Genoa, Civita Vecchia, or Malta. They were drawn to the hospitals only by their thirst for the money which they took from the patients. 'I was often obliged to clean out the slimy basements where my patients were lying on mats; that is to say, I had to pick up the rags, the kits, the hats, and the bonnets of the dead and throw them myself into the fire, which I had lit for that purpose behind the hospital.'[1] Dr. Desgenettes took the Hippocratic oath as seriously as a man possibly can, and perhaps he carried its injunctions to extremes even Hippocrates had not dreamed of. 'It was in order to calm the fears and to restore the spirit of the army,' he says, 'that one day, in the middle of the plague ward, I plunged my lancet into the pus of the bubo of a convalescent ... and made slight incisions with it in my groin and near one of my armpits, without taking any other precaution than to wash myself with water and soap. For more than three weeks the places where I had incised myself were slightly inflamed.... This incomplete experiment, which I relate only because of all the talk it caused, proves little in a medical way. It does not change the fact, demonstrated by thousands of examples, that the disease can be transmitted; it only shows that the conditions necessary for its transmission have not been well determined.'[2] Perhaps the experiment proved little in a medical way; it does prove, however, that Dr. Desgenettes was on the right track; that, had he lived half a century later, he might easily have been one of the great medical pioneers of modern times; and that he had unbelievable sang-froid and courage. He adds this interesting postscript to this episode: when the same soldier, with whose bubonic pus Desgenettes had inoculated himself, was perfectly cured, he met his doctor again during a painful march through the desert. Out of gratitude, he offered a drink of water from his flask: Desgenettes accepted it, but only after overcoming 'an extreme revulsion.' Now here was a man.

***

The histories of sieges, Homer notwithstanding, are usually tedious. To the layman, they present a monotonous succession of incomprehensible actions repeated *ad infinitum* and faintly reminiscent of Uncle Toby and Corporal Trim. It is true that the siege

---

[1] Ibid., I, 86.

[2] Ibid., I, 88

of Troy had its interesting moments; so did that other siege of Acre, when Richard Coeur de Lion confronted Saladin. General Bonaparte was no Richard, Djezzar Pasha was no Saladin, and the siege of Acre in 1799 bore more resemblance to the horrors of trench warfare in the First World War than to the prowess of chivalrous Crusaders and Saracens.

The increase of the range and power of artillery since Napoleon's days has changed the nature of siegecraft completely. Its essential features, as it was practised then, can be outlined briefly and non—technically. The besieging army would camp within sight and observation of its objective, but just outside artillery range. 'Our camp looks more like a county fair every day,' Peyrusse wrote from Acre to his mother in Carcassonne. 'Wine, liquor, figs, wheat cakes, grapes, butter, etc.... everything is here in abundance, though at exorbitant prices. But one doesn't count pennies during a campaign.'[1] The 'etc.,' it may be imagined, included things that one does not mention to one's mother in Carcassonne.

The mere setting up of a camp around a fortress was not sufficient to make the fortress fall. To attack Acre, approaches had to be made first—that is, trenches had to be dug from the camp to the walls, to shelter the assailants from the defenders' cross fire. In addition, mines had to be placed underneath the walls or towers. While these works were in progress—the various units taking turns in the digging—the defenders, if they had sufficient ammunition, would rake the diggers with cannon balls and bombs; or else, they might quietly watch them perform the work and then undo it in a massive sortie—a counter-attack from the fortress—combined with a judiciously directed fire. At Acre, both these techniques were used.

When the underground labours had progressed to a satisfactory degree, an attack would be ordered. It would open with a massive artillery barrage, directed mainly against the spot selected for the assault, although sometimes it was also directed at another point, to confuse the enemy. The object was to make a breach, and this was usually accomplished if in addition to the artillery a mine could be exploded at the desired spot. Then the signal was given for the actual assault. The first wave of assailants, usually grenadiers, would rush through the trenches and try to scale the rubble of the breach. The enemy, of course, would not stand by idle but let the assailants have everything they had—musket fire, cannon balls, bombs and rocks—and receive with sabres and bayonets

---

[1] La Jonquière, IV, 315.

those who got through. An assault, whether successful or not, usually cost many more lives than did a battle a fact which may help to explain the savage behaviour of troops in captured cities. Besides, since no sober person would dream of scaling a well-defended fortress, the assailants received, just before the attack, an extra large ration of alcoholic spirits.

If the assault succeeded, that was that., If it did not succeed, the bombing, digging, and mining would continue on both sides until the time was judged ripe for another assault or another sortie. During the siege of Acre, French and Turkish sappers sometimes worked a few yards from one another; when the siege was lifted after two months, eight major assaults had been made.

Such was the basic scheme of siegecraft. The siege of Acre had several peculiarities that deserve mention.

1. As a rule the assailants, being on the outside, are in a position to supply themselves with victuals, ammunition, and human replacements. At Acre, the French had no supply bases and no replacements. They were grateful for every bombardment from the fortress or from the British ships, because they could collect the enemy's cannon balls and use them again. Djezzar Pasha, on the other hand, received all the supplies and reinforcements he wanted, by sea. The arrival, toward the end of the siege, of several hundred gunners from Constantinople, trained by European instructors, probably was a decisive factor in the outcome.

2. Normally, when an army besieges a city, the besiegers are more numerous than the besieged. Consequently, should the siege last longer than expected, the attacking army can leave a strong enough force behind to contain the fortress and march on to another objective. At Acre, the strength of the garrison was nearly equal to that of Bonaparte's army. This, however, was not as important as the fact that the French had only 13,000 men: they could not possibly march on before the city was taken and Djezzar's troops destroyed.

5. Normally, when a fortress presents two-thirds of its walls toward the sea, it is besieged by land and by sea. At Acre, the sea was controlled by the defenders.

4. Normally, to capture a fortress, siege artillery is used. At Acre, it was used but not by the besiegers. The heavy guns which Sir Sidney Smith had captured off Cape Carmel had been landed and were used by the Turks against the French. Only toward the end of the siege did Bonaparte receive replacements for his lost artillery.

General Bonaparte hated sieges; his genius required mobility. Although he had sent to Alexandria for another shipment of siege artillery, to be landed at Jaffa, he did not wait for its arrival to order the attack. Eight days of preparations seemed an eternity to him. He ordered an attack for March 28. His subordinate commanders were sceptical about the adequacy of the works of approach. 'Damned funny trenches they have made here,' remarked the tall Kléber to the short Bonaparte when they inspected the works together, 'They may be all right for you, General, but as for me, they hardly reach up to my belly.'[1]

While the French were digging trenches fit for pygmies, Sir Sidney Smith landed 800 English Marines to reinforce Djezzar's gun crews, and Colonel Phélipeaux worked day and night placing the artillery in position and training the gunners. Bonaparte, still unaware of his former classmate's presence, could not help noticing it soon after ordering the first assault, which began at 4 a.m. on March 28 with a bombardment of the fortress. The Turks, assisted by the naval guns of Sir Sidney's squadron, replied with a cross fire so devastating that, by 6 a.m., forty French gunners were wounded or dead and all but three of their guns were out of commission. Still, a breach of sorts was made; being more than twenty feet above the moat, it was obviously impracticable, a consideration which did not prevent Bonaparte from ordering his men to scale it with ladders twelve to sixteen feet high.

At his post near the parapet, Djezzar Pasha was seated, white—bearded and fiery-eyed, ready to hand out rewards to his soldiers for every enemy head they placed before him. It was a patriarchal custom he liked to honour, but this time no opportunity presented itself: it was physically impossible for the French to scale the breach. Nevertheless, terrified by the example Bonaparte had set at Jaffa, Djezzar's men were abandoning their posts at the sight of the French charging. Djezzar herded them back and fired two pistol shots at the assailants. 'What are you afraid of?' he shouted. 'Don't you see they're on the run?'[2] The Turks returned to their posts, and a few minutes later those French who still could run were on the run indeed. This, perhaps, was the one critical moment in the whole siege of Acre. While the Turks had regained their confidence, discouragement set in among the French. 'Many

---

[1] La Jonquière, IV, 336.

[2] Miot, p. 164.

of us were of the opinion from that moment on that we could never take the place,' says Captain Doguereau in his diary.[1]

General Bonaparte did not know the meaning of discouragement. To him, unless all was lost, everything could still be gained. He set his hopes on the effect of a mine to be placed under the large tower; it was completed on March 31, despite the almost continuous artillery fire from the fortress. Another assault was ordered for April 1. Almost every man who took part in it was either wounded or killed. Among the wounded were two of Bonaparte's aides-de-camp Duroc and Eugene Beauharnais. By now, even Bonaparte realized that further attempts were useless until the siege artillery arrived.

***

In the preceding chapters, this writer has drawn repeatedly on the notes made by Adjutant-General Laugier, whom Kléber had made his chief of staff, and by Major Detroye of the Engineers. Their diaries reveal two upright, intelligent, and observant men, neither of whom could discern any plausible reason for their or for their comrades' presence in the Orient. Their testimony will no longer be heard in the sequel: Laugier was killed in the trenches during the first assault; Detroye was killed during a Turkish sortie two days later.

Captain Mailly de Chateaurenaud, of the General Staff, was killed in the moat of Acre on March 28. He had a brother, whom Bonaparte had sent on a diplomatic mission to Syria half a year earlier. That brother, also a captain, had been arrested by Djezzar and was kept a prisoner in the fortress. On March 30, two days after one of the brothers died under the walls of Acre, the other brother was strangled inside the walls on Djezzar's orders, along with several hundred other Christians. Their bodies were thrown into the sea and washed up on the beach, where the French found them. The two Maillys, who thus died within two days, separated by a medieval wall, had not seen each other for six years, except for a brief reunion at Cairo.

Considering Djezzar's temperament, one may understand easily enough why he had several hundred Christians, including Mailly, massacred after the first French attack on his fortress. It is more difficult to see why Sidney Smith and Phélipeaux were unable to prevent him from this. There can be no doubt that, throughout the siege, these two men did everything in their power

---

[1] Cited in La Jonquifere, IV, 343.

to restrain Djezzar's vile temper and to save his potential victims. How the massacre of March 30 could occur despite their efforts remains a mystery. The event led to a very unfortunate misunderstanding between Sir Sidney Smith and Bonaparte, who regarded Sir Sidney as an accomplice in the butchery. It will be seen how this misunderstanding led to the death of several hundred more men.

Although no further attack on Acre took place during the first three weeks of April, the digging, the mining, the counter digging and countermining, the artillery duels, the sorties, and all the other works and ceremonies of siegecraft continued. The rains had stopped, but the *khamsin* was beginning. At the plague hospital on Mount Carmel, new 'fever patients ' still arrived every day. Morale in the camp was low. During this lull, Bonaparte had despatched Kléber's division and several smaller units to establish French control inland and to stop the army of the Pasha of Damascus, who was marching on Acre.

***

While Bonaparte was besieging Acre, a ring was forming around him. Djezzar Pasha had addressed appeals to the warlike mountaineers of Nablus and to the pashas of Aleppo and Damascus. In the early days of April, some 7,000 warriors from the Nablus region were reported, by Christian informants, to have gathered in Galilee, and the army of the Pasha of Damascus was on the march. On April 5, a reconnaissance detachment under General Junot had repulsed a cavalry force several times its superior near Nazareth. On April 9, Bonaparte sent Kléber with part of his division to Junot's aid. Two days later, near Cana, where Jesus had once saved a wedding feast from disaster, Kléber with 1,500 men drove back a Turkish force three times that strength. More Turkish units were reported to have crossed the Jordan north of Lake Tiberias; Bonaparte despatched General Murat with two infantry battalions to meet them. On April 15, Murat's men came upon them on a height overlooking the Jordan. On the opposite side of the river, they could see the tents of the Turkish camp. Inspired by the prospect of loot, they charged, forming their usual squares. 'They did not march,' says an eyewitness, 'they ran and overthrew that splendid cavalry as they came down the slope.'[1] Having routed about 5,000 men with hardly a loss on their side, Murat's troops forded the river and camped under the Turkish tents. 'There,' says the same witness, 'our troops spent the rest of the day swapping

---

[1] Millet, p. 176.

the booty they had taken.'[1] The Jordan north of Lake Tiberias was thus cleared.

To the south, things were more difficult, for there Kléber was about to face the bulk of the Pasha of Damascus; s army. On April 16, the day after Murat's spectacular exploit on the Jordan, Kléber with about 2,000 men came upon the pasha's camp in the Plain of Esdraelon, below Mount Tabor, The pasha, with about 25,000 horse and 10,000 infantry, had a superiority of about seventeen to one; however, his was a motley army, consisting mostly of ill-trained and worse disciplined volunteers—and militia. Kléber had planned a night attack but reached the camp only at 6 a.m., thus losing the advantage of surprise. In no time, his squares were surrounded by 25,000 horsemen. All he could do was fight a defensive action. With his headquarters was the wife of General Yerdier, who commanded a brigade in the battle.

For ten hours, from 6 a.m. to 4 p.m., the French had fought without interruption and with little hope, beating back the enemy. They were running out of cartridges. 'We would gladly have given up the little bread we had for some bullets and gunpowder,' Private Millet recalls in his memoirs. 'We had not had time to eat, and even if we had had time, we could not have taken advantage of it, because we were so worn out with thirst and fatigue that we could not even speak. At a short distance there was a lake, which the division was unable to reach, so that there was no way of refreshing ourselves.'[2]

Things had reached that desperate pass when, from an elevation to the south of the battlefield, Kléber's men heard the report of a cannon which they judged to be of a French calibre. It was: the gun belonged to General Bon's division, which Bonaparte himself had led to Kléber's rescue. 'The effect was dramatic,' declares an eyewitness. [3]

When they heard the cannon shot, says Nicholas the Turk, 'the Ottomans panicked and turned to flight. Seeing this, the [French] commander had another cannon shot fired, and the rout became general. The Ottomans scattered in all directions, toward the mountains and into the valleys. The French who watched this from

---

[1] Mllet, p. 177-8.
[2] Millet, p. 104.
[3] Lavallette, I, 311.

a distance rejoiced at the spectacle and broke into peals of laughter.'[1]

The Battle of Mount Tabor, as Bonaparte chose to call this engagement, was a victory as spectacular as it was unexpected. No doubt Kléber had blundered in letting himself be placed in so desperate a situation; the victory must be credited to the men who held out against such odds for ten hours and to Bonaparte, who had grasped the necessity of a lightning intervention, had arrived just in time, and had instantly decided which would be the most effective manoeuvre. Although the Pasha of Damascus' army was not destroyed, it was dispersed; and the losses of Kléber's division, in a struggle of one against seventeen, amounted to only two killed and sixty wounded.

The instant Kléber had heard the cannon signals, he ordered his exhausted men to pursue the fleeing Turks. 'Remember, reader, what I have told you before—that we were dying of thirst,' reminisces Private Millet. 'Well, our thirst for vengeance had put out our thirst for water and kindled our thirst for blood... , Indeed, here we were, wading up to our waists in the water of that same lake of which, only a short while ago, we craved to drink a cup. But we no longer thought of drinking but only of killing and of dyeing the lake red with the blood of those barbarians, who only a moment before had hoped to cut off our heads and drown our bodies in that very same lake, where they them selves were drowned and which was filled with their corpses.'[2] Private Millet, who had lost the sight of one eye from ophthalmia and survived the plague when he took part in the battle, was an ageing schoolmaster in a French village when he wrote these lines.

That night, General Bonaparte slept at Nazareth. 'Before entering the village,' says the Comte de Lavallette, then Bonaparte's aide-de camp, 'he stopped at an ancient fountain, where a number of cattle were drinking. There, the chief personages of the village met him: everything recalled the ancient scenes that are so naïvely described in the Bible. The French were received with much joy [by the Christian population], and General Bonaparte and his staff spent the night at the monastery of Nazareth.'[3] The Fathers also opened the monastery to the French wounded, of whom they took care.

------

[1] Nicolas Turc, p. 57.

[2] Millet, p. 105.

[3] Lavallette, I, 312.

Quite suddenly the French soldiers, after filling a lake with blood and corpses, remembered that they were born Christians. Nazareth revived their childhood memories of the Gospels, of First Communion, of the church bells that had been silenced in France for six years. On the morrow of the victory, says Dr. Desgenettes, ' our victories were celebrated by a solemn *Te Deum*. There was a christening: General Bonaparte stood godfather, Madame Verdier stood godmother. A major in the 14th Squadron of Dragoons, who was ill and felt his death approaching, asked, since he was in Holy Land, to end his days with the consolations and the rites of religion.'[1] All this notwithstanding, one must not be sentimental; some of the French soldiers, more Voltairean than atheistic, regarded Nazareth as a joke. 'That building,' says Lavallette of the Church of Nazareth, 'fairly resembles our village churches, except that its chapel used to be, as we were told, the Virgin's bedroom.... The prior assured us very earnestly that when the Angel Gabriel came to announce to the Virgin her glorious and holy destiny, he touched that column [a black marble column next to the altar] with his heel, and that it broke. We started to laugh, but General Bonaparte, with a stern look, made us recover our seriousness.'[2] A French soldier who had lost a finger in the battle and, for some reason, had picked it up and kept it, buried it solemnly in the cemetery, with the remark, ' I don't know what will happen to the rest of my carcass, but at least I'll have a finger in Holy Land.'[3] Another soldier, at the point of death and pressed by the Fathers to receive the last sacrament, had his scruples and consulted his comrades. ' Don't offend these poor monks who have taken so much trouble caring for you,' they said, ' and besides, what do you risk?'[4]

While the *Te Deum* was being sung at Nazareth, the French were burning two villages and the town of Jenin, in the territory of the Nablus mountaineers.

'The joy of the Christians,' says Napoleon, 'cannot be expressed. After so many centuries of oppression, they saw people of their own religion. They loved to tell stories from the Bible, which they knew better than did the French soldiers. They had read the proclamations of the commander-in-chief, in which he had de-

---

[1] Desgenettes, Souvenirs, III, 23, cited in La Jonquière, IV, 425.

[2] Lavallette, I, 312.

[3] Desgenettes, Souvenirs, III, 237, cited in La Jonquière, IV, 425.

[4] Ibid., ibid.

clared himself to be the friend of the Moslems, and they approved
of this line of conduct; it had not diminished their trust in him.
Napoleon conferred fur-trimmed caftans on three of their chiefs.
One of them was 101 years old.... The commander-in-chief asked
him to dine with him. The old man could not say three words
without a quotation from the Bible. The loyalty of those Christians
remained firm even in bad fortune: they were useful to him
throughout the siege of Acre.[1] They also had to pay for it after the
siege was lifted, when Bonaparte wrote to the sheiks of El Azhar
that he would become a Moslem and build a magnificent mosque.

After two days among Christians, Bonaparte, leaving Kléber
behind to guard the Jordan, returned to the siege of Acre.

**

While the French had been beating back the Turks at Nazareth, Cana, Mount Tabor, and other sacred places, the preparations for another assault had made progress, though not without
interference by the besieged. On April 7, a vigorous sortie, led by
an English officer, interrupted but failed to undo the work on the
mine under the 'Damned Tower'. Fifteen Englishmen, including
their leader, were killed. Bonaparte thought that the English officer might be Colonel Phélipeaux; to make sure, he ordered the
body to be retrieved, which was done, in a grisly enough way, by
means of a harpoon. The body turned out to belong to a Captain
Thomas Oldfield, or Enfield, whose papers showed that he had
distinguished himself in the capture of Cape Town from the Dutch;
the French buried his harpooned cadaver with military honours.

Two days after this, General Caffarelli had an arm shattered by
a Turkish cannon ball; Dr. Larrey amputated the arm; soon afterwards, Caffarelli was seized with a violent fever. It was in this condition that Bonaparte found him when he returned from Nazareth.

Gaspard Monge was in almost as bad shape as Caffarelli. He
had assisted Desgenettes and Larrey in organizing the hospital and
ambulance services, had caught dysentery, and was delirious.
Bonaparte had him moved to his own tent. One cold night, Monge
recalled later, Bonaparte, thinking that he was asleep, tenderly
covered him with an extra blanket.

By mid-April, the replacement for the lost siege artillery arrived, by ship, in Jaffa. On April 19, Bonaparte wrote to Poussiel-

---

[1] Correspondence, XXX, 36-37.

gue, in Cairo, that he expected to take Acre by May 5 or 6. 'I shall leave immediately afterwards and return to Cairo', he added. [1]

Without waiting for the siege guns to be brought from Jaffa, Bonaparte ordered another assault for April 24. It began at 9 a.m. with the explosion of another mine under the large tower. 'Its only effect', Peyrusse informed his mother, 'was to blow up a corner of the tower. . . . The grenadiers boldly charged the breach, although it was clear that it was impossible to penetrate it. The enemy, installed at the top of the tower and hidden behind the battlements, flattened our troops with rocks, shells, and hand grenades. However, since nothing could turn back our troops, the Turks resorted to two or three powder kegs which they threw on them. All our men were suffocated [by the blast], although a few managed to run away half-burned.' [2]

Bonaparte, whom failure made ruthless, ordered another assault for the next morning.

This time, the French grenadiers succeeded in entering the lower gallery of the tower; the Turks, through an opening in the ceiling of the gallery, showered the French—about a hundred of them—with shells and bombs. Among those wounded in their shambles was Second- Lieutenant Fuseau of the Engineers, a sixteen-year-old student of the Ecole Polytechnique. It was the first time he had been under fire. Citizen Favier, a civil engineer on the Scientific Commission, had loved the young man. 'Favier', one of his colleagues was to recall, 'went to him in the trench, carried him back on his shoulders, and soon after wards closed his eyes. He became almost demented on that occasion and made a scene to Bonaparte which caused a great deal of talk.' [3] Bonaparte listened impassively to Favier's hysterical outburst; 'then he withdrew without the least sign of emotion, as if Favier's delirious accusations had been aimed at someone else'. [4]

At the same time, General Caffarelli began his agony. 'How is Caffarelli?' Bonaparte inquired of Bourrienne. 'He is close to the end', replied the secretary. 'He has asked me to read Voltaire's preface to [Montesquieu's] L'Esprit des Lois to him, and he fell asleep.' 'Bah!' said Bonaparte, 'he wanted to hear that preface!

---

[1] Ibid., V, 405.

[2] La Jonquiere, IV, 453.

[3] Villiers du Terrage, p. 184.

[4] Belliard, Histoire, III, 345.

That's funny.'[1] He went to see his friend that evening, and found him unconscious. Caffarelli died during the night.

Part of the siege artillery arrived at last on April 50. Bonaparte ordered another assault (the fifth) for May 1. It ended with a panic among the assailants. A night attack on May 4 also failed: Djezzar had illuminated his entire front with lanterns as a precaution. The sixth major attack, on May 6, was repulsed like the others. On May 7, all the siege artillery was in position, and another attack began at 9 a.m. Its partial success showed that Bonaparte might well have taken Acre if he had had the patience to wait for his big guns, instead of wasting his men and resources on hopeless improvised attempts. At last, the French succeeded in gaining a foothold in the 'Damned Tower'. The fighting was resumed the following morning, both on the walls and on the beach, where Sir Sidney Smith landed his crews in order to protect the passage of a contingent of European-trained Turkish gunners from their transports to the fortress. By nightfall, the French still held the tower, and some 200 Frenchmen, led by Generals Lannes and Rambaud, actually penetrated into the city; they discovered only too late that their men were not following them.

From the walls of Acre, Sir Sidney Smith, just before dark, could observe, through his spy glass, General Bonaparte and his staff directing the attack from a hill named after Richard Coeur de Lion. Bonaparte's gestures, according to Sir Sidney's report, indicated an imminent resumption of the assault. Djezzar Pasha, who stood beside Smith, decided to let the French scale the breach unhindered: Colonel Phélipeaux had constructed a second retrenchment behind the walls, where the Turks held themselves ready to receive the assailants. While Lannes, to the rear, still encouraged his men to follow him through the breach, the French who had crossed it into Djezzar's gardens were surrounded and bayoneted. From the roof tops, the Moslem women were encouraging the Turks with their peculiar strident ululations. General Rambaud was killed; Lannes was wounded by a bullet. Several English officers were mistaken for Frenchmen in the dark and fatally wounded, too; but Smith generously overlooked the incident. After twenty-five hours of uninterrupted fighting, the French gave up the assault.

The French, Sir Sidney was convinced, would renew the attack shortly. They had opened a breach big enough for a column fifty men wide to penetrate. The city, Smith reported to Lord St. Vin-

---

[1] Bourrienne, Vol. II, Ch. XV.

cent, 'is not, and never has been, defensible according to the rules of art. But, according to every other rule, it must and shall be defended; not that it is in itself worth defending, but we feel that it is by this breach Buonaparte means to march to further conquest.'[1]

***

On the following day, May 9, upon Bonaparte's orders, General Kléber with Verdier's brigade marched on Acre to reinforce the besieging forces: Bonaparte had decided on one last attack for May 10. The breach was there; throughout Palestine, tens of thousands of Christians and Druses had sworn to rally to his arms. One more effort, and he might yet march on to Constantinople. His behaviour that day suggests that he sought either victory or death. He found neither, and these moods never lasted long with him.

Madame Peyrusse, probably the best-informed lady, as to military matters, in all of Carcassonne, received the following account from her son:

Kléber's division [i.e. Verdier's brigade] was to begin the attack. Adjutant General Fouler commanded the vanguard. He was killed on the breach. This misfortune did not intimidate the 75th [Half-Brigade]; its men threw themselves into the city at the same time as Reynier's and Bon's divisions attacked the [Turkish] forces outside the walls. But the lack of co-ordination, or perhaps the endeavours of the enemy, resulted in discouraging those who had entered [the city]. Those not killed in action were either taken prisoner or assassinated, for they have not returned.

Surprised by so much disorder, we ceased fire. The troops rested for a while. All the men available were collected; the grenadiers of the 25th and the carabineers of the 2nd arrived at that point and were ordered into the trenches. The ardour and courage of these fresh troops made the commander-in-chief believe that he could order a new assault. He wanted to be first to scale the breach, and it took a great deal of trouble to restrain him.[2]

The grenadiers, Peyrusse continues, did not need Bonaparte to lead them: they threw themselves into the breach 'like madmen. It would have been impossible to charge in any other way, for in or-

[1] Barrow, I, 291.
[2] La Jonquière, IV, 496.

der to get to the breach, they had to step, quite literally, over the rotting corpses of their predecessors, who had been buried under a few inches of dirt in the trenches. (Djezzar had repeatedly refused a cease-fire to allow for a proper burial.) The thin cover of earth had worn off during the past days' fighting, and the sight and stench were hideous. At the breach, the half-crazed assailants were received by the most murderous cross fire of the entire siege. Here the division commander, General Bon, was fatally wounded; so was the aide-de-camp Croisier, whom Bonaparte had called a coward at Damanhur and who now, at last, found the death he had sought for ten months. 'Without exaggeration,' Peyrusse affirms to his mother, ' it is certain that half of the army has perished.'[1] If by 'half of the army' Peyrusse meant half of the siege force, and if by 'perished' he meant killed or seriously wounded, Peyrusse exaggerated very little. Bonaparte had gambled his last trump, and lost. No sooner was the attack beaten back than he decided to retreat. He was neither killed nor wounded. His sudden appetite for a glorious death had vanished. From now on, he exercised all hisingenuity to turn defeat into a semblance of victory.

***

On the basis of the rather incomplete figures available in the archives of the French Ministry of War, the historian La Jonquière has calculated that French casualties in the Syrian campaign amounted, at the very least, to 1,200 killed by the enemy, 1,000 dead from disease, and 2,500 ill or heavily wounded.[2] The troops Bonaparte had taken to Syria were the élite of the army; more than one third of them were dead or disabled when he returned to Egypt. After such a disaster, most other men would have either committed suicide or sought an armistice.

Sir Sidney Smith, seeing that the morale of the French troops was at its nadir, thought the time ripe for some psychological warfare. During the last days of the siege, a shower of proclamations, printed in French by the Imperial press at Constantinople, was dropped into the trenches below the walls. The proclamation bore the seal of the Imperial Divan, but its probable author was Sir Sidney. 'Can you doubt that, in sending you to such a remote country, the Directory had any aim other than to exile you from France ... and to make every one of you perish?' the pamphlet inquired of the French, who read it amidst the stench of their decaying com-

---

[1] La Jonquière, IV, 497.

[2] Ibid. 9 IV, 632-33.

rades. 'If you have landed on Egyptian soil in complete ignorance of your destination, if you have been used as tools to violate a treaty ... was this not the result of your Directors' perfidy? Yes, there can be no doubt. Yet Egypt must be freed of so wanton an invasion, and at this moment an innumerable army is on the march and a huge fleet covers the sea. Those among you, no matter what their rank, who wish to avoid the peril that is threatening you must, without delay, signify their wish to the commanders of the Allied army and navy forces. They will be guaranteed safe passage to whatever place they want to go ... Let them make haste to take advantage of the benign disposition of the Sublime Porte, and let them appreciate this propitious occasion to escape from the horrible abyss into which they have been thrown!'[1]

All French sources and historians unanimously agree that the Grand Vizier's proclamation had the opposite effect from that desired by Sidney Smith. Sir Sidney asserts that the French grabbed the broad sheets eagerly and read them with attention; yet he does not say that a single French soldier followed the invitation to surrender. None did. As is often the case in psychological warfare, the words were ill chosen: they infuriated rather than persuaded. At the same time, they lingered in the soldiers' minds. Bonaparte's unreasoning hatred of Sir Sidney and his harsh measures, a few weeks later, against 'agitators' among his troops suggest that the Turkish proclamation produced some effect.

Besides broadcasting appeals to the French army, Sidney Smith addressed himself directly to its commander-in-chief. Before leaving for Syria, Bonaparte had sent Citizen Beauchamp, the French consul at Muscat, who happened to be in Cairo, on a mission to Constantinople. Beauchamp was to go aboard the Turkish caravel anchored at Alexandria, which Bonaparte authorized to sail for that purpose, and to offer a satisfactory arrangement to the Porte, on condition that the Porte cease all hostile actions against the French. Beauchamp's instructions contain this sentence: 'If ever you are asked whether the French would agree to evacuate Egypt, [the answer is] why not?'[2] Citizen Beauchamp's mission met with no success, of course; at Rhodes, both he and his instructions fell into Sir Sidney's hands. On May 8, 1799, Sir Sidney had the following letter conveyed to Bonaparte:

Monsieur le Général,

---

[1] Ibid., IV, 528.
[2] Correspondence, V, 202.

Since your instructions to your emissary Beauchamp contain these words, 'If you are asked whether the French would agree to leave Egypt,' along with your reply, 'Why not?,' I believe I may send you the enclosed proclamation of the Ottoman Porte without your fining it out of place.

I did not want to ask you the question, 'Are the French willing to leave Syria?' before you had a chance to match your strength against ours, since you could not be persuaded, as I am, of the impracticability of your enterprise. But now ... that you can see that [this fortress] becomes stronger each day instead of being weakened by two months of siege, I do ask you this: 'Are you willing to evacuate your troops from the territory of the Ottoman Empire before the intervention of the great allied army changes the nature of this question?'

You may believe me, Monsieur le Général, that my only motive in asking you this is my desire to avoid farther bloodshed.

I have the honour, [etc.]

Sidney Smith

Perhaps Sir Sidney did not fully appreciate what sort of man he was addressing. Perhaps, also, he would not have written in this haughty fashion if, a few days earlier, Bonaparte had not accused him, in an Order of the Day, of loading French prisoners aboard plague-infected ships, of being an accomplice in Djezzar's massacre of the Christians, and of having proved, by his entire conduct throughout the siege, that he was a madman. In any event, as a result of their mutual personal animosity, all communication between the two men ceased at the precise moment when Sir Sidney's co-operation was desperately needed to help evacuate thousands of wounded and of plague victims. Such was Napoleon's fury against Sidney Smith that twenty years later he still could not mention his name without a string of violent epithets.

A retreat is often a more difficult operation than an offensive. Bonaparte's retreat from Acre presented two particularly arduous problems: how to evacuate the casualties and how to gain enough distance from his pursuers: for there could be no doubt that Djezzar would lose no time in following up his advantage. In addition, there was the problem of making the retreat look like a victory.

On May 11, the day after the final and disastrous assault on Acre, Bonaparte ordered Admiral Perée, who was off Jaffa with a small squadron, to put in at the tiny port of Tantura (a few miles south of Acre) and to evacuate 400 of the heavily wounded. Perée ignored the order, pointing out that he could not risk his ships against Sidney Smith's superior forces, and sailed back to Europe. Perhaps this decision does Perée little honour; on the other hand, it would have been easy for Bonaparte to obtain a safe-conduct for Perée's ships from Sidney Smith; but Bonaparte preferred, as will be seen, to sacrifice several thousand crippled, wounded, and plague-stricken men, for whose lives he was responsible, to asking any favour of Sir Sidney. Perée's departure, says Captain Doguereau in his diary, threw Bonaparte into considerable perplexity: ' Bonaparte was extremely worried on account [of the wounded]: there was no visible means of transportation for them.'[1] In a series of orders dated from mid-May, the commander-in-chief divided all the 2,300 sick and wounded into three categories: those who could walk, those who could ride, and litter cases. All those able to walk, including officers, regardless of rank, were to march on foot. All horses, mules, camels, and donkeys were to be used exclusively for the transportation of the invalids, except those needed for the artillery; and even a large part of the artillery was to be left behind. The most serious cases were to be transported from Jaffa to Damietta aboard the few small ships Perrée had left behind. It would be pointless to go into more details concerning Bonaparte's dispositions in this matter, for the reality of the retreat bore little resemblance to the orders he gave, possibly in full knowledge of their impracticability. The orders, on paper, would justify him before History, which is written on paper and which tends to ignore the living truth.

On May 16, the chief interpreter of the army, Venture, died of dysentery.[2] On the same day, Bonaparte had an interesting conversation with Dr. Desgenettes, in the presence of General Berthier. After a few remarks on the medical situation of the army, says the doctor in his memoirs, Bonaparte said abruptly, 'If I were in your place, I should put an end to the sufferings of our plague patients and, at the same time, to the danger they represent for us, by giving them [an overdose of] opium.' If he himself had the plague, Bonaparte continued with the utmost calm, he would ask this to be done for him as a favour. Dr. Desgenettes felt unable to agree, partly out of principle, partly because he was aware of the high percentage of cures. 'As far as I am concerned,' he replied

---

[1] 74La Jonquière, IV, 519.

[2] According to official documents; but the symptoms of his illness suggest that it may have been the plague.

simply, 'my duty is to preserve life.' Bonaparte pointed out to Desgenettes that, for his part, his aim was to preserve the army, 'I shall not try to overcome your scruples,' he added, 'but I believe I shall find people who will appreciate my intentions more than you do.'[1] During the whole conversation, General Berthier remained silent, content to bite his fingernails.

Nobody was poisoned at that time, but this was not the end of the story.

For four successive days—May 12-15—Bonaparte had Acre, and particularly Djezzar's palace, bombarded by all the artillery at his disposition. The object was partly to disguise his preparations for lifting the siege, partly to do the most damage he could, since he had to leave his heavy artillery and munitions behind, partly to be able to announce to the world that he had destroyed Acre. On May 16 he wrote to the Divan of Cairo that he was about to return from Syria. 'I shall bring many prisoners and captured flags with me,' he continued. 'I have razed Djezzar's palace and the ramparts of Acre, and I have bombarded that city in such a manner that not one stone remains in its place.... Djezzar is seriously wounded.' These lies are followed by a number of other fantastic assertions; then Sultan Kebir proceeds to conditions in Egypt: 'I am anxious to see you and to get back to Cairo, all the more so since I see that, despite your zeal, a great number of wicked men are trying to disturb the public peace. All this will vanish as soon as I arrive just as the clouds yield to the first ray of the sun.'[2]

The sheiks of the Divan of Cairo were somewhat puzzled as they read this letter, and wondered why Sultan Kebir had not bothered to take Acre after razing it; nevertheless, blatant though his lies were, they were addressed to a group of men who knew nothing of warfare, who lived several hundred miles away, and who were perfectly willing to pass them on to the ignorant people—which indeed they did.[3] It is more difficult to grasp how Bonaparte had the cheek to present the same transparent mixture of barefaced lies, sour grapes, and silver linings to his own army, as

---

[1] Desgenettes, Souvenirs, III, 256, cited in La Jonquière, IV, 555.

[2] Correspondence, V, 428.

[3] According to El-Djabarti, Bonaparte addressed a second, confidential, letter to the Divan, in which he listed his real reasons for lifting the siege of Acre. Probably El-Djabarti did not invent this letter. The official letter was intended solely to indicate to the Divan what line of propaganda Bonaparte wished them to take.

he did in his proclamation of May 17, announcing the impending retreat:

> Soldiers, you have crossed the desert which divides Africa from Asia with greater speed than an army of Arabs.
>
> The army which was marching toward Egypt has been destroyed....
>
> You have dispersed in the plain below Mount Tabor the horde of men from every corner of Asia who had gathered in the hope of looting Egypt.
>
> The thirty [Turkish] ships which you saw anchor off Acre, twelve days ago, carried aboard them the army which was to besiege Alexandria. But, since that army was obliged to come to the help of Acre, it has finished there; part of its flags will accompany you on your return to Egypt.
>
> After having maintained ourselves in the heart of Syria for three months, with only a handful of men; after capturing forty guns and 6,000 prisoners; after razing the fortifications of Gaza, Jaffa, Haifa, and Acre, we shall return to Egypt. I am obliged to go back there because it is the season of the year when hostile landings may be expected.
>
> Only a few days ago you could still hope to take [Djezzar] Pasha prisoner in his palace; but at this point the capture of the castle of Acre is not worth wasting even a few days. The brave men I might have lost in that enterprise are needed now for more important opera tions.
>
> Soldiers, there are more hardships and dangers facing us.... You will find in them new opportunities for glory. And if, in the midst of so many combats, every day is marked by the death of a hero, then new heroes must arise and take their place among those chosen few who take the lead in peril and wrest victory from it.[1]

The men to whom he addressed these words knew that Acre had not been razed, that the Turkish army had not been destroyed, and that the siege was being lifted because they had been defeated. Undoubtedly, they had been but a handful of men, and they had accomplished incredible feats; but they realized that half of them had been killed and maimed for the sake of a desperate gamble. Perhaps Bonaparte's proclamation succeeded at least partly in restoring their morale; but more certainly this blatant accumulation

---

[1] Ibid., V, 429-30.

of untruths, hypocrisy, and rhetoric was aimed not at them but at that great gallery of fools known as Posterity and History. What did he care if every man in his army shrugged off his phantasies with a cynical joke, so long as historians would quote them and send shivers of admiration down the spines of readers more credulous than the benighted sheiks of El Azhar?

The reference to the thirty Turkish ships deserves special mention. The troops they had carried had been disembarked with Sidney Smith's help and, far from being destroyed, had contributed decisively to Bonaparte's defeat. They had never been intended to lay siege to Alexandria. When the Turkish forces that were intended for that purpose suddenly turned up at Abukir not long afterwards, Bonaparte was to experience some embarrassment, having to explain the appearance of an army which he claimed he had destroyed.

But Bonaparte was not concerned with petty facts and truth; his genius was political even more than military, and what he sought was to produce an over-all effect. Thus, on May 20, the day the retreat began, orders were issued that the headquarters should march preceded by all the captured flags and that, 'every time they passed through a village, they will enter with the flags unfurled and with the band playing.'[1]

André Peyrusse reported to his mother the conditions in which the retreat began. 'We had no means of transportation whatsoever,' he wrote to her from Cairo a month later, 'and we had a thousand or twelve hundred wounded and sick to carry with us, besides about forty pieces of artillery.... All the rest, guns of every calibre, mortars, shells, bombs, muskets, bullets that is, virtually the entire ordnance had to be buried in the fields and on the beach. We blew up the gun powder we had left; all the caissons were piled up and burned in the plain.... Everything was ready for our departure ... when, on May 20, the enemy made a lively sortie; it lasted almost all day. The fire was terrible. The enemy kept on throwing himself into our trenches, but Reynier's division ... kept pushing him back with heavy losses.'[2]

At 8 p.m., after dark, the troops began to leave. On the following morning, the Turks in Acre saw that the French camp was empty.

---

[1] La Jonquière, IV, 539.

[2] Ibid., IV, 543-44.

V

Reporting to Lord Nelson on his triumph, Sir Sidney Smith adopted Nelson's peculiar ecclesiastic style: 'The Providence of Almighty God has been wonderfully manifested in the defeat and precipitate retreat of the French army.... The Plain of Nazareth has been the boundary of Buonaparte's extraordinary career.'[1] Colonel Phélipeaux, unfortunately, was unable to share in Sir Sidney's elation; he had died about a week before Bonaparte lifted the siege—either from exhaustion, as Smith asserted, or from the plague.

The retreating French army reached Haifa about midnight. 'We hoped,' Peyrusse told his mother, 'that we should no longer have before our eyes the hideous sight of dead and dying men ... when, as we entered Haifa in the dark of the night, we saw about a hundred sick and wounded who had been left in the middle of a large square. Those poor, desperate people filled the air with their screams and their curses; ... some were tearing off bandages and rolling in the dust. This spectacle petrified the army. We stopped for a moment, and men were designated in each company to carry these people in their arms to Tantura; and we continued the march.'[2]

On went the victims of the Almighty's providence. At Tantura, on the beach, they found 700 or 800 more wounded and plague cases, 'and not one single ship to transport all this,' noted Peyrusse.[3] More artillery and ammunition had to be buried and burned, to free more horses for ambulance duty. In the operation, a caisson exploded, killing and mutilating a number of bystanders.

By this time, the bands were no longer playing. 'I saw with my own eyes,' says Bourrienne, 'officers who had limbs amputated being thrown out of their litters [by their bearers].... I have seen amputated men, wounded men, plague-stricken men, or people merely suspected of having the plague, being abandoned in the fields. Our march was lit up by torches with which we set fire to the towns, the villages, the hamlets, and the rich harvests that covered the land. The entire countryside was on fire.... We were surrounded by nothing but dying men, looters, and arsonists. The dying, by the roadside, were saying in a barely audible voice, "I am

---

[1] Barrow, I, 307.
[2] La Jonquière, IV, 548.
[3] Bourrienne, Vol. II, Ch. XVI.

only wounded, I haven't got the plague ", and in order to convince those who were marching by they opened their wounds or inflicted fresh ones on themselves. Nobody believed them. People said, "He's a dead man", and passed by.... To our right was the sea; to our left and behind us, the desert we were creating; ahead of us, the sufferings and privations that awaited us.'[1]

In this description, the not always reliable Bourrienne is borne out by all other eyewitnesses.

Bonaparte had given the strictest orders that no man capable of walking was to ride. At Tantura, his groom asked him, as the march was to be resumed, 'Which horse do you wish to ride, General?' Bonaparte, infuriated, struck the groom in the face with his riding whip. 'Everybody is to go on foot, *foutre*, and I along with the rest! Don't you know my orders?' The outburst produced the desired effect. 'From then on,' says Bourrienne, 'it was a contest as to who would give up his horse first to carry the sick, provided they did not have the plague.'[2]

Among the privileged few who did not have to go on foot were Monge, Berthollet, and Costaz, all three of whom were convalescing from illness. Bonaparte had put his carriage at their disposal. They took in two plague-stricken men and a soldier's wife who was nursing a baby. Not one of them caught the plague.

Though riding in a carriage, Monge and his companions were dying of thirst. They passed Dr. Desgenettes, who walked on foot and who offered them two flasks of water. Monge, after thanking him, expressed his chagrin at seeing that Bonaparte had been rather cool toward the doctor; he promised to put in a good word for him. In reply, Desgenettes began to chant the first psalm at the top of his voice: *Beatus vir qui non abiit in consilio impiorum et in via peccatorum non stetit et in cathedra pestilentiae non sedit*: l Blessed is the man who hath not walked in the counsel of the ungodly, nor stood in the way of sinners, nor sat in the chair of pestilence'. [Douay version.]

The march continued to Jaffa, through the burning countryside, which Bonaparte had ordered devastated to slow down his pursuers and to deprive them of subsistence. The straggling columns were sniped at from the left by the peasants and bombarded from the right by Sir Sidney's gunboats. Early in the afternoon of May 24 they reached Jaffa, where only two months before they

---

[1] Ibid.
[2] Correspondence, V, 436.

had massacred at least 6,000 people. They stayed there for four days. Bonaparte's first care, upon arriving, was to order Adjutant General Boyer to leave the next day with 300 of the lightly wounded men and with several prisoners, including Abdullah Aga, who had commanded the garrison of Jaffa, and with the captured Turkish flags. They were to precede the main army into Egypt. Boyer, says Bonaparte's order, was to show the Turkish flags in every village and 'to display them as trophies of victory.

Between May 25 and May 27, 1,500 more wounded and plague patients were sent ahead by land—on foot, horse, or litter, depending on their condition—and several hundred of the most serious cases were sent by sea to Damietta on a half-dozen small ships that were utterly unequipped for the purpose. The ships were intercepted by Sir Sidney Smith, who—as he reported to Nelson—found them 'in want of every necessary, even water and provisions. They steered straight to His Majesty's ships, in full confidence of receiving the succours of humanity; in which they were not disappointed. I have sent them on to Damietta,' Sir Sidney continues, 'where they will receive such further aid as their situation requires, and which it was out of my power to bestow on so many. Their expressions of gratitude to us were mingled with execrations on the name of their general, who had, as they said, thus exposed them to perish, rather than fairly and honourably to renew the intercourse with the English, which he had broken off by a false and malicious assertion that I had intentionally exposed the former prisoners [i.e. those exchanged at Acre] to the infection of the plague.'[1] There is not one word to be added to Sir Sidney's report on the condition and morale of the French wounded or on Bonaparte's chargesof what nowadays would be called bacteriological warfare; all the available evidence supports the exact truthfulness of Sir Sidney Smith.

On May 27, Bonaparte reported on his victories in Syria to the Directory. 'The occasion seemed to favour the capture of Acre,' he wrote of the final days of the siege, 'but our spies, deserters, and our prisoners all reported that the plague was ravaging the city and that every day more than sixty persons were dying of it.... If the soldiers had entered the city ... they would have brought back into camp the germs of that horrible evil, which is more to be feared than all the armies in the world.'[2] That the plague had ravaged his own army and cost him a thousand men of this the report

[1] Barrow, I, 311-12.
[2] Correspondence, V, 440.

says not a word, nor does it mention the holocaust of the final assault: these things would have spoiled the effect of what Bonaparte called, in the same communication, 'the glorious events accomplished over the past three months in Syria in the name of the Republic.'

Bonaparte had barely finished dictating this outrage to the truth when he ordered the remaining plague patients at the hospital of Jaffa to be poisoned. Before giving this order, says Bourrienne, he visited the hospital. 'Bonaparte paced rapidly through the wards, striking the yellow cuffs of his boots with his riding whip.... "The Turks will be here in a few hours [he said]. Let all those strong enough to get up come with us; they will be carried on litters and horses".... The complete silence and apathy of the men ... announced their imminent end.'[1] [2]

There were about fifty patients left in the hospital. Dr. Desgenettes having refused to take any part in poisoning them, Bonaparte obtained the laudanum from Hadj Mustafa, a Turkish physician from Constantinople, who had arrived at Jaffa shortly after its capture by the French. The poison was administered to the patients by the chief pharmacist Royer. There is reason to believe that either Mustafa, or Royer, or both, deliberately gave the men an insufficient dose. 'Some of them threw up [the laudanum], felt relieved, recovered, and lived to tell what had happened,' asserts Dr. Desgenettes.[3] Sir Sidney Smith confirms this testimony in his report to Nelson: when the Turks entered Jaffa, he says, 'seven poor wretches [were found] left alive in the hospital; they are protected, and shall be taken care of.'[4] There is no evidence that a single man actually died of the poison; on the other hand, there can be no doubt but that Bonaparte gave orders to poison them.

A silly literature of controversy grew up around this episode. Dr. Larrey formally accused Desgenettes of lying when Desgenettes published the facts in later years, and idolaters of Napoleon tend to deny the whole story. Against them stands the testimony of Bourrienne, Jacques Miot, Marshal Marmont, the engi-

---

[1] Bourrienne, Vol. II, Ch, XVI.

[2] This second visit to the plague-stricken in Jaffa has often been confused with Bonaparte's earlier visit, which forms the subject of Gros' painting. Bourrienne's testimony is corroborated in the memoirs of Savary, Duke of Rovigo (I, 161).

[3] 88 La Jonquière, IV, 577.

[4] Barrow, I, 313.

neer Martin, Kléber, Desgenettes, Sergeant François, and at least a half dozen others. Bonaparte himself, in his version of the campaign, attenuates rather than denies these assertions: the poison, he says, was placed beside the patients before the French evacuated Jaffa, so that they could take it voluntarily to avoid falling into the hands of the Turks. It is difficult to see why this question has generated so much passion: even if Bonaparte did order the mercy-killing of two or four dozen hopeless plague patients, surely this action was more defensible than the massacre of several thousand prisoners of war, which he had ordered at Jaffa ten weeks earlier.

On May 28 the French ended their occupation of Jaffa with fireworks: they blew up the fortifications, and then resumed their long march.

'The whole track between Acre and Gaza is strewed with the dead bodies of those who have sunk under fatigue, or the effect of slight wounds,' Sir Sidney Smith informed Nelson.[1] Colonel Vigo-Roussillon, who took part in the retreat, recalls in his memoirs the violence of the troops' feelings toward their commander-in-chief: 'It was said that [the wounded] could have been evacuated by sea and that Sir Sidney Smith had offered to have them escorted to Alexandria, and that he even proposed to transport them on his own ships, to save them from the fanatic Turks. But, the soldiers said, not only did Bonaparte make no attempt to negotiate with the English on this subject but also he rejected all their offers and, out of pride, ended by forbidding all further communication with them under pain of death.'[2] It is generally believed that Napoleon's army worshipped him. This may have been true in Italy and it may have been true later; but in Egypt, the army hated him.

The retreat continued. Kléber jotted an episode in his notebook. 'Retreat from Acre. A corporal ... stops by a plague victim by the roadside and cuts off his money belt. The sick man implores him to let him keep the twelve francs he has in it: "If I give them to an Arab, they may save my life." "You're deceiving yourself," says the corporal. "Then leave me at least the hope." [An officer] made him return the belt.'[3]

May 30: the army reaches Gaza. May 31: the march through the Sinai Desert begins. June 1: having marched from sunrise to

[1] Ibid., I, 312.
[2] Vigo-Roussillon, p. 608.
[3] La Jonquière, IV, 596.

sunset for two consecutive days across the desert, the army reaches, or rather falls down in exhaustion, at El Arish, in Egyptian territory. June 5: the march through the desert is resumed.

Toward sunset, there was a brief halt. When Kléber ordered his men to continue the march, the troops remained motionless. The order was repeated. Not a man moved, but a hail of oaths was showered on the officers. An aide-de-camp strode toward the mutineers: they stopped him with their bayonets, and the aide ran back to Kléber. 'Leave them alone,' said the general. 'Let them give off steam and curse us. It's the only relief they have, you must not take it away from them. Let's pretend we don't even notice their mutiny. They'll come—you'll see. Let's march ahead.'[1] And sure enough, like rebellious children, the troops soon got up and followed their general.

In the evening of June 5, after nine hours' marching, the troops entered Katia, their starting point. Behind them was a trail of dead men and women—for a number of Palestinian Christians had shared their retreat to escape Djezzar's vengeance. They greeted Egypt with delirious joy. The diary of the Syrian campaign kept by the staff of Engineers concludes with these words: 'Egypt, the goal of all our desires, seems to us another France, a second home. Already our cruel memories are fading. We are back with our friends and our comrades, and already past sufferings are forgotten.'[2]

Not all the soldiers forgot their sufferings as quickly as did the authors of the diary. At Es Saliya, on June 9, Bonaparte issued severe orders against 'agitators' in the army. Every battalion commander was requested to make a list of them and forward it to the commander-in-chief. Every time an 'agitator' was guilty of an infraction of discipline, his punishment was to be the double of the usual sentence; every time an 'agitator' was found demoralizing the troops while under fire or during a forced march, he was to be shot without a trial. Thanks to such vigorous measures, the morale soon rose again.

***

On June 14, Bonaparte and the main part of what was left of his army entered Cairo. The wounded and the sick had been carefully distributed in a number of towns, to conceal their true number. Only those in good health took part in the triumphal return.

---

[1] Richardot, Nouveaux Memoires, p. 178

[2] La Jonquière, IV, 609.

It was a triumphal return, staged magnificently by General Dugua, to whom Bonaparte had issued detailed instructions. The army entered through the Bab el-Nasr—the Gate of Victory. On its path, palm leaves had been strewn, and every soldier wore a palm frond stuck in his hat or cap. The members of the Divan, the French garrison and native militia, and all the civil and military authorities of Cairo escorted the victors to Esbekiya Square, with the bands playing and the captured flags in display. The streets were crowded with an immense throng. 'They seemed,' observes Captain Doguereau, 'extremely curious to find out how many there were left of us.'[1]

Everybody taking a part in this show played his role admirably well; nobody was deceived by it.

Ten days after the triumphal entry into Cairo, André Peyrusse, whose memories were still fresh, wrote to his mother his long account of the campaign, which has been quoted abundantly in the preceding pages. 'Today,' Peyrusse concludes, 'the army is resting from its fatigues. Already a proclamation by the commander-in-chief announces more battles to come. When, God, shall we stop this fighting? ... The notes I took down during the Syrian campaign are scrupulously truthful. The report of the commander-in-chief, which I enclose, will prove to you how much a man must lie to be in politics.'[2]

---

[1] La Jonquière, IV, 625
[2] La Jonquière, IV, 625-26

Chapter Ten
The God of War and
The God of Luck?

ON the day he left Acre, Bonaparte had held a staff meeting. | After the conference, Kléber wrote in his private notebook,

'Lost all illusions.'[1] What Bonaparte said to make Kléber lose what few illusions he had left is not known; on the other hand, it is easy to see in retrospect what was on his mind, and all his subsequent actions could only intensify Kléber's disillusionment and contempt.

Having lost his bloody gamble at Acre, Bonaparte had made up his mind to return to Europe at the first opportunity, lest he lose an even bigger stake. To understand his reasoning, it is necessary to return briefly to the origins of the expedition. When Bonaparte determined to undertake it, the European continent was at peace. His inspection of the French armaments against England convinced him that an invasion of the British Isles was doomed, and he had no intention of identifying himself with failure. The only way to get out of this predicament was to put himself at the head of another great enterprise—the expedition to Egypt. At that time, indeed, the enterprise seemed great; Egypt was to become the stage of world history, where he would deal a mortal blow to England, found a colonial empire, and revolutionize world trade. It

---

[1] La Jonquière, IV, 634. 6

was an enterprise worthy of him, and it was hailed in the French press of 1798 as the beginning of a new era.

The loss of the fleet at Abukir, the Ottoman declaration of war, the failure of the French government to send aid, and now the disaster of Acre had changed the picture completely; Egypt was no longer the stage of world history but its backwash, while in Europe momentous decisions were about to be made, both on the battlefield and at the furtive gatherings of conspiring politicians. Egypt and Asia offered no more opportunities, but the mole hill Europe, of which he had spoken so contemptuously only a year before, beckoned him to greater glory. If he remained in Egypt much longer, the opportunity might be lost forever. Egypt had served its purpose as far as he was concerned, though its continued possession might be of some use to France in the event of negotiations for a general peace.

Bonaparte's secret decision to return to Europe was based partly on his appraisal of the local situation, partly on some sparse but significant news he had received from Europe. A few days before leaving Cairo for Syria, he had interviewed a French merchant named Hamelin, who had just arrived from Trieste. It was from Hamelin that he learned of the outbreak of war in Italy, the capture of Rome by the Neapolitan army, the Forte's formal declaration of war on France, and the Russo-Turkish blockade of Corfu. It seemed to Bonaparte that a resumption of general hostilities, involving most of the European powers, was imminent. 'The day he left [for Syria],' asserts Bourrienne, 'he said that if in the course of March he received positive news of France being at war with a European coalition, he would return.'[1]

On March 25, while besieging Acre, Bonaparte received additional information from Wynand Mourveau, who brought him the Directors' letter of November 4. The news in the letter was stale, and although Mourveau could report more recent events, he did not know that France and Austria were once more at war. However, by April 18 Bonaparte had learned from some other source that the French had recaptured Rome and taken Naples, a development which made war with Austria a virtual certainty. This may help to explain Bonaparte's impatience to take Acre at almost any cost, so that he could get the Syrian campaign over, return to Egypt more or less victorious, and go on to bigger things from there.

---

[1] Bourrienne, Vol. II, Ch. XIII. 7

Acre did not fall, but he managed to disguise his failure under some cheap yet effective stage trappings. On June 21, one week after his triumphal entry into Cairo, he instructed Admiral Ganteaume to keep two frigates, *La Muiron* and La Carrère, in constant readiness to leave for France. It was with them that he sailed two months later.

There were several reasons for his spending two more months in Egypt. For one thing, he hoped to be recalled officially; as early as the preceding November, he had sent his brother Louis back to France with the mission of working for his return in cooperation with brothers Joseph and Lucien and possibly also with Talleyrand. A second reason was that he was waiting for more positive news. Moreover, an opportune moment had to be found during which he could slip by the British cruising squadron with relative safety. Lastly, and most important, he was expecting an allied landing on the Egyptian coast. If he could repulse it, he would make Egypt safe from attack for several months to come, and he would return to France with another victory to his credit. The army, of course, would stay behind. It was capable of defending Egypt for at least another year and should be held as a trump in the event of peace negotiations.

In the meantime, he would continue to govern Egypt just as before, and act as if he intended to stay forever.

***

The premises of General Kléber's reasoning were the same as Bonaparte's. He had come to Egypt because he had been convinced of the importance of the enterprise, and he realized the expedition had failed in every purpose save that of preparing the next phase of General Bonaparte's career. Since he was not only indifferent but actively hostile to Bonaparte's ambitions, it seemed to him that the sooner the army was brought back to France, the better. It was needed in France, and it was wasting away in Egypt. The idea of sacrificing thousands of soldiers' lives for the mere sake of holding a diplomatic trump card struck him as an indefensible, a monstrous notion. Bonaparte was a calculating politician, Kléber an emotional soldier. This contrast of point of view and temperament offers the key to all the baffling actions of Bonaparte and of Kléber in the course of the year.

II

Although Bonaparte had announced to the Divan of Cairo that all troubles in Egypt would vanish upon his return like clouds under the sun's first rays, his countenance was anything but sunny when he con fronted the Divan. 'I understand,' he said by way of preamble, 'that according to the rumours spread by my enemies I am dead. Take a good look at me, and make sure that I am really Bonaparte.'[1] If their eyes did not convince them, his actions in the following weeks left no doubt as to his identity.

While Bonaparte was losing half his army in Syria, Desaix had more or less pacified Upper Egypt, and Dugua and Poussielgue, by their tact and moderation, had kept good order in Cairo. The troubles had taken place in Lower Egypt, and they had been suppressed before Bonaparte brought back his sunshine. Apart from the standard Bedouin raids and peasant ambushes, two dangerous rebellions had broken out. They did not lead to anything except the usual massacres, but they were significant in that they demonstrated the continued restlessness of the population and the tenuousness of French control.

The lesser of the two rebellions was provoked by the Emir al-Hadj Mustafa, who was supposed to follow Bonaparte into Syria with the Grand Judge of Cairo, several sheiks, and an escort of Moorish Janissaries. On a number of pretexts, instead of going to Syria, the Emir moved about from place to place in the province of Sharkiya, recruiting, by means of bribes, some 2,000 Bedouin Arabs, who attacked a French convoy and generally threatened the French supply line to Syria. When there could be no more doubt about Mustafa's treason, Dugua sent several detachments to track him and his allies down. By that time, the Cairo sheiks had given Mustafa the slip—more out of caution than out of loyalty to the French—and only the Kadi Asker, or Grand Judge, of Cairo remained with him among the notables. (The Kadi, like the Emir, was an Ottoman Turk.) At the approach of the French punitive forces, Mustafa's Bedouin allies also vanished, with all the money he had given them, and Mustafa, according to General Lanusse's report, 'took the road to Syria and tore out his beard in despair.'[2] Needless to say, neither the Emir nor the Kadi joined Bonaparte in Syria.

The sheiks of Cairo had given the Emir no support, although they sympathized with him. They were prudent men. At the same time they were traditionalists: it was only after considerable pressure had been exerted on him that the Egyptian sheik El-Arishi

---

[1] Nicolas Turc, p. 65. 8
[2] La Jonquière, V, 51. 9

accepted the post of the fugitive Kadi Asker, which since time immemorial had been held by Turks.

The more serious rebellion broke out near Alexandria and was stirred up by a fanatic named Ahmed, a fakir or dervish from Derna, in Libya, who claimed to be the Mahdi—that is, the promised envoy of the Prophet, sent to lead the Faithful in the destruction of the Infidel. (Mahdis kept cropping up in Egypt and in the Sudan every once in a while: the best-known is the one who, several decades later, caused Kitchener so much inconvenience.)

The Mahdi's preachings to the credulous Bedouins and peasants of Beheira soon stirred up the entire province. Practically naked and barely coherent, he impressed his audiences with claims so bold as only a true prophet can be expected to make: he could make the French disintegrate into dust by merely looking at them, stop cannon balls in mid-air, prevent cannons from firing by breathing at them, and transform anything he touched into gold; bullets could do no harm to him or his followers; his body was all spiritual, and he sustained himself by dipping two fingers into a jar of milk once a day and rubbing them over his lips; besides, he was the son of the King of Morocco. The Mahdi's qualifications appealed to the fellahin and desert Arabs, several thou sand of whom he recruited. They took Damanhur on the night of April 24-25, massacred the French garrison, and marched into the Delta. A French punitive expedition caught up with them at Damanhur on May 9. At their first contact with bullets and cannon balls, the Mahdi's followers saw the error of their ways and fled into the desert. As usual, it was against the local population that the French exercised their vengeance: 'Damanhur is no more, and twelve to fifteen hundred of its inhabitants have been burned or shot,' General Lanusse reported to Dugua.[1] It is not sure whether the Mahdi himself escaped or was among the victims.

The Mahdi's rebellion brings to mind a short story Bonaparte had written at the age of nineteen, when he still had literary ambitions. Called 'The Masked Prophet,' it relates the end of an eighth-century Mahdi named Hakim. Blinded in a battle against the Caliph's men, Hakim covers his face with a silver mask to hide his infirmity, while asserting that without the mask his radiance would blind anyone who looked at him. He then persuades his followers to dig a deep trench, into which his enemies would fall when they attacked. This done, he invites his men to a feast, poisons them one and all, drags their corpses into the trench, lights a

---

[1] Ibid., V, 87. 10

huge fire to burn them, and throws himself into the flames. 'This,' young Bonaparte concludes, 'is an incredible example of the extremes to which the mania for fame can push a man.'[1] It is an odd story; considering the author's subsequent career, it seems even odder.

***

Although both rebellions had been suppressed before Bonaparte's return, French soldiers continued to be ambushed, supplies continued to be raided, and Murad Bey was once again on the war path. The plague had abated, but the pox was on the increase, and the French forces were dwindling slowly but surely. In his report of June 29, 1799, to the Directory, Bonaparte admitted having lost 5,344 men since the beginning of the campaign (i.e. about 15 per cent of his land forces) and expected that, in the spring of 1800, there would be only 15,000 men left, 3,000 of them unfit for combat duty. In view of his later polemics with Kléber (who could not answer, being dead), it is good to emphasize these figures, given by Bonaparte himself. For the first time, he mentioned the plague epidemic; for the first time, he asked for reinforcements—a minimum of 6,000 men.

Meanwhile, he resorted to every conceivable device to increase his manpower. In addition to requesting shipments of black slaves from the Sultan of Darfur, he directed that, wherever possible, administrative work should be given to disabled soldiers, and that the administrative employees thus freed from their duties be incorporated into the army. At the same time, he took a sudden interest in the lot of the French soldiers detained at the Citadel of Cairo for various offences and ordered a revision of their sentences. The obvious purpose was to restore as many as possible to active service. Such tenderness was not habitual with him.

As for the Moslem prisoners at the Citadel, Bonaparte set a term to their tribulations by a simple but effective expedient. Between the 19th and the 22nd of June he ordered thirty-two of them to be shot by firing squad, with no other legal formality than his signature. Some of them were prisoners of war taken in Syria, who had outlived their usefulness once they had been paraded in his triumphal procession; others were followers of the Emir al-Hadj; some were Mamelukes who had returned to Cairo without buying safe-conducts from the French authorities. The motives given by Bonaparte for several of the death sentences sound a trifle cava-

---

[1] Masson and Biagi, II, 19.

lier: 'Mohammed el-Tar, accused of speaking against the French, is to be executed.... You will order the execution, Citizen General [Dugua], of the seven men in Omar's company [of Janissaries] whom you have reported to me as obstreperous individuals.'[1] By June 25, General Dugua, a man of benign disposition but obviously exasperated, proposed to Bonaparte: 'Since executions are becoming frequent at the Citadel, I intend to substitute a head-amputator (*un coupeur de têtes*) for the firing squad. This will save us ammunition and make less noise.' 'Agreed,' Bonaparte wrote in the margin.'[2]

It was on July 8 that Bonaparte wrote the most astounding death sentence of this grisly series: 'Citizen General, you will order the beheading of Abdullah Aga, former commandant of Jaffa, now detained at the Citadel. Judging from everything the inhabitants of Syria have told us about him, he is a monster that must be removed from the earth.'[3]

Abdullah Aga, it may be recalled, was the commander of the several thousand Turks whom Bonaparte had had massacred in cold blood on the beach of Jaffa. He had been spared to encourage Djezzar Pasha to surrender and to be displayed to the people of Cairo. Since there was no judicial procedure, it has never been established what had been his crimes in Syria or whether the French were competent to sentence him for them. His head was cut off at dawn on July 9.

The heads were still rolling at the Citadel when, on June 29, Bonaparte convened the first session of the Institute of Egypt since his departure for Syria. The Institute had three of its members to mourn—Caffarelli, Venture, and Horace Say, all three buried below the walls of Acre. It was not to pay tribute to the dead, however, that Bonaparte attended the session, but in order to appoint a committee to make a report on the bubonic plague in Syria. The committee's purpose, he clearly hinted, was to blame the failure of his campaign on it. The one man who could have spoken on the subject with some authority, Dr. Desgenettes, was not nominated to serve on the committee. In the resulting discussion, Bonaparte allowed himself some cheap witticisms at the expense of the medical profession. Desgenettes leapt to his feet and, 'with a vehemence that astounded the numerous audience,' spoke his mind. His

[1] La Jonquière, V, 231.
[2] Ibid
[3] Ibid., V, 233.

crime, he declared, was to have refused to give poison to the plague victims at Jaffa. And there were other things which the General, in his contempt of all principles of morality, had omitted to mention. Ignoring Bonaparte's and Monge's attempts to silence him, Desgenettes went on to fulminate against 'mercenary adulation,' 'Oriental despotism,' and 'armed guards stationed within the very precincts of a peaceful society of scholars.' By this time, the peaceful society of scholars was about to come to blows. 'I know, gentlemen,' Desgenettes continued in a calmer voice, 'I know, General—for you are here in another quality than that of a simple member of the Institute, and you want to lord it over everything—I know that I have been carried away and have said things that will have their repercussions far from here. But I will not retract one single word.... I take refuge in the army's gratitude to me.'[1]

Immediately after this scene, Desgentetes requested authorization to return to France, for reasons of health and family. Bonaparte turned down the request, and the doctor stayed on until the French capitulation of 1801. Apart from this, Bonaparte never took any steps against Desgenettes. As Madame de Staël was to point out, 'He is a man whom true resistance appeases. Those who have borne his despotism are just as guilty as he.'[2]

***

While Bonaparte was killing time in Cairo, waiting for something to do, signing death sentences, sleeping with Madame Fourès, ordering capital levies, and arguing about the plague, Murad Bey, with 200 or 300 men, had become restless in the Kharga Oasis and left it. In a dazzling succession of zigzags and feints, he had dodged all the forces sent to intercept him, entered Beheira province, found it disappointingly calm since the Mahdi's defeat, and doubled back to stop near the Great Pyramids. His purpose, no doubt, was to join the Turkish landing forces whose imminent arrival had been announced to him. On July 13, it seems, Murad and his wife signalled to each other from, respectively, the top of Cheops' Pyramid and the roof of her Cairo mansion. Having learned this, Bonaparte decided that for want of more important things to do, he might as well direct the elusive bey's pursuit in person. To catch the uncatchable would add to his glory.

On July 14, Bonaparte shifted his headquarters to the Pyramids. Murad, of course, was gone by then. On the next morning

---

[1] Victoires, conqultes, X, 313.

[2] Stael, p. 334. 46

Bonaparte, still encamped at the Pyramids, received word from Alexandria that a Turkish fleet had arrived off shore and was about to disembark an army estimated at 12,000 to 13,000 men. It was the army which, in his bulletins from Acre, he claimed to have destroyed; it was also the occasion he had been waiting for. He did not waste a moment. After dictating a series of orders to the commanders of his troops, which were scattered all over Egypt, he broke up the camp at 12.30 p.m. Three days later, he was at El Rahmaniya, a hundred miles to the north, concentrating a striking force against the Turks. The precision of his timing, the speed of the execution, the instantaneous grasp of all the essential elements in the situation border on the miraculous.

On the day Bonaparte looked for Murad at the Pyramids, five Turkish battleships, three frigates, and fifty or sixty transports anchored off Abukir Bay and began to disembark their troops on the beach. With them were several British ships under Commodore Sidney Smith. The Turks stormed a French redoubt east of the village of Abukir, massacred its 300 defenders, laid siege to the fort at the tip of the peninsula, which was held by only thirty-five Frenchmen, and set up camp. Three days later, the garrison of the fort surrendered, having waited in vain for General Marmont to bring succour from Alexandria. Even then, the Turks made no further move but entrenched themselves instead. What their commander, Mustafa Pasha, Seraskier of Rumelia —a venerable, white-bearded man—expected to accomplish in this manner remains a mystery. The position he chose was strong, but all he could do in it was wait to be either driven or starved out.

While the Turks squatted, the French moved. On July 24, nine days after receiving news of the Turkish landing, Bonaparte had assembled close to 10,000 French troops in the vicinity of Abukir. Although Kléber's division had not yet reached the rendezvous, he ordered the Turkish camp to be attacked the next morning. This may seem rash—or bold—to those who accept the figures Bonaparte gave later for the strength of the Turkish forces; it seems perfectly normal, however, if one realizes that in fact the number of Turks was equal or even inferior to that of the French, that the Turks had no cavalry, and that Bonaparte had a thousand horse.[1]

During the night, Bonaparte summoned General Murat, who commanded the cavalry, to his tent. After discussing his plans for the attack, he exclaimed, 'This battle will decide the fate of the world.' Murat was dumbfounded. 'Well, at any rate,' he answered, 'it will decide the fate of the army.'[2] This was not what Bonaparte had in mind; he was already thinking of France, and he had begun to identify his personal career with world history.

The French began their attack in the early morning. The Turkish position was strong. Three successive lines of entrenchments cut across the neck of Abukir Peninsula, allowing only a direct frontal attack, and the gunboats off shore lent them effective support. At the same time, it was a perilous position, since it left the Turks no retreat except into the small fort at the tip of the peninsula or into the sea. Bonaparte's victory was due largely to the impetuosity of his attack, which forced the Turks back despite their very brave resistance. The decisive moment came shortly after midday, when Murat's cavalry charged with such speed and momentum that it reached the fort within a matter of minutes, while two infantry battalions led by Lannes were still dislodging the Turks from their main redoubt. From that moment, the battle turned into a shambles. Some thousand Turks managed to reach the fort; about 2,000 were cut down with sabres and bayonets; at least twice that number sought to swim to their ships and either drowned or were shot from the shore. Among the few who reached the ship was a young officer who rose to fame not many years later as the Khedive Mehemet Ali, founder of modern Egypt and of a dynasty that ended not too gloriously with King Farouk.

***

---

[1] 'We have only 7,000 men fit for combat,' Mustafa wrote to his government on the eve of the battle. Bonaparte himself, in his letter of July 28 to the Directory, says that 9,000 Turks were killed, and that this meant virtually the entire Turkish army; it was only in his second report (August 2) that he raised the figure to 18,000. Sir Sidney Smith gives the Turkish strength as 7,000; Smith's secretary, as 8,000-9,000; Kléber, as 9,000. All standard history books and reference works, however, persist in accepting Napoleon's inflated figure, which goes to show that it pays to lie.

[2] La Jonquière, V, 405. 51

By one o'clock, the battle was over. 'This was one of the most beautiful battles I ever saw,' Bonaparte wrote to Dugua; he called it 'the most terrible sight I ever saw' in his report to the Directors.[1]

It was Murat in person—according to most accounts—who captured the Turkish commander-in-chief. Before surrendering, Mustafa wounded Murat's lower jaw with a pistol shot, but Murat knocked the weapon out of the pasha's hand with his sabre, taking a couple of fingers with it. Bonaparte received the defeated pasha most courteously and even bandaged the old man's hand with his handkerchief—a kindness that was not wasted, for Mustafa was to do the French more than one good turn before his death a year later.

In the fort, about 2,500 Turks, commanded by Mustafa's son, continued to resist. On the morning after his victory, Bonaparte called on the captive pasha in his tent and persuaded him to join in an appeal to the garrison, promising it safe passage to the Turkish ships if it surrendered. The pasha's son and his chief officers agreed to the pro position, but the men, mindful of what Bonaparte had done at Jaffa, mutinied and insisted on defending their lives to the end. They held out for a week, despite the most incredible hardships. On August 2, with a thousand of them dead—many, crazed by thirst, had tried to drink sea water—the rest came out at last. 'They looked like ghosts,' says Sergeant François. 'They all bowed down and asked for death.... We gave them water and food.'[2] The Turks gorged themselves so ravenously that 400 of them died of indigestion even before they were evacuated to Alexandria.

In the week's fighting, the French had 220 men killed and about 750 wounded. Compared to the Turkish losses, these were few casualties, but the Turks could replace them easily, whereas the French could not. As Sidney Smith wrote to Lord Nelson, 'Under these untoward circumstances, we have the satisfaction of observing the enemy's losses to be such that a few more victories like this will annihilate the French army.'[3] In other words, all England had to do was sacrifice about 100,000 more Turks, and there would not be a Frenchman left in Egypt.

---

[1] Correspondance, V, 537, 541. 52

[2] François, I, 359. 53

[3] Barrow, I, 364. 54

Sir Sidney's report to Nelson was dated August 2, 1799. On August 2, 1798, in the same Abukir Bay, Nelson had dictated the victory bulletin beginning with the words, 'Almighty God has made me the happy instrument in destroying the Enemy's Fleet.' In his account of the second battle of Abukir, Sir Sidney had nothing to say of Almighty God, who had been fickle on this particular occasion. 'I am sorry,' he wrote instead, ' to have to acquaint your lordship of the entire defeat of the first division of the Ottoman army.'[1] It was Bonaparte's turn to invoke the Almighty's name in vain. Back in Cairo on August 11, he received the Divan's congratulations on his victory. The sheiks' simulated joy did not conceal their consternation: they had counted on the destruction of the French. Bonaparte eyed them coldly while his interpreter read his message to them. He was astounded by their discomfiture. Had he not told them time and again that he was a true Moslem, that he hated the Christians, whose altars and crosses he had overthrown, and that he had abjured his former faith? Would God grant him victory upon victory if he were not His chosen instrument? And yet, despite all this, the sheiks had stubbornly questioned his sincerity but the day would come when they would 'disinter the bones of the French in order to wet them with their tears.'

Though troubled and terrified by this outburst, the sheiks continued to be sceptical in private. 'All this,' Nicholas the Turk quotes them as saying, 'is mere ruse and deceit, designed to soften us up. Bonaparte is just a Christian, the son of a Christian.'[2]

Even as he was chiding the sheiks for doubting his sincerity, Bonaparte was secretly preparing his departure. A week later, he was gone. A year later, he restored the Roman Catholic Church in France.

***

After his victory at Abukir, Bonaparte had sent two officers aboard H.M.S. *Tigre* to arrange for an exchange of prisoners with Sir Sidney Smith. The ever-courteous Sir Sidney had presented them with two sets of European newspapers. In them, Bonaparte read the news up to June 10—precisely the bad news he had been waiting for: on every front, France was on the brink of disaster. According to his own account of the story—which has been parroted by nearly every history text-toot—Bonaparte decided then and there that he must return to France and save her from the de-

---

[1] Ibid. 55
[2] Nicolas Turc, p. 78. 56

feat and anarchy into which a handful of lawyers and politicians were plunging her.

There is just enough truth in this version to commend it to the kind of historians who like to present their facts simply. Smith *did* send the papers to Bonaparte; the news was bad; Bonaparte did return to France and save her from anarchy and defeat. Since he succeeded, he was right. (Historians are lenient to those who succeed and stern with those who fail; in this, and this alone, they display strong political sense.) The facts, of course, are that Bonaparte had only been waiting for this news in order to leave; that his exclamations of shock and dismay at the incompetence of French generals and politicians, genuine though they were, concealed an equally strong dose of delight; and that he was terrified lest someone other than he should pick the overripe pear that was waiting for him. So convinced was he of the need France had for him, he wrote to the Directors, that he braved the danger of capture by the British, and if he had not had his frigates to take him back, he would have wrapped himself in his cloak and sailed on a bark.

The question whether his motive in returning was to save France or to save his career is meaningless. A man's motives must be judged on the basis of his entire character. To Bonaparte, he and France were one and the same thing. He could not be great without her; he would make her great. 'Power is my mistress,' he said once; and, on another occasion, to the same interlocutor, 'I have only one passion, only one mistress, and that is France: I sleep with her. She has never failed me.... If I need five hundred thousand men, she gives them to me.'[1] France and Power were merely two different pet names for the same mistress, and it was to conquer that mistress that he was about to leave Egypt and his army, just as a lover quits a passing amour for the sake of a great love.

Others, of course, saw his action in a different light. Some spoke of desertion. Whether or not Bonaparte had the right to return alone and without specific authorization from his government is a question that may be debated forever. If a military tribunal had tried him, its decision would have rested on reasons of expediency rather than of justice. From the moral point of view, Bonaparte may be absolved from responsibility toward a government that had given him only ambiguous advice and no help, and the problem may be reduced to this simple question: to whom was Bonaparte responsible—to what he called his destiny or to his

[1] Roederer, pp. 212, 240.

men? Both generals—Bonaparte and Kléber—answered this question unambiguously, each for himself.

***

Among the news that Bonaparte gathered from the papers sent him by Sidney Smith was that France and Austria had been at war since March; that the French were being driven out of Germany by Archduke Charles and out of Italy by Marshal Suvarov, and that the French government were moving from one political and economic crisis to another, with the probable prospect of a complete overthrow of the Republic. On the positive side, he learned that the French Atlantic fleet, commanded by the Minister of Marine, Admiral Bruix, had entered the Mediterranean and was at Toulon, and that a Spanish squadron under Admiral Mazarredo had left Cadiz and was at Cartagena. This last bit of news, which presaged a joint Franco-Spanish action in the Mediterranean, should perhaps have induced Bonaparte to remain in Egypt in order to await its issue. It did not so induce him, and the outcome of Bruix's expedition tended to justify him.

Bruix's original instructions were to co-operate with the Spanish fleet in supplying beleaguered Malta and Corfu and then to bring supplies and several thousand reinforcements to Alexandria. On June 22, after helping to evacuate French troops from various Italian ports, Bruix joined Mazarredo at Cartagena. The combined Franco-Spanish fleet comprised forty-two battleships. Since the sixty English ships of the line in the Mediterranean were scattered among several squadrons, Bruix had a unique opportunity to expel the British from that sea and to take his fleet to Egypt.

Meanwhile, on May 26, the directory had issued new instructions to Bruix and Bonaparte: in view of the alarming Austrian and Russian victories, France had to concentrate her forces; Bruix was to use every possible means to gain temporary control over the Mediterranean and to evacuate the French army from Egypt. 'You yourself, Citizen General,' Talleyrand wrote to Bonaparte, 'will be able to judge whether you can safely leave behind a part of your forces, and the Directory authorizes you, in that event, to entrust your command to anyone you see fit.'[1] Needless to say, it would have been impossible for Bonaparte to leave part of his forces behind safely. As it turned out, the question remained purely academic, since Mazarredo refused to co-operate in any enterprise save the reconquest of Minorca from the English. Bruix appealed

---

[1] La Jonquière, V, 166. 58

to the Spanish government; the Spanish government upheld Mazarredo and ordered him back into the Atlantic, where Bruix followed him. Thus the last chance of gaining mastery over the Mediterranean was lost without a single shot being fired.

Probably the two most remarkable events in Admiral Mazarredo's life were his offering 500,000 francs a month to a dancer
for being his mistress and his refusal to co-operate with Bruix in
1799. If he had been more co-operative and presented himself with
Bruix and forty-two ships of the line before Alexandria in late July
or early August 1799, the consequences in all likelihood would
have been momentous. Among other things, Bonaparte would
have been faced with the choice of returning to France with his
army or refusing to evacuate Egypt. In either case, history would
have taken a somewhat different course.

Bonaparte stayed in Cairo for only a week from August 11,
when he returned from Abukir, to August 18, when he left for
good. Only five of the men whom he had selected to take with him
to France were in his confidence: Admiral Ganteaume (who had
remained in Alexandria to prepare the departure), General Berthier, Bourrienne, Monge, and Berthollet. Of those who were to stay
behind, not one—not even his successor—was forewarned. In fact,
every precaution was taken to avoid giving alarm. Until the last
day, Bonaparte busied him self with routine matters—the fortifications of Es Saliya and El Arishj the appointment of two scientific
committees, to be headed by Fourier and Costaz, for the systematic exploration of the monuments of Upper Egypt; the accelera-
tion of tax collecting; the issue of new cloth uniforms to the entire
army. (The series of orders issued for that last purpose specified
every detail except how to pay the contractors.) On August 15 he
celebrated the Feast of the Prophet with the usual pomp and dined
at the house of the sheik El-Bekri, with Mustafa Pasha and the
other high Turkish officers captured at Abukir attending as guests
of honour and all agog at the sight of Bonaparte performing the
ritual prayers with the sheiks.

On August 17, Ganteaume reported that the Anglo-Turkish
fleet had left Egyptian waters, presumably to renew their supplies
in Cyprus; the coast, for the next few days, could be expected to
stay relatively clear. Bonaparte decided to leave Cairo that very
night. To forestall rumours, he had announced his imminent departure for a tour of inspection in the Delta, but his last instructions to Poussielgue suggested that his absence might be prolonged. 'I urge you to take energetic measures to speed up the collection of rents and taxes; ... to remain on good terms with the

sheiks; and to maintain order in Cairo. I urge General Dugua to strike hard at the first sign of trouble. Let him chop off six heads per day, but always keep smiling.'[1]

On the same day he wrote to the Grand Vizier a letter of which more will have to be said later. It offered peace: 'What the Porte can never attain by force of arms, it can achieve by negotiation.... You want Egypt, I understand. But France never intended to take her away from you... , Everything can be settled in a couple of hours' talk.'[2]

At 10 p.m. Bonaparte's carriage called for Monge and Berthollet at the headquarters of the Institute of Egypt. For several days, the Institute had been buzzing with rumours of the commander-in-chief's imminent departure for France. The savants, assembled in the dining hall when the carriage was announced, were aghast to see their two most eminent colleagues sprint away to pack their trunks. A barrage of questions broke loose as soon as Monge and Berthollet came back down stairs. 'Well, Citizen Monge,' asked Costaz, 'shall we hold our next meeting in the ruins of Thebes?' (There had been some talk of Bonaparte visiting Upper Egypt.) Monge, in his embarrassment, became incoherent: 'Yes, we shall meet at Dandara—at-above-below Dandara.' 'Will you pass through Damietta?' enquired Parseval-Grandmaison. 'I don't know a thing,' Monge stammered; 'I believe we're going to Lower Egypt.' At last, pressed by Costaz and Fourier, who pursued him and Berthollet all the way to the carriage, Monge let four-fifths of the cat out of the bag. 'My friends,' he said, 'if we are leaving for France, I assure you we knew nothing about it until noon today.'[3] The members of the Institute were still discussing this strange reply when one of them —Parseval—was already packing his bags. It was the first time he had shown any activity since his arrival in Egypt: he, at least, would not be left behind if he could help it.

Shortly before midnight, Monge and Berthollet joined Bonaparte in the garden of Elfi Bey's palace. Denon, also among the chosen, was there too. Strolling up and down, Bonaparte chatted casually with the savants; every once in a while he would leave them to join and amicably pinch Madame Fourès, who, dressed in a hussar's tunic and tight trousers, was strolling along another path, suspecting nothing. Bonaparte's stepson, Eugène Beauhar-

---

[1] Ibid., V, 576. 59

[2] Correspondance, V, 565. 60

[3] Jomard, p. 54. 61

nais, and three other aides-de-camp—Duroc, Lavalette, and Merlin—who were of the party, also stood in readiness. So did Bourrienne and a new member of the household, who from that moment until 1814 practically never left Napoleon's side.

Napoleon's famous Mameluke, the Armenian Roustam Raza, was then about nineteen years old. He had been kidnapped at the age of seven by what he calls, in his quaint memoirs, 'un marchand de petits enfants.' After a number of traumatic experiences, he was brought to Constantinople and to Cairo, by a route no other traveller—with the possible exception of Lewis Carroll's Bellman [1]—can conceivably have taken: 'We passed the very dangerous straits where the Nile re-enters the Black Sea and where the two rivers knock against each other,' declares Roustam.[2] In Cairo, he was bought by Salih Bey, then the Emir al-Hadj, who took him to Mecca in 1797. On the return journey, Salih learned that the French had taken Egypt and decided to join Ibrahim Bey in Syria; he made the mistake of going on to Acre in order to seek reconciliation with his old arch-enemy, Djezzar Pasha. Djezzar offered him a cup of coffee, and Salih died half an hour later. Disguised as a peasant, Roustam made his way to Cairo, where he found 'many French troops, and handsome old grenadiers with big moustaches.'[3]

Eventually he found service in the household of the sheik El-Bekri, who 'held a high post in the civilian department.' El-Bekri's wives pampered him, and El-Bekri did to him what he should have done to his wives, until another young Mameluke attracted his favours. There were scenes of dissension, and when Bonaparte returned from Syria in June 1799, El-Bekri presented him with Roustam, along with a fine black stallion. Henceforth, always dressed in Mameluke clothes, Roustam served Napoleon as bodyguard, valet, and procurer. His figure became almost as familiar as that of the Emperor himself, and he has been immortalized in many a painting, astride a prancing horse by his master's side. Having acquired a handsome fortune by means of intimidation and influence-peddling, Roustam left his master just before his abdication without so much as a goodbye, married a French girl, and wrote his memoirs, which reveal a naïve, illiterate, shrewd, and bullying lackey.

---

[1] The captain in the mock-epic poem "The Hunting of the Snark" by Lewis Carroll. Navigation is not one of the Bellman's skills.— [Ed.]

[2] Roustam, p. 35. 62

[3] Ibid., p. 43. 63

In addition to the three academicians, his four aides-de-camp, his secretary, his Mameluke, and his cook, Bonaparte had picked several generals to accompany him on his journey—his chief of staff Berthier, already palpitating at the prospect of his reunion with Madame Visconti, and Generals Andréossy, Lannes, Marmont, and Murat, who joined him after his departure from Cairo. A detachment of Guides, commanded by the future Marshal Bessières, was to form the escort. All of these were young men and devoted to him, unlike most of the senior generals whom he left behind.

Pauline Fourès was not of the party. When all was ready, Bonaparte bade her farewell with a casual pat and kiss. Then the small group rode off to Bulaq, where they took ship at three in the morning. It was thus unceremoniously—*sans tambour ni trompette*, as the French saying goes—that the hero slipped away from the capital and from the mistress he had conquered. The 'most ideal time' of his life was over.

Bonaparte and his suite arrived at Alexandria on August 22. They did not enter the city but halted a few miles to the east, somewhere between the present Sporting Club and Montazah Palace. Here, on the beach, they were joined by Admiral Ganteaume and General Marmont, who came from Alexandria, and by General Menou, who had been summoned from Rosetta.

On the horizon, the sails of a presumably English ship were clearly visible. She was going east, at a fast clip. Ganteaume urged Bonaparte to take ship that very night, lest the British return before he could leave. *La Muiron* and *La Carrère* had already sailed out of the New Port and were anchored off shore.

While waiting for the sun to set, Bonaparte paced up and down with General Menou, whom he let into the secret only then and to whom he handed a parcel of papers. It contained a terse proclamation to the army, a letter to the Divan, and a set of instructions for Kléber. Kléber him self, during that time, was racing from Damietta to Rosetta, where Bonaparte had ordered him to be on August 24 to confer 'on some matters of extreme importance.'[1] On August 24, of course, Bonaparte was already on the open sea: the hero had not dared to face his unwitting and unwilling successor.

Both in his proclamation to the soldiers and in his letter to the Divan, Bonaparte promised to return shortly. This may have been politic, but it was hardly honest.

---

[1] Correspondance, V, 569. 64

Night fell—it falls early in Egypt—and still the sloops had not arrived to take the passengers to their ships. It was a moonless night: at the risk of arousing suspicion, the travellers lit flares to guide the sloops. At about eight o'clock, they arrived at last, and an hour later Bonaparte went aboard *La Muiron*. There was not a breath of wind. Supper was served, and the party proceeded to the dining room.

No wind could be expected before sunrise, and the ships remained at anchor through the night. At five in the morning a boat pulled along side *La Muiron;* Parseval-Grandmaison, the indefatigable and homesick translator of Tasso and Camoëns, had made it in the nick of time. At first, Bonaparte absolutely refused to admit him on board. He held a particular grudge against Parseval, who had refused to edit the *Courrier de L'Egypte* or to write a single poem in his honour; instead, almost as if out of malice, Parseval had begun work on an epic poem glorifying the capture of Acre by Richard Coeur de Lion—a subject that must have made Bonaparte wince for more reasons than one. However, with Monge and Berthollet pleading in their colleague's favour, Bonaparte relented and, with a cheap joke, allowed the poet to board La *Carrère*. At 8 a.m. the flotilla set sail. By noon, the arid dunes and sparse palm trees of the Egyptian coast had vanished from view.

III

Bonaparte's journey took forty-seven days. It was uneventful. Admiral Ganteaume, who commanded the flotilla—two frigates and two courier shipskept his course close to the Barbary coast until he came opposite Sardinia. These waters were relatively free of English cruisers; the danger of capture was greatest on the last lap of the journey.

Undoubtedly Bonaparte needed a little luck to reach France without falling into English hands, but the danger has been considerably exaggerated by Bonaparte and by most historians after him. The two frigates were heavily armed: unless they blundered into a superior enemy squadron, they risked meeting only individual English cruisers, which they could easily outshoot. The risk was worth the stake, for even if Bonaparte had been captured, he would have been no worse off, from the point of view of his career, than he would have been in Egypt. And yet even anti-Bonapartist historians keep repeating that he risked his life for the sake of returning—a claim that does not stand up for a minute to common sense.

Far greater were the dangers he faced once back in France. There lay the real risk. He might be given a hero's welcome and swept into the government on a wave of enthusiasm, or he might be shot as a deserter. He was prepared to meet any contingency, but he could make no plans until he had familiarized himself with the situation. 'To be great means to be dependent on everything,' he told his travel companions. 'As for me, I depend on events, and events depend on chance.'[1]

The political situation he was to find in France had been extremely fluid for several months.

Under the Constitution of 1795—a grotesque structure devised for the protection of politicians and profiteers—France was governed by an executive board of five Directors, to whom the cabinet ministers were responsible, and by a legislature consisting of two chambers the Council of Ancients and the Council of Five Hundred. Both chambers were chosen by a small electorate based on narrow property qualifications. The Directors had nothing in common except mutual detestation and distrust and a tendency to kick each other out of office. In the Council of Ancients, the centre and the moderate and royalist right predominated; in the Council of Five Hundred —of which Bonaparte's brother Lucien was a member—the Jacobin left still constituted a powerful minority that threatened to sweep the centre to its side.

The military disasters of the spring of 1799 and a number of highly unpopular fiscal measures placed the Directory under the cross fire of both right and left. At the same time—on May 16—the most outspoken critic of the existing Constitution was elected to replace one of the Directors. That man was Sieyès, a former priest, who had been the chief spokesman of the insurgent middle class in 1789. He passed for a profound political theorist. From the day of his election, Sieyès concentrated all his efforts on the overthrow of his own government. What France needed, he argued to those in his confidence, was a stronger and more stable authority. Depending on whose support he was trying to enlist, he hinted either at a three-man Executive and a Legislature made tame and manageable by various devices, or at a constitutional monarchy.

Three out of his four colleagues in the Directory stood in Sieyès' way; so did the leftist bloc in the Council of Five Hundred. The clever thing to do was to use that leftist bloc in order to unseat

----

[1] Ollivier, p. 131. 65

the three Directors. For that purpose Sieyès needed a willing tool in the Council of Five Hundred. He found it in Lucien Bonaparte.

The one Director whom Sieyès did not wish to displace was Barras, ex-nobleman, ex-lover of Josephine Beauharnais, present lover of Madame Tallien and of every handsome young man he could put his hands on, venal and rotten to the fingertips, once a rabid Jacobin, now a crypto-monarchist. He had been negotiating for several months with the exiled King of France, Louis XVIII, to restore him on the throne, in exchange for a gratuity of 12 million francs. Though aware of Barras' activities, Sieyès did not mention them to Lucien. For the time being, it suited his scheme to keep Barras, who could be bought off easily at any time.

Lucien performed his mission well. A series of parliamentary attacks resulted in the replacement of the Director Treilhard by Gohier on June 17, of Merlin by Ducos on June 19, and of La Revellière-Lépaux by General Moulins on June 20. Ducos was to make common cause with Sieyès in the following months: Gohier, whose main distinction it was to have been Minister of Justice during the Reign of Terror, was to prove an obstacle, but not a very stubborn one; as for Moulins, who was totally unknown, he possessed the merit of being on excellent terms with the radical wing of the Jacobins without sharing their ardour. In the weeks following, several cabinet ministers were also replaced. General Bernadotte, officially an ardent Jacobin, became Minister of War; Robert Lindet, once a member of Robespierre's Committee of Public Safety, became Minister of Finance; and the ex-monk Fouché, who had played a not inconsiderable part in the Reign of Terror, became Minister of Police. In appointing three notorious Jacobins to these posts, Sieyès and Barras expected to lull the leftist opposition without much danger to themselves. One of Fouché's first actions was to close down the Jacobin Club. To make a rightist coup d'état look like a leftist one was no mean feat, but Sieyès had managed it.

A fourth minister had to resign on July 20—Talleyrand. His downfall—which was about as real as the murder of a stage king—was the result of the combined propaganda efforts of the Jacobins and of the English. Ever since Nelson's victory at the Nile, the English government had encouraged the notion that the Directory had sent General Bonaparte and his army to certain destruction in Egypt simply to be rid of them. It was for the purpose of lending some plausibility to this line of propaganda that Pitt arranged for the publication of the intercepted letters written by the French in Egypt. The editor of these letters, whose footnotes are longer than the text proper, neglected nothing to hammer home the point that Bonaparte's army had been deliberately sacrificed. To counteract the propaganda, the French government also had the letters published, with footnotes refuting the footnotes of the English editor. Nevertheless, when the French armies were being routed on every front in Europe, the Jacobin patriots seized that opportunity to accuse the Directory of laxness and treason, and incidentally brought up the charge that the Directors had 'deported into the deserts of Arabia forty thousand men—the élite of our troops, General Bonaparte, and the cream of our savants, scholars and artists.'[1] The same people who had hailed the Egyptian expedition as the beginning of a new era and as a revolution in world commerce (already then the Suez Canal had captivated the public imagination) now were suddenly denouncing it as a folly or even a conspiracy.

The chief instigator of the Egyptian scheme was, of course, Talleyrand. At first, however, the attack was directed mainly against Barras, the only Director left in power of the five who had approved the expedition. Barras stopped the attack simply by privately pointing out to Lucien Bonaparte certain irregularities in his election, which Barras had chosen to overlook but which ___. A word to the wise was enough for Lucien. Henceforth, the attacks singled out Talleyrand. Talleyrand denied all responsibility, claiming that he had inherited the Egyptian scheme from his predecessor in the Foreign Office—a classic line of argument, especially among French cabinet ministers. The predecessor, Charles Delacroix, vigorously rejected this charge in the press, as well he might. (It is piquant to note that Talleyrand, who credited Delacroix with the Egyptian project, has himself been credited—on much better grounds—with the paternity of Delacroix's son Eugène, the painter.)

Unwilling to pursue the argument, Talleyrand resigned. However, he appointed his own successor, who was entirely his man, the French ambassador to Switzerland, Reinhard. Pending Reinhard's return, Talleyrand remained at his post until September 5. During that period he drew up a memorandum, approved by the Directory on September 10, which recommended that negotiations be opened with the Ottoman Porte, through the good offices of the Spanish ambassador in Constantinople, for the purpose of restoring Egypt to Turkish control and of evacuating the French army.

---

[1] Ibid., p. 121. 66

By September 10, General Bonaparte had been at sea for eighteen days on his way to France. He, too, had started negotiations with the Porte, but he had not waited to be evacuated.

In order to carry out his coup d'état—or constitutional reform, as he put it—the ex-abbé Sieyès needed not only a docile legislature but also what he called 'a sword.' In the jargon of the time, a sword meant a kind of bravo, a general willing to lend his muscle to a politician's not entirely constitutional schemes. When the time was ripe, a decree of the Council of Ancients would give the general command over the forces of the interior; his troops would encourage the legislature to vote in the desired way; and, this accomplished, the politician would reward the general with anything save a share in the government. The general on whom Sieyès and Lucien Bonaparte pinned their hopes was Joubert, who was handed the command of the French forces in Italy on July 28. Joubert was a wise choice: he passed for a good republican, he secretly enjoyed the confidence of the royalist exiles, he was willing to play his part, and he was less dangerous than either Bernadotte or Bonaparte. Unfortunately, on August 15, Joubert was defeated by Suvarov at Novi and was killed in the battle. France had a new hero, but Sieyès had lost his sword. Sieyès was disconsolate. 'We are lost,' he cried. 'We'll never find another general who can reconquer Italy and, at the same time, help us overthrow the government in co-operation with the royalists.'[1] One sympathizes with Sieyès, for although another sword was on its way from Alexandria, that sword was too big for him to handle.

Bonaparte was still somewhere off the Barbary coast, and Barras and Sieyès were still pursuing their separate conspiracies in uneasy co operation, when General Bernadotte, the Minister of War, was plotting a coup d'état on his own account. His plan was simply to have Barras and Sieyès arrested and to set up a Jacobin regime with himself at its head. For this purpose that staunch republican, who was to end up as King of Sweden, had enlisted the co-operation of General Jourdan, a deputy in the Council of Five Hundred. On September 15 Jourdan, after painting a grim picture of the military situation abroad and of royalist plots at home, invited his colleagues to pass a motion declaring a state of national emergency. Passing the motion would have been tantamount to deposing the Directory. It is true that three out of the five Directors also wanted to depose the Directory, but they wanted to do the deposing themselves. The moment was critical; Lucien Bona-

---

[1] Ibid., p. 130. 67

parte saved the situation. Certainly the Republic was in danger, he admitted. However, an official declaration to that effect was no solution. 'When a state is in danger, it can be saved only by strengthening the existing government or by changing it.' There were cries of 'Set up a dictatorship!' 'I hear the word " dictatorship,"' Lucien continued solemnly. 'There is not one among us who would not be ready to plunge his dagger into the first man who should dare to want to be the dictator of France.'[1] The phrase was greeted by unanimous, though largely reluctant, applause; it was to be recalled in a different spirit on another occasion, two months later.

The danger was past, and the session was adjourned without a vote on the motion. One hour before midnight, Bernadotte resigned as Minister of War.

***

On September 30, Bonaparte's flotilla was just outside the harbour of his native city of Ajaccio, in Corsica. On the same day, at Zurich, General Masséna defeated the Austro-Russian forces, thereby turning the tide of the war. Suvarov began his epic retreat through the Alps, and soon afterwards Tsar Paul declared Russia's neutrality. It was an unfortunate coincidence for Bonaparte: the indispensable man had become a little less indispensable.

On October 1, *La Muiron* cast anchor at Ajaccio. In no time she was surrounded by a multitude of boats carrying half the local population. Ignoring the quarantine rules, the crowd poured aboard the frigate to cheer the native hero. Among them was a little elderly woman, dressed in black and highly excited. 'Caro figlio!' she shouted. 'Madre!' cried Bonaparte. She was his wetnurse: a touching moment. Not a single government official turned up, however. The reason for their absence, it was explained to the astonished Bonaparte, was that the municipal and departmental officers had thrown each other in jail; the political confusion in Paris was reflected at Ajaccio in a peculiarly Corsican manner.

The flotilla left Ajaccio on October 7 and sighted the French coast the next evening, along with an English squadron of twenty-two sail, Admiral Keith's fleet. The Englishmen went on their way, ignoring the French: they had seen them, but in the dusk they had mistaken them for two of their own frigates. By such threads history hangs. In the morning of October 9, Bonaparte landed at Fréjus. Again the quarantine regulations were ignored, Bonaparte

---

[1] Ibid., p. 137. 68

was carried in triumph to the town, and an hour later a carriage stood ready for him. After a week's triumphal procession, Bonaparte drove up before his house in Paris, rue de la Victoire, on October 16, at 6 a.m. The bulletin of his victory at Abukir had preceded him by just a few days.

In the evening of October 13, while Lyons was illuminated in honour of General Bonaparte, the General's wife was dining in Paris with President Gohier of the Directory. They were still at table when a telegraphic message was brought in: Bonaparte had landed. Gohier was thunderstruck; Josephine was in consternation. 'I must meet him on the way,' she stammered. 'It is very important for me to head off his brothers, who have always detested me.'[1] And off she went.

Josephine had every reason to be concerned. Apart from her open affair with Citizen Charles, she had contracted several hundred thousand francs' worth of debts, and if Bonaparte divorced her, she would not have a penny to her name. So eager was she to rush into her husband's arms that she took the wrong road and missed him.

The same evening (October 13), in another apartment of the Luxembourg Palace, where the Directors had their residence, Sieyès also received the telegram announcing Bonaparte's return. 'Too late,' he muttered to Lucien, who was with him. Indeed, since Joubert's untimely death, the pair had settled on General Moreau to serve them as a sword. But Moreau was not eager. When he arrived a little later and heard the news, 'Well,' he remarked drily, 'there's your man. He'll make a better job of your coup d'état than I could.' No question about it; but, as Lucien remarks in his memoirs, although Sieyès needed a sword, 'that of Moreau, Jourdan, or Joubert would have answered his need.... Bonaparte's sword was too long.'[2]

Those who rely on Nicholas the Turk for their information on European history—their number must be small—will emerge from their studies with a highly original version of Bonaparte's rise to power. 'At the news of his return,' says Nicholas, 'the five heads of the French government decreed that Bonaparte was a rebel ... and that he be deprived of his rank and obliged to stand guard duty as a simple private at the door of the [legislative] assembly.... He

---

[1] Gohier, I, 199. 69
[2] Ollivier, p. 152. 70

submitted and was a sentry at the door of the Divan until he took steps to overthrow it.'[1]

This may not be history, but it missed being so by a narrow margin. The Directory met on October 14—two days before Bonaparte arrived in Paris to discuss what to do with him. 'Well,' grumbled Sieyès, 'it's just one more general. But, before we go any further, has the general been authorized by the government to come back?' The deputy Boulay de la Meurthe, who was present at the discussion, offered to move that Bonaparte be outlawed.

'But,' squirmed Sieyès, 'this would mean shooting him—which would be a serious matter, though he deserves it.' 'These are details I don't want to go into,' replied Boulay. 'Once he has been outlawed, let him be guillotined, shot, or hanged, I don't care which—it's just a formality of execution.'[2] (One week later, the same Boulay de la Meurthe joined the circle of Bonaparte's intimate advisers who urged him to seize the power.)

The reaction of the Council of Five Hundred to the news of Bonaparte's return was such that there could be no more question—in the immediate future, at least—of shooting Bonaparte or even of putting him on guard duty. The deputies, dressed in their quaint robes and toques, greeted the announcement with an ovation, while the band struck up a patriotic hymn. (Indeed, that strange parliament had an orchestra in readiness to punctuate its patriotic seizures.) In the evening of October 14, all Paris was illuminated. To the public, the name Bonaparte still stood for victory and, especially, peace.

The popular enthusiasm cannot be said to have infected the Directory. On the evening of his arrival, Bonaparte called on its President, Gohier, whose weakness for Madame Bonaparte did not extend to her husband. (Madame Bonaparte, at that time, was still looking for her husband on the highways.) 'The news that reached me in Egypt was so alarming,' said the General, 'that I did not hesitate to leave my army in order to share your dangers. 'Ah yes, nodded Gohier, the dangers had been great, but luckily they were over. General Brune had repulsed the English in Holland, Masséna had beaten the Austro-Russians at Zurich, 'and you come just in time to celebrate the victories of your comrades in arms.'[3]

---

[1] Nicolas Turc, p. 120. 71

[2] Barras, IV, 29. 72

[3] Ollivier, p. 156. 73

The next day, dressed in his plainest uniform, Bonaparte reported officially to the Directors, resplendent in their pseudo-Roman mantles and tricoloured ostrich plumes. He was putting himself at their service, Bonaparte told them modestly at the head of an army if they gave him one, or as a simple artillery man. He did not mention guard duty. The Directors responded coolly and noncommittally, but they did not dare question the legality of his return.

More setbacks were in store before the final triumph. The first of these was domestic. On October 18 Josephine returned at last. Bonaparte, after ordering all her belongings to be placed in the entrance hall, locked himself up in his room and told her to get out. The whole day long, she knocked at his door, crying and pleading. All in vain: he was determined to divorce her. At last, prompted by her maid, she tried a new line of attack. Her children, Eugène and Hortense, were thrown into the trenches; they made a breach through which Josephine entered victoriously. In the morning, Lucien—Josephine's chief enemy—called on his brother, expecting to find his sister-in-law routed and in full flight; instead, he found them in bed together. At least, so the story goes. It takes little imagination to suppose that Josephine's cordial relations with two of the Directors Barras and Gohier helped to put her husband into a forgiving mood for the time being. Her connections were to prove very useful to him during the next three weeks.

***

On October 21 Lucien Bonaparte came to speak to his brother Napoleon on behalf of Sieyès. If Napoleon supported Sieyès' projected coup d'état, he would be made one of the three consuls—the executive triumvirate—that was to govern France. The General was noncommittal. He was equally noncommittal when, in the course of the next three weeks, similar baits were presented to him by the other two conspirators—Barras for the royalists and Bernadotte for the Jacobins. He would not serve as anybody's 'sword.' He would not identify himself with any party. He would act only for himself, or for France as a whole: it amounted to the same thing. Although the politicians mistook him for a general, the General was a statesman. Why use force for the benefit of a Sieyès or a Barras, when he felt sure that he himself could take over the government, without the use of force, by uniting a parliamentary majority behind him? What Bonaparte really wanted was a strong presidential regime on the American model (minus the federalism), with himself in the role of George Washington (minus the stepping down after the second term). In this view he was supported and encouraged by his private circle of advisers, among whom Talleyrand and the journalist Roederer were the most influential and the cleverest.

However, despite all his political genius, the General was inexperienced in politics. Until the very last moment, it seemed as if the routine politicians would have the better of him. He might have a theoretical parliamentary majority behind him, but what was the good of that once he had put the Directory solidly against him? He discovered this truth on October 23, when the Directors Gohier and Moulins evaded his suggestion that he might replace Sieyès in the Directory: the General was ten years short of the age of forty, which the Constitution prescribed for membership in that body. By this time, after only one week in Paris, Bonaparte's stock was already beginning to fall. Masséna was the hero of the day; the conquest of Egypt was forgotten or denounced as a folly by the same leftist press which had hailed it a year earlier. The only reason for Bonaparte's suddenly leaving Egypt was to escape an imminent mutiny of his entire army, *Le Messager* of October 20 suggested. On the other hand, Lucien's stock was rising: on October 25 he was elected President of the Council of Five Hundred.

Since none of the political leaders was willing to co-operate with the General on the General's terms, the General had no choice but to change his terms. On November 1 he consented at last to a private interview with Sieyès, held at Lucien's house. Still, the terms he sprung on Sieyès and on his brother were not exactly what they had expected. He would co-operate in overthrowing the Directory, he declared, and he even consented to be one of the three Consuls, with Sieyès and Ducos—but only if the new government were a provisional one. Sieyès could not impose a ready-made constitution on the nation; the new constitution would have to be worked out by a legislative committee. If Sieyès was not satisfied with this, he concluded, 'don't count on me. There is no lack of generals to execute the decrees of the Council of Ancients.' Sieyès was stunned. 'The General seems to have chosen his terrain as on a battlefield,' he sighed to Lucien as he left. 'We'll have to follow his opinion. If he backed out, everything would be lost.'[1]

There was no time to waste: both Barras and Bernadotte were getting ready for coups d'état of their own. With Talleyrand and Roederer acting as liaison between Bonaparte and Sieyès, the details of the plot were worked out in a series of furtive nocturnal conferences. It was a complicated business, since all five Directors

---

[1] Iung, I, 295. 74

resided at the Luxembourg and kept a jealous eye on each other's apartments. However, the fact that the Minister of Police, Fouché, had joined the conspirators gave them a comfortable feeling of security. Financial backing was also assured, thanks to the banker Collot, with whom Bonaparte had had mutually profitable dealings during the Italian campaign. Within five days, everything was ready. The text by which the Council of Ancients would transfer the seat of the two chambers to Saint-Cloud had been worked out, as had the text of the decree giving Bonaparte the command of the troops. Once at Saint-Cloud, with their meeting halls surrounded by soldiers, the deputies would be persuaded to depose the Directory and to vote in the new provisional regime: it seemed as if Bonaparte's role in this revolution would be that of a mere 'sword' after all. The day was set for 16 Brumaire (November 7).

Conspiracies may be dramatic, but they usually have their moments of farce. On November 6, the day before the planned coup, the deputies of the two chambers, whom Bonaparte was about to overthrow, gave a gigantic banquet in honour of Generals Bonaparte and Moreau in the Church of Saint-Sulpice, which had been converted during the Revolution into a 'Temple of Victory.' Seven hundred and fifty plates were set in the chilly church. The dishes cooled rapidly, fog kept creeping in through the doors, and the mood was even more glacial than the food. A number of Jacobins, notably Bernadotte, were conspicuously absent. Bonaparte touched none of the food except two boiled eggs and a pear. Meanwhile, the orchestra was playing a tune called 'Where could one be happier than in the bosom of the family?' Then came the toasts. Bonaparte's was 'To the union of all Frenchmen!' He left less than an hour after arriving. Outside, he was greeted by a crowd of united Frenchmen with mixed boos and cheers.

Discouraged by the fiasco of the banquet, Bonaparte postponed the coup d'état until 18 Brumaire. Before venturing all, he intended to take some additional tactical precautions, especially to make sure of the co-operation of the troops and their commanders. Also, he was having a number of tracts and proclamations printed which came rather as a surprise to Sieyès on the great day.

Sieyès spent most of 17 Brumaire taking riding lessons. He planned to ride, the next morning, to the Tuileries palace, where the Council of Ancients was sitting, at the head of the Directorial Guards and preceded by their band. He was surprised to find, at dawn on 18 Brumaire, that the Directorial Guard had vanished from the precincts of the Luxembourg: Bonaparte, anticipating the

authority to be conferred on him the next day, had quietly removed it.

During the night, the Ancients received summonses to meet at
the Tuileries at the ungodly hour of 5 a.m. At 7.30 a.m. the groggy
senators obediently voted the transfer of the legislature to Saint-
Cloud and invited General Bonaparte to present himself in order
to be sworn in as commander of the troops. The decree reached
Bonaparte about an hour later. He calmly amended it, adding to
the list of units placed under his command the Directorial Guard,
which Sieyès had reserved for himself. Sieyès had to ride to the
Tuileries alone.

The commanders of the units, in dress uniform, had been waiting at Bonaparte's house for the past hour, amazed to see themselves so numerous and wondering for what purpose they had
been convoked. Bernadotte—'the obstacle man,' as Bonaparte
called him—arrived last, in civilian clothes, with his brother-in-law
Joseph Bonaparte. He refused to take any part in the enterprise
but, after a few sharp words, allowed himself to be dragged away
to breakfast at Joseph's house. With the obstacle thus disposed of,
Bonaparte emerged at his doorstep, received the acclamations of
the assembled officers, and rode off to the Tuileries.

About the same time Barras was taking a bath. When he got
out of it, he found two visitors, Talleyrand and Admiral Bruix, who
presented him with a letter of resignation. All it needed was his
signature. So effectively did Bonaparte's envoys intimidate him
that he signed it before they had a chance to offer him the 2 million francs which Collot had advanced for that purpose.

At the Tuileries, after being sworn in, Bonaparte made a short
speech. 'Let no one search the past for examples that might slow
down our advance! Nothing in all history resembles the last years
of the eighteenth century; nothing in the last years of the eighteenth century resembles the present moment.'[1] Then, in the Tuileries gardens, he addressed the troops at greater length, lambast-
ing the administration and promising national unity. None of this
speech-making entered into Sieyès' plans, nor did the tracts,
drawn up for Bonaparte by Roederer, which were beginning to cir-
culate in Paris. The sword was getting out of hand.

Of the five Directors, two—Sieyès and Ducos—had set up their
head quarters at the Tuileries to overthrow the Directory. Another,
Barras, had obligingly resigned. The remaining two—Gohier and

---

[1] Correspondance, VI, 1. 75

Moulins—having gone to the Tuileries to see what was happening, were informed by Bonaparte that there was no more Directory. Reluctant to see things in that light, they refused to resign and went back to the Luxembourg, where Bonaparte put a guard on them.

After midnight, the General returned to his house. 'It didn't go too badly,' he said to Bourrienne. 'We'll see about tomorrow.'[1] Then he went to sleep, after putting two loaded pistols near his pillow.

Tomorrow went very badly indeed. Bonaparte arrived at Saint-Cloud shortly before noon. 'Vive Bonaparte!' the troops cried at his appearance; the deputies shouted, 'Vive la Constitution!'

At half past one, the Ancients opened their session in the great hall of the château of Saint-Cloud. Many of them felt that they had been hoodwinked the day before. There were shouts of 'No dictatorship!,' and a motion calling on each member to swear allegiance to the Constitution was adopted with only one dissenting vote.

Meanwhile, in a drawing room of the château, Bonaparte, awaiting the results of the deliberations, became increasingly nervous. At half past three, word came that the Ancients had passed a resolution calling for the election of a new Directory. To Bonaparte, everything seemed lost. White with rage, he stalked into the great hall, followed by an escort of grenadiers. The hostile glares of the red-robed senators sent him into a frenzy. He blurted out an incoherent speech which, interrupted by the questions of several hecklers, soon turned into gibberish. 'And if some speaker, bribed by foreign gold, should propose to outlaw me,' he screamed, 'let the thunderbolt of war crush him instantly! ... I would appeal to you, my brave comrades in arms, to you, brave soldiers, whom I have led to so many victories! ... Remember that the god of war and the god of luck are marching alongside me!'[2] 'Get out of here, General,' whispered Bourrienne. 'You no longer know what you're saying.'[3] But Bonaparte raved on for several more minutes before he withdrew.

His only salvation was to win over the Council of Five Hundred. The deputies were in the midst of their discussion of the last twenty-four hours' baffling events when Bonaparte burst in, with a clatter of arms. The grenadiers remained at the door. At the sight

---

[1] Bourrienne, Vol. III, Ch. VII. 76

[2] Correspondance, VI, 4. 77

[3] Bourrienne, Vol. III, Ch. VII. 78

of the soldiers, the deputies leaped on to their benches. There were cries of 'Outlaw the dictator!' while Lucien, from the presidential chair, vainly tried to calm the commotion. Several deputies grabbed the General by the collar, pushed him around, and, it seems, even hit him in the face. At last, four grenadiers dragged him away to safety. There were scratches on his cheeks.

Panting and inarticulate, Bonaparte came running to Sieyès. 'General,' he cried, 'they want to outlaw me!'[1] It must have given the ex-abbé a moment of wry satisfaction to hear *the* General address him as 'General.'

What to do? Bonaparte had never known a rout before. He was paralysed.

Meanwhile, at the Five Hundred, brother Lucien was going through a rather rough half hour. Several times he stepped down from the presidential chair, and each time the infuriated assembly ordered him to get back. Was he to preside over the outlawing of his own brother? A platoon of grenadiers suddenly materialized like a *deus ex machina*, grabbed him bodily, and kidnapped him. The deputies, stunned at first by the sudden disappearance of their President, soon resumed their debate without him.

Lucien burst into the room where Sieyès and Bonaparte were sitting. 'They want to outlaw us?' Sieyès said calmly. 'Well General, just put them out of their hall.'[2] The suggestion struck the brothers with all the force of its simplicity. They ran downstairs together, leaped on horseback, and cantered up to the troops of the Legislative Guard, who stood in formation. Lucien addressed them first. 'Frenchmen,' he said, 'the President of the Council of Five Hundred declares to you that the overwhelming majority of the Council are, at the present moment, being terrorized by a few representatives armed with stilettoes.' The 'handful of raving madmen' had put themselves outside the law. In the name of the people, Lucien requested the troops to protect the majority from the stilettoes—with their bayonets.

The repetition of the word 'stiletto' gave General Bonaparte an idea. He himself now began to address the troops. 'I wanted to speak to them [the deputies],' he cried, 'and they answered me with daggers![3] The troops were persuaded. To the accompaniment of drum rolls, they marched to the Orangerie, where the Five

---

[1] Ollivier, p. 215. 79

[2] Ibid., p. 218. 80

[3] Ibid., p. 220. 81

Hundred, in the absence of their President, were engaged in chaotic argument. As the soldiers advanced into the hall, bayonets fixed, the representatives leaped out of the windows and ran, leaving their togas in the shrubbery.

Except for a few formalities, all was over. A few hours later, the Ancients voted to establish a provisional government, and the remnants of the Five Hundred, reconvened by Lucien for that purpose, followed suit. Bonaparte, Sieyès and Ducos were created consuls of the provisional government. It was at about this point that Talleyrand arrived from Paris. 'Let us have dinner,' he said. [1]

***

General Bonaparte had obtained what he wanted, but not in the way he had intended. It was not thus that George Washington became President, and it did not require a Napoleon Bonaparte to expel 500 deputies from their hall with bayonets. 'Is it to do this, General, that you have won your victories?' one of the deputies had shouted at him that afternoon. [2] The question was well taken. Was it for this that some 15,000 men had been killed or maimed in Egypt, or died of thirst, or lost their eyesight? Was it for this that severed times that number of Turks, Arabs, and fellahin had died? Yes and no: it was not so much for this as for the sake of what was to follow, for the sake of a glory unrivaled in modern times and paid for with the price of several million more lives.

Were the battles of Egypt and of Syria necessary to win the Battle of Saint-Cloud? Hardly, except in a peculiarly negative way. If Bonaparte had not gone to Egypt and won a few battles there, if he had not lost the Battle of the Nile, thereby setting in motion the events that led to the resumption of a general war, he might well have become known simply as the man who had failed to take the British Isles, a reputation which would not have opened to him the road to power.

To speculate on what might have happened if ... is a fascinating pastime. But it is equally interesting to point out simple facts that others have overlooked. One of those facts is this: When he left Egypt, Bonaparte wrote to General Kléber, 'I shall remain with you in spirit and in heart.... I shall regard as ill-spent every day in my life that I do not do something for the army which I leave in your command.' [3] Throughout the month elapsed from his landing in

---

[1] Ibid., p. 224. 82

[2] Ibid., p. 214. 83

[3] Correspondance, V, 575.

France (October 9) to his nomination as Consul (November 10), Bonaparte neither did nor said anything whatever to help the plight of the army he had left behind. He was too busy with more important things, and he went on being too busy.

'Friends,' General Kléber is reported to have said when he learned that Bonaparte was gone, 'that b_ has left us with his breeches full of s_t. We'll go back to Europe and rub them in his face.'[1] It was a tempting prospect, and many may regret that Kléber could not carry it out.

IV

Ordinarily, when a general is appointed commander-in-chief of an army, he is more pleased than angry. General Kléber, when he learned that he was to command the Army of the Orient, was extremely angry. As he saw it, Bonaparte had fled, leaving him to face the music and to pay the bills. He had not even dared to confront his successor, who would either have refused the command or accepted it only on very specific conditions. By making Kléber dash to Rosetta for a rendezvous that he had no intention of keeping, Bonaparte had not only played a cheap trick on him: he had also shown himself a moral coward, and he had tied Kléber's hands with a set of instructions without giving Kléber a chance to discuss or modify them. When Kléber studied the instructions, their almost complete irrelevancy to the situation as he saw it made him gasp with unbelief.

The larger part of the instructions consisted of four memoranda—on the internal administration, the fortifications, the defence, and the political situation of Egypt. They either set forth elementary principles which it was unnecessary to spell out for so experienced a general as Kléber and which, in addition, all of Bonaparte's subordinates had heard him repeat *ad nauseam*; or else they bore only a tenuous relationship to things as they really were. Kléber could shrug them off with one of his pungent witticisms, but posterity would be impressed by the depth of their acumen and vision: 'Cambyses, Xerxes, Alexander the Great, Amr, and Selim I entered Egypt ... through the Gaza Desert.... Turkey is no longer a state but a collection of independent pashaliks.... The plague is one of the army's most redoubtable foes.... Mecca is the centre of Islam.... Do not lose sight of the fact that Alexandria must eventually become the capital of Egypt.... Permanent fortifi-

---

[1] La Revelliere-Lepaux, II, 348.

cations, storehouses, hospitals, arsenals, windmills, and factories should be established preferably at Alexandria'[1] And so forth. It requires little effort to imagine the comments with which Kléber, a talented satirist, greeted this egregious collection of platitudes and pipe dreams. Bonaparte had left him an army half its original combat strength, demoralized, sapped by disease, clothed in rags, and mutinous; a deficit of 12 million francs, with no regular revenues in prospect for several months; a country seething with discontent, which could never be effectively controlled by the forces at Kléber's disposition; and a military situation in which every victory would bring him closer to disaster, what with England commanding the seas and Turkey (though 'no longer a state,' according to Bonaparte) sending an army of 80,000 men against him. In such circumstances, to speak of strengthening the defences, keeping on good terms with the religious leaders, issuing new uniforms, founding hospitals, arsenals, and factories, and preparing for a permanent stay seemed a little unrealistic. Surely Bonaparte did not expect Kléber to be deceived by all this, nor was he deceiving himself: while leaving Kléber holding the bag, he was already laying the foundation for the legend of his grandness of vision and foresight.

It was public knowledge that Kléber was the outstanding spokesman for those generals and officials who regarded the Egyptian venture as a hopeless failure and favoured as prompt an evacuation as possible, provided it could be accomplished on honourable terms. This party formed the majority of the high officials as well as the rank and file. Among the 'colonial' faction—those who still had faith in making Egypt into a permanent and prosperous establishment—the foremost advocates were General Davout, a pathologically ambitious young man, and the middle-aged General Menou, who pushed colonial enthusiasm to the point of becoming a Moslem convert and calling himself Jacques Abdallah Menou. Desaix, although he drew up admirable memoranda on how to administer a region which he could not even control, probably should not be counted among the 'colonialists'; but then he was not an 'evacuationist' either. Why did Bonaparte choose Kléber, of all people, to succeed him? The only plausible answer is that the securest way of tying Kléber down in Egypt and of preventing an open split among the high command was to make Kléber commander-in-chief. Also, apart from Desaix, Kléber was the most capable and popular of the generals, and Bonaparte wished

---

[1] Correspondance, XXX, 8493.

Desaix to follow him to France in November. He had issued specific instructions to that effect.[1]

Under the abundant sauce of good advice, grandiose visions,
references to Cambyses and Alexander the Great, and elaborate
specifications on the execution of unrealizable projects, General
Bonaparte had concealed a hare that was very much alive and real:
'If by next May you have received neither help nor news from
France,' he wrote to Kléber, 'and if, in the coming year, despite all
precautions, the plague should kill more than 1,500 men ... you are
authorized to make peace with the Ottoman Porte, even if the
evacuation of Egypt should be the principal condition.'[2] Several
observations may be made on this passage, and they will be made
presently. It is enough at this point to quote Kléber's own comment on it, in a celebrated letter he wrote to the Directory: 'I draw
your attention to this passage, Citizen Directors,' he wrote, 'because it is characteristic in more ways than one, and because it il-
lustrates the critical situation in which I find myself.'[3]

Along with his instructions, Bonaparte had sent Kléber a copy
of his letter of August 17 to the Grand Vizier, in which he had assured the Sultan's Minister that France had never wanted to take
Egypt away from the Sultan, and that everything could be settled
in a couple of hours' chat. To Kléber, however, he made it clear
that an agreement to evacuate should not necessarily be followed
by an actual evacuation. 'You should simply delay the fulfillment
of that agreement, if possible, until the conclusion of a general
peace treaty,' he wrote. 'The Turkish Empire ... is crumbling, and
the evacuation of Egypt would be all the more disastrous for
France since we would see that fertile country fall into the hands
of some other European power in our lifetime.'[4] This, of course,
was precisely the reasoning that had started the whole unfortunate
campaign—a fact which did not escape Kléber.

---

[1] Since he was relinquishing his command, Bonaparte had no right, of
course, to order a general to be sent back to France after his own departure. Consequently, he used this peculiar wording: 'It is the intention of
the *government* [italics mine] that General Desaix should leave for
Europe in November.' Needless to say, 'the government' had expressed
no such intention. It is by equivocations of this kind that Bonaparte
hoped to suggest that he was returning to France under government orders.

[2] Ibid., V, 577.

[3] Rousseau, p. 80.

[4] Correspondance, V, 577.

In Kléber's opinion, Bonaparte's instructions could be disregarded as a whole. In the first place, it was questionable whether a commander-in-chief who left his army without the authorization of his government had the right to issue instructions to his successor; by appointing Kléber commander-in-chief, Bonaparte implicitly transferred all his powers to him. In the second place, Kléber had not even been asked whether he wanted the command. And, lastly, the instructions were based on false premises and impossible to execute. The only document among the papers Bonaparte had sent him that held any positive significance for Kléber was the copy of the letter to the Grand Vizier. Bonaparte had opened the way for negotiations, and Kléber was determined to bring them to a successful conclusion as soon as he possibly could. In the meantime, his first duty was to see to it that his army was paid, clothed, and fed, even if this meant treading on the toes of those people who until then had enjoyed Bonaparte's indulgence—the sheiks, the big merchants, the Coptic tax collectors, and the profiteers in his own administration. 'Soldiers, have no doubt of it, your pressing needs will always be the object of my greatest solicitude;'[1] with these words Kléber ended his first proclamation to the army, and he meant what he said.

It has been asserted by many writers that the French soldiers in Egypt received the news of Bonaparte's departure with sorrow and consternation. If this was so, this was not because he had left but because they had stayed behind. The available evidence indicates that their feeling of bereavement was more than compensated by their rejoicing when they learned that Kléber was their new commander. Kléber was at least as popular as Desaix; he had their complete confidence as a leader; and Ms strong stand in favour of giving up Egypt was well known,

As for the reaction of the population—and, especially, of the sheiks—to the change of command, Kléber preferred to take no chances. When he made his solemn entry into Cairo on August 31, he displayed a regal pomp and a sternness of countenance that contrasted sharply with Bonaparte's informality and affability. A double column of 500 Janissaries preceded him, striking the soil with their long poles and crying out, 'Here comes the lord commander-in-chief! Moslems, bow down before him!' Arms crossed over chests, the people bowed as he passed. When the sheiks were presented to him, reports El-Djabarti, 'they found him

---

[1] Rousseau, p. 8.

less amiable than Bonaparte, who was very easy-going and who liked to chat and jest with his visitors.'[1]

***

General Kléber lacked the politician's gift for easy familiarity, which Bonaparte possessed to a high degree. A man of imposing build and presence, close to six foot tall, slightly corpulent, lion-maned, Teutonic in his broad and open features, endowed with a powerful voice and a commanding eye, Kléber was the very image of the handsome warrior in his maturity and offered a striking contrast to the awkward, sallow-faced little Corsican. Bonaparte's personality was magnetic; Kléber's merely inspired respect. To those who knew him only in an official capacity, Kléber seemed calm, cold, and stern to the point of harshness. Undoubtedly he was capable of great severity, both toward his troops and toward the nation whose government had been placed on his reluctant shoulders. Yet his severity manifested itself as a steady pressure, unspectacular but firm, rather than by the kind of erratic and brutal 'examples' with which Bonaparte had been so lavish.

Kléber's spectacular entry into Cairo marked a change in the French occupation policy. It had been his contention from the start of the campaign that any attempt to win the affection of the Moslem population by a show of brotherliness was futile: the people would see through the pretence; they would also mistake indulgence for weakness. The only thing they respected or understood was force. Since he regarded the French occupation of Egypt as a mere passing phase, he saw no point in trying to reform the national character, which was the product of thousands of years of oppression, exploitation, and anarchy. He agreed with Bonaparte's policy of respect for local institutions and for Islam; he did not agree with his predecessor's posturing as a Moslem. Egypt, to him, was merely a territory under temporary military occupation, not the core of a potential colonial empire. Perhaps he lacked Bonaparte's grandness of vision, but he showed considerably more sagacity.

In one respect, however, his policy was mistaken. Bonaparte's formula was to cut off six heads per day and to keep smiling. Under Kléber's administration, few heads were cut off, but there were no smiles either. In the eyes of the more influential part of the population, he did worse than cutting off heads: he systematically soaked the rich. One of his first actions Was to make the Coptic tax

---

[1] El-Djabarti, VI, 154.

collectors disgorge 800,000 francs, on the theory that if they made a 10 per cent profit on their business that was sufficient. The Copts protested, argued, and wept, but Kléber remained adamant. Later, when he had every reason to chop off several sheiks' heads, he spared their lives but imposed heavy fines on them. It is true everywhere in the world that men will readily accept the remote risk of having their heads cut off but not, if they can help it, the certainty of being taxed more than they are used to paying: the great American and French revolutions illustrate this general rule. In Egypt, however, this truth held even more than anywhere else. The esteem in which an Egyptian fellah or sheik el-beled was held in his village depended on the number of strokes he would take on the soles of his feet before paying the tax he was assessed, and this characteristic extended even to the sheiks when Kléber had the notion of assessing them. It is true that under Kléber the poor were squeezed less than under any previous administration; but to squeeze the poor was safe, whereas to squeeze the rich beyond certain accepted limits was decidedly dangerous.

To his intimate circle, Kléber was an entirely different man from what he seemed in his official capacity. With them, he discarded all formality and caution. His dinner parties were as convivial and lusty as Bonaparte's were frigid. His language could be earthy, to say the least, in a military and scatological way, but his wit was caustic rather than coarse, and he exercised it unstintingly at Bonaparte's expense. His sallies about the ' Hero,' the 'Almighty,' made the rounds of the officer corps, as did his caricatures, which he sketched with a quick and gifted hand.

Kléber's unconcealed detestation of Bonaparte has been ascribed by some to his republican convictions, by others to jealousy. Just how sincerely republican was a man who had served under Louis XVI and under Maria Theresa before joining the Revolutionary army it is difficult to determine. As for jealousy, if allowance is made for the normal dose of invidiousness that exists in all professions, there is no reason to believe that Kléber was particularly jealous of Bonaparte, whose boldness and military genius he admired. When he arrived at Abukir just after Bonaparte's victory, he embraced him and exclaimed, 'General, you're as big as the world, and the world isn't big enough for you'[1]—a fair tribute, though perhaps it contained a touch of malice. What Kléber could not abide in Bonaparte was his ambition. He could not help despising a man who calmly sacrificed thousands of lives entrusted

[1] Denon, I, 351.

to his care for the sake of his career. Bonaparte had gambled an
army and lost; he had then sneaked away like a coward, leaving
the army to pay his debts, and returned to France as a hero to
capitalize on his empty victories. So, at least, it seemed to General
Kléber. His dislike for Bonaparte turned into positive hatred. Not
only was he determined to take his army out of Egypt, but he also
sought to damage Bonaparte's reputation in France by every
means at his disposal.

Some of these means were, perhaps, below his dignity, though
they undoubtedly reflect his sense of humour. Thus he seemed
very anxious to satisfy Madame Fourès' demand to be sent back to
France: her return would embarrass 'the hero and lover whom she
has lost.'[1]

Madame Fourès did leave aboard the United States ship *America* but was removed from it by H.M.S. *Theseus* and brought back
to Egypt (Bonaparte's luck was truly incredible), where she had to
stay for several months before she finally reached France. Of a far
more serious nature was the letter which Kléber addressed to the
Directory on October 8, one copy of which reached Bonaparte after he became First Consul, and another copy of which fell into the
hands of the British, with results disastrous to everybody concerned.

Kléber's letter painted an exaggeratedly gloomy picture of his
situation. The comments Napoleon made on it later are, however,
far more exaggerated in the opposite direction. The army, wrote
Kléber, was reduced to half its strength. (This was not true,
claimed Bonaparte, who by some specious calculations arrived at
the result that Kléber at that point had 28,500 men; yet in his own
letter to the Directory, dated June 28, Bonaparte stated that by the
year 1800 the army would be reduced to 15,000 men, including
3,000 unfit for combat duty!) Moreover, Kléber continued, disease
was prevalent, and the soldiers were in rags. It is true that Bonaparte had ordered new uniforms to be issued, 'but, in this as in
many other things, he had left it at that. Lack of funds ... no doubt,
obliged him to postpone the execution of that useful project.'[2]

As for lack of funds: 'When Bonaparte sailed, he did not leave a
penny in the till, nor any cash equivalent. On the contrary, he left a
deficit of almost 10 million.... The soldiers' pay in arrears accounts

---

[1] Rousseau, p. 70.

[2] Ibid., p. 78.

for 4 million alone.'[1] (According to Bonaparte's comments, the deficit amounted to only 1.5 million francs. Actually, the balance drawn up on October 8, 1799, shows a deficit of almost 12 million francs. To be sure, this was two months after Bonaparte left.)

The internal political situation in Egypt, Kléber wrote without exaggeration, was precarious at best. Moreover, a large Turkish army commanded by the Grand Vizier had already reached Gaza. (To this point, Bonaparte objected that by October 8 the Grand Vizier had not yet entered Syria. This is a mere quibble: the Grand Vizier turned up at Gaza soon enough.)

Such was the situation, Kléber continues, that he had inherited from General Bonaparte. 'He saw the fatal crisis approaching.'[2] It was because of this inevitable crisis that Bonaparte had started to negotiate with the Grand Vizier. What was there left for Kléber but to follow up this beginning without waiting for the plague to kill 1,500 more of his men? Accordingly, Kléber had written to the Grand Vizier and sent him a duplicate of Bonaparte's letter.

In his separate financial report, Poussielgue went Kléber one better, suggesting that Bonaparte had taken 2 million francs of the treasury for his own use.

When Kléber's and Poussielgue's reports reached Paris, the Directory no longer existed. Bonaparte, by then First Consul, answered Kléber through General Berthier, his Minister of War. Kléber's information was incorrect, Berthier wrote to him, and at any rate Kléber must not sign any treaty of capitulation. Berthier's letter was dated January 12, 1800. It reached Kléber only some time after the capitulation was signed and ratified.

***

Kléber's first letter to the Grand Vizier Yussef was dated September 17. It repeated Bonaparte's letter of August 17 in that it invited the Porte to enter into negotiations for the restoration of Egypt to Turkey and for the resumption of the traditional Franco-Turkish alliance. Its tone, however, was less declamatory and more tactful. A week later, in his proclamation to the army of September 25 (the first day of the Year VIII), Kléber optimistically promised peace: 'Your flags, my comrades in arms, are bending under the weight of your laurels. So much travail must have an end; so much glory deserves a reward. Persevere for just a little longer, for you have almost reached this end and you are about to obtain the re-

---

[1] Ibid.

[2] Rousseau, p. 80

ward, by giving the world a lasting peace after fighting it for so long.'[1]

Kléber's optimism was founded on conversations he had had with Mustafa Pasha, the captive commander of the Turkish army that had been defeated at Abukir. Mustafa, who had been won over to the French point of view, was to serve as an intermediary between Kléber and the Grand Vizier for several months to come. He remained in French hands, it is true more as a hostage than as a prisoner but he wrote to the Grand Vizier on several critical occasions, always in a conciliatory sense. The Grand Vizier, however, was less tractable. Bonaparte's optimistic assumption (which Kléber shared at the beginning), that the Porte was eager to break away from its British and Russian allies and to make peace with France, turned out to be a piece of wishful thinking. The Turks were more adamant in their demands than either of their allies. Unexpectedly enough, it was Sir Sidney Smith who took upon himself the role of mediator and who, after considerable effort, convinced the Grand Vizier that an army that requested a truce was not necessarily a beaten army, and that con cessions had to be made on both sides.

Sidney Smith's intervention in the negotiations began in late October, with a letter in which he pointed out to Kléber that the Anglo-Turkish treaty of alliance forbade a separate peace, that England must be a partner to any agreement between the French and the Turks, and that Egypt must be evacuated before any general peace treaty could be signed. Kléber's reply (of October 30) started out haughtily enough. The French forces in Egypt, he asserted, could resist any army for a long time, and, if they received the least reinforcements, forever. (For obvious reasons, his language toward Sir Sidney contrasted sharply with his language toward the Directory.) The French would never quit Egypt merely to go home, but they would leave 'with pleasure and alacrity if this evacuation were the price that must be paid for a general peace.'[2] This sounds like a condition; actually, it was a major con cession. Indeed, a few lines later, Kléber conceded explicitly that the evacuation of Egypt by the French must be a preliminary to a general peace, and in doing so he not only ignored Bonaparte's instructions, which he had every right to ignore, but also his own assurances to the Directory, that he would insist on occupying a number of cities and fortresses until a peace treaty was signed. All

---

[1] Ibid., p. 59.

[2] Rousseau, p. 102

subsequent concessions—and there were many—were subsidiary to this one.

It must have been quite clear to Kléber that, of the three parties concerned—himself, Smith, and the Grand Vizier—only the Grand Vizier had authority to negotiate any matter regarding a general peace treaty. Sir Sidney Smith was a mere captain in the English navy, with the temporary rank of commodore and with full powers to negotiate with the Porte but not with the French. As for Kléber, he had no diplomatic status whatsoever, although he could invoke the precedent of General Bonaparte, who had negotiated a preliminary peace with Austria in 1797 without being authorized to do so; but that peace had been a victorious one. Thus, when General Kléber wrote to Captain Smith that the time had come 'for the two most civilized nations of Europe to cease fighting one another,'[1] he ventured out on rather dangerous terrain. Normally, commanders of enemy forces in wartime do not exchange letters on the desirability of making peace without taking the risk of being charged with treason.

To commit treason was far from Kléber's mind. He had gauged Sir Sidney quite accurately as a highly emotional and impressionable man who was burning to play a role far above his actual station. All Kléber wished to do was to leave Egypt on honourable terms that is, with arms and baggage, neither victor nor defeated. In appealing to Sidney Smith to bring about this result and thus to lay the foundations of an international peace, he transformed him from an enemy into his warmest spokesman. It was through Smith's intervention that, in December 1799, the Grand Vizier consented at last to issue safe-conducts to the French negotiators.

In the meantime, on November 1, General Verdier with about a thousand men had routed another sea-borne Turkish invasion force several times the number of his, near Damietta. The Grand Vizier, with an army of 80,000 (at least half of whom were servants, cooks, and other non-combatants) was advancing through Syria; however, since Djezzar Pasha had refused to co-operate with him in any way whatsoever (the Butcher was hostile to all intruders, whether Turkish or French), the Vizier's army was in sorry shape, starving and dying of thirst. Though inclined to take alarm unnecessarily, Kléber must have realized that he was capable of inflicting a crushing defeat on the Turks. Nevertheless, he chose to negotiate. His correspondence indicates his motives clearly enough: any victory he might win, no matter how brilliant, would

[1] Rousseau, p. 104

385

be of a Pyrrhic nature. He would merely lose more men, both by battle and by disease, and sooner or later he would inevitably succumb under the repeated blows of an inexhaustible enemy. It was better to negotiate from a position of strength than to wait until 1,500 men had died of the plague and as many more in battle.

On December 22, Kléber's two negotiators went aboard H.M.S. *Tigre*, where they immediately began preliminary talks with Sir Sidney Smith. They were Citizen Poussielgue, who had had some diplomatic experience, and General Desaix. Poussielgue was an out spoken 'evacuationist.' As for Desaix, he had accepted his mission with great reluctance and after considerable soul-searching. It was clear to him that if he refused the task entrusted to him by Kléber, an 'evacuationist' general would be assigned to it and consent to even less favourable terms than Desaix was prepared to accept. Throughout the negotiations, Poussielgue carried the initiative, with Desaix acting as an occasional brake.

There is every indication that Poussielgue, during the three weeks he spent as Smith's guest aboard the *Tigre*, wound his host around his little finger. There was, between the two men, a complete sympathy of views, and perhaps also of tastes. In Sir Sidney's eyes, Poussielgue was a gentleman, the kind one could do business with, endowed with states manlike vision and destined to play an important role in France. They shared an intense dislike for General Bonaparte. Also, Poussielgue convinced Smith that Kléber was 'a liberal humane man,' the kind that was needed in France to replace the existing belligerent government. As Smith wrote to Admiral Keith, there was 'most positive ground for saying that Kléber is Buonaparte's most determined and dreaded opponent.... France can be set to rights only by Frenchmen, and till she is set to rights, in the internal springs of government, we never can have peace.'[1] It was Captain Smith's notion—in which Poussielgue was encouraging him—that he could, by negotiating a limited agreement in the Middle East, bring about a change of government in France and put an end to a war that had lasted for seven years. Judging from Desaix's reports, Smith's anxiety to push the negotiations and to emerge from them as the saviour of Europe drove him to near—hysteria: when things were going too slowly, he would have trembling fits and stamp his foot like a frustrated prima donna.

While the Frenchmen and Sir Sidney exchanged views aboard the *Tigre*, the Grand Vizier's army reached Gaza. Desaix insisted on an immediate halt to the Turkish advance if negotiations were

---

[1] Barrow, I, 380, 385, 387.

to proceed. Smith agreed and notified the Grand Vizier accordingly; the Grand Vizier ignored Smith's message and marched on to El Arish, held by a French garrison of about 250 men. Their commandant, Major Cazal, ordered them to resist. Instead, his men mutinied, looted the liquor store, tore down the tricolour flag, and threw ropes to the Turks to facilitate their entry. To the horror of Colonel Douglas, a British officer attached to the Turkish headquarters, the Turks proceeded to massacre the surrendered garrison before his eyes; he managed to save about a hundred of them.

The incident, in different circumstances, would have caused the French to break off negotiations. Its actual result was, if anything, the exact opposite. Not that Kléber regarded the loss of the fortress as a serious blow: but the behaviour of the troops was characteristic of the morale in the French army. There had been mutinies in several coastal cities. The men were determined not to fight. In Alexandria, the troops had rioted to prevent the departure of several officials for France. 'Either we'll die all together or we'll get out all together,' they had cried, according to Nicholas the Turk. 'You are escaping one by one, and abandoning us little soldiers in this faraway country.'[1] The rats were leaving the sinking ship, it seemed to them, and General Bonaparte had led the procession of rats.

Just as mere talk of war often causes nations to slide into war, so do peace talks generate a momentum of their own. On January 13, Desaix and Poussielgue, accompanied by Sir Sidney Smith, arrived at the Grand Vizier's camp at El Arish to start the main part of the negotiations. There they received instructions from Kléber not to insist on the return of El Arish, provided the Grand Vizier guaranteed that the cease-fire would be observed in the future. The main terms of the treaty had already been worked out by correspondence between Kléber and the Grand Vizier. The Vizier had agreed to let the French leave with all their arms and property and with full honours of war as well as to provide the necessary transports and supplies. The main points still outstanding were Kléber's demands that Turkey withdraw from her alliance with England and Russia; that no Turkish troops enter Egypt until the Turkish navy had provided the transports to take the French home; and that, in the meantime, Turkey guarantee the funds required to maintain the French army in Egypt. To facilitate his communications with the Grand Vizier—and, also, in order to see to the de-

---

[1] Nicolas Turc, p. 86.

fence of the Egyptian frontier in case the talks broke down— Kléber moved his headquarters to Es Saliya in mid-January.

At El Arish, Poussielgue and Desaix found the Turks quite stubborn about the last two of these points. As to the first, they met opposition from Sidney Smith, who pointed out that the withdrawal of Turkey from the Triple Alliance could not take place until a general peace had been signed. Kléber yielded on all points save the matter of money. The importance he attached to that condition was so great, he wrote to his emissaries on January 19, 'that I am tempted to authorize you to break off negotiations if it is refused. His military position was precarious, he continued, but the financial situation was such that he lived 'not from day to day, but from second to second.' He had submitted the entire problem to 'an exact mathematical calculation.' The result of the calculation was 'that we must not fight but that we must compromise with those barbarians while we are still strong enough to enforce the faithful execution of the terms agreed upon.' It could be objected, he continued, that reinforcements might be on their way from France; however, he did not feel that there was any hope of this happening. (He was quite correct.) 'Since Bonaparte's return to France, there has been time enough to send us not one but ten courier ships. None was sent, because the government had nothing to promise me.... If I win a victory, all I gain is a three-month respite.... If I am beaten, I am responsible toward the Republic for 20,000 citizens, who will be unable to escape being massacred by a lawless and infuriated soldiery ... [especially] since, in this respect, we have set a fatal example for them to follow.'[1]

Nowhere has Kléber stated his reasoning more clearly. The passage also explains his reluctance to make an issue of the massacre of the garrison of El Arish: he remembered Jaffa. To a rational mind, his argument is unassailable. To those who hold that 'Theirs not to reason why, theirs but to do and die' (a school of thought more prevalent than ever in the world's war offices), Kléber was guilty of reasoning—an unforgivable offence in a soldier. In order to strengthen his position, Kléber convened a council of eight generals. All but one (Davout) supported Kléber. Menou would have opposed him had he been present.

The treaty was drawn up in the following few days and ratified by Kléber on January 28. According to its terms, the French undertook to evacuate Katia, Es Saliya, and Bilbeis ten days after ratification, and Cairo one month later. All French forces were to

---

[1] Rousseau, pp. 197, 198.

withdraw to Alexandria, Abukir, and Rosetta and there to await the arrival of the Turkish transports. The Turks undertook to bring the French army, with arms and baggage, to France and, in the meantime, to allow about 2 million francs for its maintenance in Egypt. Only one minor matter remained to be settled before the negotiators parted: Desaix insisted that a French *cantiniere*, the widow of a sergeant killed in battle, be returned by the Pasha of Jerusalem, who had confiscated her for his harem. The Grand Vizier agreed—but the sergeant's widow did not. She was perfectly happy where she was, she declared, and indeed she remained at Jerusalem and lived happily ever after into old age.

***

Kléber felt very uneasy, not about what he had done, but about the reception his action would be given. His uneasiness is quite apparent in a dozen or so letters he wrote to the Directory (of whose demise he had not yet been informed), to Desaix, and to Dugua. Yet, no matter how much he searched his conscience, it always led him to the same conclusion: reason, humanity, and a true understanding of his country's interests had dictated his conduct; to persevere in his determination for peace had required more effort and courage than any battle he had fought. Whether he was right in this or not is, perhaps, a matter of personal opinion. It is the unequivocal opinion of this writer that Kléber was right.

During the month following the agreement, Kléber had carried out its terms punctiliously, with the approval of the overwhelming majority of his army. Among the minority who disapproved was Sergeant François, who had been transferred to the Dromedary Corps and henceforth referred to his unit only as 'we, the dromedaries' a habit which earned him, for the rest of his life, the nickname 'the Dromedary of Egypt.' According to François, 'We, the dromedaries, knew that General Desaix was ashamed of the role he had been made to play in that negotiation.'[1] In the first days of March, events took a turn which seemed to justify the party of the dromedaries against that of *homo sapiens*. On March 2 Brigadier Latour-Maubourg arrived in Cairo fresh from Paris and brought Kléber the news of 18 Brumaire and a copy of the new Constitution, which made Bonaparte First Consul. He also brought a few newspapers, pamphlets, books, and promotions, but not a single letter of instructions nor the least promise of reinforcements. The letter which Kléber wrote to Berthier in response vibrates with his

---

[1] François, I, 384.

sense of outrage. 'They are making fools of us,' he wrote to Dugua.[1] 'Bonaparte's omnipotence may squash the truth for a moment,' he wrote to Poussielgue, 'but sooner or later the truth will be known.... If I had to start all over again, I would do exactly what I did.'[2] Those, however, who saw in Bonaparte's rise to power an argument against Kléber were quick in disavowing him. At their head was Menou, who instantly wrote to Bonaparte, to Berthier, to every powerful friend in Paris, letters worthy of a lackey. Kléber's agreement with Smith and the Grand Vizier, he informed everybody, had 'plunged all those who love honour and fatherland into the deepest sorrow.'[3] While Menou thus impugned the honour of Kléber, Kléber requested Poussielgue to send to him or to destroy the minutes of the council of war which had approved the agreement, in order to avoid compromising the generals who had signed them.

At almost the same time as the despatches from Paris, Kléber received even more disquieting news from Poussielgue, who had remained with Sir Sidney Smith as a special armistice commissioner. Admiral Keith had informed Sir Sidney that he had received positive instructions from the English government to disregard any agreement reached between the Grand Vizier and the French. Any shipments of French troops would be intercepted by the British fleet and treated as prisoners of war. This blow threw Sir Sidney into a consternation even greater than Kléber's: his entire scheme was about to collapse and his honour and reputation were at stake. 'My lord,' he wrote to Keith, 'I own, in my office of mediator in this business, it never entered into my ideas that we could put any obstacle in the way of an arrangement so very beneficial to us in a *general* view, and which evidently could not take place on any terms disgraceful to a veteran, unbeaten, and uninvested army.'[4] The British government's disavowal of the Convention of El Arish was, indeed a blunder which eventually cost England a heavy price. It was brought about by one of those monumental muddles which, it appears, the British government needs once in a while in order to function properly the rest of the time. (The attack on Egypt in 1956 is the most recent example.)

---

[1] Rousseau, p. 231.

[2] Ibid., p. 233

[3] Ibid., p. 226.

[4] Barrow, I, 384-85.

One of the copies of Kléber's letter of October 8 to the Directory, in which he criticized Bonaparte and drew a pessimistic picture of the French position in Egypt, had fallen into British hands. The British cabinet, on the strength of that somewhat exaggerated letter, had reached the conclusion that Kléber was on the verge of total defeat and consequently had instructed Keith to ignore any agreement reached between the French and the Turks, thereby forcing the Turks to resume hostilities and to consummate the destruction of the French expeditionary force. This egregious piece of foolishness Lord Keith passed on to Smith, without even bothering to question his government about it. In the meantime, the cabinet had changed their minds and advised Lord Elgin, the British ambassador in Constantinople, to accept the Convention of El Arish with only minor modifications and to issue safe-conducts to the French troop transports. Unfortunately, neither Lord Grenville, the Foreign Secretary, nor Lord Elgin had informed Lord Keith of this new development.[1]

If Sidney Smith had chosen to do so, he could have kept the contents of Keith's instructions from the French until they had evacuated Cairo and were unable to resume hostilities. 'I had both armies, as it were, dependent on my notification of the non-ratification,' he wrote to Lord Spencer. But, 'however true it may be that the French army, with which we have still to contend, would now be a set of skeletons bleaching on the sand, if I had led them step by step to perdition, as was certainly and evidently in my power, I pity the man that can wish it at the expense of our national honour.'[2] Indeed, Sir Sidney loyally informed Poussielgue of the obstacle that had arisen. 'Smith,' Poussielgue wrote to Kléber, 'seemed sincerely distressed. He told me that he risked his life in not following the orders he had received, but that he would rather lose it a thousand times than not to try every means without exception to facilitate the complete execution of the agreement.'[3]

---

[1] A great deal has been made of the technical question whether Sidney Smith had proper powers to sign the Convention of El Arish, and of the French plenipotentiaries' neglecting to verify Smith's powers. Since the Convention was an agreement *ad hoc*, reached in a remote part of the world, this technicality was of little importance. The orders received by Lord Keith were issued before the British government were aware of Smith's being a party to the negotiations, and the instructions sent to Lord Elgin essentially endorsed Smith's conduct. Even if Smith's credentials had been impeccable, the result would have been the same.

[2] Ibid., II, 55, 51.

[3] Rousseau, pp. 238-39.

This Smith did (without too much risk to his life, it is true) by trying to persuade the Grand Vizier to halt his advance until the difficulty raised by Keith's letter had been cleared up; also, he wrote to Lord Elgin, requesting safe-conducts for the French troops to be evacuated. 'The great national object is attained,' he wrote to the ambassador, 'if we can get the French army *out of the country*, even if they took the Pyramids with them.'[1]

To Kléber as to Sidney Smith it seemed, not unreasonably, that the whole difficulty rested on a misunderstanding that could be removed in a short time, provided that the Turks agreed to stop their advance. Accordingly, he requested the Grand Vizier to withdraw his troops from Bilbeis, which the French had already evacuated, and proposed to freeze the positions of their respective troops until the obstacle had been lifted through negotiation. But, despite Smith's efforts, the Grand Vizier would listen to nothing, insisted on the punctual execution of the treaty despite the altered circumstances, and continued his march toward Cairo.

On March 18 Kléber received from Lord Keith a personal letter[2] couched in brutal and insulting language, in which he notified the General that His Majesty could not consent to any capitulation on any terms save unconditional surrender. By that time, the Grand Vizier with 40,000 men was almost at the gates of Cairo.

It was at this point that Kléber, in Bonaparte's words, had his 'lion's awakening.' Nicholas the Turk, using a different simile, says that 'General Kléber, when he read this message, roared like an infuriated camel.'[3] There can be no question but that Kléber's reaction was spectacular. Within forty-eight hours, he countermanded all orders regarding the evacuation, notified the Grand Vizier that the armistice was terminated; issued a proclamation to his army which, apart from the full text of Keith's letter, contains only two lines: 'Soldiers, the only answer to such insolence is victory: prepare yourself for battle'; and, at 2 a.m. on March 20, sallied forth from Cairo to meet the Grand Vizier. Before night fell, he had routed an army four times as large as his, near the ruins of Heliopolis: his attack had taken the Turks completely by surprise. A week later, he had driven the Turkish army out of Egypt.

---

[1] Barrow, II, 22.

[2] It is dated aboard Keith's flagship, the Charlotte, off Minorca, January 8, thus antedating the signature of the Convention of El Arish.

[3] Nicolas Turc, p. 97.

General Menou, the most flat-footed of flatterers, congratulated Kléber on his victory in somewhat tactless terms. 'Yes, General,' he wrote, 'if, in my opinion, the capitulation signed at El Arish was a political mistake, the brilliant victory you have won and the reconquest of Egypt you have accomplished cover you with glory. General, I have no desire save to share in your glory and your labours.... Remember who you are, and you will be the founder of a magnificent colony.'[1] Kléber's reply was crushing: 'I have just received your letter, Citizen General. My stupidity is so enormous that even today I do not believe that the Convention of El Arish was a political mistake or that there is any reason to lose one's head over the victory I have won with my army. Even today, I am profoundly convinced that, by means of that treaty, I had succeeded in putting a reasonable end to an insane enterprise. Even today I remain convinced that we shall receive no help from France and that we shall never ... found any colonies in Egypt unless the cotton plants and palm trees should soon produce soldiers and bullets. You, General, have your face turned toward the East; mine is turned to the West. We shall never understand each other.'[2]

Few generals ever won so brilliant a victory as Kléber's at Heliopolis; few reconquered a country the size of Lower Egypt in a week; none, in all likelihood, ever looked at their victory with as much detachment and sadness. To him, Heliopolis was not a glorious feat of arms but the bloody result of a stupid mistake: it should never have happened; it was as gratuitous as the entire war.

***

Kléber's victory at Heliopolis, though spectacular, was incomplete. While Kléber pursued the Grand Vizier, who was in full flight, the Vizier's son, Nassif Pasha, with part of the Turkish forces, managed to elude the French, made straight for Cairo, and announced that the French army had been routed. In an instant, the populace rose in rebellion. The few French troops left in Cairo were soon isolated in the Citadel, in a couple of forts, in the headquarters at Esbekiya Square, and in a few isolated houses. From that moment until the recapture of Cairo by Kléber five weeks later, the city was plunged into an apocalyptic nightmare and chaos. Incited by Nassif and by the Grand Vizier's lieutenant Osman, the mob invaded the Christian quarters, killing, raping, and

---

[1] Rousseau, p. 299.

[2] Ibid., pp. 301-2.

looting. Only the Coptic quarter held out, under Moallem Jacob's plucky leadership. The Turkish soldiery, for their part, instead of halting the disorder, joined in the raping and looting. Nassif and Osman soon came to regret having roused and armed the mob; they lost all control of the situation.

When Kléber returned to Cairo on March 27, he was barely able to make his way into his headquarters through the garden entrance. While waiting for the arrival of the ordnance needed to bombard the rebellious quarters, he ordered his troops to draw a ring around the city, cutting it off from all food supply. At the same time he invited the Turks to capitulate. The Turkish commanders, by that time, were willing enough to comply but were prevented by the mob. Kléber offered an amnesty to the population: the population killed his emissary. There was no choice but to bomb and starve the city into submission.

With the Turks, all the remaining Mameluke beys save one had re-entered the city. The lone exception was Murad, who remained at the outskirts as a neutral spectator. When his fellow beys invited him to join them, he replied evasively and advised them to negotiate with the French. The beys sent one of theirs, Osman Bey, to bring him back to his senses. After a talk with Murad, Osman returned to Cairo completely converted to Murad's views.

Murad's puzzling behaviour had a very simple explanation. As early as March 14, before the resumption of hostilities, Kléber had sent the mathematician Fourier to sound out Murad's wife Nafissa about the possibility of bringing Murad to the French side, in exchange for the governorship of Upper Egypt. Lady Nafissa received the proposal favourably and, by some mysterious means, passed it on to her husband. Murad, who had not paid tribute to the Porte for a great many years, was not eager to meet the Turks and not displeased to see the Grand Vizier routed. He agreed to the French proposal and, on April 5, sent Osman Bey to Kléber to conclude an alliance with him. The circle was complete: two years earlier, the French had attacked Murad in the name of their ally, the Sultan; Murad had resisted the French in the name of that same Sultan, his overlord; he had eluded the pursuing French for almost a year, leading them a merry chase from Cairo to Aswan and back; and now he joined his forces to the French in order to avoid paying taxes to the Sultan in whose name he had fought them.

Thanks partly to Murad Bey, who intercepted a food convoy including 4,000 sheep, Cairo was starving by mid-April. With starvation came more looting, more torture and extortion, accompanied by daily house-to-house fighting and incessant bombardments night and day. The entire Esbekiya section of the city, with its palaces and gardens, was reduced to rubble. Fires broke out throughout the city. 'The women and children,' says Nicholas the Turk, 'ran in panic terror to take refuge under stone arches and protect themselves from the bombs.... Every night the screams of the women and children could be heard.'[1] Despite all this, resistance continued; a handful of demagogues who had emerged from nowhere were threatening to kill anyone who spoke of surrender.

On April 14, Kléber ordered a major assault on the city. According to El-Djabarti, the French used a primitive kind of flamethrower which emitted a 'liquid whose flame gained in intensity at the contact with water'—no doubt an invention of some member of the Scientific Commission—in addition to their field artillery.[2] At the same time a heavy rain and thunderstorm—an extremely rare phenomenon in Cairo—added to the noise and the terror. 'The French,' says El-Djabarti, 'were gaining ground and spread the conflagration as they advanced. The people who were enveloped by the circle of flames burned to death. The terrified women and children leapt over the walls and mixed their confused cries with the roar of the thunder and of the guns.'[3] Throughout this inferno, negotiations between Kléber and Nassif Pasha were in progress, with Murad Bey as the intermediary. The fighting died down the following day, with the larger part of Cairo still in rebel hands. Kléber turned his efforts against Bulaq, which had refused to surrender after being promised an amnesty. In Bulaq, which they took by assault, the French went berserk. 'The streets,' says El-Djabarti, 'were littered with corpses and the houses were reduced to rubble and ashes.'[4] Whatever property they could find, the soldiers took with them, including a large part of the women, with whom they set up house throughout the remaining year of occupation.

On April 22, at last, sanity prevailed. The people, terrified and weary, no longer put an obstacle to Nassif Pasha's acceptance of Kléber's quite generous conditions. The Turkish troops were allowed to leave with arms and baggage and were to proceed under escort as far as Es Saliya, whence they were to march on to Syria.

---

[1] Nicolas Turc, p. 107.

[2] El-Djabarti is the only source in which this engine is mentioned. His description of it and of its effects is specific enough, however, to lend his account some plausibility.

[3] El-Djabarti, VI, 193-94.

[4] Ibid., VI, 194.

The Mamelukes were to proceed to Upper Egypt, but the larger number of the beys, including Ibrahim, chose to follow the Grand Vizier to Syria. During the march to Es Saliya, General Reynier, who commanded the French escort, astonished the defeated Turks by offering mounts to the wounded and stragglers among them,

Mustafa Pasha, who had remained in French hands throughout the siege of Cairo, was not allowed to go with the rest of the Turks but was kept in the anticipation of an exchange of prisoners. Kléber, expecting that a prompt agreement would be reached on that subject, sent him and several other Turkish officers captured at Abukir to Damietta. The Turks put all sorts of obstacles in the way of an exchange, and Mustafa died at Damietta before an agreement was reached of chagrin, says Nicholas the Turk. The French gave him a military funeral with the same honours as for a French general.

At the same time as he accepted the Turkish capitulation, Kléber promised a general pardon to the people of Cairo. Even before recapturing the city, he had written to the Turkish government proposing the renewal of negotiations leading to the evacuation of Egypt. Napoleon's assertion, that 'Kléber, after his victory ... did all he could to consolidate the colony; his conduct was in every respect the opposite of what it had been before,'[1] is utterly unfounded. Kléber had not changed his mind about anything.

Although, contrary to Napoleon's opinion, Kléber continued to regard the evacuation of Egypt as his ultimate goal, he was undoubtedly reluctant to proceed without the authorization of his government, now that he knew that Bonaparte was in power. As a result, he felt compelled to prepare himself for a longer stay than he intended. He ordered the construction of elaborate fortifications, simplified the administration of finances and supplies (mainly with a view to preventing waste), and reorganized the Divan of Cairo. Several of the sheiks notably El-Bekri, whom the rebels had very nearly put to death were restored to office, but others were ordered to pay astronomic fines. Though he refrained from physical reprisals, having promised a pardon, Kléber took advantage of the rebellion to replenish the army's coffers by the most brutal means. When the sheik El-Sadat declared himself unable to pay his fine, Kléber had him imprisoned in the Citadel and beaten daily on the soles of his feet, until Murad Bey interceded in the venerable old man's favour. Kléber's regime, which was not to last long, may be characterized as fiscal terror. By the end of May,

---

[1] Correspondance, XXX, 125.

according to Sergeant François, the army received ten months of pay in arrears. Far from wishing to establish a permanent colony in Egypt, Kléber was deter mined 'to squeeze Egypt as the lemonade vendor squeezes the lemon' (the expression is his own) in order to fulfil his obligations toward the army until the happy day when it could leave.

IV

On March 5, 1800, General Desaix, provided with a passport signed by the Grand Vizier and Commodore Sidney Smith, left Alexandria aboard a Ragusan merchantman which her owner had tersely christened *The House of Grace of Saint Anthony of Padua.* General Junot followed him aboard the brig *L'Etoile.* Late in March both ships were almost within sight of the French coast when an English frigate boarded them. The commander of the frigate declared Desaix's and Junot's passports to be invalid, unless countersigned by Lord Keith, and took both ships to Leghorn. There Lord Keith had the two French generals locked up in a hospital. His treatment of them was something less than generous and would have shocked the chivalrous Sir Sidney Smith. At last, on April 29, Keith was obliged to release them, having received orders to that effect from London. They resumed their journey on the same ships. Once more Desaix was in sight of France; once more his ship was boarded—this time by Tunisian corsairs. The corsairs, however, showed more respect for the Grand Vizier's signature than had Lord Keith. After giving Desaix many marks of their esteem, they let him continue his journey. He reached Toulon on May 5.

He had barely landed when, that same day, he wrote to General Bonaparte, now First Consul of the Republic. 'Yes, General,' declared that indefatigable warrior, 'I have an intense desire to fight—preferably the English. I have vowed them my eternal hatred. Their insolence, the ill-treatment I received at their hands, are ever-present to my mind. Whatever grade you give me, I shall be content.... I shall serve equally gladly as a private volunteer or as a general.... Every day not well employed is a day wasted.'[1]

Desaix's most recent biographer sees in these lines 'abnegation and disinterestedness, dedication to duty and passion for combat.'[2] Perhaps so; it is humbly suggested, however, that one

---

[1] Sauzet, pp. 267-68.

[2] Ibid., p. 268.

may also see in them vindictiveness and an unpleasant anxious-
ness to make up with patriotic zeal for whatever grudge the First
Consul might bear one of the signatories of the Convention of El
Arish.

The First Consul received this letter on May 14, at Lausanne,
on Lake Geneva. He was about to lead his army across the Great
Saint Bernard pass to meet the Austrian forces in the plains of Italy. In his reply, Bonaparte, after chiding Desaix for his part in the
capitulation, makes the astonishing assertion that he was about to
send thirty-six ships with supplies and reinforcements to Egypt
when the news of the Convention of El Arish caused him to cancel
the convoy. Actually, all he had done was entertain the fleeting
thought of sending a squadron into the Mediterranean, primarily
to relieve Malta—a project which never materialized because it was
impossible. However this may be, Bonaparte assured Desaix that
bygones were bygones. 'Come and join me as fast as you can,
wherever I am,' he continued.[1]

Desaix lost no time. After a thirty-day quarantine at Toulon he
left on June 5, accompanied by his Mameluke Ismail and his Negro boy Baqil, and five days later joined Bonaparte at his headquarters at Montebello. After a long private conversation, during
which, no doubt, little good was said of Kléber, Bonaparte gave
Desaix the command of a corps comprising two divisions. A decisive battle was expected within the next few days. It was fought on
June 14, and it turned out to be decisive indeed, both for Bonaparte and for Desaix.

***

In January 1800 a Moslem Arab resident in Aleppo named Soliman, twenty-four years of age and a public writer by trade, went
on a pilgrim age to Jerusalem. If the testimony he gave at his trial
half a year later is correct, he must have been a very pious young
man, since he claimed to have spent three years at Mecca. In April,
he went to make a complaint to a Turkish officer, Ahmed Aga, who
was then in Jerusalem, about some unjust exactions that had been
demanded of his father, a butter merchant. After some conversation with Soliman, the Aga promised to put in a good word for his
father with Ibrahim Pasha of Aleppo, in exchange for a little service; Soliman was asked nothing less than to murder the
commander-in-chief of the French army in Egypt. Soliman did not
agree until they had had two more interviews. Ahmed Aga recom-

---

[1] Correspondance, VI, 273.

mended him to another officer, Yassin Aga, at Gaza, who would give him money. From that moment, Soliman stated later, it seemed to him that he had lost his sanity.

Soliman arrived in Cairo about mid-May and, for the whole month following, made the Mosque El Azhar his residence—as did many pilgrims and students—trying to find work as a public writer and reading the Koran with one of the teachers. Almost from his arrival, he confided in three young sheiks of El Azhar, all compatriots of his. As one of them was to testify, he told them that 'he wanted to do battle for the glory of God, which signifies that he wanted to kill a Christian,'[1] All three claimed that they tried to dissuade him, since they had doubted whether he was the right man for that commendable task. They did not warn the authorities, however, and every day they discussed and argued about the planned deed.

The sheiks' scepticism, if genuine, was misplaced. It took Soliman a full month to find the courage and the opportunity to commit his crime for God, but he was a man possessed by his fate. Fate also willed it that Kléber and Desaix, though 1,500 miles distant from one another, should be cut down at almost the same instant. Desaix was rushing to his rendezvous with death like an impatient lover. Kléber had done all he could to avoid it: but for the English cabinet's disavowal of the Convention of El Arish, he would be on his way to France instead of being shadowed by his assassin.

Fate—or death—seemed to favour Bonaparte. The god of war and the god of luck, as he had said, were marching alongside him. The price for his future victories was about to be paid by Desaix, the price for his past ones by Kléber.

---

[1] El-Djabarti, VI, 231

Chapter Eleven
The Vanities of Death

IN June 1800, all eyes were fixed on the military events to take place in the plains of Piedmont: if Bonaparte lost, his downfall was inevitable. From royalists to Jacobins, the leaders of the opposition in Paris were merely waiting for his first defeat to be rid of him. At Coppet, Madame de Staël received couriers every hour from Geneva, so anxious was she for the first bad news.

At three o'clock in the afternoon of June 14, Field-Marshal Melas, who commanded the Austrian army, sent out a message of victory: Bonaparte had been defeated near the village of Marengo. Melas had won by the simple expedient of spending five days doing absolutely nothing: puzzled as to Melas' whereabouts, Bonaparte had divided his army, sending his corps in various directions to look for him. On the morning of the 14th, instead of being surprised by Bonaparte, Melas surprised him.

At the same time as Melas sent his victory message, General Desaix with his corps joined Bonaparte, after marching all day in pursuit of the elusive Austrians. It seemed just a little too late. 'Well, General Desaix,' said the First Consul, 'we've had quite a brawl.' Desaix pulled his watch from his pocket. 'It is three o'clock,' he observed, 'the battle has been lost. There is time to win another.'[1]

---

[1] Sauzet, pp. 289, 290.

The Austrians and Hungarians, still within view, were marching off singing, with their bands playing. Less than half an hour later, Desaix's infantry charged at a run, screaming wildly as they went, while the cavalry of General Kellermann *fils* attacked the Austrians' flank. Before sundown the Austrian victory turned into a rout. But when Bonaparte asked for Desaix, to embrace his saviour, Desaix could not be found. Only an aide-de-camp and a sergeant had noticed him sliding from his horse at the beginning of the charge.

General Desaix's body was discovered, by lantern light, among a heap of others; it was recognized by his long, black hair, still tied with a ribbon. A large bullet had literally torn his heart to pieces. 'Why have I not the right to cry?'[1] Bonaparte is reported to have remarked when he viewed the corpse. Baqil, Desaix's black boy, and Ismail, his young Mameluke, felt no such inhibitions as they wailed over their dead master.

Napoleon never forgot his debt toward Desaix, and since Desaix was dead, he acknowledged it generously. The general whose death, at the age of thirty-two, was the pedestal of Napoleon's glory deserved a very special tomb. 'To so much virtue and heroism, I wish to pay such homage as no other man has received,' Napoleon proclaimed. 'Desaix's tomb shall have the Alps for its pedestal and the monks of the Saint Bernard for its guardians.'[2] On June 14, 1805, Desaix was solemnly buried in the chapel of the Hospice of Saint Bernard. The military Requiem was celebrated by the abbot; musketry punctuated the chant of the friars. Denon and Berthier pronounced Desaix's eulogy. 'Here is the man,' said Berthier, 'whom the Orient called "the Just", his fatherland "the Brave", his century "the Wise", and whom Napoleon has honoured with a monument.'[3] A more fatuous climax it would be difficult to imagine.

***

On June 14, General Kléber began the day by reviewing some troops on Rodah Island. Among the crowd was young Soliman, with a knife concealed under his galabiya. He followed the general back to Cairo, to the house of General Damas, where Kléber invited himself to lunch. It was a gay meal; Kléber enlivened it by drawing a caricature of Bonaparte expelling the Directors. Mean-

[1] Ibid., p. 296.
[2] Ibid., p. 308.
[3] Ibid., p. 309.

while Soliman loitered about Damas' house, until told to go away. Later in the afternoon Kléber left the party, which was still in progress; he had an appointment with the architect Protain, who was planning to build an addition to Elfi Bey's palace. It was a warm day and the two men decided to take a stroll in the garden. Kléber wore only his shirt and trousers. There were no guards in sight.

An Arab, dressed like a labourer, appeared on the path and walked toward the General. Taking him for a beggar, Kléber motioned him to go away, while Protain went on toward the house to call a sentry.

Soliman the Aleppan kept advancing and held out his left hand to Kléber, as if to seize the General's hand in order to carry it to his lips a custom generally followed by petitioners. Kléber gave him his hand. In an instant, Soliman lashed out with his right, which he had held concealed, and stabbed Kléber in the chest. At that moment Protain was glancing over his shoulder; he saw the murderer withdraw his knife and, as Kléber staggered, plunge it into his victim's abdomen, then through his left arm and into his right cheek. Protain's first reaction was to throw himself to the ground. He heard Kléber give a roar and fall. At this, Protain rose again, ran toward the assassin, and beat him over the head with his stick. The murderer stabbed wildly at Protain six times, left him nearly unconscious, and ran away. According to Protain's testimony, six minutes elapsed before any help arrived. Kléber died shortly afterwards.

A drum roll gave the alarm from Esbekiya Square. Within a few minutes, all the drums in Cairo called the soldiers to their stations. The news of Kléber's murder spread with incredible speed. Terrified of the consequences, the population sought safety in their houses, while the soldiers, seized by fury (and, perhaps, mistaking the murder for the beginning of another rebellion) ran amuck in the streets. 'We cut down with our sabres and daggers all the men and children we came across,' reminisces Sergeant François, apparently without shame.[1] Fortunately, the disorder stopped as soon as the murderer was apprehended. He had not fled far from the scene. A woman, who saw him from the roof of a neighbouring house, pointed him out to the soldiers, who found him crouching by a ruined garden wall, his head bruised by Protain's blows, his garments sticky with blood, praying. The knife was discovered near him, still bloody, covered with a little earth.

---

[1] François, I, 430.

A preliminary investigation was held by a commission headed by General Menou, who by right of seniority succeeded Kléber as commander-in-chief. In the teeth of circumstantial evidence, Soliman at first disclaimed any connection with the crime. Then, according to the transcript of the proceedings, 'the commander-in-chief ordered him put to torture, a measure authorized by local custom. He was beaten until he begged for mercy and promised a full confession,'[1]

Confessions under torture are open to doubt, but they are not necessarily false. The record of Soliman's trial leaves no doubt as to his guilt, and his confession—including the part about the two Turkish officers who had assigned him the mission—was most probably accurate. On the other hand, the reasoning by which the special court (composed entirely of Frenchmen) pinned the ultimate responsibility for Kléber's murder on the Grand Vizier is specious and laboured and has no basis in Soliman's confession.

In his chronicle, the sheik El-Djabarti reproduces the full record of Soliman's trial. 'The record,' he says, 'has some importance because it contains all the details of the crime and because it gives an idea of how justice is practised by the French, a nation which has no religion but follows the rules of reason.'[2] What astonished El-Djabarti was that a man whose guilt was manifest should be given a regular trial instead of being put to death instantly. Actually, however, the procedure adopted in the case differed widely from normal French practice (for one thing, the defendants were not represented by counsel), and the purpose of the trial was not to be fair to the defendants but to discover accomplices.

Apart from Soliman, four others were tried—the three sheiks of El Azhar to whom he had confided his project, and an old teacher of the Koran, the Turk Mustafa Effendi of Bursa, with whom Soliman had studied. Cross examination and confrontation of the three sheiks established plainly that they were accessories before the fact, having failed to inform the authorities of Soliman's intent to commit a crime. Mustafa Effendi was found innocent and released. The three sheiks were sentenced to be decapitated; as for Soliman, the court chose to apply a penalty permitted by local custom but scarcely in keeping with the enlightened principles of the French Republic. To order a man to have his right hand burned off

---

[1] El-Djabarti, VI, 227.

[2] Ibid., VI, 223-24.

and to be impaled alive may strike some as too zealous a gesture of respect for indigenous tradition.

For three days, since Kléber's death, a cannon shot had been fired every thirty minutes from the Citadel. On June 17 Kléber's coffin, bearing his hat, his sword, and his murderer's knife, was carried to the burial place with military pomp. General Menou led the procession. The drums were muffled and covered with black crepe; the troops carried their muskets upside down and wore ribbons of black crepe on their sleeves. A deputation of Mameluke horsemen, representing Murad Bey, and the Moslem and Christian dignitaries of Cairo followed the lead coffin. The procession halted, and the coffin was put down, on the hill where Soliman and his accomplices were awaiting execution. An artillery salvo gave the signal for that part of the ceremony to begin.

In the life of Barthelmy the Greek, this must have been the supreme day. He began by hacking off the heads of the three sheiks. In the meantime, coals had been heating in a brazier. Soliman made no complaint while his hand was being roasted, but when a lump of red—hot coal rolled to his elbow, he drew Barthelmy's attention to the fact that his sentence did not mention the elbow—only the hand. Barthelmy expressed the opinion that Soliman was quibbling. Soliman called Barthelmy a Christian dog and insisted on his rights until the coal was removed. The surgical details of Soliman's impaling, which followed, have been recorded by Sergeant François, who claims to have observed them from a distance of five paces: amateurs of such matters are free to look them up in his memoirs. It is interesting to note that everyone present, including the patient, seems to have regarded the bestial procedure as altogether normal. When Barthelmy had completed the preliminary part of the operation, the pole with Soliman on it was set upright and planted in the ground. Soliman begged a French soldier who stood nearby for water. The soldier was about to hand him his canteen when Barthelmy prevented him: the least bit of water, he pointed out, would cause instantaneous death and thus frustrate the due course of justice.

The funeral procession resumed its march, leaving the impaled Soliman to pray to God. At Kléber's tomb, Fourier delivered an endless oration whose hollow bombast did the great mathematician little honour. Four hours later, Soliman died. What had he accomplished? He had killed the man whose sole desire it was to end the French occupation of Egypt, and in his place he had put an imperialistic maniac who was determined to make Egypt a part of France. This, of course, he did not know: all he knew was that he had ' done battle for the glory of God,' and that his reward would be paradise. In this respect he showed far more confidence than had his victim Kléber, who had written to a friend several months earlier, 'What I fear least is the battle; what I fear most is the day after.'[1]

II

If Kléber looked every inch a soldier, his successor, Jacques Abdallah Menou, looked every inch the proprietor or headwaiter of a rustic bistro. Only the napkin and apron are missing from the portrait Dutertre sketched of him in Egypt. With his balding and greying hair, his undistinguished features, his pot belly and un-martial stance, it is difficult to visualize him commanding an army, though one can readily imagine him bowing to his patrons and tyrannizing over his staff. As so often happens with character judgments based on physiognomy, the impression would be abso-lutely accurate, except for the detail that Menou, issued from an ancient noble house, was the son of a marquis.

Like many of his fellow nobles, he had greeted the Revolution enthusiastically in 1789. Though suspected of royalist leanings during the Reign of Terror, he survived the storm, fought against the royalist insurrection in the Vendée, was wounded, and in 1794 was appointed to command the Army of the Interior. In this ca-pacity he brutally suppressed the working men's riots of May 1795 but balked at taking similar measures against a rightist insurrec-tion in September. As a result, he was sacked and replaced by Bonaparte, who saved the day with his famous 'whiff of grapeshot.' Menou remained in disgrace until April 1798, when Bonaparte gave him a divisional command in the Egyptian expedition.

Menou, at that time, was in his fifty-first year—only three years older than Kléber —yet for some reason all his comrades in arms, in their memoirs, describe him as an old man; so do the Arabic chroniclers, and Napoleon in his history of the campaign flatly as-serts that Menou was sixty. Apart from having been wounded in the Vendée and during the capture of Alexandria, Menou's record was undistinguished—and to receive a wound is not necessarily a sign of military competence. It is doubtful whether Bonaparte ever intended him to command a division; in any event, Menou's wound gave him an opportunity to transfer the divisional com-mand to Vial (and later to Lannes) and to make Menou governor

[1] Rousseau, p. 195.

of Rosetta. From July 1798 to March 1801, Menou took part in no military operations save punitive raids.

Beginning in February 1799, Menou's behaviour showed signs of eccentricity. Just before Bonaparte left for Syria, he appointed Menou governor of Cairo; Menou asked for a delay, on the ground that the British squadron was bombarding Alexandria and that his presence on the coast might be necessary. Dugua took temporary command of Cairo, and the matter was dropped. A month later, Bonaparte ordered Menou to follow him to Syria and to take over the governorship of Palestine; a snail would have reached Syria faster than did General Menou, who in fact never even reached the border. By June 3, he had progressed as far as Katia, where Bonaparte met him on his way back from Syria. Bonaparte did not reprimand him: as things turned out, Menou's presence in Palestine would have been unnecessary in any event; moreover, the motives that kept the general at Rosetta, though unconventional, fitted very well Into Bonaparte's schemes for Egypt.

Among the French leaders in Egypt, Menou had always been the most sanguine champion of colonization and assimilation. Others shared his enthusiasm, but none acted upon it with Menou's literal-minded optimism. Bonaparte had declared himself a Moslem at heart and hinted at a conversion in the future; Menou actually became a Moslem.

Whether, as some have asserted, he did this merely in order to marry the daughter of a hat-keeper in Rosetta, or whether his reasons were primarily political, it is difficult to say; in any event, religious conviction had little to do with his conversion.

Testimony regarding Menou's bride, Zobeida, varies widely. According to some, she was young and alluring, and her charms had reawakened the 'senescent' Menou's appetites to the point of making a fool of him. According to others, he had never seen her before the wedding, and she turned out not so young, not so pretty, and not so rich as Menou had been led to believe. Menou himself declared to every body that she came from a sherifian family, both her father and mother being descendants of Mohammed. 'I must let you know, my dear General, that I have just taken a wife.' he wrote to Dugua. 'I believe this measure will be useful to the public interest.'[1] Marmont, whom he had apprised of his 'measure' in a similar vein, congratulated him, adding most likely with tongue in cheek: 'You are right in saying that your marriage

---

[1] La Jonquière, V, 15.

will surprise many people. As far as I am concerned, my dear General, I regard it as a sign of your great devotion to the interests of the French army.' A week later, Marmont enquired with a straight face, 'I am impatient to know whether Madame Menou is pretty, and whether you intend, in the near future, to follow local customs and to give her some companions.' 'My dear General,' answered Menou, 'my wife ... is tall, large, and in every respect quite good-looking. She has very beautiful eyes, the usual Egyptian complexion, and long, extremely black hair. She is good-natured, and I find that she accepts many French customs with less repugnance than I expected.... I have not yet urged her to show herself unveiled among men; this will come little by little.... I shall not make use of Mohammed's permission to have four wives, not counting concubines: Moslem females have vehement appetites; one wife will more than suffice me.'[1]

Menou had received dispensation from circumcision, but in every other respect he practised his new religion punctiliously. He studied the Koran, went to pray at the mosque every Friday, and performed his five daily prayers with ostensible devotion. Still, El-Djabarti is probably quite right when he asserts that Menou's conversion was merely feigned for political reasons. It is clear from Menou's letters that his religious beliefs, if any, did not go beyond the tolerant and vague eighteenth-century deism in which he had been brought up.

Bonaparte, who realized that Abdallah Menou's action lent some plausibility to his promise of an imminent -conversion of the entire French army, congratulated Menou on his sacrifice to the patriotic cause. Needless to say, this official blessing of the union did not stop the irrepressibly ribald comments in the army.

When Kléber succeeded Bonaparte as command-in-chief, a clash between him and Menou became inevitable. While Kléber was pre paring to evacuate Egypt, Menou was drafting memoranda on the dazzling prospects of a permanent French establishment. Menou' s patronizing advice, his pretentious and foolish excursions into inter national politics and political economy irritated Kléber, whose sarcastic replies must have wounded Menou. At the same time, Menou was beginning to show mild signs of paranoia. His patriotism and republicanism, he thought, had been questioned by certain people because he had the misfortune of being born a noble. He wrote letters to every body, protesting his staunch republicanism; he wrote to Bonaparte and to Berthier,

---

[1] Ibid. 9 V, 662-63.

condemning Kléber's conduct as unpatriotic and dishonourable; he wrote to Kléber, begging to be employed as a simple grenadier. Somewhat harshly, Kléber answered that he had believed Menou to be too busy writing memoranda on colonial trade to serve in a military capacity. He, Kléber, was more interested in finding ways to pay and feed his army than in learning how much cotton, sugar cane, and indigo could be grown in Egypt. However, he would give Menou the military command of Cairo, on the condition that Menou did not engage him in arguments about political economy. This offer Menou rejected, but late in May 1800 he agreed to accept the governorship of the provinces of Beni Suef and Faiyum in Middle Egypt. He was about to take this post when Kléber's death called him to the supreme command.

Even if he had possessed the gift of leadership, Menou would have laboured under several handicaps when he succeeded the immensely popular Kléber: he was widely regarded as a comic figure, he had no military reputation; and he championed the unpopular cause of a permanent occupation of Egypt. In addition, his outstanding talent was for making enemies. It became apparent very soon that, though he might be ridiculous, he was by no means to be laughed at. No sooner had he occupied his new post than he fancied himself in the role of Hercules cleaning out the Aegean stables. Kléber's administration, in his eyes, had been a disastrous mixture of indolence, defeatism, and corruption; but he, Menou, would restore discipline, punish the thieves (a class which, according to him, comprised all the Copts save Moallem Jacob and virtually the entire army administration save the Chief Paymaster Estève), smite all enemy armies, be they ever so numerous, and transform Egypt into a prosperous province of France. To carry out this ambitious project, Menou thought it expedient to begin by discrediting his predecessor and by making insulting insinuations against those who had enjoyed Kléber's confidence. To those who dared to defend themselves or to speak up in favour of a comrade, Menou would address long epistles disclaiming any personal animosity: they did not know what sort of man he was; if they knew him better, they would realize that he was guided only by the principles of honour, integrity, patriotism, and duty, in which he had been brought up since childhood. His passion for self-justification leaves one with the impression of an emotionally and mentally unbalanced personality.

Although he courted his subordinates' approval in a manner unbecoming a commander-in-chief, Abdallah Menou was not tolerant of contradiction. To antagonize him was dangerous. General

Damas (Kléber's chief of staff), Poussielgue, Tallien, the Chief Army Commissioner Daure, and others were dismissed from their posts and sent back to France. Their careers were ruined. Tallien (who had done Menou more than one good turn during the Reign of Terror) was even arrested on Bonaparte's orders after his landing. In due course, Menou was surrounded only by yes-men; his belief that he had restored unity and morale in his command proved utterly unrealistic as soon as his administration met with its first and last crisis.

Menou had not been in charge of Egypt for long when he discerned a spectacular change for the better since the days of Kléber. He lost no opportunity to point out the success of his policies in his letters and in his Orders of the Day. The improvement was real enough, and undoubtedly it was due in part to Menou's administrative measures, some of which were very sound. In the main, however, Menou owed his success to his predecessor. Thanks to Kléber's victory at Heliopolis, Egypt enjoyed nine months of peace; thanks to the alliance Kléber had made with Murad Bey, the French received a fixed tribute from Upper Egypt without having to administer it; thanks to the same alliance and to Murad's prestige, subversion in Cairo and Lower Egypt ceased. Yet, in his blindness, Menou refused to see the true reasons of the sudden peace and prosperity. He never missed a chance to deplore Kléber's treaty with Murad, which he pretended to honour only because he could not go back on Kléber's word, and he went so far as to forbid the erection of a monument to Kléber. In this, he was worse than ungrateful: by taking all the credit for himself, he lost touch with political reality and slowly but surely moved toward catastrophe. Those who mistake their good luck for their merit are inevitably bound for disaster.

Less than a week before Kléber's murder, Sir Sidney Smith—who had received new instructions from his government—wrote to the French commander-in-chief to propose negotiating a new treaty on the same basis as the Convention of El Arish. Menou rejected the offer peremptorily and even made the grotesque insinuation that Smith might have had a hand in Kléber's murder. It would have been sufficient if he had replied that the terms acceptable before Heliopolis were no longer quite good enough after that victory; but to keep the doors open to negotiation was far from his intentions. As the months passed by and none of the expected English or Turkish attacks materialized, Menou's self-confidence took on maniacal proportions. 'As for our possession of Egypt,' he wrote to Talleyrand in January 1801, 'the Republic and the First

Consul may rest assured that no power on earth can wrest that conquest from the Army of the Orient. If need be, we shall fight all the hordes of Asia and defeat them.... I dare affirm that we shall not negotiate except with bullets and cannon balls.'[1]

Since his wishes were his convictions, Menou considered Egypt a part of French territory, officially declared it to be so, and proceeded to transform the country in the image of France. He had entire quarters of Cairo demolished to make room for vast avenues; he took the tax collection out of the hands of the Copts and imposed a single land tax; he abolished feudal dues and changed the Moslem laws of inheritance; he abolished Moslem criminal law and set up criminal courts under French control, he ordered the compulsory registration of births and deaths; he set up the first newspaper printed in Arabic. All these were praiseworthy reforms, but Menou lacked the two only means that can make reforms effective—power and persuasion. The population for whose benefit they were intended saw in them mere attempts, perpetrated by a pseudo-Moslem, at uprooting all their institutions; Menou's confused philosophical-theological lucubrations, with which he prefaced his edicts, only added to the general bewilderment. If Menou believed that his being a Moslem would make his precipitate and ill-prepared reforms more acceptable to the nation, he was deceiving himself. The Moslems regarded him as an impostor and realized with a sure instinct that all Menou wanted was to make Egypt French a desire they did not share. According to El-Djabarti, who became a member of the Divan under Menou's administration, Moslems fared far less well under Abdallah Menou than they had under either of his non-Moslem predecessors. 'The commander-in-chief no longer showed himself in public and received no one among the Moslems,' declares El-DjabartL 'The Moslems were treated with contempt. The French as well as the Coptic, Syrian, and Greek Christians insulted and maltreated them.'[2]

As long as Murad Bey's prestige prevented a rebellion, as long as no invader tested the discipline and morale of his army or his own military competence, as long as time had not yet exposed the utter ineptitude of his reforms, the ex-nobleman, ex-Christian Menou, now faithful servant of Mohammed's God and Bonaparte's Republic, could afford to withdraw from reality into a world of wishful dreams. To him, the future prosperity of an *Egypte*

[1] Rousseau, p. 394.
[2] El-Djabarti, VI, 255.

française, the Suez Canal, the flourishing cotton and indigo plantations, the lucrative trade with central Africa in black slaves, ivory, gold dust, and spices, and the brotherhood between happily sweating fellahin and benevolently profit-taking French colonists were already a reality. To doubt it was treason in a Frenchman and blasphemy in a Moslem: 'Take note,' he admonished the Divan, 'that Egypt has definitely become a possession of France. You must convince yourself of this truth and believe in it with the absolute faith with which you believe in the unity of God.'[1] A few weeks after writing this, he lost Egypt.

III

It was only a week after Marengo—ten months after his departure from Egypt—that Bonaparte gave any sign of remembering the army he had left behind. It is true that he had not wasted his time during those ten months: he had made himself the master of France, given her a new Constitution, pacified the rebellious Vendée, stabilized the franc, laid the foundations for a new Civil Code, and won a major victory. This accomplished, he was able to address himself to problems of less immediate urgency, and Egypt was one of them. Even then, and throughout the second half of the year 1800, the aid he sent to the Army of the Orient was not in keeping with the promises he had made. A few courier ships carrying despatches, newspapers, books, medicine, spirits, seeds, ammunition, and a handful of specialists, notably surgeons and artisans—that was all. Nevertheless, it was a great deal more than the Directory had done for him. Then, in January 1801, his Egyptian policy underwent a marked change. Several frigates were despatched to Alexandria carrying close to a thousand troops, and on January 23 Admiral Ganteaume left Brest with a squadron including seven ships of the line, with the mission of transporting about 5,000 men to Egypt.

The most obvious of the many reasons for this change of policy was the spectacular improvement of France's military and political position over the past few months. The Kingdom of the Two Sicilies had been forced out of the war; its ports were open to French ships and closed to the English. General Moreau had inflicted another crushing defeat on Austria at Hohenlinden, and Austria was obliged to make peace. Spain was coaxed into a closer alliance and

[1] Ibid., VII, 15.

retroceding Louisiana and her half of Santo Domingo to France. Most important of all, Tsar Paul of Russia, an eccentric if not a madman, had changed sides in the war and turned into a fanatical worshipper of Bonaparte. These gains more than made up for the one important loss suffered by France—the capitulation of Malta to the English on September 5, 1800.

Only two great powers remained in the field—England and Turkey. Bonaparte had written a personal letter, offering peace, to King George III as early as January 25, 1800. He had also re-opened negotiations with Turkey, offering the eventual evacuation of Egypt—and that at a time when General Menou had proclaimed Egypt a permanent French possession and was laying plans with a confidence in the future unrivalled since the building of the Pyramids. With the European continent at peace, Bonaparte was free to despatch a few thousand men to the Eastern theatre of war, which once again became the centre of operations.

The English government realized no less clearly than did Bonaparte that the terms of a peace treaty between England and France would depend to a large degree on the outcome of a test of strength in the eastern Mediterranean. As early as October 1800, the English cabinet instructed Admiral Keith to be prepared to transport an expeditionary force of 17,000 men, commanded by General Sir Ralph Abercromby, to Egypt. Another force—3,000 Indian troops and 2,000 troops to be picked up at the Cape—under the command of General Baird, was to land at Kosseir, on the Red Sea coast of Egypt. The British landings were to be supported by a Turkish army under the Kapitan Pasha—the Ottoman First Lord of the Admiralty. These plans, though impressive, were based on a very inadequate estimate of French strength in Egypt. Deceived partly by Kléber's letter to the Directory and even more so by their own propaganda, the British government estimated Menou's forces at only about two thirds of their actual number and vastly over estimated the efficiency of the Turkish army. It is true, as luck would have it, that General Menou's ineptitude more than compensated for the error in the British calculations.

Bonaparte was well informed of the British plans; hence the urgency of the orders he issued to Ganteaume. There was, however, yet another and larger project at the back of his mind, which gave Egypt paramount importance. On December 16, 1800, Tsar Paul had concluded with Prussia, Sweden, and Denmark a League of Armed Neutrality whose purpose, in simple terms, was to challenge Britain's interference with neutral shipping on the open seas. A virtual state of warfare resulted between Britain and the League, culminating in the destruction of the Danish navy by Nelson in the Battle of Copenhagen in 1801. The creation of the League represented a diplomatic triumph for Bonaparte. Not content with this, the First Consul persuaded the impressionable Tsar to deal an even heavier blow to British hegemony by agreeing to a joint attack directed at the English possessions in Asia. Russian troops were ready to march on India when, on March 24, the entire scheme collapsed with Paul's assassination.

Even if Paul had not been murdered, Bonaparte's revived Asiatic dream was bound to dissolve under the sober reality of Ganteaume's timorousness, Menou's ineptitude, and British naval superiority. As for Bonaparte's belief that Egypt was a valuable asset in his peace negotiations with England (which were then being conducted in the wings), it was also based on an illusion: as long as the French were in possession of Egypt, England would make no peace. What Bonaparte regarded as an asset, what Menou swore to defend to the last man, was in fact the principal obstacle to peace. This simple proposition, which Kléber had grasped a year earlier, was proved beyond any doubt by the events of the summer and autumn of 1801. Bonaparte failed to see it until the end of his life. Even then, writing the history of the campaign in St. Helena, he persisted in speculating on what would have happened if Ganteaume had reached Egypt, *if* Menou had made better use of his forces, and so forth. According to him, France would have obtained better peace terms. The truth is that, when peace was made in 1802, France obtained the best terms she could get, and that if Egypt had remained French, there would have been no peace at all. Bonaparte judged most things and most people acutely, with the exception of the English. In this, of course, he is in a very large company.

***

The British expeditionary force for Egypt was assembled at Malta late in November 1800. It left a month later—not for Egypt but for the small bay of Marmorice, on the coast of Asia Minor opposite Rhodes. Unlike Bonaparte in 1798, Sir Ralph Abercromby was a man of method and of caution: at the staging area of Marmorice his men recuperated from their long and strenuous voyage and were given a thorough training course in landing tactics. At the same time Major-General Sir John Moore was despatched to Jaffa to co-ordinate the British campaign with the movements of the Grand Vizier, who had reconstituted the remnants of his army after his rout at Heliopolis. Sir John was gloomy when he returned to Marmorice on January 20. The Grand Vizier's supply system was chaos, he reported; his army was a horde; and the Vizier him-self was an old man who did not know the first thing about war. In addition, a thousand Turkish soldiers were dying every month of the plague. Hearing this, Sir Ralph decided to write off the Grand Vizier, to rely mainly on his own forces and on the more disci-plined army of the Kapitan Pasha, and to concentrate his attack on Alexandria. On February 21, the English fleet left Marmorice.

On February 20, Bonaparte issued a proclamation to the Army of the Orient, announcing an imminent Anglo-Turkish invasion. 'Every man who disembarks must be either killed or captured,' he wrote. 'The desert of Katia must become the grave of the Grand Vizier.'[1] On the same day, Admiral Ganteaume returned to Toulon, having judged the risks of a crossing to Alexandria too heavy to take upon himself. The First Consul was infuriated. 'You must, at any price whatever, bring aid to the Army of the Orient,' he ad-monished Ganteaume on February 25.[2] Ganteaume felt that this was more easily said than done. Nevertheless, he set sail again on March 19, ran into the squadron of Admiral Warren, which had recently entered the Mediterranean, escaped it, and returned to Toulon for the second time. While Ganteaume was testing the Mediterranean with his big toe, as it were, and finding it too wet, Bonaparte wrote optimistically to Tsar Paul: 'The English are at-tempting a landing in Egypt. It is in the interest of all Mediterra-nean and Black Sea powers that Egypt remain French. The Suez Canal ... has already been traced: it is an easy enterprise which will require little time and which will bring incalculable advantages to Russian commerce.'[3] It would be difficult to pile up a more impos-ing heap of—to put it mildly—questionable assertions, but then the First Consul was addressing a maniac. It so happened that when the message reached St. Petersburg, the maniac had been shot dead by the friends of the maniac's son, who at that time did not yet share his father's enthusiasm for Bonaparte. Also, on March 8, Sir Ralph Abercromby's army had landed in Abukir Bay.

The landing was carried out with brilliance and dash. 'We were fired upon from fifteen pieces of artillery as soon as we were within reach,' Sir John Moore recorded in his diary, 'first by round shot, afterwards with grape, and at last by the infantry. The boats continued to row in steadily, and the sailors and soldiers occasion-ally huzzaed. Numbers were killed and wounded, and some boats

[1] Correspondance, VII, 40.
[2] Ibid., VII, 48.
[3] Correspondance, VII, 50.

were sunk. The fire of grape-shot and musketry was really most severe.'[1] The training the troops had received at Marmorice paid off: despite their heavy casualties—600, according to Moore—the English established a beachhead and stormed the steep dunes. The French, too inferior in numbers to resist, withdrew. After consolidating his position and unloading his artillery, Abercromby advanced in the direction of Alexandria, leaving a force behind to invest Fort Abukir, whose garrison of about 200 men capitulated on March 20.

The main body of the English army ran into heavy resistance a few miles west of Abukir but succeeded in dislodging the French from their position after a severe combat on March 15. It was here, near the ruins of ancient Canopus, that Menou attacked them a week later.

***

For several months, General Menou had been warned that a British landing was imminent. It is difficult to explain what prevented him from reinforcing the units stationed along and near the coast. It is even more difficult to understand why, for almost two weeks, he did nothing even after he received the news that the British had arrived. Indeed, the English fleet had been sighted off Abukir as early as March 1; heavy weather prevented the landing until a week later, but Menou must have been notified of its presence by March 3, and he left Cairo only on March 12. Speed was not Menou's outstanding quality, yet even his slowness would not have been fatal had it not been complicated with overconfidence.

The most sensible course for Menou to take would have been to march without delay on Abukir with all his available forces (which were far superior to Sir Ralph Abercromby; s) and, after repulsing the English, to march east and head off the Grand Vizier. He could then have returned to Cairo, which Murad Bey would have held for him in the meantime, and made mincemeat of General Baird's Anglo-Indian army. Even if Murad had proved disloyal, Menou could have recaptured Cairo just as Kléber had done a year earlier. The essential thing was to strike at each invading force successively and with superior numbers, beginning with Abercromby's army at Abukir. This is what Bonaparte or Kléber would have done. Instead, Menou made every mistake in the book. He gave Abercromby time to consolidate his position; he left nearly half of his forces in Cairo under General Belliard, and he

---

[1] Moore, II, 2.

spurned Murad Bey's co-operation. On March 21 three weeks after the English appeared off the coast Menou gave battle to them near the site of ancient Canopus, between Abukir and Alexandria. Sir Ralph disposed of about 15,000 men fit for combat, Menou of about 12,000. It is doubtful whether Menou's recipe for victory was to get there the slowest with the fewest. More likely, he mistook the Englishmen for Turks and himself for a Bonaparte: other wise, it is difficult to imagine a reason for his choosing to attack Abercromby at the time and in the place he did.

The battle of Canopus was murderous for both sides. According to Lieutenant-Colonel Wilson, French losses amounted to 4,000 killed, wounded, and captured; 1,040 Frenchmen were buried by the English during the two days following. The English losses were at least 240 killed and 1,250 wounded, but Wilson seems to underestimate them. 'I never saw a field so strewed with dead,' Sir John Moore noted succinctly in his diary.[1] Sir John himself was wounded in the leg; so was the English commander-in-chief, Sir Ralph Abercromby, who soon became delirious and died a week later.

On the French side, two generals were fatally wounded—Roize and Lanusse. When Menou came to Lanusse's bedside—so Nicholas the Turk reports—the dying man showed little gratitude for his superior's concern. His last words—addressed to Menou—were to the effect that Menou was not fit to be an onion peeler in the kitchen of the Republic. It must have done the brave man some good to expire with a truth on his lips.

Having lost the battle and one third of his forces, General Menou did what he should have done in the first place: he withdrew to Alexandria. As Lieutenant-Colonel Wilson, who took part in the action, puts it convincingly, Menou's chief error had been 'his eagerness to be the aggressor.... The wish of France was to preserve Egypt, not fight for victories, bought at an expense in the event as ruinous as defeat.'[2] If Menou, instead of attacking, had awaited the English at Alexandria, Wilson suggests, the English army might well have been forced to abandon its enterprise.

What would have been right on March 20 was wrong on March 22. Having lost to the British at Canopus, Menou with his reduced forces should never have locked himself up in Alexandria and given the enemy time to pursue his advantage. While Menou pre-

---

[1] Moore, II, 16

[2] Wilson, I, 62-63.

pared his defences and engaged in acrimonious recriminations with his subordinates, whom he blamed for his defeat, the Kapitan Pasha landed 6,000 Janissaries at Abukir (March. 25), and General Hutchinson, Sir Ralph's successor, took Rosetta with an Anglo-Turkish force (April 2). On April 15, the English engineers cut through the narrow isthmus between Lake Ma'addiya (now dried up, but then communicating with the Mediterranean), and the partially dried-up bed of Lake Maryut, south of Alexandria. General Hutchinson had long opposed the scheme, which was extremely destructive of property, but had given way at last to military considerations. Four cuts were made. 'At seven o'clock in the evening,' reports Wilson, 'the last fascine was removed and joy was universal. The water rushed in with a fall of six feet, and the pride and peculiar care of Egypt, the consolidation of ages, was in a few hours destroyed by the devastating hand of man.... An immense body of water rushed in, which continued entering for a month with considerable force.'[1] The inundation cut off Alexandria very effectively, facilitated the task of the English siege force, and enabled a number of small English vessels to enter Lake Maryut.

With part of the British units thus relieved from siege duty, a combined Anglo-Turkish force under General Hutchinson and the Kapitan Pasha marched up the left bank of the Nile; on May 9, in an engagement at El Rahmaniya, they obliged a French force under General Lagrange to withdraw to Cairo. Thus Belliard's army at Cairo (about 12,000 men after Lagrange joined it) was cut off from Menou's army at Alexandria. At the same time the Grand Vizier with 15,000 men entered Egypt from Syria, took Damietta and Es Saliya, and marched up the right bank of the Nile.

Cut off from the coast, with two armies advancing toward Cairo, and with the plague raging throughout Lower and Middle Egypt, General Belliard considered the possibility of giving up Cairo and withdrawing into Upper Egypt, where he would join forces with Murad Bey's Mamelukes. This plan was frustrated when Murad Bey, on his way to Cairo, died of the plague. Murad's successor, Osman Bey Tambordji; with 1,500 Mameluke horsemen (amongst them a number of French deserters) passed over to the

---

[1] Wilson, I, 6

British on May 28.[1] On June 19, the combined armies of Hutchinson, the Kapitan Pasha, and the Grand Vizier, reinforced by Mamelukes and Bedouins, were encamped almost within cannon range from Cairo, on both sides of the Nile; a boat bridge had been thrown across the river by the British.

Throughout the Anglo-Turkish advance and the manoeuvres preparatory to an investment of Cairo and Giza, General Belliard had remained absolutely passive. His main concern seems to have been the prevention of a popular rebellion. To this effect he sent Fourier to warn the sheiks that the strictest neutrality was expected of the people of Cairo in the event of fighting. Let everyone stay at home and keep quiet, and no one would be harmed; otherwise, the just would inevitably have to pay the same price as the wicked. The sheiks disagreed with the mathematician's logic, but Fourier ended the debate with the remark that 'bombs and bullets do not read the Koran.'[2] As it turned out, there was neither fighting nor rebellion. On June 22, an emissary from Belliard arrived in the British camp. After five days of negotiating, Belliard signed the capitulation of Cairo without a shot being fired. The terms were essentially the same as those of the Convention of El Arish, except that the document contained guarantees for the safety of the native Egyptians who had co-operated with the French. It was only on July 10 that the actual evacuation took place. In the meantime, the main preoccupation of the French troops was to liquidate all their possessions for cash, including their concubines.

---

[1] It appears, both from the papers of Sir Sidney Smith and from a letter of Osman Bey quoted by Sir Robert Wilson, that it was Murad Bey's intention, just before his death, to pass over to the English if they guaranteed that there would be no reprisals against him on the part of the Grand Vizier. 'We know very well,' wrote Osman to Smith, 'that Murad Bey was very much afraid of the Sublime Porte, and that he put himself under your protection. We are no less afraid, and you know that there is no power in the world in which we can put more perfect confidence than in the Court of Great Britain. We are all brethren, trust first in God the Almighty, and then in you, we put ourselves under your protection, we wish to stay with our children and our families in Cairo, under the orders of the Sublime Porte, and under the guarantee of the English' (Wilson, History of the British Expedition to Egypt, II, 201). On the other hand, French sources assert unanimously that Murad Bey remained loyal to the French until the end. If this was his intention, General Menou made it difficult for him to carry it out.

[2] El-Djabarti, VI, 281.

On July 4 or 5—one week after the signing of the capitulation—an order from General Menou reached General Belliard: the French troops must either defeat the enemy or die. 'This order could not have been given by anyone but a madman,'[1] commented Malus in his diary. Perhaps so; but Belliard's decision to capitulate without resistance, although approved by the majority of a council of war convened to that effect, was nonetheless astonishing. It took the English command completely by surprise. The position of the Anglo-Turkish forces was by no means as brilliant as it appeared. Ophthalmia and dysentery had incapacitated a good part of the English, who were also short of siege artillery; as for the Turks, they were for the most part an undisciplined horde. In the opinion of the larger part of the British staff, General Hutchinson had acted recklessly in venturing so far inland. They regarded Belliard's capitulation as an incredible piece of luck.

It is true that Belliard, despite all the excuses he found for his action, could easily have held out for a considerable time, if not in Cairo itself, then at least in the Citadel and in several of the forts surrounding the city. Nevertheless, if he capitulated without a fight, this was not from cowardice: he had amply proved his bravery in Upper Egypt under Desaix. He capitulated for precisely the same reasons that had made Kléber capitulate at El Arish. To sacrifice thousands of lives for a patently hopeless cause seemed to him not honourable but criminal. According to El-Djabarti, thirty to forty Frenchmen were dying of the plague at the Citadel every day. There was barely any water—one glass per day for each soldier, if the *Gazette de Leyde* may be relied upon. Was Belliard to prolong a siege under such conditions, merely to flatter General Menou's colonial dreams and in the vain hope of reinforcements being brought from France? If he had taken this course, several thousand dead men would have been proclaimed heroes, and Egypt would have been lost just the same. As in Kléber's case, the verdict depends entirely on the question whether reason in a general is treason.

The French left Cairo with full honours of war, with all their weapons, equipment, and whatever possessions they could carry. Not counting their women and children, there were nearly 15,000 of them—11,168 land troops fit for duty, 1,500 sick, 544 seamen, and 82 civilians; in addition, there were 760 Copts, Greeks, and Mamelukes who elected to accompany them to France. Thanks to the efforts of all the commanders concerned—French, British, and

---

[1] Malus, p. 218.

Turkish—the evacuation was effected in the greatest order, without any incident. 'The English,' noted the diarist Malus, 'are behaving very decently. The Turks are tired of the whole business and want to put an end to it at any price.'[1]

It seemed fitting that the body of General Kléber, which the French carried with them, should be paid special respect by all three belligerents. While the French troops, lined up in two ranks, presented arms at its passage, the English and Turkish artillery saluted the procession. 'It was not the muffled beat, the trappings of the ceremony, the imposing stillness of parade, but the silent manliness of unaffected grief which diffused the mournful solemnity. Every soldier, as the coffin passed, felt that therein their benefactor's, their father's bones reposed.'[2] These words were written, not by a Frenchman, but by an English officer, Sir Robert Wilson, who witnessed the scene.

Unfortunately, his tribute to Kléber was motivated largely by his hatred of Bonaparte. Nevertheless, no intelligent person, whether Frenchman, Englishman, or Turk, could have failed to reflect, as Kléber's body passed, how many of their comrades would still be alive if Kléber's counsel had prevailed. The blame for his failure must fall very squarely on the British cabinet.

Just before the French left Cairo, the Chief Paymaster Estève addressed a farewell letter to the Divan. Adding one more lie to so many, he promised that the French would return soon. The sheiks' reply, as quoted by one of them, El-Djabarti, was not without dignity. 'Power belongs to God,' they said. 'To Him belongs the dominion of the world. He alone can grant it to whom He chooses.'[3]

***

On July 15, the French evacuated Giza. By that time, General Baird had landed some 5,000 Indian and British troops at Kosseir, and his advance units had reached Cairo. Their journey had been unnecessary, but the magnificence of the Indians uniforms impressed the population vastly.

The march of the French troops from Cairo to Rosetta, where they were to embark for France aboard British transports, was not an easy operation. It was directed by General Sir John Moore, General Hutchinson being too ill to take charge. With great tact and sagacity, Sir John managed to keep sufficient distance be-

[1] Ibid., pp. 218-19.
[2] Wilson, I, 230.
[3] El-Djabarti, VII, 29.

tween the French and their British and Turkish escorts to prevent a clash. Indeed, what with 10,000 fully armed French soldiers, it was not at all certain, in case there was trouble, who would come out the victor. The situation was, perhaps, unique in military history. However, the French showed not the least inclination to fight their escort. By all accounts, the prospect of returning home after three rather strenuous years put them in excellent humour, and they fraternized most happily with the British.

Between July 31 and August 7, all of Belliard's army, including its followers and even some horses, were embarked at Rosetta. They reached France in October. Only one man among them was refused admittance to the mainland—General Kléber. An order issued by Bonaparte on October 9 prescribed that his body be temporarily detained at the prison fortress on the island of If, opposite Marseilles. It was left there until Napoleon's downfall.

Meanwhile, in Cairo, the Grand Vizier did his best to prevent his troops from looting the city, a reward they had been dreaming of for some time. The amnesty clause of the treaty of capitulation was generally observed, at least in the case of men; as for women, the case of the sheik El-Bekri's daughter, decapitated with her father's consent for having liked the French too much, was by no means unique. Nor was the Turkish soldiery completely at a loss on account of the Grand Vizier's injunction against looting. 'There is a suspicion,' says Lieutenant-Colonel Wilson, 'that the Turkish soldiers, individually taking advantage of the panic of the inhabitants ... persuaded the shopkeepers that they would protect them ... but stipulated that in the interim they must be considered partners in their trade.... Certainly the universal appearance of a Janissary seated on the shopboard of each house, earnestly welcoming customers, was strong presumptive, if not positive, evidence of the fact being as represented.'[1] Whatever changes may have taken place in Egypt for the past few thousand years, there can be no doubt that the Egyptians invariably bore the costs.

***

In Alexandria, Menou held out until the end of August. Although he had more than 7,000 troops at his disposition, against a siege force of about 4,000 under General Coote, he made no attempt at attacking the enemy and confined his military operations to heroic phrases and to a lightning police action against his own generals. His wrath was aroused most particularly against General

---

[1] Wilson, I, 236.

Reynier, his second in command, who had dared criticize his conduct. In one of the most grotesque episodes of the campaign, Menou, with an escort of grenadiers, personally arrested Reynier for treason, had him forcibly embarked, together with General Damas, the Chief Commissioner Daure, Adjutant General Boyer, and several others, and sent the lot of them back to France for trial. These men, he wrote to Bonaparte, 'were not friends either of the Republic, or of its government, or of the colony.'[1] Before leaving, Reynier relieved his feelings in a letter to Menou, a copy of which he had conveyed to his friends in Cairo. 'Personally,' he wrote among other things, 'I should be pleased to be removed from the disgusting spectacle of your operations and from the necessity of communicating with a man whom I sincerely despise.... You have set up a regime similar to that of [the Reign of Terror in] 1795.... By your incredible obstinacy in committing every conceivable folly you have reduced the army to a pitiful state.'[2] No doubt Reynier's language was as intemperate as Menou's action. However, regardless of their respective rights and wrongs, it stands to reason that an army in whose command such arguments could take place was doomed.

Not content to wage war on his subordinates, Menou also picked a quarrel with the Scientific Commission, a number of whose members had requested to be sent to France with their collections. To begin with, Menou forbade them to take their collections with them, declaring them to be 'a sacred trust.' Then, after some argument, he allowed them to embark aboard the brig *L'Oiseau*, which left Alexandria on July 15. Refused passage by the British, *L'Oiseau* attempted to re-enter the port when Menou, whose brain had been addled by the surrender of Cairo, ordered two of his frigates to fire upon the brig if she returned. According to him, the tiny *L'Oiseau*, with her cargo of scholars, should have defended the honour of the French flag by firing upon the British battleships that blocked her way and let herself be captured rather than come back without fighting. His stand was too ludicrous to be maintained for long, and the scientists were allowed to return.

Menou's conception of honour reflected a pathological state of mind. On the occasion of the affair of *L'Oiseau*, he wrote a long letter of apology to Admiral Keith; a few days later, he addressed a letter taking up five printed pages to Sir Sidney Smith, all about points of honour, according to Menou, or points of petty vanity, by

---

[1] Rousseau, p. 408.
[2] Wilson, II, 203, 205.

more reasonable standards. A few days earlier he had written to Bonaparte, shaking with indignation at the news of Belliard's capitulation at Cairo. 'I shall defend myself to the last extremity within the walls of Alexandria,' he concluded. 'I know how to die, but not how to capitulate.'[1] Seven weeks later he capitulated, and he remained alive for nine more years.

Two weeks after Menou promised to die in the defence of Egypt, on July 25, Bonaparte in a note for Lord Hawkesbury, who represented the English government in the current negotiations, stated succinctly: 'Egypt will be restored to the Porte.'[2]

Menou's continued resistance at Alexandria was justified (apart from his notions of honour) by one single hope—the expected arrival of Admiral Ganteaume with reinforcements. Indeed, after Ganteaume's second inglorious return to Toulon, Bonaparte had ordered the Admiral to take his seven battleships and 5,000 troops to Derna, in Libya, whence they were to make their way to Egypt by land, across the desert. Just how he imagined that the troops, after the agonies of spending three months at sea, cooped up in their ships, could achieve that feat of endurance, is one of the many perplexing things about Napoleon. Ganteaume left Toulon rather belatedly, in May, and soon afterwards had to send back three of his ships, an epidemic having broken out aboard them. The rest of his squadron reached Derna on June 8, but the hostile attitude of the local authorities made a landing inadvisable. Ganteaume continued toward Crete, captured the English battleship *Swiftsure*, and content with this triumph, returned to Toulon on July 22. If his brief proximity to Egypt justified General Menou's hopes of receiving reinforcements, the fact remains that *almost* is not good enough: General Belliard was even more justified in not counting on Ganteaume.

At precisely the moment when Ganteaume's squadron was off the Libyan coast, within a day's journey from Alexandria, desperately awaited by Menou and dreaded by the feeble forces of General Coote, another reinforcement from France was intercepted by Admiral Keith. The Admiral very gallantly offered to let the shipment through to Alexandria, for it consisted neither of soldiers nor of munitions but of a troupe of actors and actresses, sent by the First Consul to raise the morale of the Army of the Orient. In a way, the arrival of this troupe at such a juncture represented the

---

[1] Rousseau, pp. 412-13.

[2] Correspondence, VII, 203.

most irrefutable, though posthumous, justification of the conduct of General Kléber. Menou politely thanked Lord Keith for his offer to let the actors through but pointed out that the moment was not propitious and begged him ('for certainly you are a friend of the arts')[1] to send them back to France.

By mid-August, the main English forces, under Hutchinson and Moore, having conducted Belliard's army to Rosetta, joined the siege of Alexandria. The siege operations, rather languid up to that point, immediately took on a more lively nature. The details, for the most part, hold only technical interest; the main operation was the landing of part of the British troops at Fort Marabut, west of Alexandria, which completed the encirclement of the city. The British themselves, however, were short of supplies, especially of fodder, a circumstance which forced them to remove their field artillery and all their draft animals—camels, horses, and asses—to Rosetta. The removal of the donkeys did more for British morale than the arrival of the troupe of actors could have done for the French. 'These jack-asses were removed,' says Lieutenant-Colonel Wilson, 'to the great joy of every one but their proprietors. The serenade of at least a thousand such voices, continuing incessantly during the night, was not desirable.'[2] The detail may seem trivial, but Sir Robert's gift for understatement deserves praise.

The braying asses had been removed only to be succeeded by an intensification of mutual cannonades, a music more martial but not more conducive to sleep. After several weeks of alarums and excursions, General Menou decided at last that negotiations might be in order. For some time, indeed, the French outposts had reassured the English, with whom they were in informal communication, that their commander-in-chief's oath to be buried in the ruins of Alexandria rather than capitulate was merely a *façon de parler*. A French emissary appeared in the English camp on August 26, proposing a three-day armistice to negotiate the terms of the capitulation. The armistice was extended, and on August 30 General Hope entered Alexandria to sign the agreed-upon terms. General Menou invited him to a repast consisting only of horse meat. On September 2, Admiral Keith came on shore to ratify the treaty.

The terms obtained by General Menou were precisely those obtained nineteen months earlier by Kléber at El Arish arid two months earlier at Cairo by Belliard—the same terms which Menou

---

[1] Rousseau, p. 410.

[2] Wilson, II, 15.

had never tired of qualifying as shameful and atrocious. The difference was that Menou accepted them only after a sufficient number of men had been killed and maimed on both sides—a margin which represented his conception of honour.

To conclude any transaction without acrimony and polemics was one thing of which General Menou proved incapable. No sooner had the capitulation been signed than a duel of verbal pinpricks followed between him and General Hutchinson concerning the disposition of the savants' collections and of several antiquities, including the Rosetta Stone, which Menou declared to be his private property. Hutchinson claimed all these objects under Article XVI of the treaty of capitulation. Menou was ready enough to relinquish the scientists' collections; the scientists, however, led by Geoffroy Saint-Hilaire, declared that they preferred to follow their collections to England rather than give them up. Menou granted their request with ill grace, as appears from his letter dated September 13 to General Hutchinson: 'I have just been informed that several among our collection-makers (*faiseurs de collections*) wish to follow their seeds, minerals, birds, butterflies, or reptiles wherever you choose to ship their crates. I do not know if they wish to have themselves stuffed for the purpose, but I can assure you that if the idea should appeal to them, I shall not prevent them. I have authorized them to address themselves to you.'[1] Hutchinson allowed the scientists to keep their collections but insisted on the Rosetta Stone, which Menou relinquished grudgingly. 'You want it, Monsieur le général?' he wrote. 'You can have it, since you are the stronger of us two.... You may pick it up whenever you please.'[2] If honour was General Menou's strong point, dignity was not.[3]

On September 14, says Sir Robert Wilson, 'the first division of French troops marched to Abukir and embarked. The troops seemed in high spirits.'[4] The other units followed, including General Menou. Menou's wife and small son, after a rather perilous

---

[1] Rousseau, p. 427.

[2] Ibid., p. 424.

[3] According to General Reynier's account, which is understandably prejudiced against Menou, Menou insisted on keeping the scientists' collections only after the scientists threatened to destroy them rather than let them pass into British hands. There is no corroboration of this implausible story, which Sir Robert Wilson denies specifically in his history of the campaign. Reynier, of course, was no longer in Alexandria when these events occurred.

[4] Wilson, II, 74.

journey from Rosetta to Cairo and from Cairo to Alexandria, had joined him at last and embarked with him.

Two weeks later, on October 1, at London, the French and English negotiators signed a preliminary peace treaty. On December 1, Bonaparte wrote to Menou, who had just returned to France: 'I know that if the event had depended on your will and on your love for the beautiful country of Egypt, the Republic would have kept that conquest. Your long resistance at Alexandria was useful in the negotiations.'[1] Though meant in a kindly and consoling spirit, the statement merely added an untruth to so many others. If anything, it was the end rather than the length of Menou's resistance at Alexandria which made the preliminary peace of London possible.

***

In his history of the Egyptian campaign, Napoleon managed, by means of a statistical sleight-of-hand, to make it appear that five sixths of the army he had taken to Egypt returned to France alive. This astonishing result is easily explained by the fact that he left the sailors and marines out of his account. The true figures, properly interpreted, tell a different story. In July 1798, Bonaparte had a little over 34,000 land troops and about 16,000 sailors and marines in Egypt. In September 1801, about 21,500 land troops (3,000 of them sick or wounded) were being repatriated, but the 16,000 sailors and marines had shrunk to 1,866. Thus, of a total of more than 50,000 only a little over 23,000 returned, including 3,000 invalids. The discrepancy may be explained by the incorporation of a large part of the naval forces into the army units after the Battle of the Nile. The number of casualties must be set at even several hundred more than these figures indicate, since almost a thousand reinforcements had arrived in Egypt in February 1801 and since a number of the sick and wounded died on their way to France. (Among them was Moallem Jacob.) On the other hand, several hundred wounded had been transported to France before the capitulation. Thus, while it is impossible to tabulate the French losses exactly, it is safe to say that one half of the expeditionary force (including the naval personnel) perished in the course of the expedition, either in combat or from disease, and that several thousand more were blinded or crippled.

Whatever the gains bought at this price, they had nothing to do with the purposes for which the expedition was undertaken, in all of which it failed.

---

[1] Correspondance, VII, 346.

The troops and the cripples were still on their way to France, thanks to the English navy, when General Bonaparte, First Consul of the French Republic, wrote Egypt off as a loss and turned his eyes to other stakes on the gaming table. On September 13, 1801, he requested his Minister of Marine to compile a memorandum on Madagascar. On October 25, he appointed his brother-in-law, General Leclerc, commander-in-chief of the expeditionary force to Santo Domingo. On November 8, he addressed a proclamation to the inhabitants of Santo Domingo, in a style he had perfected in Egypt: 'Rally to the Captain General [Leclerc] ... Whoever dares separate himself from the Captain General's cause is a traitor to his country, and the wrath of the Republic shall devour him as fire devours your cane fields in a drought.'[1]

Thus one futile chapter of colonial history closed, only to open another. The horrors of the Dominican campaign were to make a worthy sequel to those of the Egyptian expedition, and the words Napoleon spoke at St. Helena by way of epitaph might be applied with equal aptness to both ventures: 'The Santo Domingo affair was a very—foolish business on my part. If it had succeeded, it would have done no good except that it would have made the Noailles and La Rochefoucaulds still richer.'[2] These words sum up the results of nineteenth-century colonialism in a nutshell.

IV

Apart from the loss of lives, the destruction, the cruelty, what were the achievements of the Egyptian campaign? For Bonaparte, it had opened the way to power. For France, far from accomplishing the expected results, it meant the loss of her superiority in the Near and Middle East, to the profit of England. For Egypt, it had more lasting significance. The power of the Mamelukes was broken, despite British efforts to reinstate them, and a decade later Mehemet Ali managed to eliminate them altogether by the simple expedient of massacring what was left of them. Many of the projects first conceived by the French to make Egypt into a modern country were carried out under Mehemet Ali and his successors, and French cultural and technological influence remained manifest to the present day. As in Italy, Germany, and Spain, so in Egypt Napoleon had set in motion the forces that work for change against the inert mass of past tradition.

---

[1] Ibid., VII, 315.
[2] Gourgaud, I, 402.

J. Christopher Herold

While all these results, some of them positive, cannot be denied, it would be idle to dwell on them. Egypt would have changed even if Bonaparte had never appeared; the splendours of Luxor and Karnak would have been discovered even if Desaix had never marched up the Nile; the hieroglyphs would have been deciphered even if the Rosetta Stone had been found only a few decades later; the Suez Canal would have been built even if Bonaparte had not ordered the Isthmus to be surveyed. There is a tendency among historians to see silver linings surrounding everything, even futile wars: to be sure, every evil accidentally carries some good with it, but this does not always mean that the evil is necessary to produce the good.

It is more to the point to regard the Egyptian campaign as the first massive European attempt to colonize the countries which, in recent times, have been labelled 'underdeveloped areas.' Of all colonial campaigns, it was perhaps the most remarkable, not only because of the personalities involved in it, not only because of the scope of its planning or the excitement of its adventure, but more especially because of the earnestness with which Bonaparte and his two successors sought to bring about a fusion of the secular West and the Islamic East on equal terms. No such attempt has been made since.

If one considers Bonaparte's Egyptian campaign in this context, it is more tempting to speculate what would have been its results had it succeeded than to condemn it as futile because it failed. A great deal of argument is possible on this subject, yet the field of speculation tends to narrow as one takes a longer view. If France had established herself in Egypt as she did, thirty years later, in Algeria, the event would have seemed tremendously important to nineteenth-century minds. In 1962, it would seem less important. After fighting each other for a century and a half over the possession of the world, the colonial powers are liquidating their empires, sometimes voluntarily, sometimes under compulsion; unable to divide the earth among themselves, they are forced by circumstances more than by good sense to draw together in Europe. Their resigning themselves to working together at home rather than fighting each other abroad is the silver lining of colonial history. The effect of the colonial age is likely to be felt more lastingly in the former colonies than in their metropoles: perversely enough, the main result of domination and exploitation was emancipation. The world-wide collapse of the colonial dream tends to justify General Kléber's defeatism, which may have seemed short-sighted to his contemporaries.

If the long-range effects of the Egyptian campaign are a trifle nebulous and uncertain, the immediate results for the survivors were very definite. Some were crippled for life, others won promotions or financial gains, or both; many relived their adventures by writing their memoirs (more or less truthfully); the savants spent the next quarter of the century compiling their findings; Vivant Denon became the first Director of the Louvre and founded its Egyptian collection; several of the Mameluke beys were massacred by the Turks almost immediately after being guaranteed their safety, and the others went on fighting each other until they too were massacred by the Turks; a few hundred Egyptian women were decapitated to warn the others against adopting the ways of Infidels; those among the Mamelukes, Copts, and Syrians who had followed the French to France and were fit for military service were formed into a Mameluke corps, and the rest eked out a melancholy existence on insufficient pensions.

More picturesque were the careers of some of the several hundred Frenchmen who chose to remain behind in Egypt—most of them deserters. The Chief Pharmacist Royer—the man who had administered opium to the plague-stricken in Jaffa—chose to stay and eventually became physician to Mehemet Ali. Some 130 deserters and stragglers were rounded up by the Pasha of Cairo and put in charge of training Negro and Nubian recruits to serve as the Pasha's Guards (an idea taken over by the Pasha from the French). The French-trained Guards distinguished themselves in 1805 in an action against a number of rebellious Mameluke beys, who also had French deserters among their forces, notably one Selim Combe, a native of Avignon. Selim, who directed the Mamelukes' artillery, later helped the American expedition against the Barbary pirates of Derna, and he and his men wore United States uniforms. When Mehemet Ali, in 1811, invited all the Mameluke officers to a banquet at the Citadel of Cairo in order to ambush them, he excepted the French from the massacre, with the intention of attaching them to him. The most successful career of any Frenchman left in Egypt was undoubtedly that of a drummer boy from Toulon whom the Bedouins captured in 1799, when he was about twelve years old. The Bedouins sold him to the Pasha of Tripoli, in whose service he rose under the name of Abdallah. He took part in the Turkish conquest of Fezzan and was made the governor of a desert area which enabled him to pay a yearly tribute of 10,000 Spanish piastres, levied on the date harvest.

The record for longevity among survivors of the Egyptian campaign was held, in all probability, by Pauline Fourès. She had managed to return to France in 1800. Bonaparte refused to see her but presented her with a mansion near Paris and with repeated gifts of cash. During the year of her return she met and married one Henry de Ranchoup, who had formerly served as a major in the Turkish army and for whom she obtained several modest consular posts, first in Santander, then in Cartagena, and finally in Gothenburg. Madame de Ranchoup's sentiments for her second husband appear to have been less than passionate. While Monsieur de Ranchoup languished in Spain and in Sweden, she spent most of her time in Paris, leading very much her own life. She took up writing, published a novel in two volumes, entitled *Lord Wentworth*, and also began to paint. Her self-portrait shows her plucking the petals of a daisy and still pretty enough to be loved.

According to Napoleon's reminiscences at St. Helena, he met Pauline once, in 1811, at a masked ball. He reminded her that she had been called Cleopatra in Egypt; if his testimony is truthful, she spoke with warmth of Caesar, without recognizing him—but this is a most unlikely story. Certain it is that, in the same year, Napoleon had 60,000 francs paid to her out of the receipts of the state theatres. From 1812 until Napoleon's abdication two years later, Madame de Ranchoup appears to have lived in exile in the small town of Craponne in Haute-Loire; it is not far-fetched to suppose that the Emperor thought he had paid enough. Pauline startled the people of Craponne by letting herself be seen sitting at her window smoking a pipe and by taking long walks alone with her silky-haired dog, whom she also took to Mass each Sunday.

Napoleon's downfall does not seem to have caused Madame de Ranchoup any strong emotions; neither did his return from Elba, nor his second abdication after the Hundred Days. She did not like to be reminded of her Egyptian romance and, in her political opinions, she staunchly supported the restored Louis XVIII. In 1816, in her mid-thirties, she seems to have begun a new life. She obtained a separation from her husband, sold all her furniture, and went off to Brazil with one Jean-Auguste Bellard, a former officer in the Imperial Guards. A rumour had it that she was hoping to establish contact with her former lover on his lonely rock in the South Atlantic, and perhaps even to help him escape. Nothing was farther from her thoughts. Her object in going to Brazil was, from all appearances, purely commercial: she took some French merchandise with her, sold it, and with the proceeds bought precious woods, with which she returned to France, Engaged in this lucrative trade, she shuttled back and forth between France and Brazil until 1857, when she settled in Paris with an assortment of monkeys and parrots who ran and flew about her flat with complete freedom.

By this time, Napoleon had been dead for sixteen years. Madame de Ranchoup was still very much alive. She wrote another historical novel (*Une Châtelaine du douxième siècle*) which created as little stir as her first; she painted; she played the harp agreeably. She also formed a circle of friends, among them the painter Rosa Bonheur, who liked to wear men's clothes, and she kept her wits intact for the next twenty-two years. Her ex-lover's body was brought back from St. Helena to France by King Louis Philippe; King Louis Philippe was overthrown; her ex-lover's nephew became Emperor as Napoleon III and, like his uncle half a century earlier, dreamed of an Empire in the East. Instead of campaigning in Egypt, he acquired for France the controlling interest in the Suez Canal, then under construction. At last, in 1869, the Canal was opened by the Khedive Ismail, Mehemet Ali's descendant: bankers and engineers had accomplished what General Bonaparte had attempted too hastily by force of arms. In the same year, approaching her nineties, Pauline de Ranchoup died. Had she lived one year longer, she could have witnessed the collapse of the second Napoleonic Empire and looked down upon a century of history.

APPENDIX A

CASABIANCA [1]
by
Felicia Dorothea Hemans

The boy stood on the burning deck
    Whence all but he had fled;
The flame that lit the battle's wreck
    Shone round him o'er the dead.

Yet beautiful and bright he stood,
    As born to rule the storm;
A creature of heroic blood,
    A proud, though child-like form.

The flames rolled on–he would not go
    Without his Father's word;
That father, faint in death below,
    His voice no longer heard.

He called aloud–'say, Father, say
    If yet my task is done?'
He knew not that the chieftain lay
    Unconscious of his son.

'Speak, father!' once again he cried,
    'If I may yet be gone!'
And but the booming shots replied,
    And fast the flames rolled on.

---

[1] From Hemans, Felicia Dorothea. The Poetical Works of Felicia Dorothea Hemans London: Oxford University Press, 1914. p. 396.

Upon his brow he felt their breath,
  And in his waving hair,
And looked from that lone post of death
  In still yet brave despair.

And shouted but once more aloud,
  'My father! must I stay?'
While o'er him fast, through sail and shroud,
  The wreathing fires made way.

They wrapt the ship in splendour wild,
  They caught the flag on high,
And streamed above the gallant child,
  Like banners in the sky.

There came a burst of thunder sound—
  The boy—oh! where was he?
Ask of the winds that far around
  With fragments strewed the sea!—

With mast, and helm, and pennon fair,
  That well had borne their part—
But the noblest thing which perished there
  Was that young faithful heart.

GLOSSARY OF ARABIC
AND TURKISH TERMS

AGA. Turkish title meaning 'elder brother,' 'chief, or 'master'; in the Ottoman army, it was held by superior officers, but it has no precise equivalent in the West. The Aga of the Janissaries was the commanding general of the regular Turkish infantry.

BEY. Turkish title meaning 'lord' and given to a variety of high officials. In Eygpt, it was given to the Mameluke chiefs who ruled as suzerain princes.

CHEBEK. A Levantine sailing ship, with three masts, which can also be rowed.

DIVAN. Turkish word of Persian origin, meaning either a government office or a high council, as a council of ministers or of notables.

DJERM. Typical sailing ship of the Nile, with lateen sails, similar to the felucca.

DRAGOMAN. An interpreter. The Dragoman of the Porte was the chief official under the Reis Effendi in charge of relations with European powers; his office was traditionally held by a Greek. The First Dragoman of an embassy held a position equivalent to First Secretary.

EFFENDI. Turkish title, derived from the Greek, meaning 'master' and given to persons with a literary education.

EMIR. Arabic title meaning 'commander 1 , 'governor,' or 'prince'.

EMIR AL-HADJ. Leader of the annual pilgrimage from Cairo to Mecca.

FELLAH (plural: FELLAHIN). The Egyptian peasant.

FETFA or FATWA. A legal opinion concerning religious law, given by a mufti in answer to a question specifically submitted to him.

FIRMAN. An imperial command or rescript, issued by the Ottoman Porte and written in a special hand. In times of war, army commanders sometimes had authority to issue firmans.

FUNDUK. Generally, an inn or hostel; more specifically, in North Africa, a compound of warehouses and living quarters used by foreign merchants.

GRAND VIZIER. The chief minister of an Ottoman Sultan. In times of war, he was also the supreme military commander.

HADJ. The annual pilgrimage to Mecca; title of one who has made the pilgrimage.

IMAM. Arabic title meaning 'leader' or 'guide.' Applied originally to the Prophet himself, later to the Caliphs, it came to mean any religious official who led the Faithful in prayers. Every mosque has at least one imam.

JANISSARIES. The regular Turkish infantry until 1826. They were originally recruited from Christian children, but later membership in the Corps of Janissaries became hereditary. The Janissaries in Egypt were only nominally under the Pasha's command but were in fact under their Aga and controlled by the Mamelukes.

KADI. A judge, particularly in matters relating to Moslem law, including the law of inheritance. The Kadi Asker (Grand Judge) was the superior judge of Cairo.

KAPITAN PASHA. In the Ottoman Empire, the supreme commander of the Turkish fleet and governor of the Greek Archipelago.

KHAMSIN. Sand storm.

KHEDIVE. Viceroy of Egypt. The title was given by the Ottoman Sultan to the hereditary pashas of Egypt in 1867.

KIBLAH. The direction of Mecca. In a mosque, it is usually marked by a niche flanked by pillars.

KYACHEFF or KASHIFF. Under the Mameluke regime of Egypt, a bey's delegate governing a province and responsible for the collection of its revenues.

MIRY. The principal land tax collected in Egypt from the fellahin under the Mameluke regime.

MOALLEM. Title given to educated persons of the Christian faith.

MUEZZIN. Religious official calling the Faithful to prayer and with the functions of a cantor or deacon during prayer service.

MUFTI. A person learned in Moslem canon law.

MULTAZIM. In Egypt under the Mameluke-Ottoman regime, the landlords holding property in military fee.

NAHIB EL-ASHRAF. The head of the sherifs; marshal of the nobility. PASHA. Title given in the Ottoman Empire to certain high civil and military officials and to governors of provinces.

PORTE: see SUBLIME PORTE.

REIS EFFENDI. In the Ottoman Empire, the Secretary of State for Foreign Affairs.

SERRADJ. A foot soldier in attendance on a mounted Mameluke warrior.

SERASKJER. In the Ottoman Empire, a commander-in-chief. A vizier commanding an army in time of war was called a seraskier.

SHEIK, Arabic title of respect meaning 'elder' and given, often regardless of age, to the head of a family or a tribe, to high religious dignitaries, to teachers and scholars, or to any person notable in a religious or civil (but not military) capacity,

SHEIK EL-BELED. In Egypt, the title ordinarily denoted a village elder or mayor. However, the Sheik el-Beled of Cairo was the 'head of the

country,' i.e. the acknowledged head of the Mameluke beys. At the time of the French invasion, the title was borne by Ibrahim Bey.

SHERJF (plural-. ASHRAF). Person of noble descent, i.e. in theory, a descendant of the Prophet's family. In Egypt, the sherifs or ashraf wore green turbans. In Arabia, the rulers of certain places (e.g. Mecca) were also called sherifs.

SUBLIME PORTE. The seat of the Ottoman government at the Seraglio in Constantinople; by extension, the Ottoman government itself.

ULEMA. A scholar of recognized eminence, custodian of Islamic tradition and law. As a body, the ulemas represented the doctrinal idjma (agreement, unity) of the Moslem peoples. In the Ottoman Empire, they were the only spiritual counterforce to the military and temporal rulers.

VIZIER. A Turkish minister of state, member of the Grand Vizier's divan. A pasha of three horse tails (i.e. a pasha of several provinces) also was given the title vizier.

BIBLIOGRAPHY

Abd el—Rahman el-Djabarti: see El-Djabarti.

Abrantes, Laure Junot, Duchesse d; . Mémoires. 10 vols. Paris, n.d.

Arnault, Antoine-Vincent. Souvenirs d'un sexagénaire. 4 vols. Paris, 1833.

Aubry, Charles. Le Ravitaillement des armes de Frédéric le Grand et de Napoléon. Paris, 1894.

Aubry, Paul V. Monge. Paris, 1954.

Bainville, Jacques. Bonaparte en Egypte. Paris, 1936.

Barras, P.-J.-F.-N. Mémoires. 4 vols. Paris, 1895-96.

Barrow, John. The Life and Correspondance of Admiral Sir William Sidney Smith. 2 vols. London, 1848.

Beauharnais, Prince Eugène de. Mémoires et correspondance politiques et militaires. 10 vols. Paris, 1858-60.

Belliard, Augustin Daniel, Comte, et al. Histoire scientifique et militaire de l'expédition française en Egypte. 10 vols. Paris, 1830-36. .

——- Mémoires du Comte Belliard. 3 vols. Paris, 1842.

Bergell, P., and Klitscher, K. Larrey, der Chefchirurg Napoléons I. Berlin, 1913.

Berthier, Louis-Alexandre. Relation des campagnes du général Bonaparte en Egypte et en Syrie. Paris, Year VIII.

Bertrand, Henri-Gratien. Cottiers de Sainte-Helene. Ed. by Paul Fleuriot de Langle. 3 vols. Paris, 1949-59.

Borelli, Octave. Notes à propos de documents relatifs a l'expédition française en Egypte. Cairo, 1888.

Boselli, Count. 'La Prise de Malte en 1798 racontée par un témoin oculaire,' Rivista del Collegia Araldico (Rome, 1909), pp. 556-58.

Boulay de la Meurthe, Alfred, Comte. Le Directoire et l'expédition d'Egypte. Paris, 1885.

Bourrienne, Louis-Antoine Fauvelet de. Mémoires.; vols. Paris, n.d.

Brehier, Louis. L'Egypte de 1789 a 1900. Paris, 1903.

Brun, V. Guerres maritimes de la France. Porte Toulon. Vol. II. Paris; 1861. Caulaincourt, Louis, Marquis de, Due de Vicence. Mémoires. 3 vols. Paris, 1933. Cavaliero, Roderick. The Last of the Crusaders: The Knights of Malta in the Eighteenth Century. London, 1960.

Charles-Roux, François. L'Angleterre et l'expédition française en Egypte. 2 vols. Cairo, 1925.

——- Bonaparte; gouverneur d'Egypte. Paris, 1935.

Charles-Roux, François. Les Origines de l'expédition d' Egypte. Paris, 1901.

Chauvin, Victor. La Légende égyptienne de Bonaparte. Mons, 1902.

Cherfils, Christian. Bonaparte et l'Islam. Paris, 1914.

Chuquet, Arthur. Etudes d'histoire. Fourth series. Paris, 1911.

Copies of Original Letters from the Army of Général Buonaparte in Egypt, Intercepted by the Fleet under the Command of Admiral Lord Nelson. London, 1798.

Correspondance de L'armée Française en Egypte. (French edition of the work listed above.) Paris, Year VII.

Correspondence: for the work thus referred to in the Notes, see Napoléon I. Correspondance inédite, officielle et confidentielle: see Napoléon I.

Courrier de l'Egypte, Le.

Damas Hinard, ed. Dictionnaire Napoléon. Paris, 1854.

Dard, Emile. Napoléon et Talleyrand. Paris, 1935.

Décade Égyptienne, La.

Dehérain, H. L'Exploration de la Haute Egypte ... en 1799,' Revue Historique, 1931.

Denon, Dominique Vivant, Baron. Voyages dans la Basse et la Haute Egypte pendant les campagnes de Bonaparte en 1798 et 1799. 2 vols. London, 1807.

Desgenettes, René Nicolas, Baron. Histoire médicale de l'armée d'Orient. Paris, 1802.

——- Souvenirs d'un médecin de l'expédition d'Egypte. Paris, 1893. (This seems to be an abridged version of Desgenettes' Souvenirs, a virtually unfindable work from which, however, C. de La Jonquiere quotes abundantly.)

Description de L'Egypte. 10 vols. of text, 14 vols. of plates. Paris, 1809-28.

Desvernois, Nicolas-Philibert, Baron. Mémoires du Général Baron Desvernois. Paris, 1898.

Doguereau, Jean-Pierre. Journal de l'expédition d' Egypte. Paris, 1904.

Doublet, P.-J.-O. Mémoires historiques sur l'invasion et l'occupation de Malte par une armée française, en 1798. Paris, 1883.

Douin, Georges. La Flotte de Bonaparte sur les côtes d ; Egypte. Cairo, 1922.

Driault, Edouard. Mohammed Ali et Napoléon. Cairo, 1925.

Du Casse, Albert, ed. Mémoires et correspondance politique et militaire du roi Joseph. 2d ed. 10 vols. Paris, 1854-55. .

——- Les Rois frères de Napoléon 1st. Paris, 1883.

El-Djabarti, Abd el-Rahman. Merveilles biographiques et historiques, ou Chroniques. Tr. from the Arabic. 9 vols. Cairo, 1888-96.

Elgood, Percival George. Bonaparte's Adventure in Egypt. London, 1931.

Fouché, Joseph, Duc d'Otrante. Mémoires. 2 vols. Paris, 1824.

François, C. Journal du Capitaine François, dit le Dromadaire d'Egypte, 1792-1830. 2 vols. Paris, 1903.

Galea, Joseph. l'Occupation de Malte par les François: Etude bibliographique. Geneva 1959.

Galland, A. Tableau de l'Egypte pendant le séjour de L'armée Française. 2 vols. Paris, 1804.

Geoffrey Saint-Hilaire, Etienne. Lettres Writes d'Egypte. Paris, 1901.

Gohier, Louis-Jerome. Mémoires. 2 vols. Paris, 1824.

Gourgaud, Gaspard. Sainte-Helene: Journal inédit. 2 vols. Paris, n.d.

Guémard, Gabriel. Aventuriers Mamelouks d'Egypte. Societ Royale d'Archéologie d'Alexandrie, n.d. .

——- Histoire et bibliographique critique de la commission des sciences et arts de l'lnstitut d'Egypte. Cairo, 1936.

Guerrini, Domenico. La spedizione française in Egitto. Turin, 1904.

Hallberg, Charles Williams. The Suez Canal: Its History and Its Diplomatic Importance. New York, 1931,

Homsy, Gaston. Le Général Jacob et l'expédition de 'Bonaparte en Egypte. Bergerac and Marseilles, 1921.

Horndasch, Max. Der Chirurg Napoléons: Das Leben des Jean-Dominique Larrey. Bonn, 1949

Inglis, Charles. 'Operations on the Coast of Egypt, 1801,' in Navy Records Society, XL (London, 1912), 333-49.

Institut d'Egypte. Mémoires sur L'Egypte. 4 vols. Paris, Years VIII-XL

Iung, Theodore. Lucien Bonaparte et ses Mémoires. 3 vols. Paris, 1882-83.

Ivray, Jehan d' [Mme Jeanne Fahmi-Bey]. Bonaparte et L'Egypte. Paris, 1914.

Jollois, J.-B.-P. Journal d'un ingénieur attache a I'expédition d'Egypte, 1798—1801, Paris, 1904.

Jomard, Edme-Francois. Souvenirs sur Gaspard Monge. Paris, 1853.

Keith, George Elphinstone, Viscount. The Keith Papers. 3 vols. London, Navy Records Society, 1927-55.

Kircheisen, Friedrich M. Napoléon L Vol. III. Munich and Leipzig, 1914.

Kircheisen, Gertrude. Die Frauen urn Napoléon. Munich and Leipzig, 1912.

Lacorre, A. Journal inédit d'un commis de vivres pendant l'expédition d'Egypte. Bordeaux, 1852.

Lacroix, Alfred. Deodat Dolomieu. 2 vols. Paris, 1921.

——- Dolomieu en Egypte. Cairo, 1922.

Lacroix, Desire. Bonaparte en Egypte. Paris, 1899.

La Jonquiere, C, de. L'Expédition en Egypte, 1798-1801. 5 vols. Paris, 1899-1907.

La Revellere-Lepaux, Louis-Marie de. Mémoires. 3 vols. Paris, 1873.

Larrey, Dominique-Jean. Mémoires de chirurgie militaire et campagnes. 4 vols. Paris, 1812-17.

Las Cases, Emmanuel, Comte de. Mémorial de Sainte-Helene. Pleiade ed. 2 vols. Paris, 1948.

Lavallette, Antoine-Marie Chamans, Comte de. Mémoires et souvenirs. 2 vols. Paris, 1831.

Lee, Sir John Theophilus. Mémoires. London, 1836.

Lefebvre, Georges. Le Directoire. Paris, 1946.

Lichtenberger, Andre. 'Le Général Caffarelli du Falga', in Le Socialisme utopique, pp. 260-76. Paris, 1898.

Malus, Etienne-Louis. L'Agenda de Malus. Paris, 1892.

Marmont, A.-F.-L. Wiesse de, Duc de Raguse. Mémoires. Vols. I and II. Paris, 1857.

Marquiset, Alfred, ed. Napoléon sténographié au Conseil d'Etat. Paris, 1913.

Martha-Beker, Felix-Victor. Etudes sur Desaix. Clermont, 1852.

Martin, P.-D. Histoire de l'expédition française en Egypte. 2 vols. Paris, 1815.

Masson, Frederic. Mme Bonaparte (1796-1804). Paris, 1920.

——- Napoléon et les femmes. Paris, 1894.

——- Napoléon et sa famille. Vol. I (1769-1802). Paris, 1897.

Masson, Frederic, and Biagi, Guido, eds. Napoléon inconnu: papiers inédits (1786-1793). 2 vols. Paris, 1895.

Mathiez, Albert. Le Directoire. Paris, 1934.

Maurel, Andre. Les Trois Dumas. Paris, 1896.

Maurois, Andre. Les Trois Dumas. Paris, 1957.

Meneval, Claude-François, Baron de. Mémoires pour servir a l'histoire de

Napoléon 1st. 3 vols. Paris, 1894.

Millet, P.-J.-S. Le Chasseur P. Millet: Souvenirs de la campagne d'Egypte,

1898-1901. Paris, 1903.

Miot, Jacques-Francois. Mémoires pour servir a l'histoire des expéditions en Egypte et en Syrie. 2d ed. Paris, 1814.

Moore, Sir John. Diary. 2 vols. London, 1904.

Morier, John Philip. Memoir of a Campaign with the Ottoman Army in Egypt. London, 1801.

Napoléon I, Emperor of the French. Correspondance de Napoléon 1st publiée par ordre de l'Empereur Napoléon III. 32 vols. Paris, 1858-70.

——- Correspondance inédite, officielle et confidentielle de Napoléon Bonaparte. Vols. V-VII: Egypte. 3 vols. Paris, 1819-20.

——- Dernieres lettres inédites de. Napoléon 1st. Ed. by Leonce de Brotonne. 2 vols. Paris, 1903.

——- Lettres de Napoléon a Joséphine. Ed. by Leon Cerf. Paris, 1929.

——- Lettres inédites de Napoléon 1st. Ed. by Leonce de Brotonne. Paris, 1898.

——- Lettres inédites de Napoléon 1st. Ed. by Leon Lecestre. 2nd ed. 2 vols. Paris, 1897.

——- Supplement a la Correspondance de Napoléon 1st: Lettres curieuses omises par le comitee de publication. Paris, 1887.

——- See also: Masson and Biagi, eds., Napoléon inconnu.

Nelson, Horatio, Viscount Nelson. Dispatches and Letters. Ed. by Sir Nicholas Harris Nicolas. Vol. III. London, 1895.

Nicholas the Turk: see Nicolas Turc.

Nicol, John. The Life and Adventures of John Nicol, Mariner. Edinburgh, 1822.

Nicolas Turc [Nicholas the Turk; Nikula ibn Yusuf, al-Turki], Chronique d'Egypte, 1798-1804. Ed. and tr. from the Arabic by Gaston Wiet. Cairo, 1950.

Norden, Friedrich Lewis. Travels in Egypt and Nubia. 2 vols. London, 1757.

Norry, Charles. Relation de l'expédition d'Egypte. Paris, Year X.

Ollivier, Albert. Le Dix-huit Brumaire. Paris, 1959.

O'Meara, Barry Edward. Napoléon in Exile; or, A Voice from St. Helena. 2 vols. Philadelphia, 1822.

Pastre, J.-L. Gaston. Bonaparte en Egypte. Paris, 1932.

Pelet [de la Lozere], Baron, ed. Opinions de Napoléon sur divers sujets de politique et d'administration. Paris, 1835.

Peyre, Roger. l'expédition d'Egypte. Paris, 1890.

Phipps, Ramsay Weston. The Armies of the First French Republic. 5 vols. London, 1926-39.

Rapp, Jean, Comte. Mémoires. Paris, 1823.

Remusat, Claire de Vergennes, Comtesse de. Mémoires. 24th ed. 3 vols. Paris, 1893.

Reynier, J.-L.-E. De l'Egypte apres la bataille d'Heliopolis. Paris, 1802.

Richardot, Charles. Nouveaux Mémoires sur I'armee française en Egypte et en Syrie. Paris, 1848.

——- Relation de la campagne de Syrie. Paris, 1839,

Rigault, Georges. Le Général Abdallah Menou et la derniere phase de l'expédition d'Egypte. Paris, 1911.

Roederer, Pierre-Louis, Comte. Autour de Bonaparte: Journal du Comte P.-L. Roederer. Paris, 1909.

Rousseau, Frangois. Kléber et Menou en Egypte depuis le départ de Bonaparte. Paris, 1900.

Roustam Raza. Souvenirs de Roustam, mamelouk de Napoléon 1st. Paris, 1911.

Sauzet, Armand. Desaix, le 'Sultan Juste'. Paris, 1954.

Savant, Jean. Les Mamelouks de Napoléon, Paris, 1949.

Savary, A.-J.-M.-R., Due de Rovigo. Mémoires. 8 vols. Paris, 1828.

Savary, Claude. Lettres sur l'Egypte. 2nd ed. 3 vols. Paris, 1786.

Segur, Philippe-Paul, Comte de. Mémoires. 3 vols. Paris, 1894-95.

Six, Georges. Dictionnaire biographique des généraux et amiraux de la Révolution et de l'Empire. 2 vols. Paris, 1934.

Skalkowski, Adam. Les Polonais en Egypte, 1798-1801. Paris, 1910.

Stael, Germaine Necker, Baronne de. Considérations sur les principaux événements de la Revolution française. Paris, 1845.

Talleyrand, Charles-Maurice de, Prince de Benevent. Mémoires. 5 vols. Paris, 1891-92.

Thurman, Louis. Bonaparte en Egypte. Paris, 1902.

Triaire, Paul. Napoléon et Larrey. Tours, 1902.

Tott, Frangois Baron de. Memoirs of the Turks and Tartars. Eng. tr. 2 vols. London, 1786.

Vandal, Albert. L'Avènement de Bonaparte. 2 vols. Paris, 1903.

Vendryes, Pierre. De la Probabilité en histoire: l'exemple de l'expédition d'Egypte. Paris, 1952.

Vertray, Captain. Journal d'un officier de l'armée d'Egypte. Paris, 1883.

Victoires, conquêtes, désastres, revers et guerres civiles des Français de 1792 a 1815. Vols. VIII-XIV. Paris, 1818-19.

Vigo-Roussillon, P. 'Mémoires militaires', Revue des Deux Mondes (August 1 and 15, 1890), pp. 576-607, 721-50.

Villiers du Terrage, René-Edouard de. Journal et souvenirs sur l'expédition d'Egypte. Paris, 1899.

Volney, Constantin-François, Comte de. Voyage en Egypte et en Syrie. 2 vols. Paris, 1787.

Walsh, Thomas. Journal of the Late Campaign in Egypt. London, 1803.

Warner, Oliver. The Battle of the Nile. London and New York, 1960.

Wheeler, H. F. B., and Broadley, R. M. Napoléon and the Invasion of England. Vol. I. London and New York, 1908.

Wiet, Gaston. Deux Mémoires inédits sur l'expédition d'Egypte. Cairo, 1941.

Wilson, Sir Robert Thomas, History of the British Expedition to Egypt. 2 vols. London, 1803.

ABOUT THE AUTHOR

Born in Brünn, Czechoslovakia, in 1919, J. Christopher Herold attended schools in Berlin and Geneva, and received his M.A. degree at Columbia University in New York. After serving from 1943 to 1945 in the United States Intelligence Service in Europe, he joined Columbia University Press as editor and remained there for ten years. From 1956 to 1960 he was editor-in-chief of Stanford University Press. In 1960 he was granted a Guggenheim Memorial Foundation Fellowship for a year's research on the Romantic movement.

His previous books were: *The Swiss Without Halos*, a survey of Switzerland; *Joan, Maid of France*, a biography for children; *The Mind of Napoleon; Mistress to an Age: A Life of Madame de Staël;* and *Love in Five Temperaments. Mistress to an Age* was a Book-of-the-Month Club selection and a Book Society choice in England, and for this book Mr. Herold received the 1959 National Book Award for nonfiction and the Gold Medal for Literature awarded by the Commonwealth Club of California.

Mr. Herold, along with his wife and son, made their home in Los Altos, California, where he passed away in 1964.

Other fine Napoleonic Era books from www.FireshipPress.com

Breinigsville, PA USA
13 January 2010
230705BV00005B/4/P